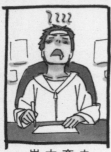

岸本斉史

I'm trying to come up with the author's note for this volume right now, but I have a fever, so nothing's coming to mind... It's been a while since I've been sick. Argh... I can't think of anything...

—*Masashi Kishimoto, 2009*

Author/artist Masashi Kishimoto was born in 1974 in rural Okayama Prefecture, Japan. After spending time in art college, he won the Hop Step Award for new manga artists with his manga **Karakuri** (Mechanism). Kishimoto decided to base his next story on traditional Japanese culture. His first version of **Naruto**, drawn in 1997, was a one-shot story about fox spirits; his final version, which debuted in **Weekly Shonen Jump** in 1999, quickly became the most popular ninja manga in Japan.

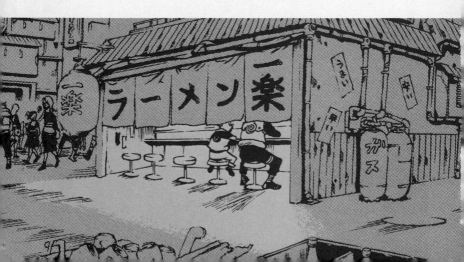

NARUTO VOL. 46
SHONEN JUMP Manga Edition
This graphic novel contains material that was originally published in
English in SHONEN JUMP #77–79. Artwork in the magazine may have
been slightly altered from that presented here.

STORY AND ART BY MASASHI KISHIMOTO

Translation/Mari Morimoto
Series Touch-up Art & Lettering/Annaliese Christman, Inori Fukuda Trant
Additional Touch-up Art & Lettering/Sabrina Heep
Design/Sean Lee
Series Editor/Joel Enos
Graphic Novel Editor/Megan Bates

Published by VIZ Media, LLC
P.O. Box 77010
San Francisco, CA 94107

10 9 8 7 6 5 4 3
First printing, October 2009
Third printing, June 2015

PARENTAL ADVISORY
NARUTO is rated T for Teen and is recommended
for ages 13 and up. This volume contains realistic
and fantasy violence.
ratings.viz.com

SHONEN JUMP MANGA EDITION

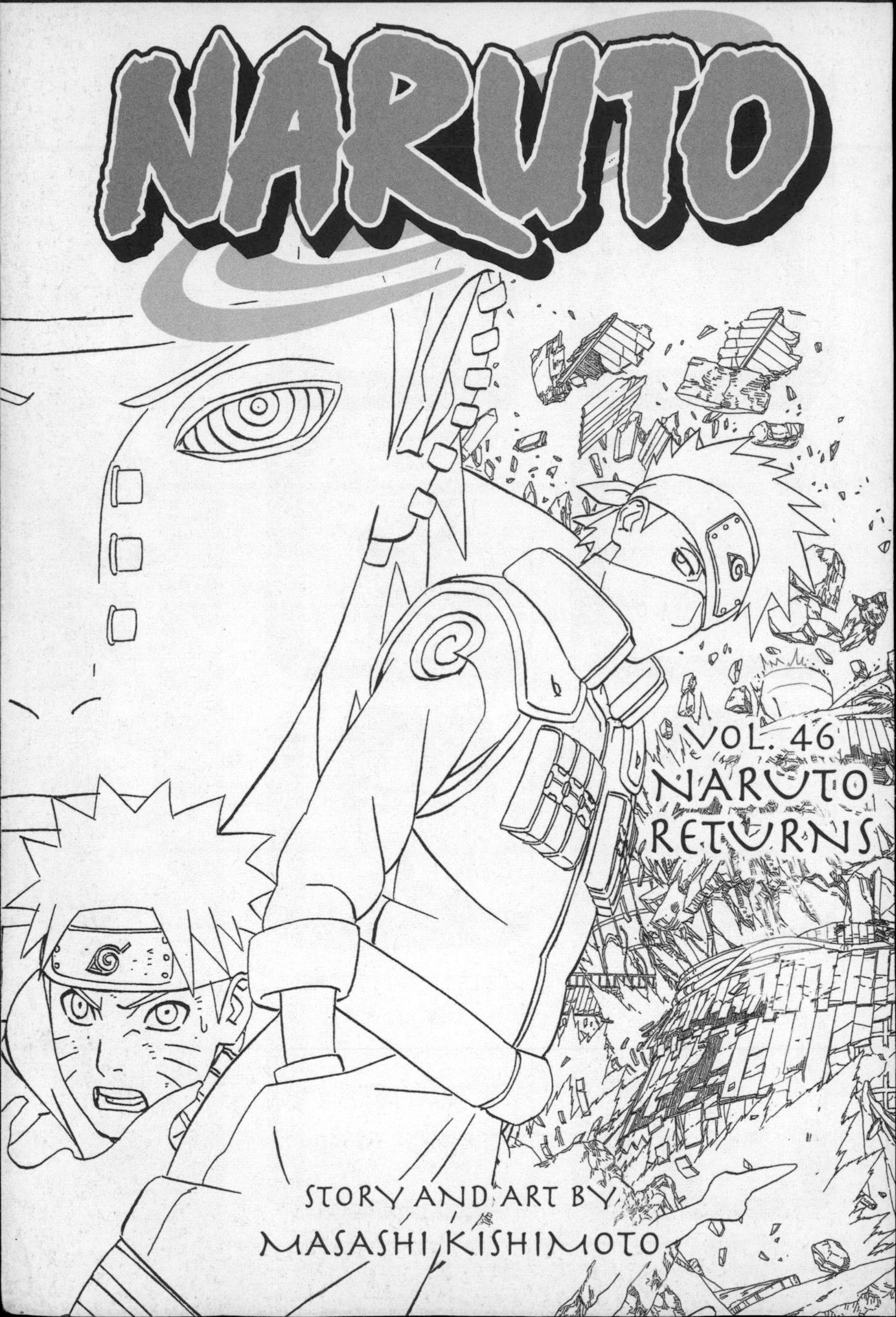
NARUTO
VOL. 46
NARUTO RETURNS
STORY AND ART BY
MASASHI KISHIMOTO

CHARACTERS

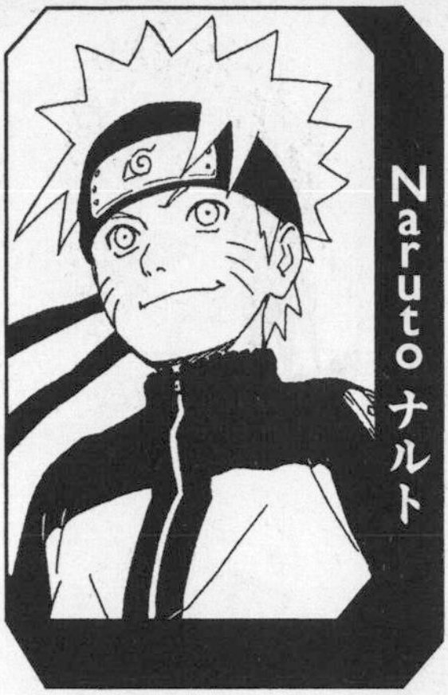

Naruto ナルト

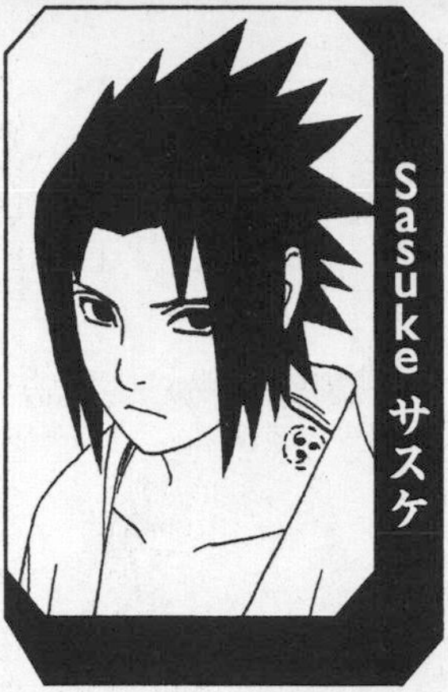

Sasuke サスケ

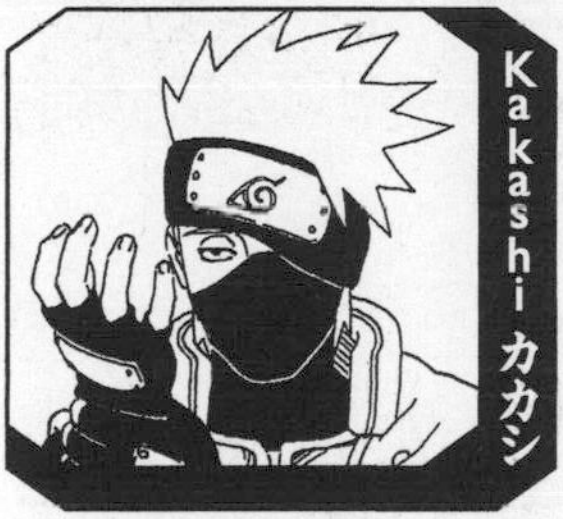

Kakashi カカシ

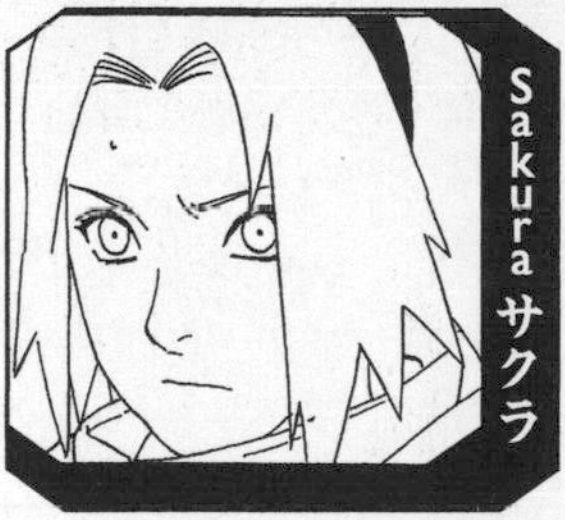

Sakura サクラ

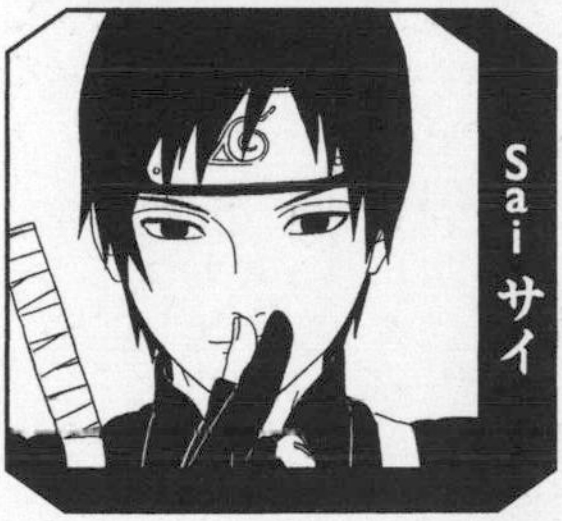

Sai サイ

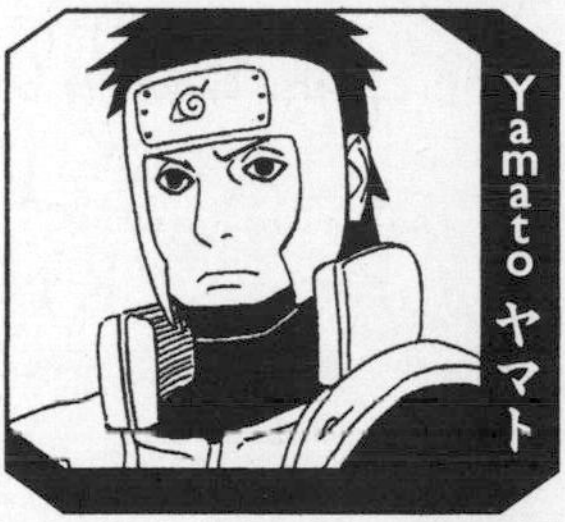

Yamato ヤマト

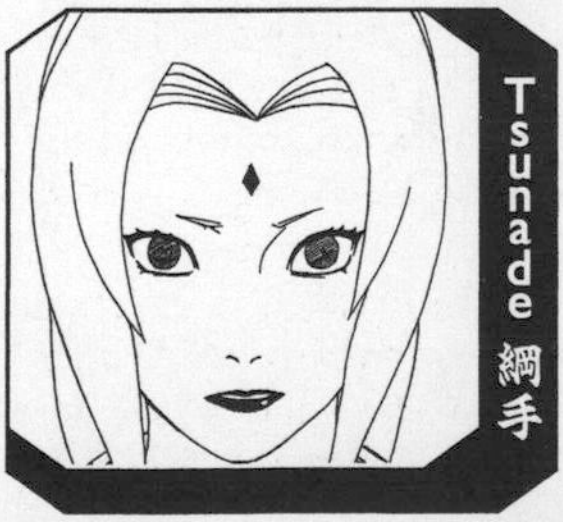

Tsunade 綱手

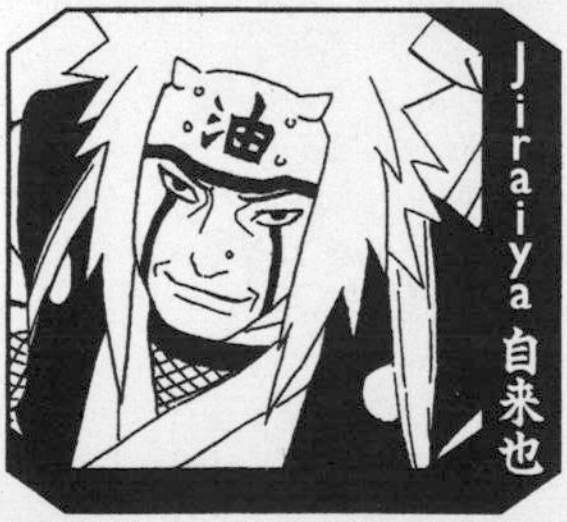

Jiraiya 自来也

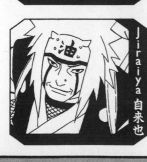

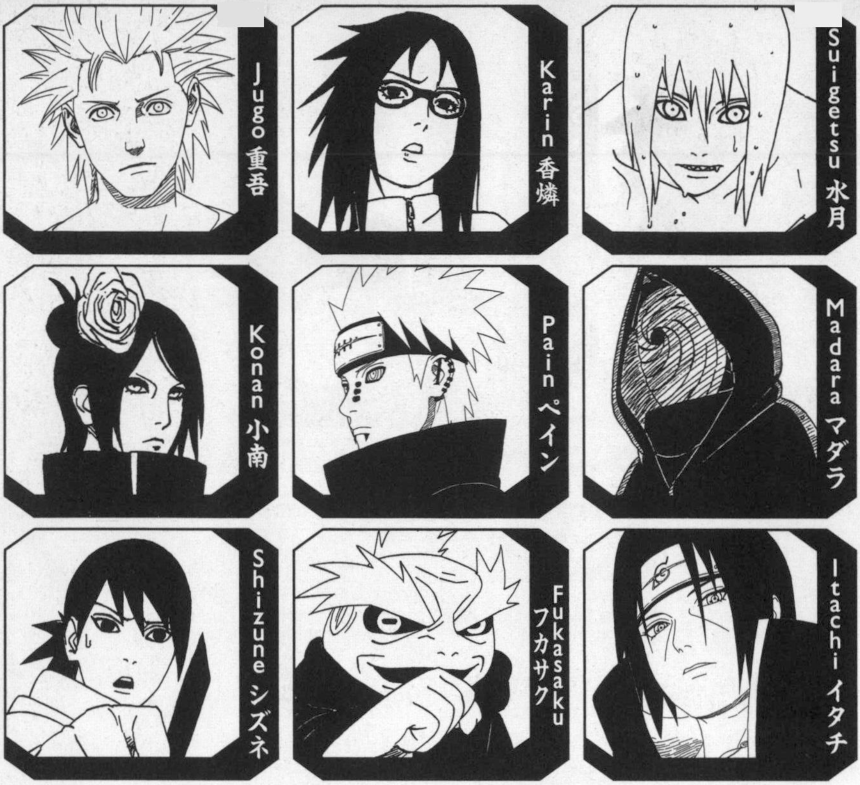
Suigetsu 水月
Karin 香燐
Jugo 重吾
Madara マダラ
Pain ペイン
Konan 小南
Itachi イタチ
Fukasaku フカサク
Shizune シズネ

THE STORY SO FAR...

Naruto, the biggest troublemaker at the Ninja Academy in the Village of Konohagakure, finally becomes a ninja along with his classmates Sasuke and Sakura. They grow and mature through countless trials and battles. However, Sasuke, unable to give up his quest for vengeance, leaves Konohagakure to seek Orochimaru and his power...

Two years pass. Naruto and his comrades grow up and head out once more. As their fierce battles against the Tailed Beast-targeting Akatsuki rage on, Sasuke rebels against Orochimaru and takes everything from him. Sasuke then gathers new companions and chases after his brother Itachi. The heroic battle concludes with Sasuke fulfilling his long-cherished goal. But after learning of his older brother's true intentions, Sasuke allies with the Akatsuki and sets out to destroy Konoha! Naruto trains in senjutsu with Fukasaku at Mount Myoboku. Meanwhile, Pain finally begins his assault against Konoha in search of Naruto!

NARUTO

VOL. 46
NARUTO RETURNS

CONTENTS

Number 423: Tendo's Ability!!

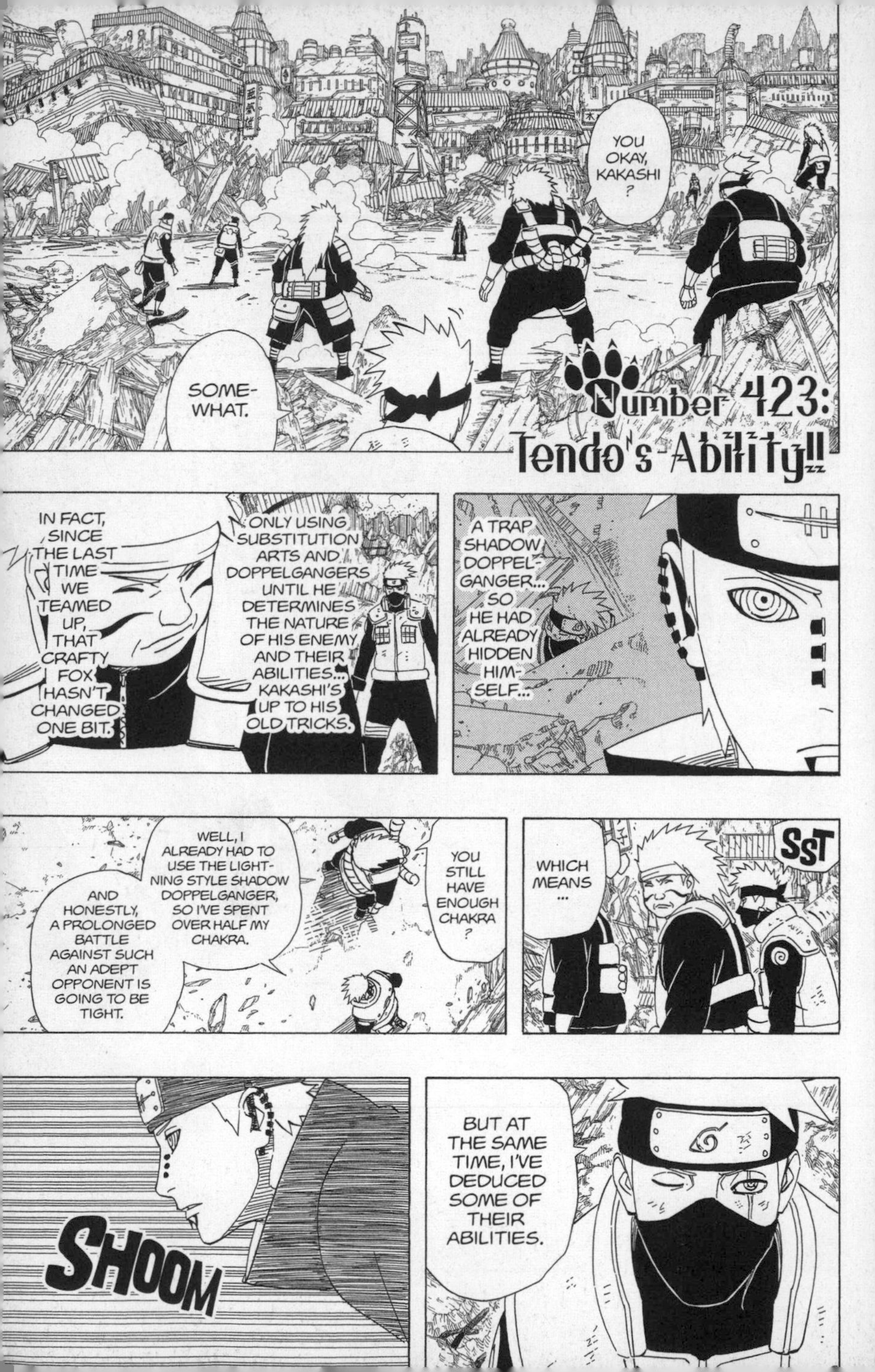
YOU OKAY, KAKASHI?
SOME-WHAT.
A TRAP SHADOW DOPPELGANGER... SO HE HAD ALREADY HIDDEN HIMSELF...
ONLY USING SUBSTITUTION ARTS AND DOPPELGANGERS UNTIL HE DETERMINES THE NATURE OF HIS ENEMY AND THEIR ABILITIES... KAKASHI'S UP TO HIS OLD TRICKS.
IN FACT, SINCE THE LAST TIME WE TEAMED UP, THAT CRAFTY FOX HASN'T CHANGED ONE BIT.
SST
WHICH MEANS ...
YOU STILL HAVE ENOUGH CHAKRA?
WELL, I ALREADY HAD TO USE THE LIGHTNING STYLE SHADOW DOPPELGANGER, SO I'VE SPENT OVER HALF MY CHAKRA.
AND HONESTLY, A PROLONGED BATTLE AGAINST SUCH AN ADEPT OPPONENT IS GOING TO BE TIGHT.
BUT AT THE SAME TIME, I'VE DEDUCED SOME OF THEIR ABILITIES.
SHOOM

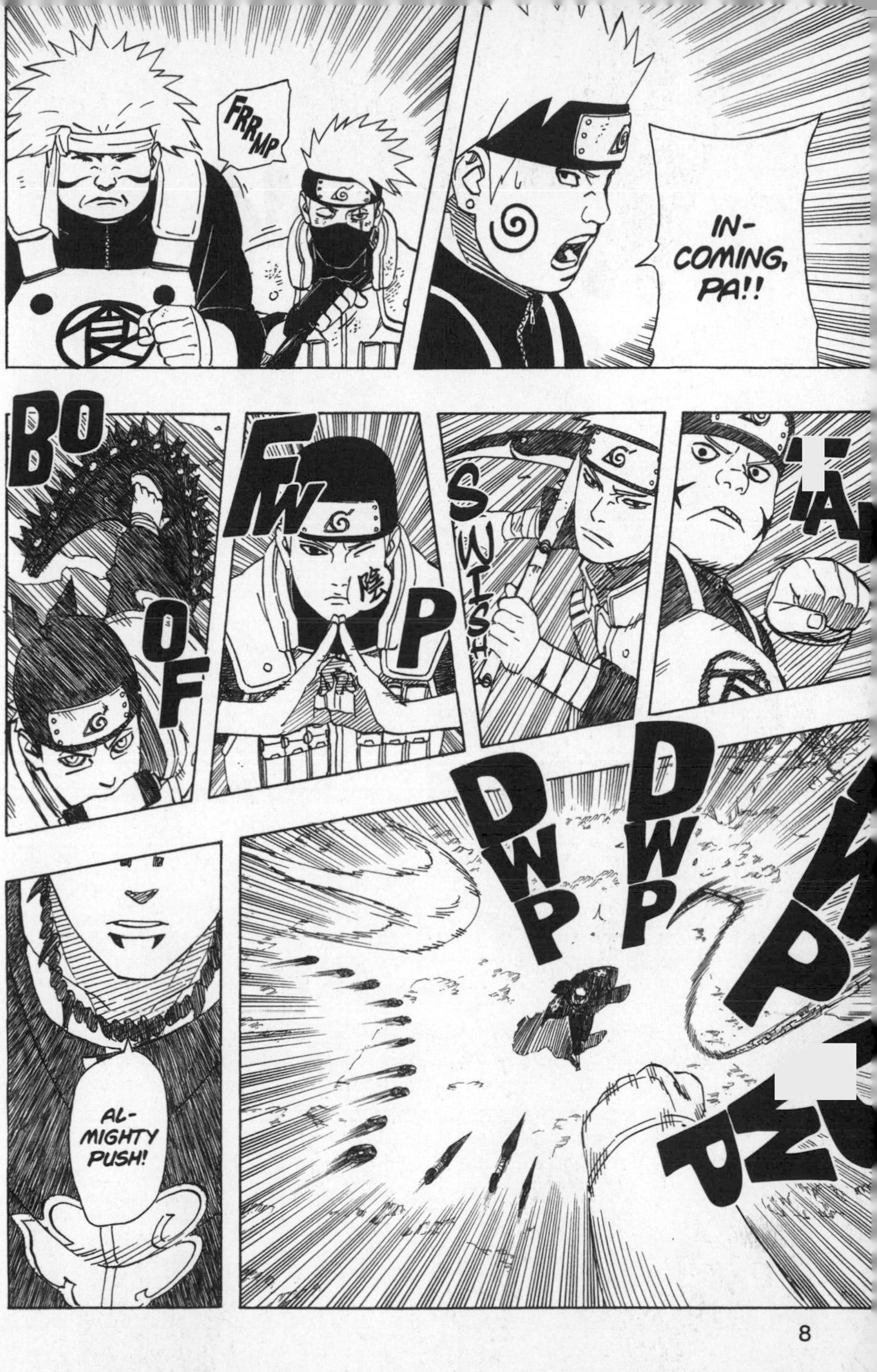
IN-COMING, PA!!
FRRMP
SWISH
FWP
BOOF
DWP
DWP
AL-MIGHTY PUSH!

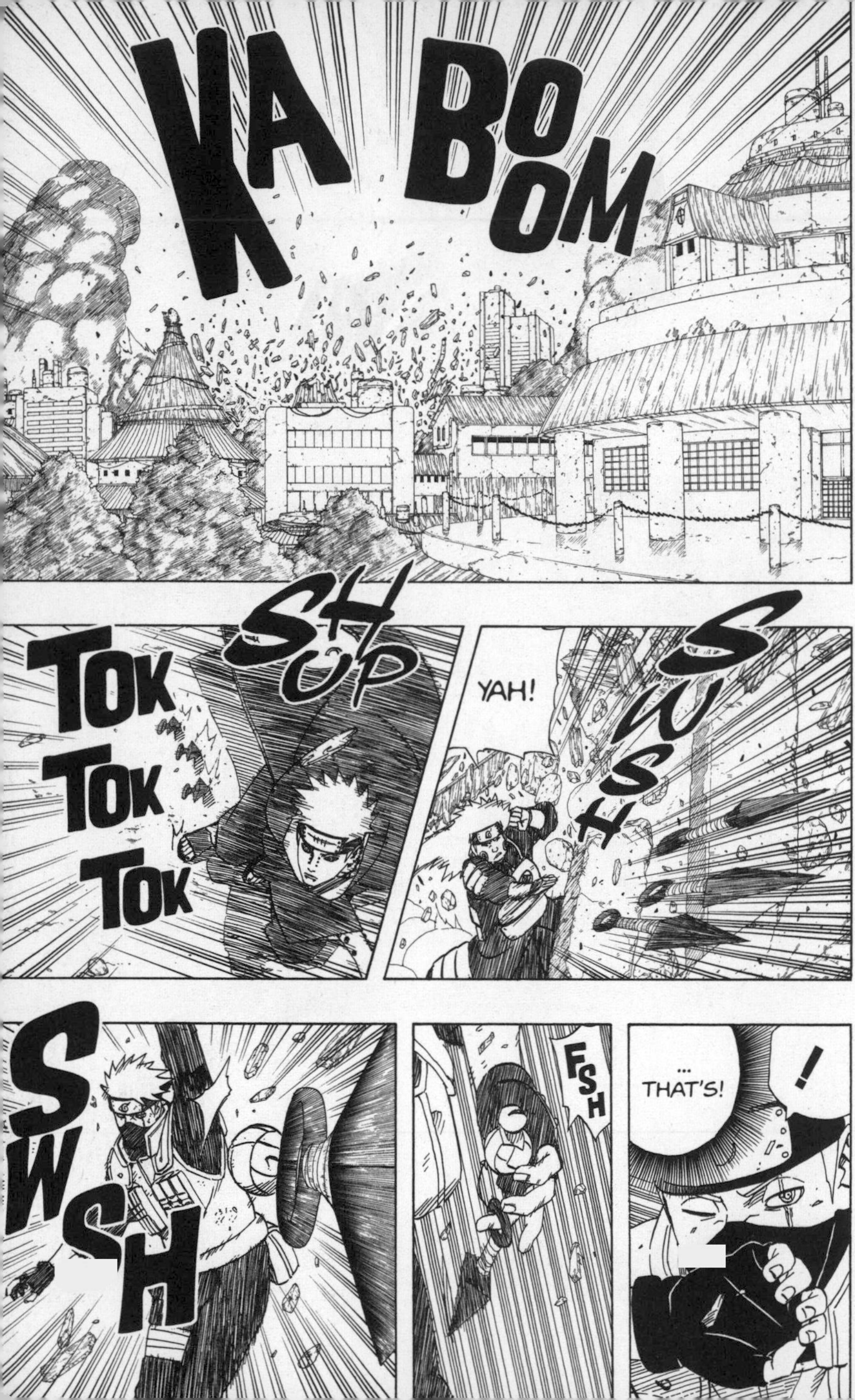
KABOOM
SWSH
YAH!
SHUP
TOK
TOK
TOK
... THAT'S!
!
FSH
SWSH

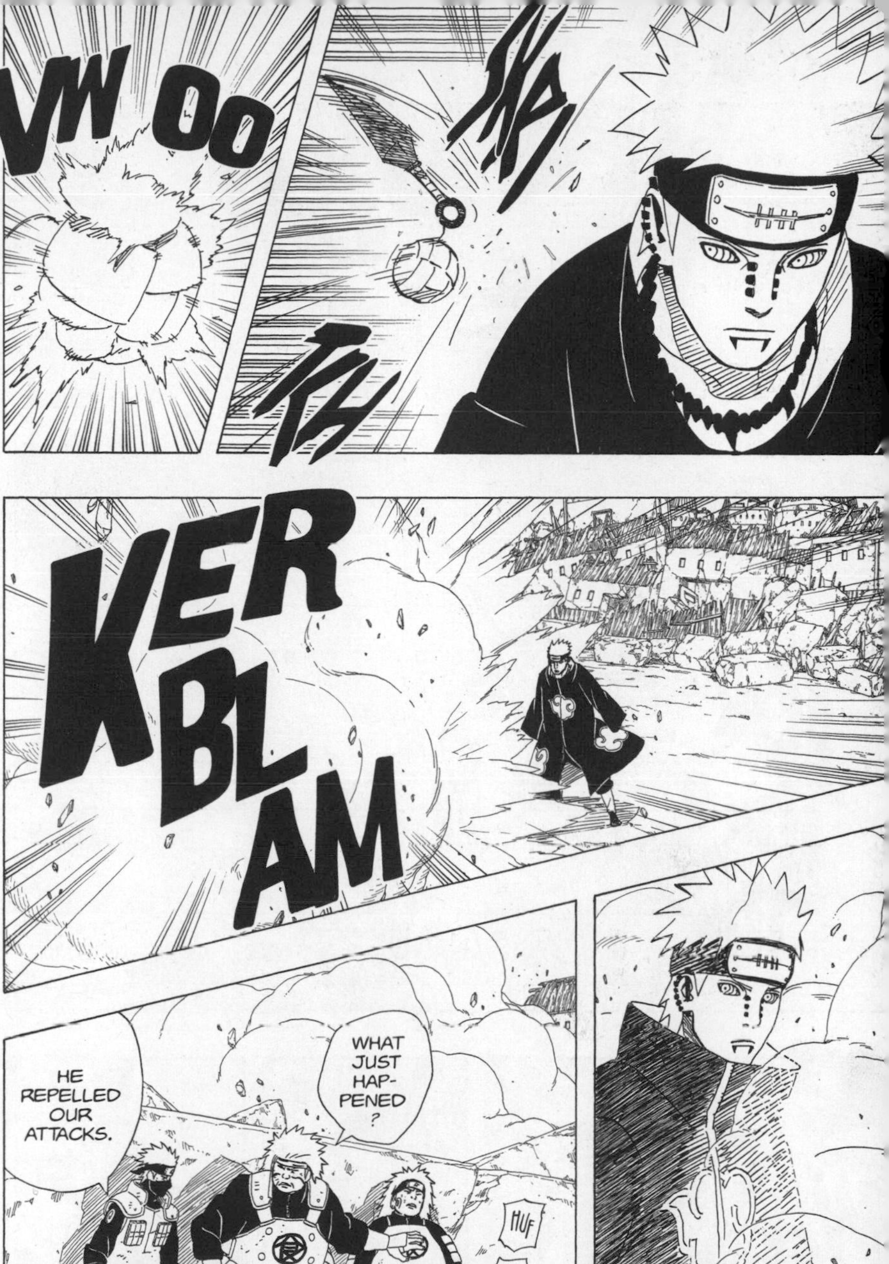
VWOO
KERBLAM
WHAT JUST HAP-PENED?
HE REPELLED OUR ATTACKS.
HUF
HUF

READ THIS WAY

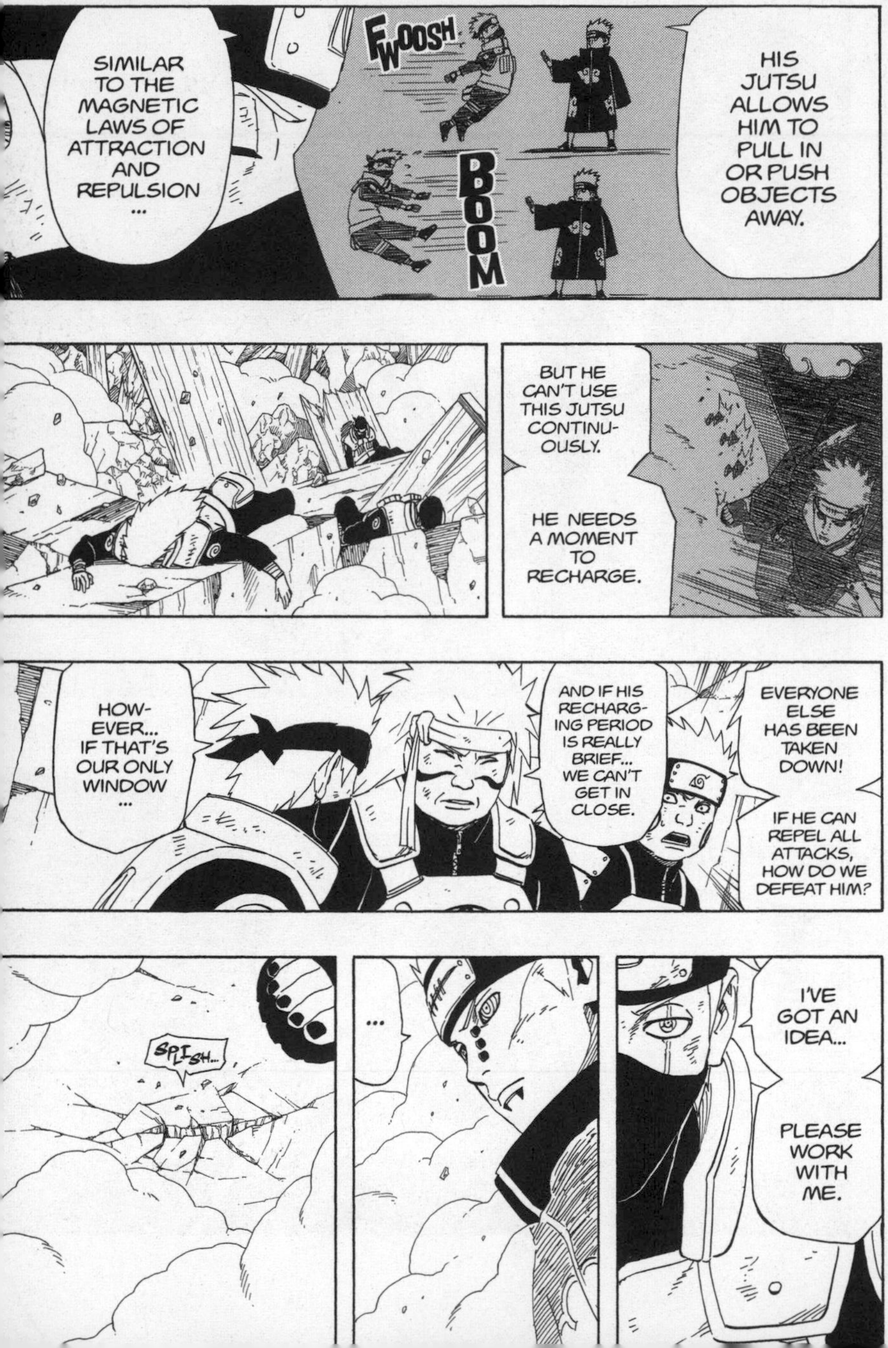
HIS JUTSU ALLOWS HIM TO PULL IN OR PUSH OBJECTS AWAY.
FWOOSH
BOOM
SIMILAR TO THE MAGNETIC LAWS OF ATTRACTION AND REPULSION ...
BUT HE CAN'T USE THIS JUTSU CONTINU-OUSLY.
HE NEEDS A MOMENT TO RECHARGE.
EVERYONE ELSE HAS BEEN TAKEN DOWN!
IF HE CAN REPEL ALL ATTACKS, HOW DO WE DEFEAT HIM?
AND IF HIS RECHARG-ING PERIOD IS REALLY BRIEF... WE CAN'T GET IN CLOSE.
HOW-EVER... IF THAT'S OUR ONLY WINDOW ...
I'VE GOT AN IDEA...
PLEASE WORK WITH ME.
...
SPLISH...

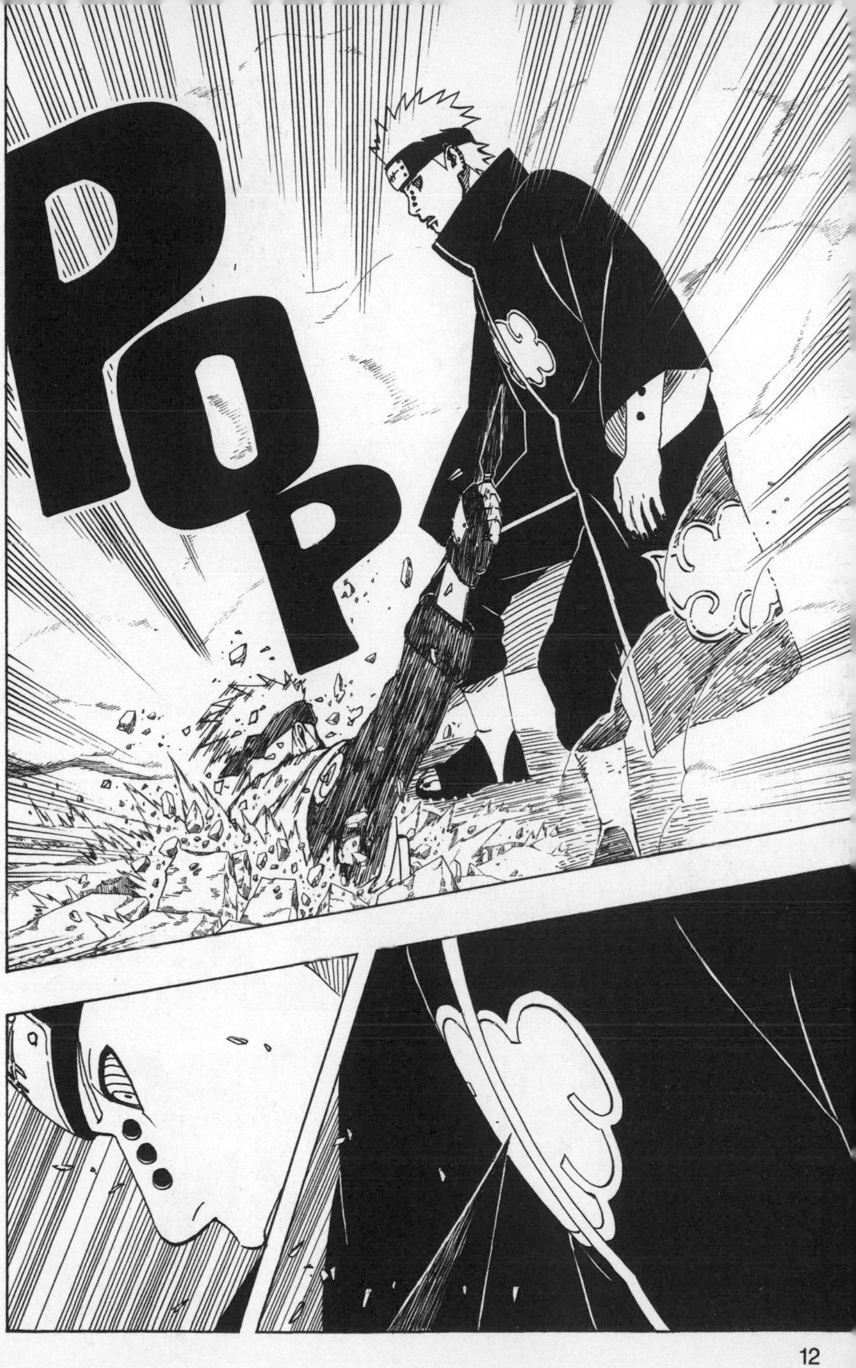

POP

READ THIS WAY

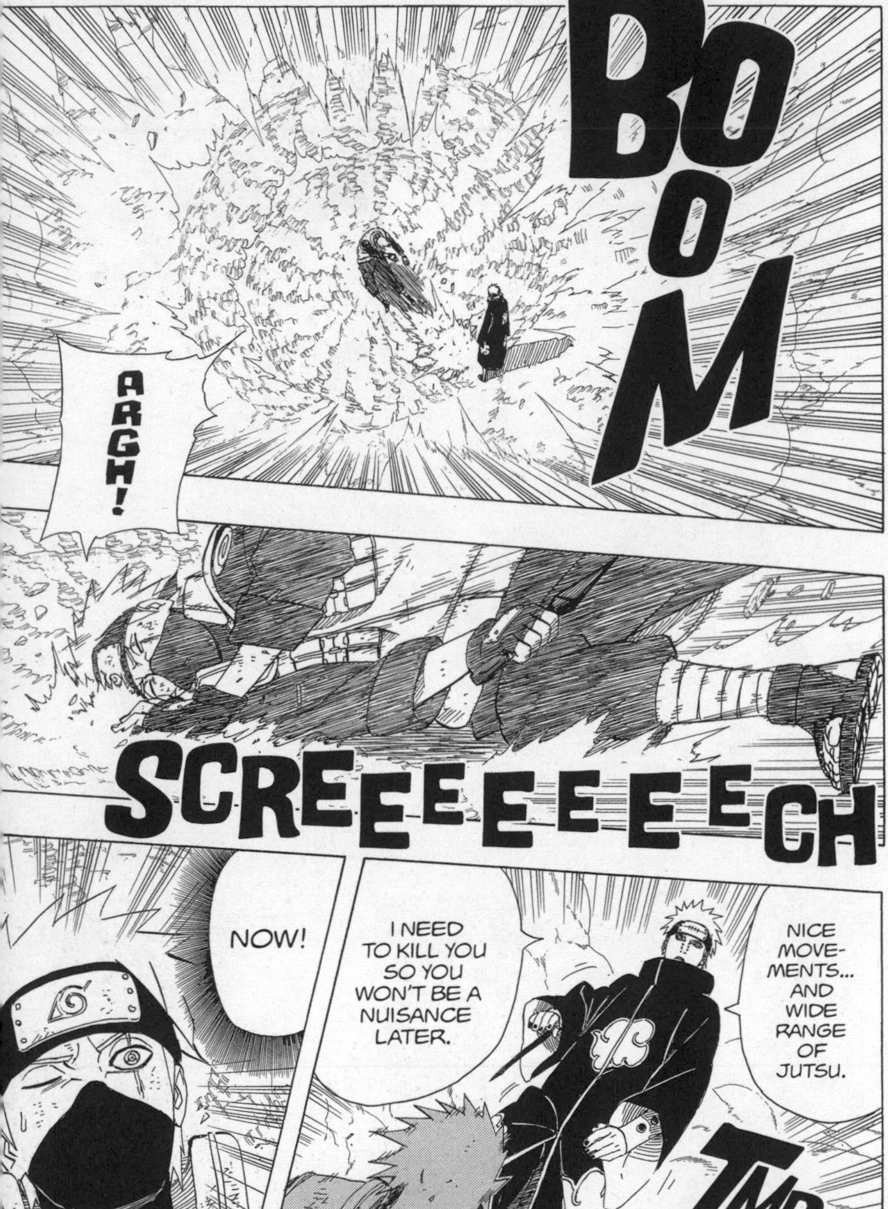
BOOM
ARGH!
SCREEEEEEECH
NICE MOVEMENTS... AND WIDE RANGE OF JUTSU.
I NEED TO KILL YOU SO YOU WON'T BE A NUISANCE LATER.
TMP
NOW!

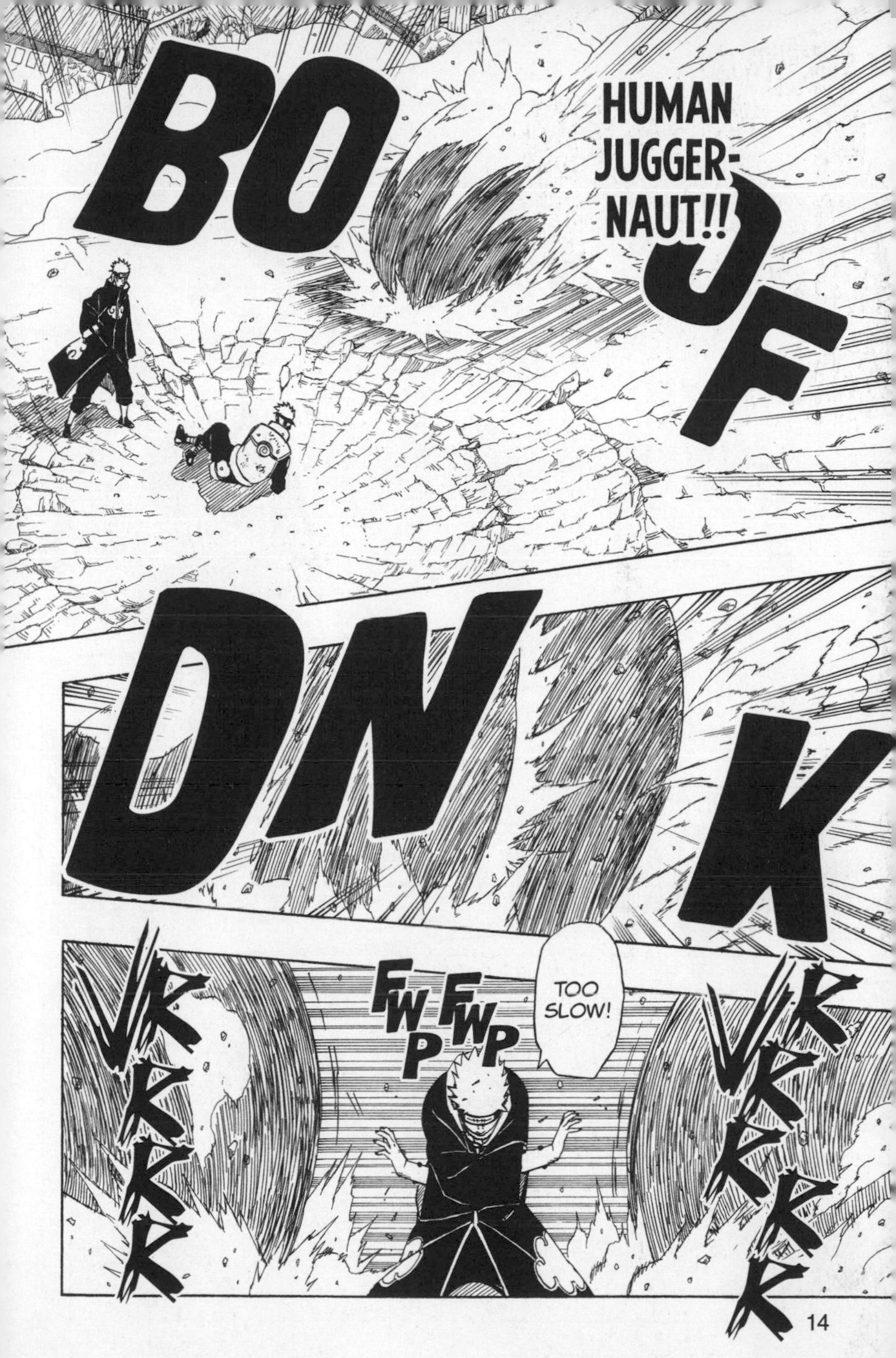
BOOF
HUMAN JUGGER-NAUT!!
DNK
TOO SLOW!
FWP FWP
VRKKKKK
VRKKKKK

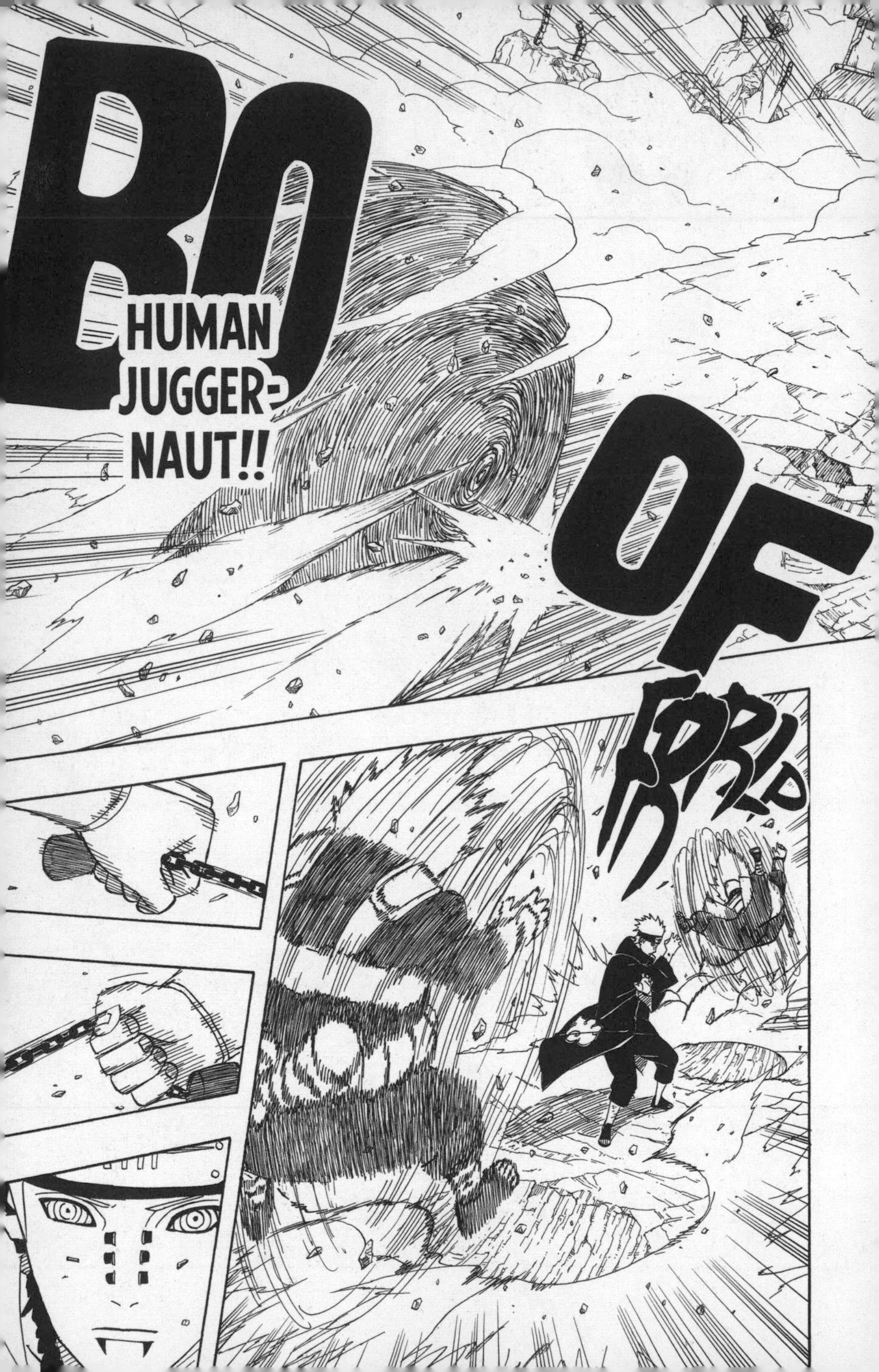
RO
HUMAN JUGGER-NAUT!!
OF
FDRI.D

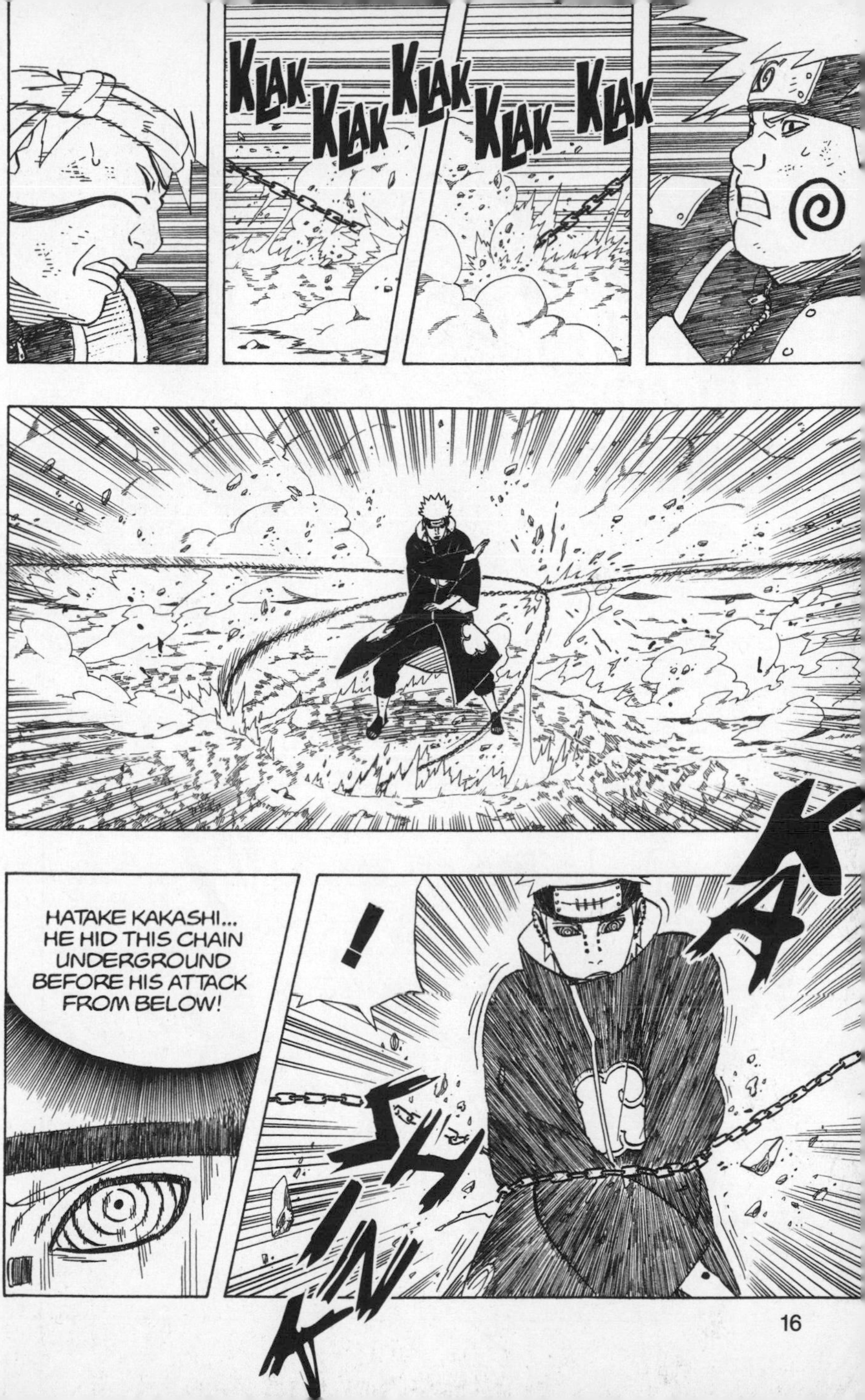
KLAK
KLAK
KLAK
KLAK
KLAK
!
KA
SHINK
HATAKE KAKASHI... HE HID THIS CHAIN UNDERGROUND BEFORE HIS ATTACK FROM BELOW!

READ THIS WAY

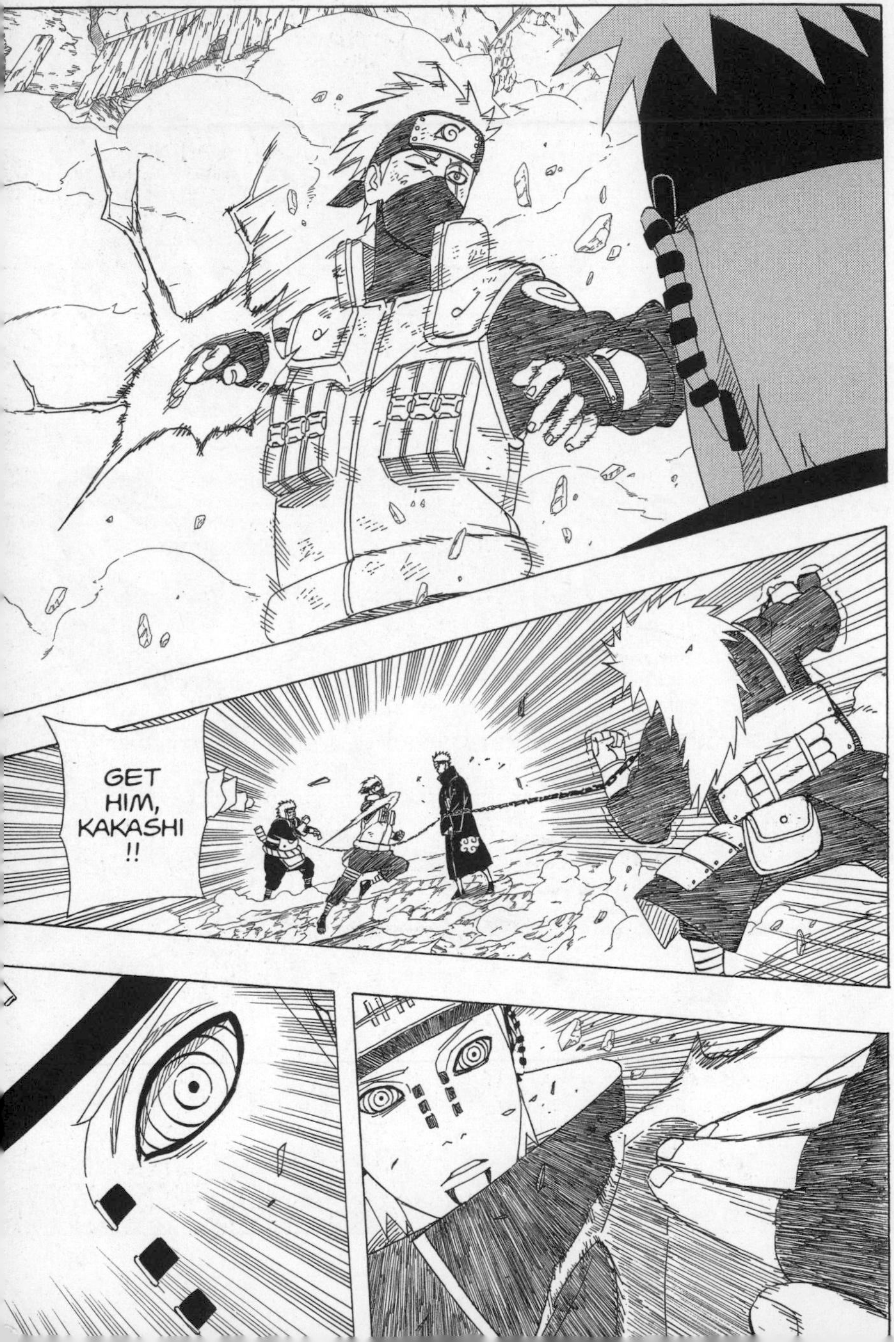
GET HIM, KAKASHI !!

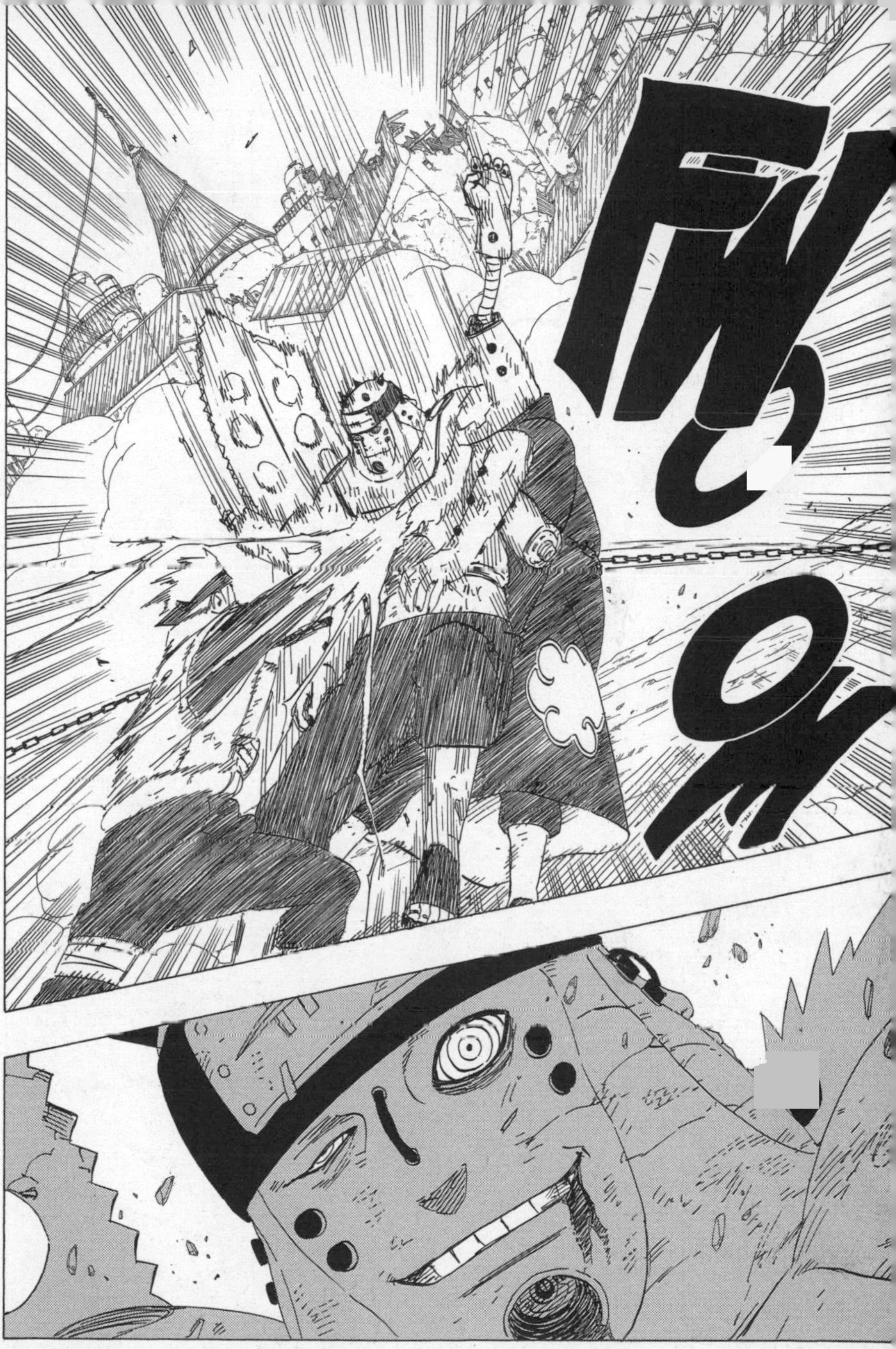
FWOOM

READ THIS WAY

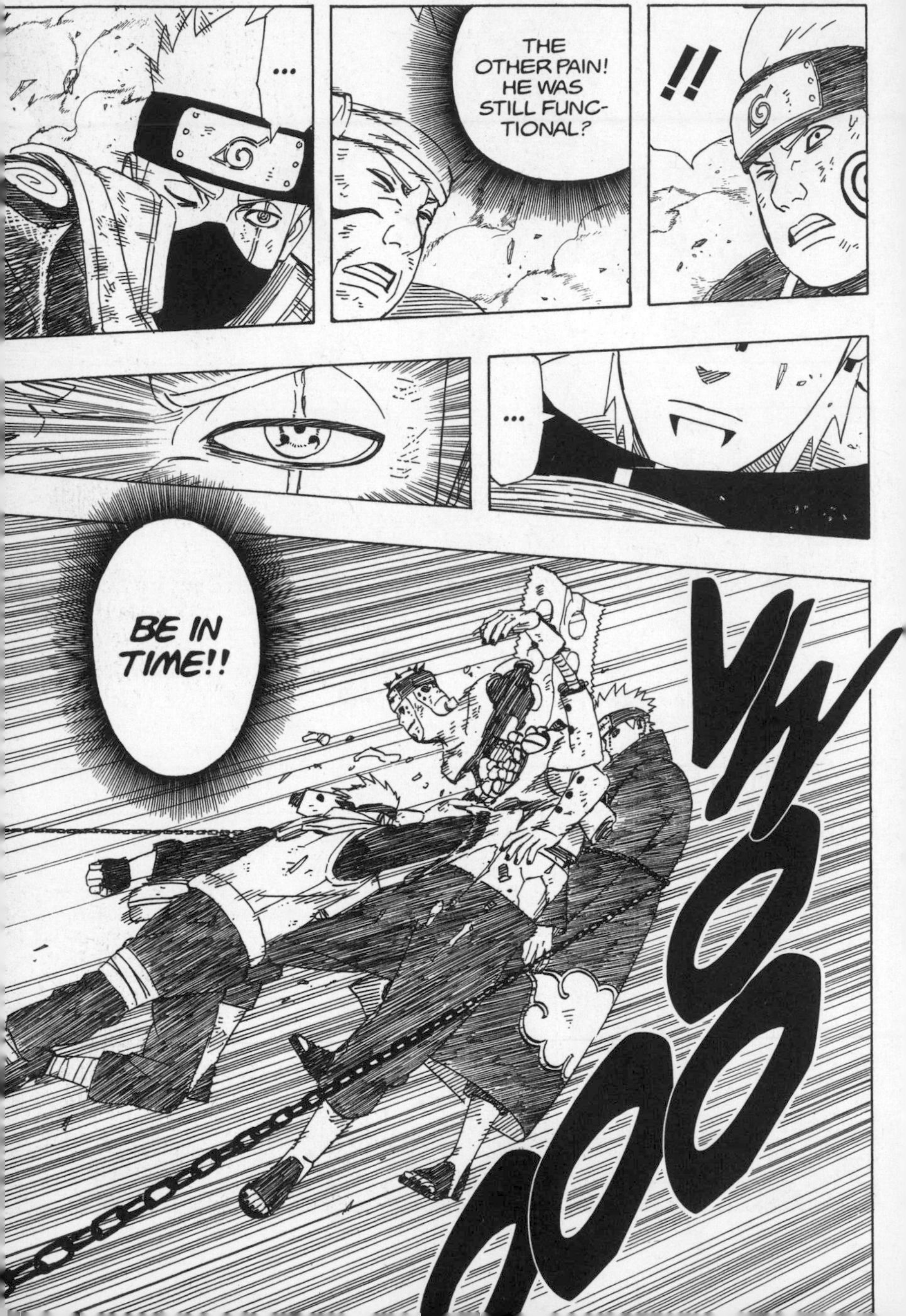
!!
THE OTHER PAIN! HE WAS STILL FUNCTIONAL?
...
...
BE IN TIME!!

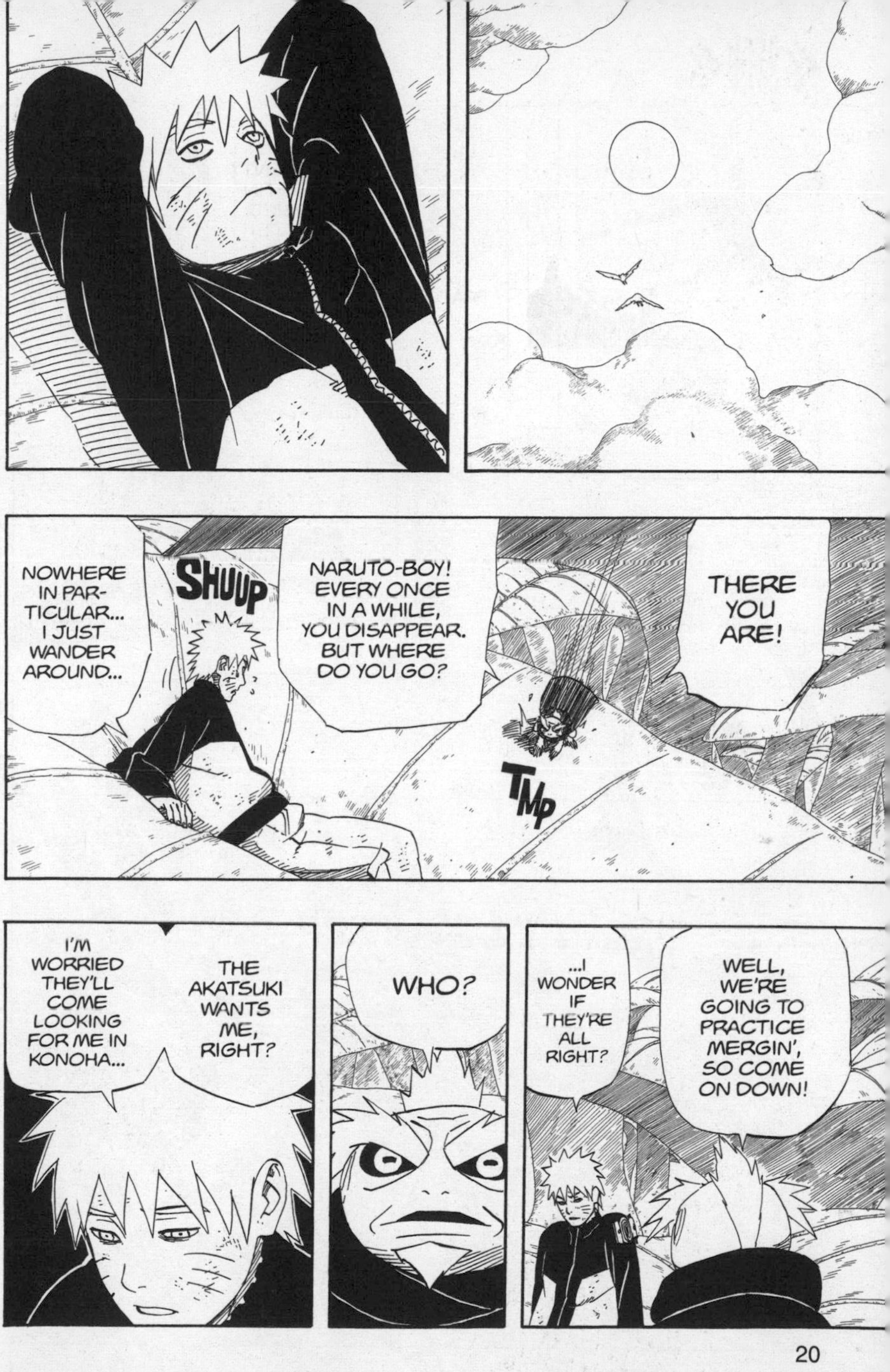
THERE YOU ARE!
TMP
NARUTO-BOY! EVERY ONCE IN A WHILE, YOU DISAPPEAR. BUT WHERE DO YOU GO?
SHUUP
NOWHERE IN PARTICULAR... I JUST WANDER AROUND...
WELL, WE'RE GOING TO PRACTICE MERGIN', SO COME ON DOWN!
...I WONDER IF THEY'RE ALL RIGHT?
WHO?
THE AKATSUKI WANTS ME, RIGHT?
I'M WORRIED THEY'LL COME LOOKING FOR ME IN KONOHA...

READ THIS WAY

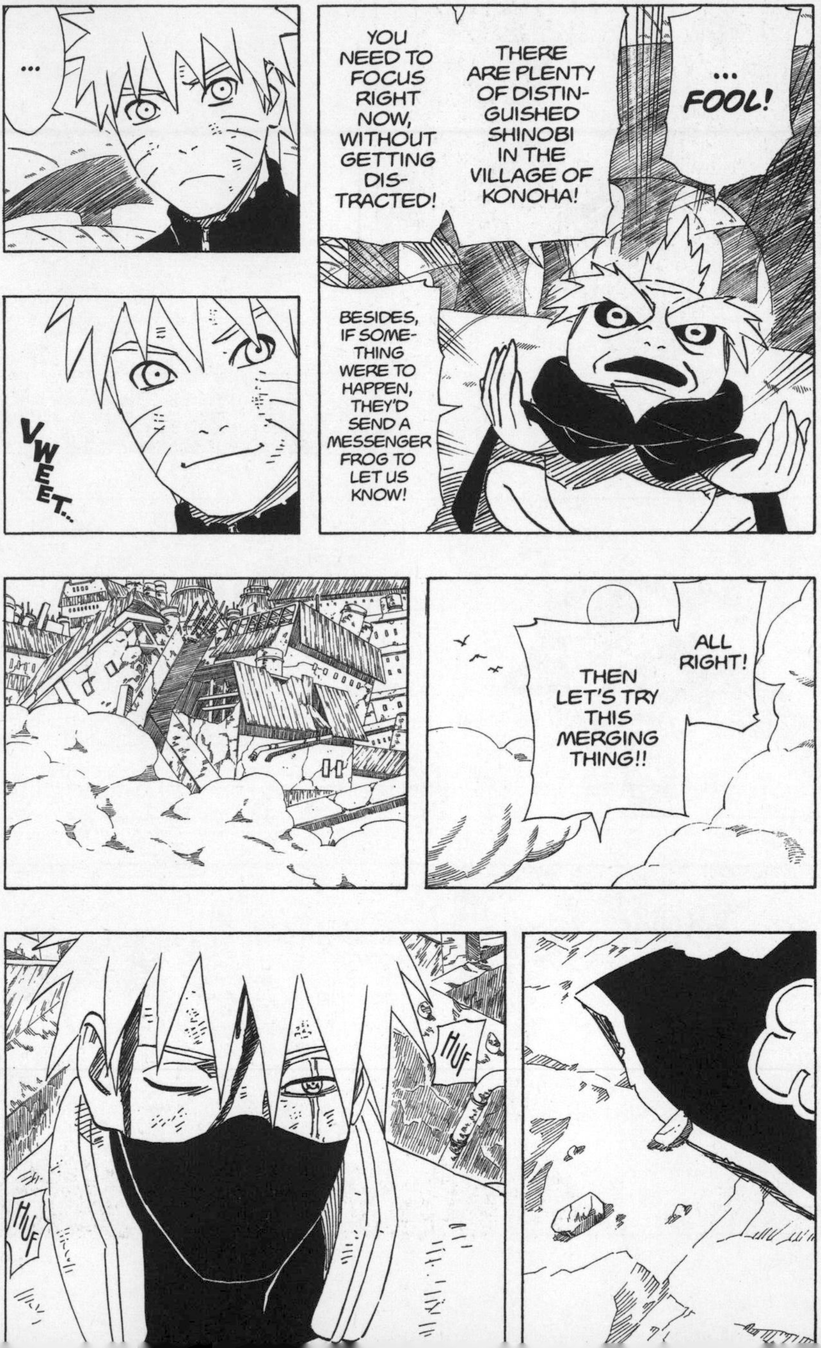
... FOOL!
THERE ARE PLENTY OF DISTIN-GUISHED SHINOBI IN THE VILLAGE OF KONOHA!
YOU NEED TO FOCUS RIGHT NOW, WITHOUT GETTING DIS-TRACTED!
BESIDES, IF SOME-THING WERE TO HAPPEN, THEY'D SEND A MESSENGER FROG TO LET US KNOW!
...
VWEET...
ALL RIGHT!
THEN LET'S TRY THIS MERGING THING!!
HUF
HUF

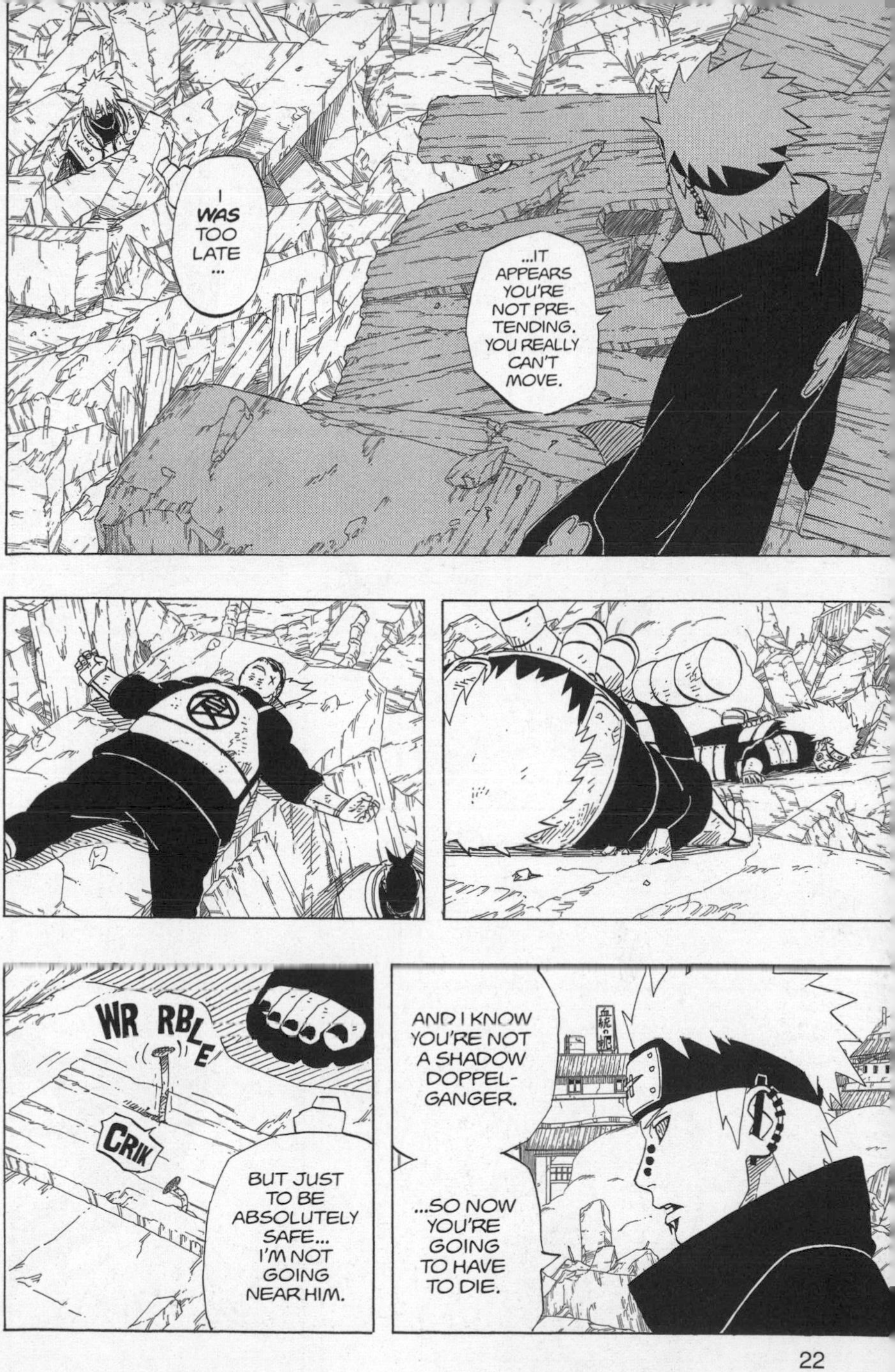
...IT APPEARS YOU'RE NOT PRETENDING. YOU REALLY CAN'T MOVE.
I WAS TOO LATE ...
AND I KNOW YOU'RE NOT A SHADOW DOPPEL-GANGER.
...SO NOW YOU'RE GOING TO HAVE TO DIE.
WR RBLE
CRIK
BUT JUST TO BE ABSOLUTELY SAFE... I'M NOT GOING NEAR HIM.

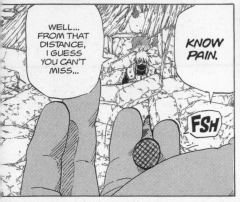

WELL... FROM THAT DISTANCE, I GUESS YOU CAN'T MISS...

KNOW PAIN.

FSH

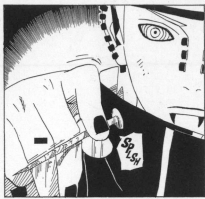

SPLSH

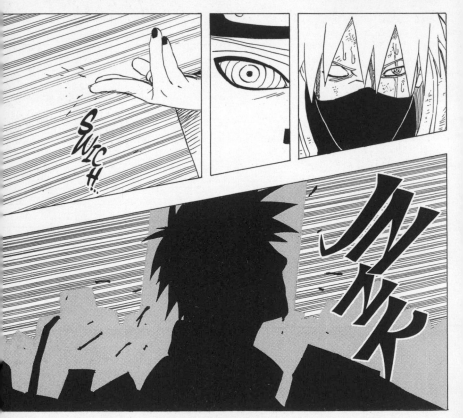

SWICH!!

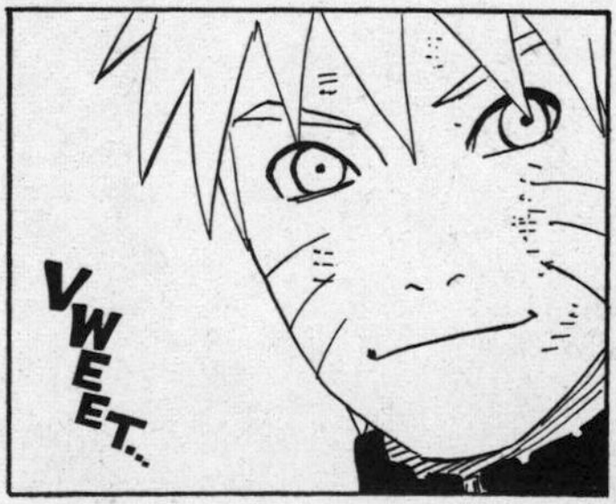
VWEET...

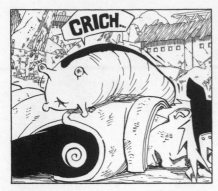

CRICH...

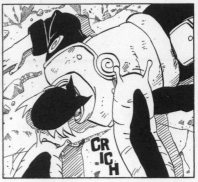

CRICH

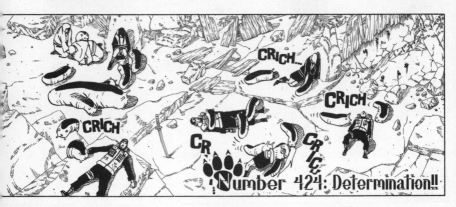

CRICH...

CRICH

CRICH

CR

CR
ICH

Number 424: Determination!!

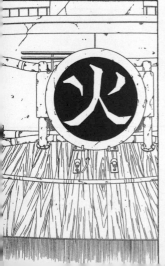

PLICH...

UNH...

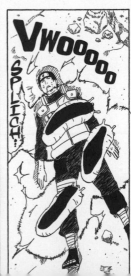

VWOOOOO

SPLICH...

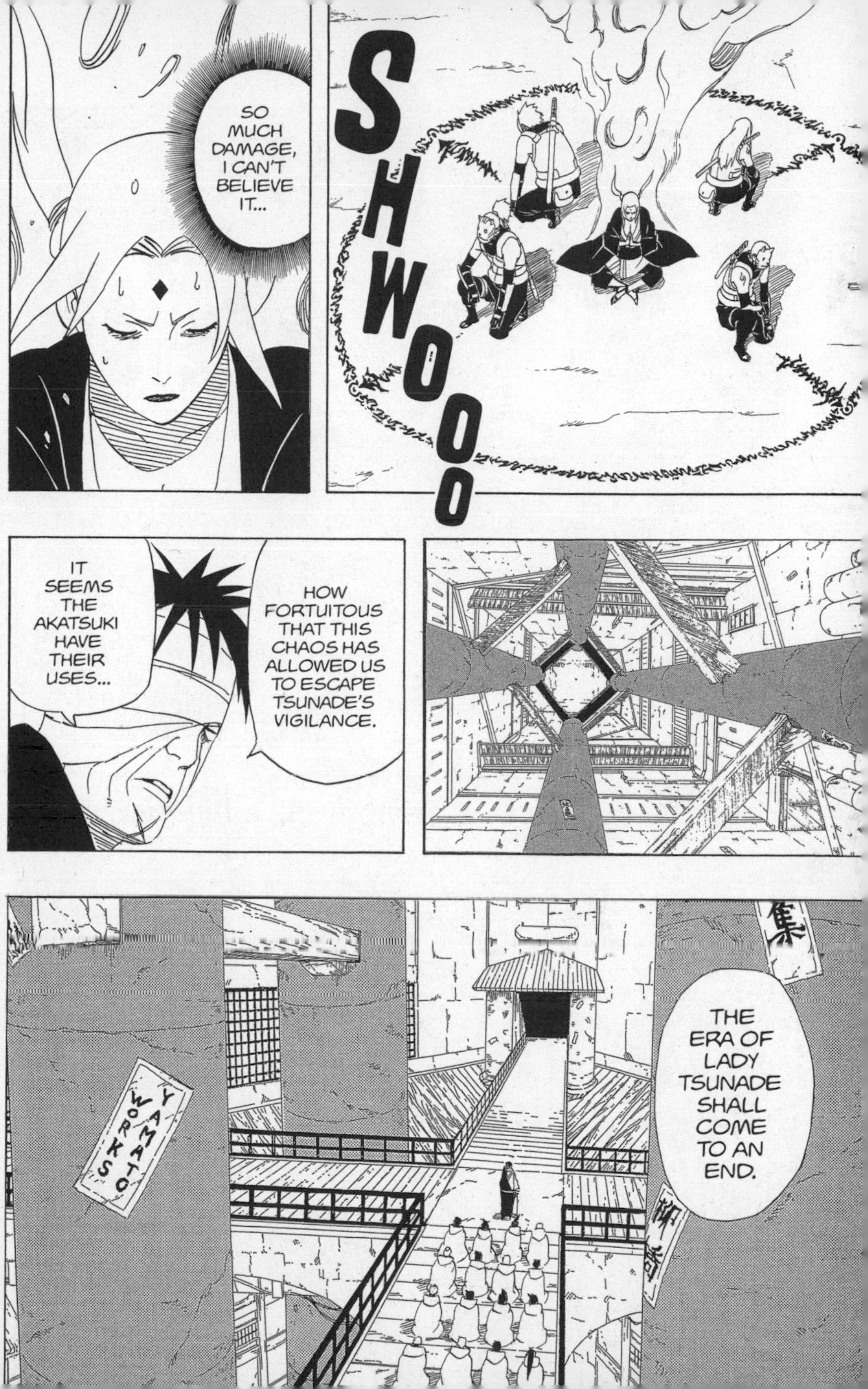
SHWOOO
SO MUCH DAMAGE, I CAN'T BELIEVE IT...
HOW FORTUITOUS THAT THIS CHAOS HAS ALLOWED US TO ESCAPE TSUNADE'S VIGILANCE.
IT SEEMS THE AKATSUKI HAVE THEIR USES...
集
THE ERA OF LADY TSUNADE SHALL COME TO AN END.
YAMATO WORKS

READ THIS WAY

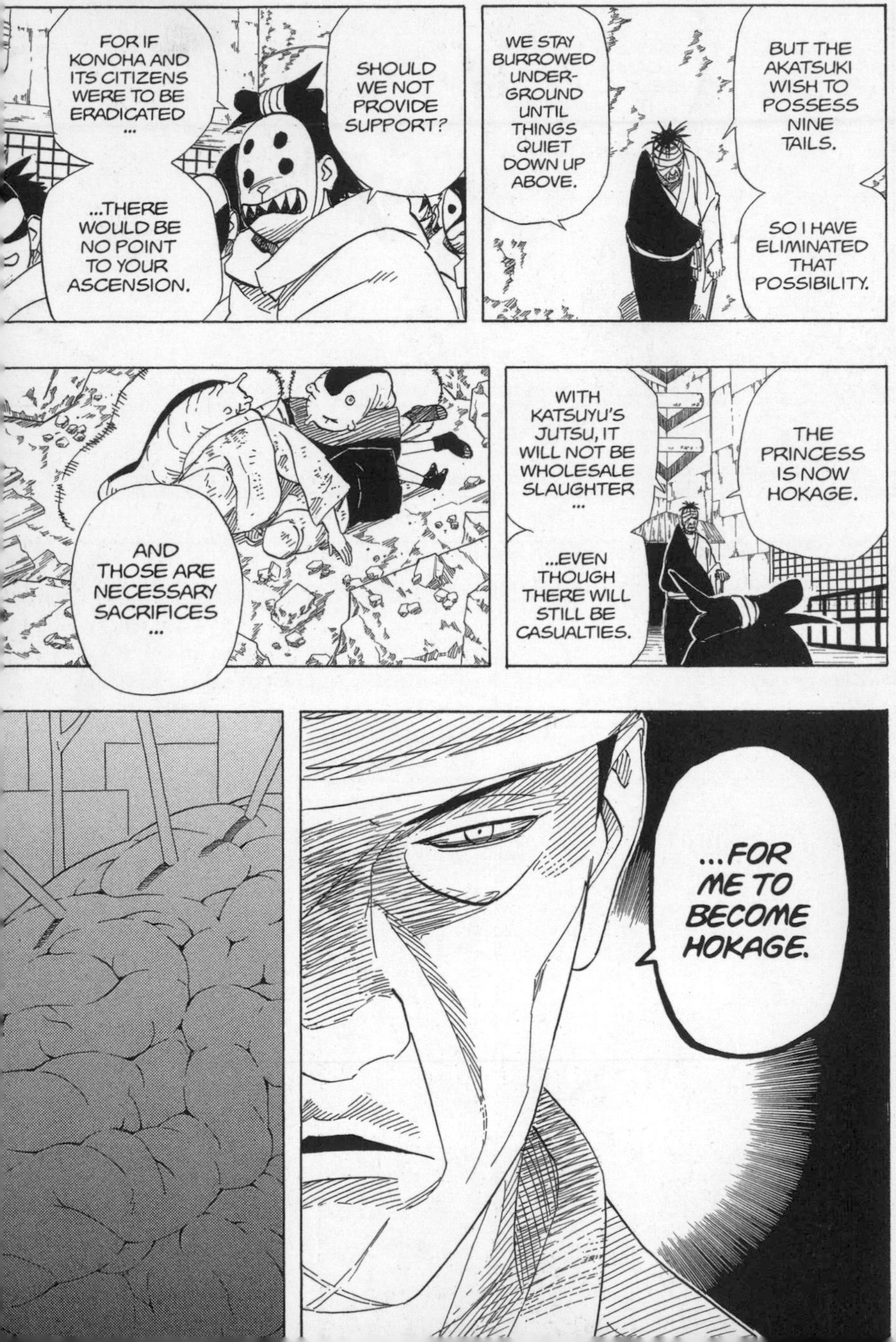

BUT THE AKATSUKI WISH TO POSSESS NINE TAILS.
SO I HAVE ELIMINATED THAT POSSIBILITY.
WE STAY BURROWED UNDER-GROUND UNTIL THINGS QUIET DOWN UP ABOVE.
SHOULD WE NOT PROVIDE SUPPORT?
FOR IF KONOHA AND ITS CITIZENS WERE TO BE ERADICATED ...
...THERE WOULD BE NO POINT TO YOUR ASCENSION.
THE PRINCESS IS NOW HOKAGE.
WITH KATSUYU'S JUTSU, IT WILL NOT BE WHOLESALE SLAUGHTER ...
...EVEN THOUGH THERE WILL STILL BE CASUALTIES.
AND THOSE ARE NECESSARY SACRIFICES ...
...FOR ME TO BECOME HOKAGE.

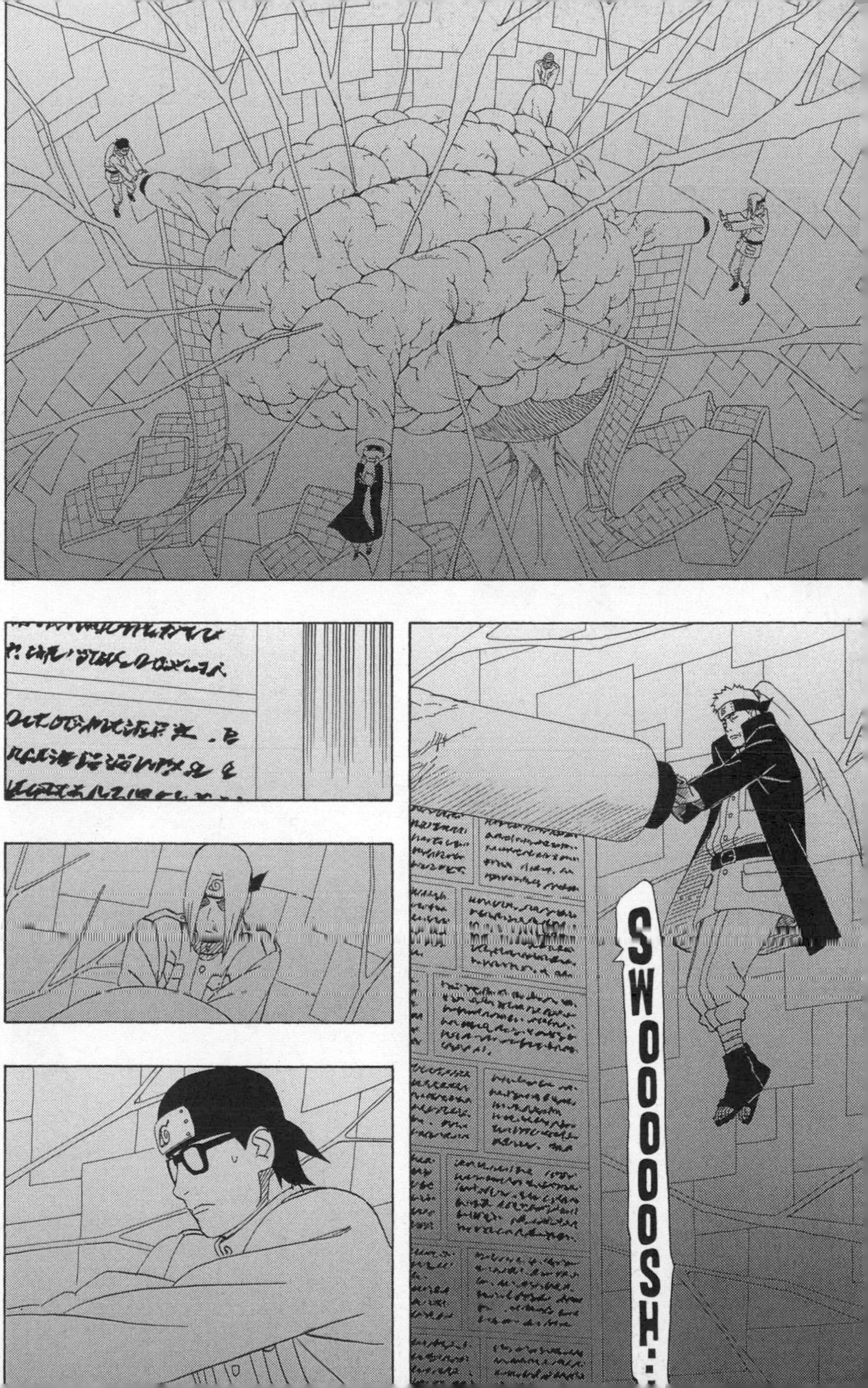
SWOOOOOOSH..

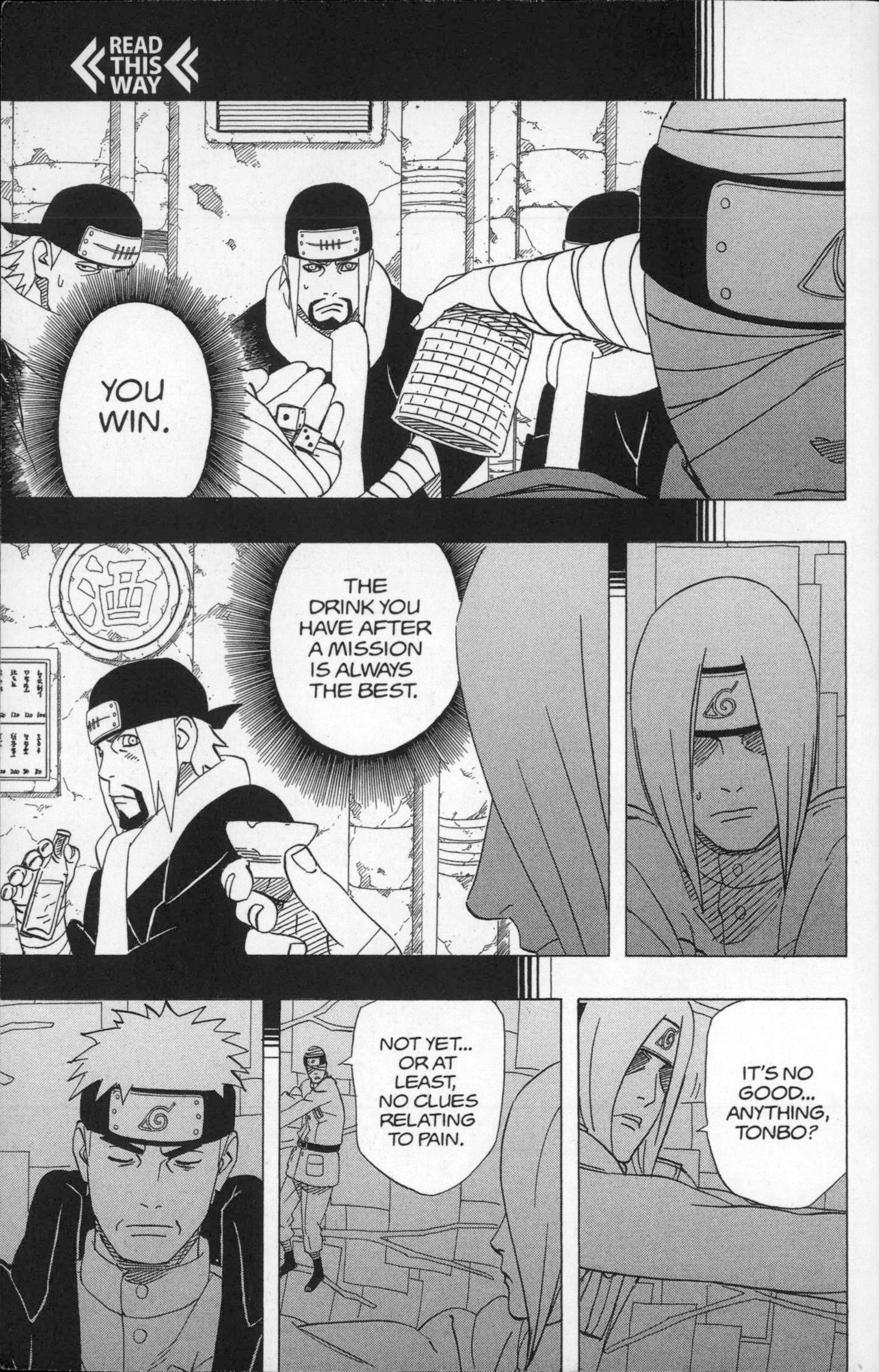
READ THIS WAY
YOU WIN.
THE DRINK YOU HAVE AFTER A MISSION IS ALWAYS THE BEST.
IT'S NO GOOD... ANYTHING, TONBO?
NOT YET... OR AT LEAST, NO CLUES RELATING TO PAIN.

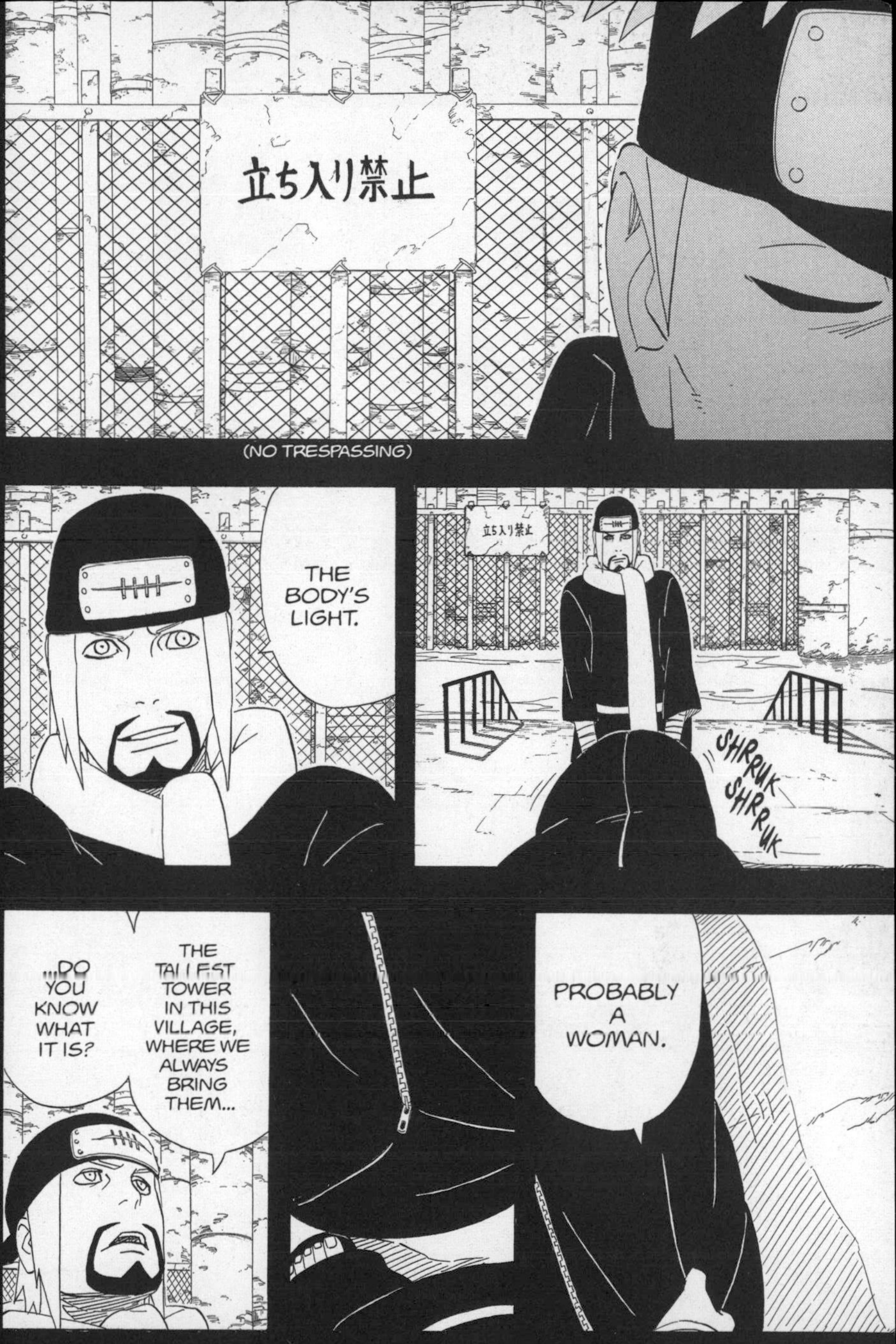

立ち入り禁止
(NO TRESPASSING)
立ち入り禁止
SHRRUK SHRRUK
THE BODY'S LIGHT.
PROBABLY A WOMAN.
THE TALLEST TOWER IN THIS VILLAGE, WHERE WE ALWAYS BRING THEM...
...DO YOU KNOW WHAT IT IS?

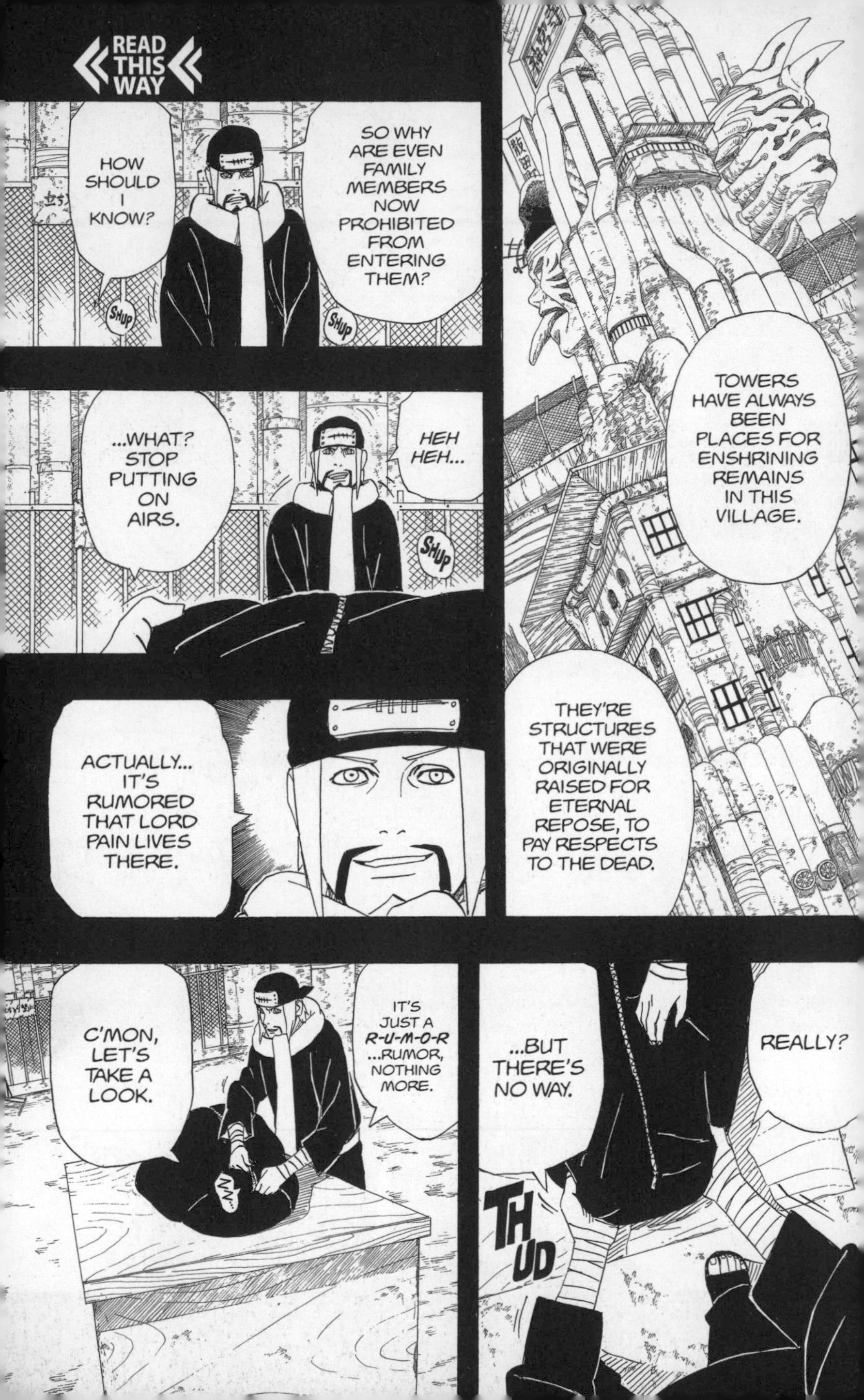
READ THIS WAY
TOWERS HAVE ALWAYS BEEN PLACES FOR ENSHRINING REMAINS IN THIS VILLAGE.
THEY'RE STRUCTURES THAT WERE ORIGINALLY RAISED FOR ETERNAL REPOSE, TO PAY RESPECTS TO THE DEAD.
SO WHY ARE EVEN FAMILY MEMBERS NOW PROHIBITED FROM ENTERING THEM?
HOW SHOULD I KNOW?
SHUP
SHUP
HEH HEH...
...WHAT? STOP PUTTING ON AIRS.
SHUP
ACTUALLY... IT'S RUMORED THAT LORD PAIN LIVES THERE.
REALLY?
...BUT THERE'S NO WAY.
THUD
IT'S JUST A R-U-M-O-R ...RUMOR, NOTHING MORE.
C'MON, LET'S TAKE A LOOK.

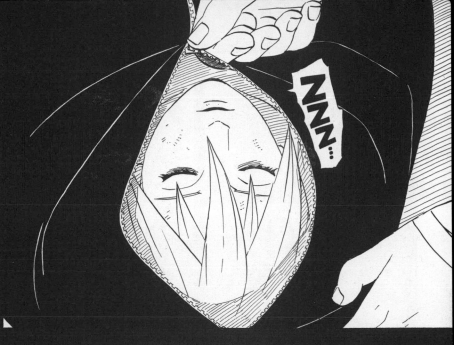

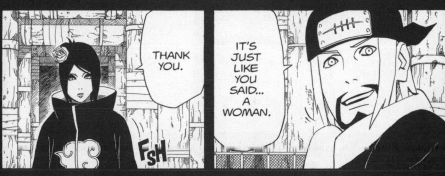

THANK YOU.

IT'S JUST LIKE YOU SAID... A WOMAN.

FSH

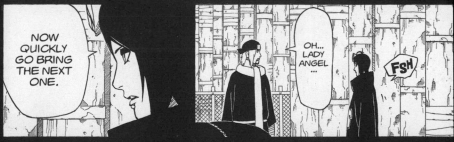

NOW QUICKLY GO BRING THE NEXT ONE.

OH... LADY ANGEL ...

FSH

READ THIS WAY

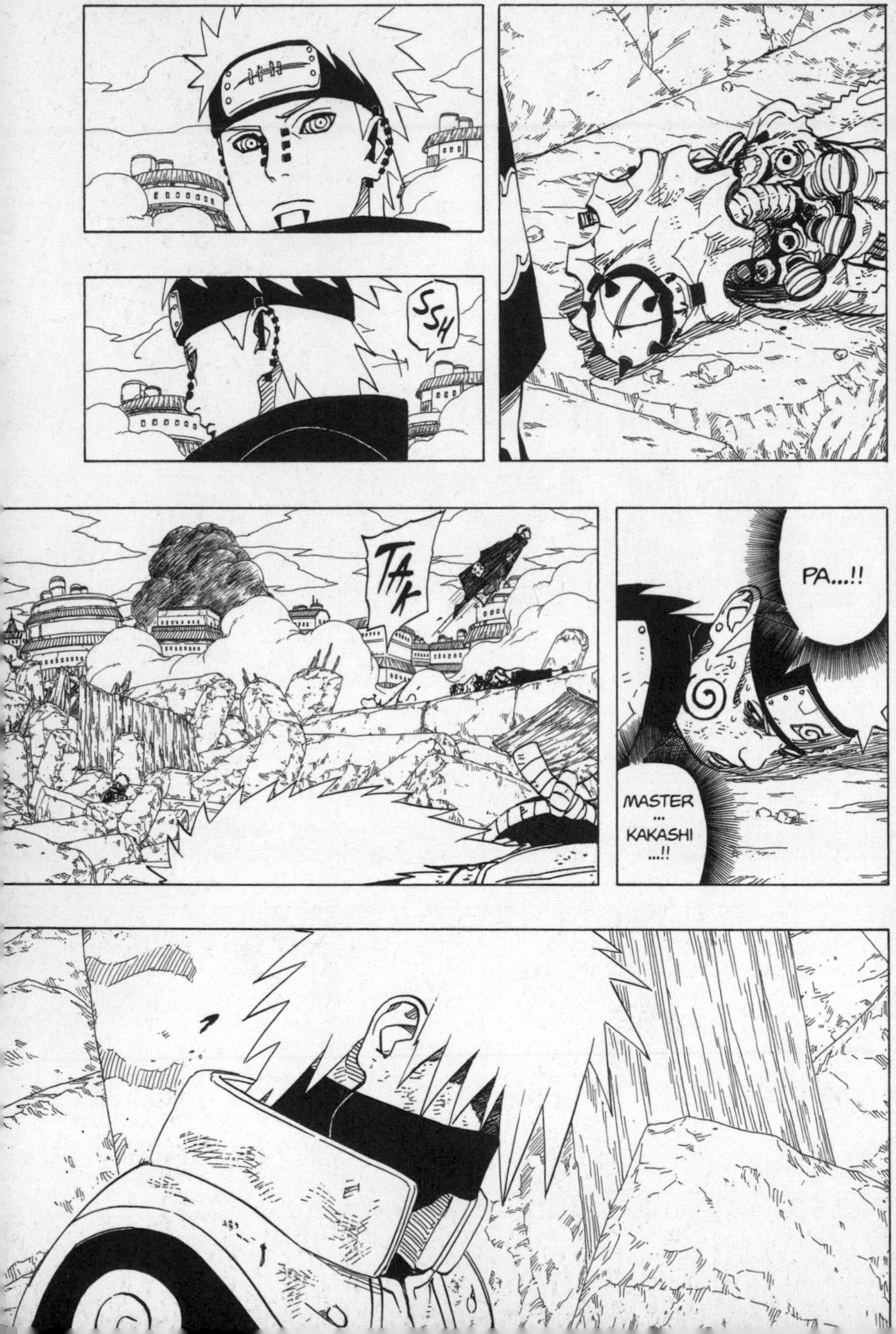
SSH
PA...!!
MASTER ... KAKASHI ...!!
TAK

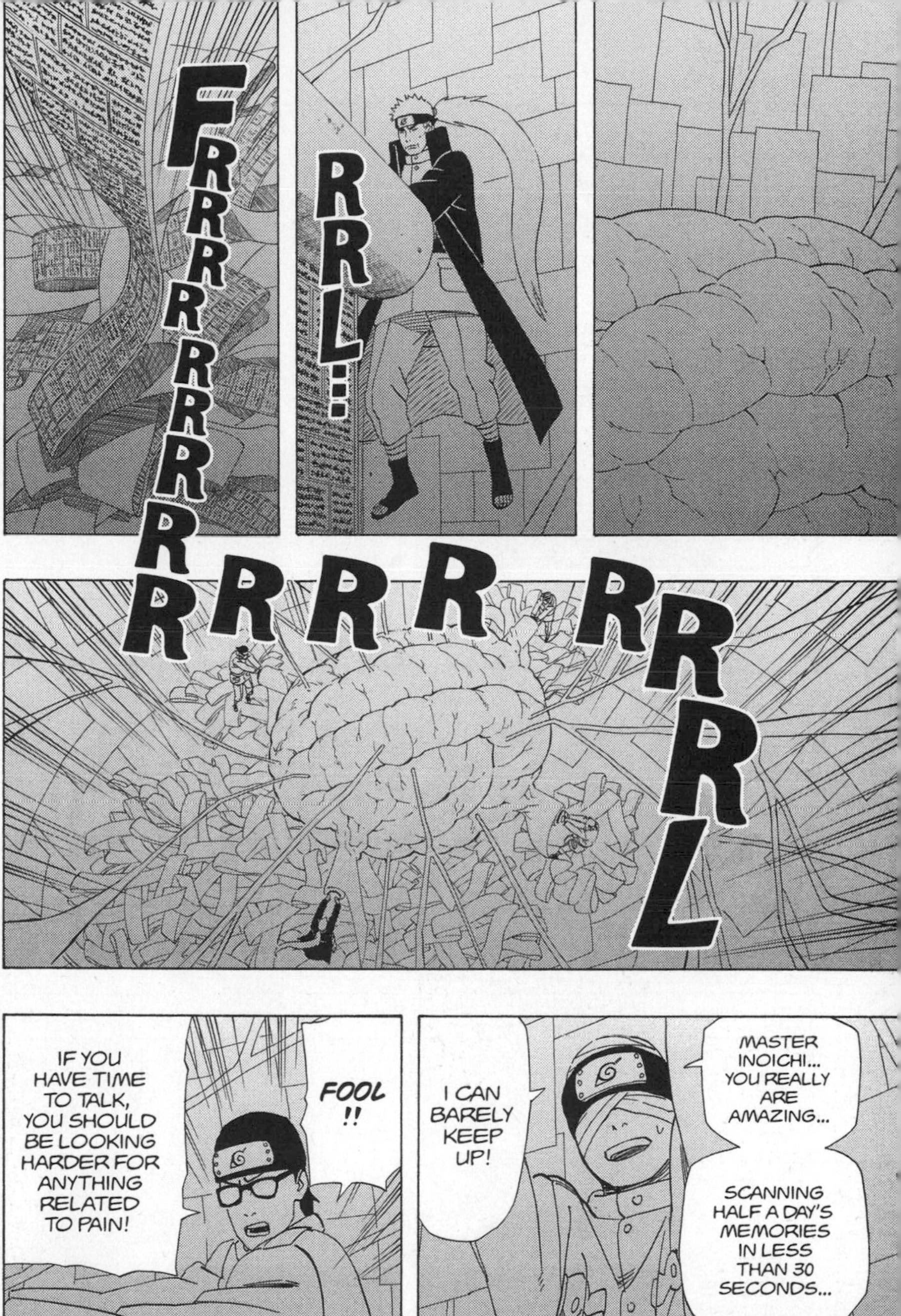
RRRL..
FRRRRRRRRRRRRRRRRRRRL
MASTER INOICHI... YOU REALLY ARE AMAZING...
SCANNING HALF A DAY'S MEMORIES IN LESS THAN 30 SECONDS...
I CAN BARELY KEEP UP!
FOOL!!
IF YOU HAVE TIME TO TALK, YOU SHOULD BE LOOKING HARDER FOR ANYTHING RELATED TO PAIN!

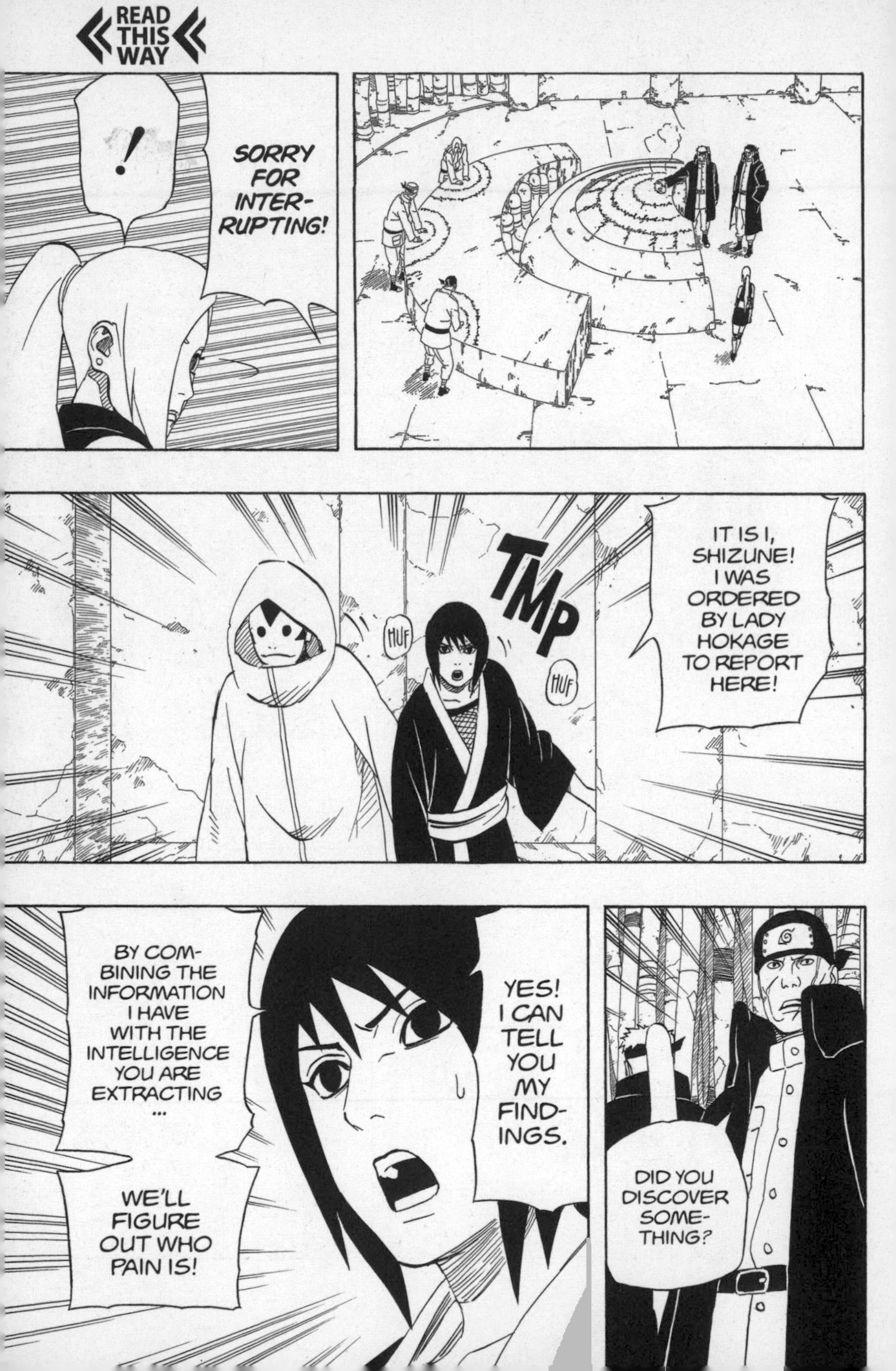
READ THIS WAY
!
SORRY FOR INTER-RUPTING!
IT IS I, SHIZUNE! I WAS ORDERED BY LADY HOKAGE TO REPORT HERE!
TMP
HUF
HUF
DID YOU DISCOVER SOME-THING?
YES! I CAN TELL YOU MY FIND-INGS.
BY COM-BINING THE INFORMATION I HAVE WITH THE INTELLIGENCE YOU ARE EXTRACTING ...
WE'LL FIGURE OUT WHO PAIN IS!

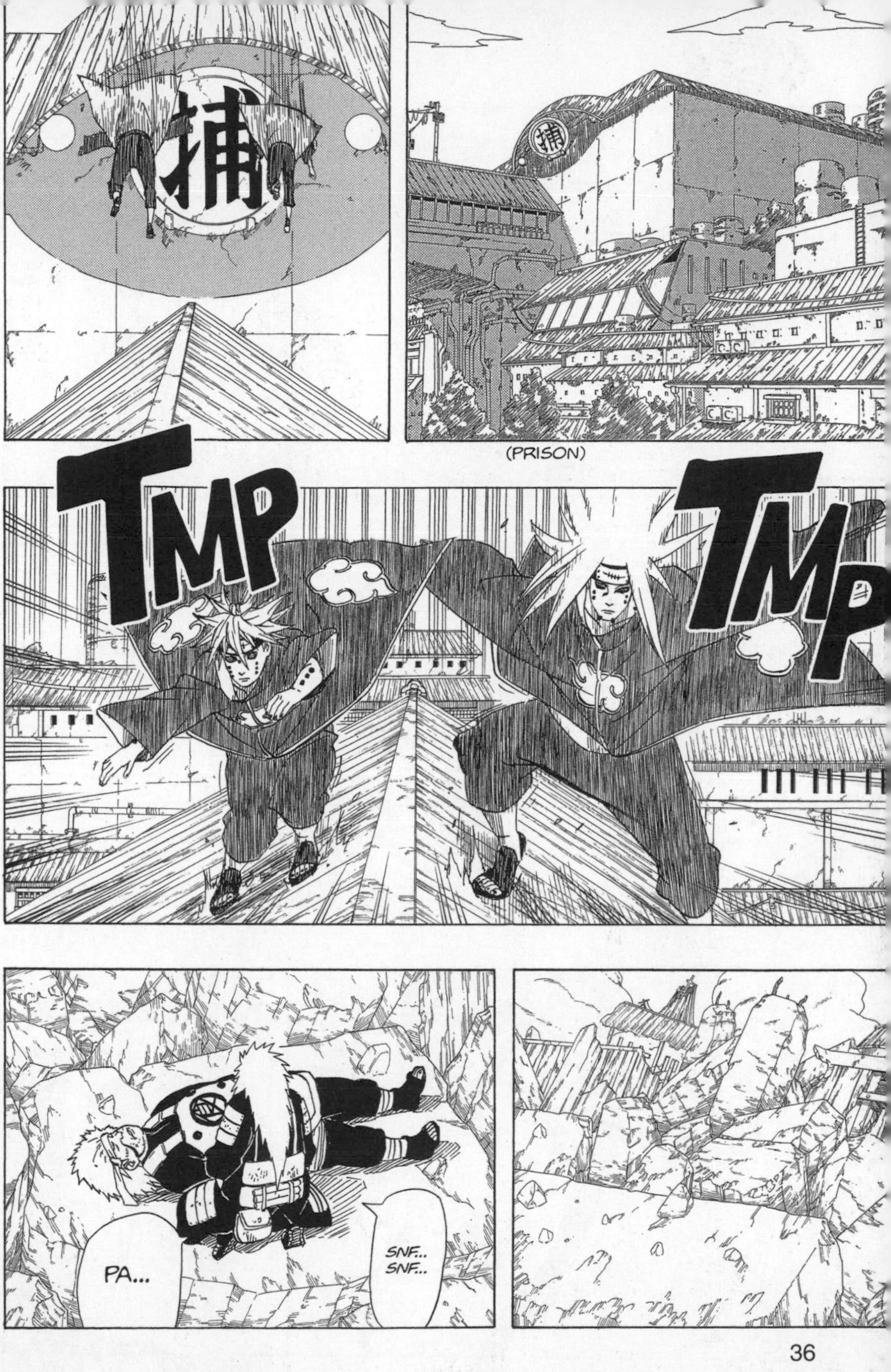
(PRISON)
TMP
TMP
SNF... SNF...
PA...

READ THIS WAY

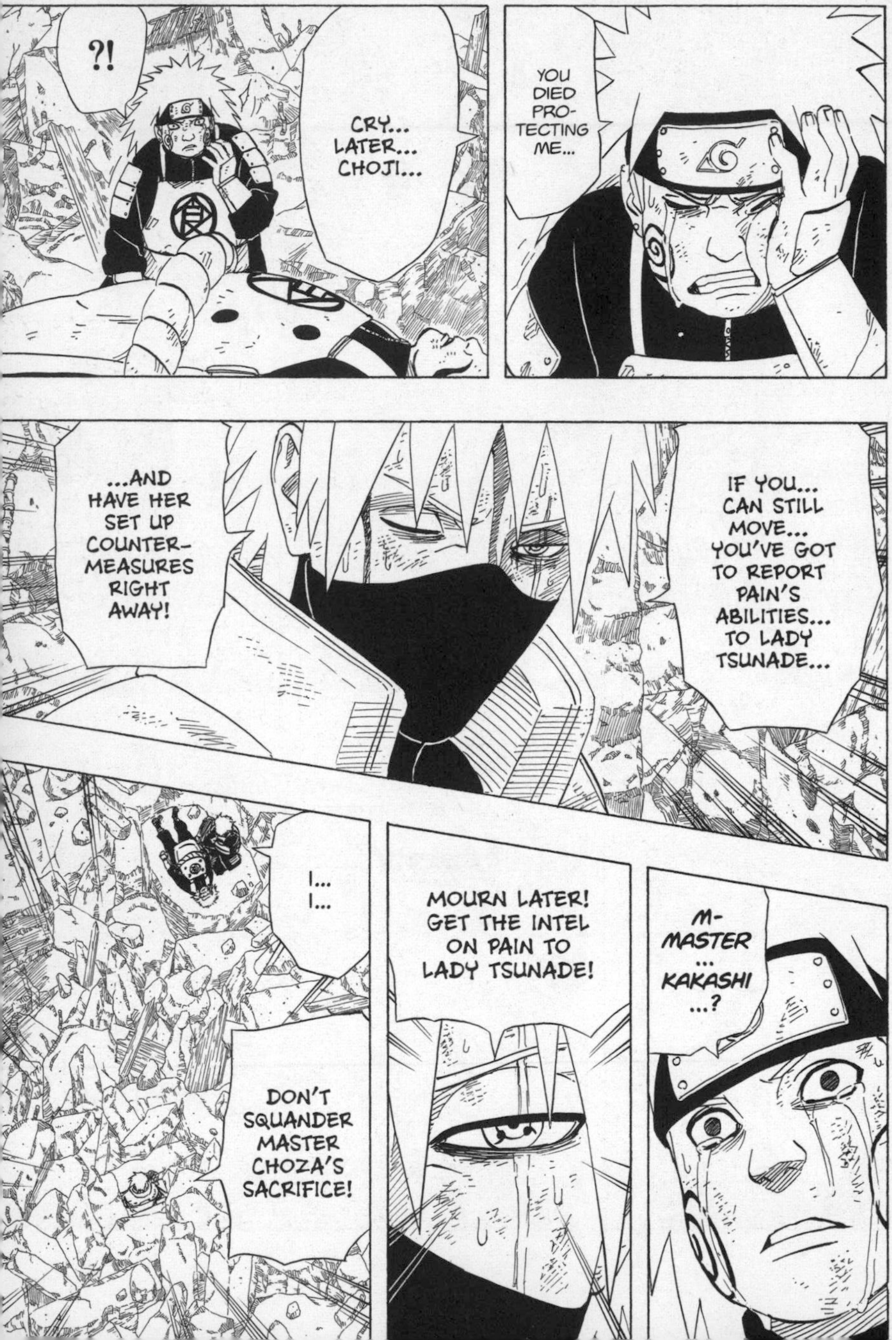
YOU DIED PRO-TECTING ME...
CRY... LATER... CHOJI...
?!
IF YOU... CAN STILL MOVE... YOU'VE GOT TO REPORT PAIN'S ABILITIES... TO LADY TSUNADE...
...AND HAVE HER SET UP COUNTER-MEASURES RIGHT AWAY!
M-MASTER ... KAKASHI ...?
MOURN LATER! GET THE INTEL ON PAIN TO LADY TSUNADE!
I... I...
DON'T SQUANDER MASTER CHOZA'S SACRIFICE!

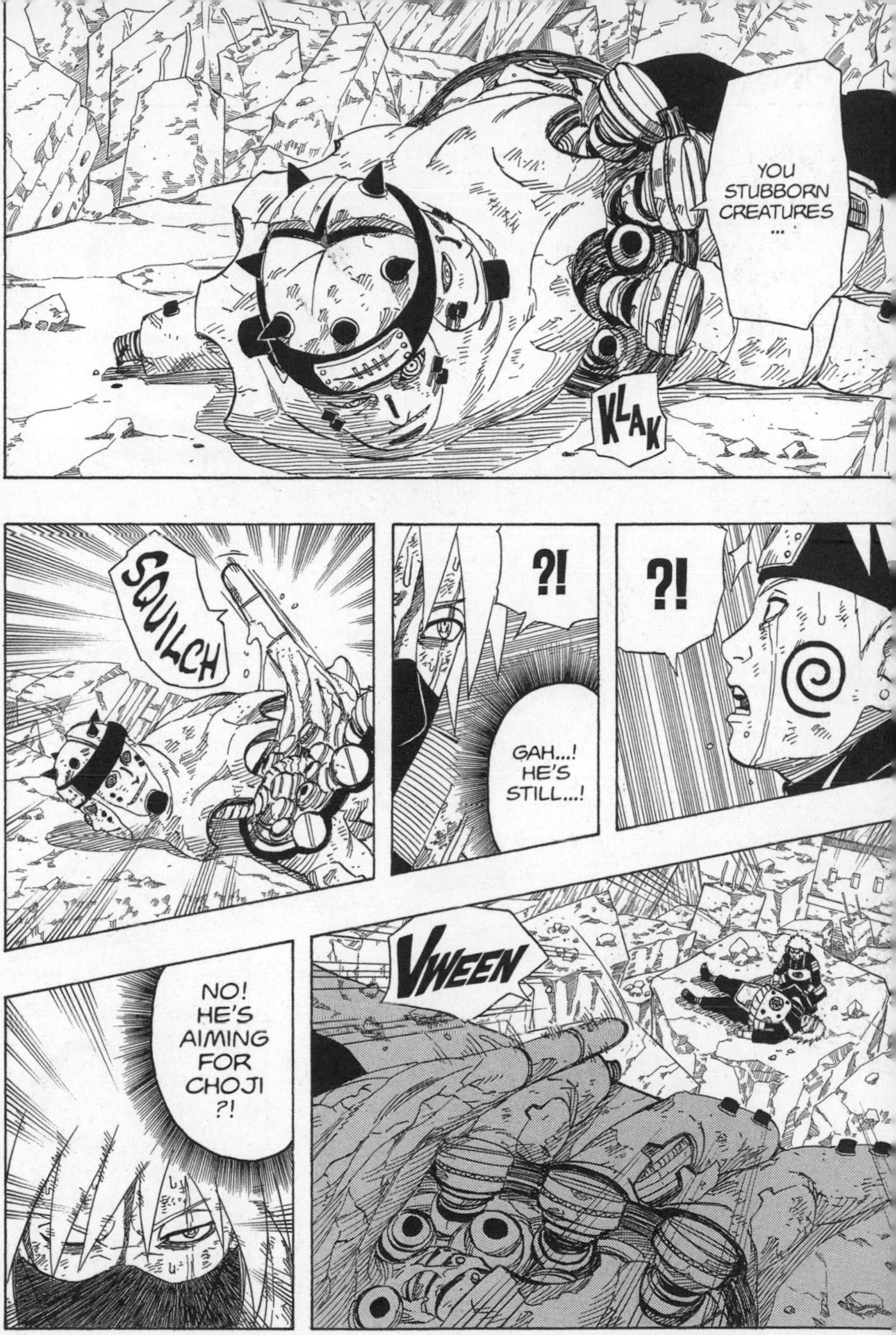
YOU STUBBORN CREATURES ...
KLAK
?!
?!
GAH...! HE'S STILL...!
SQUILCH
VWEEN
NO! HE'S AIMING FOR CHOJI ?!

READ THIS WAY

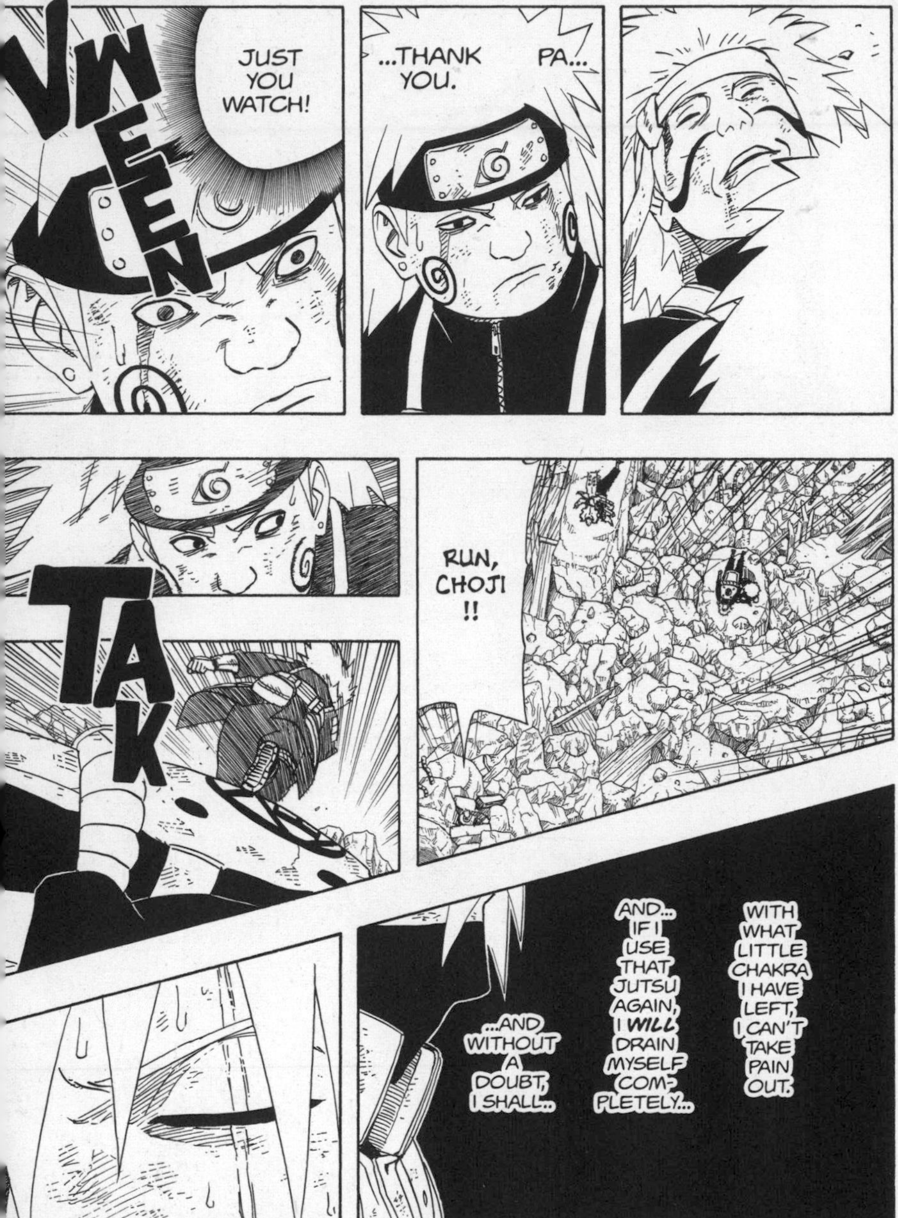
PA...
...THANK YOU.
VWEEN
JUST YOU WATCH!
RUN, CHOJI !!
TAK
WITH WHAT LITTLE CHAKRA I HAVE LEFT, I CAN'T TAKE PAIN OUT.
AND... IF I USE THAT JUTSU AGAIN, I **WILL** DRAIN MYSELF COMPLETELY...
...AND WITHOUT A DOUBT, I SHALL...

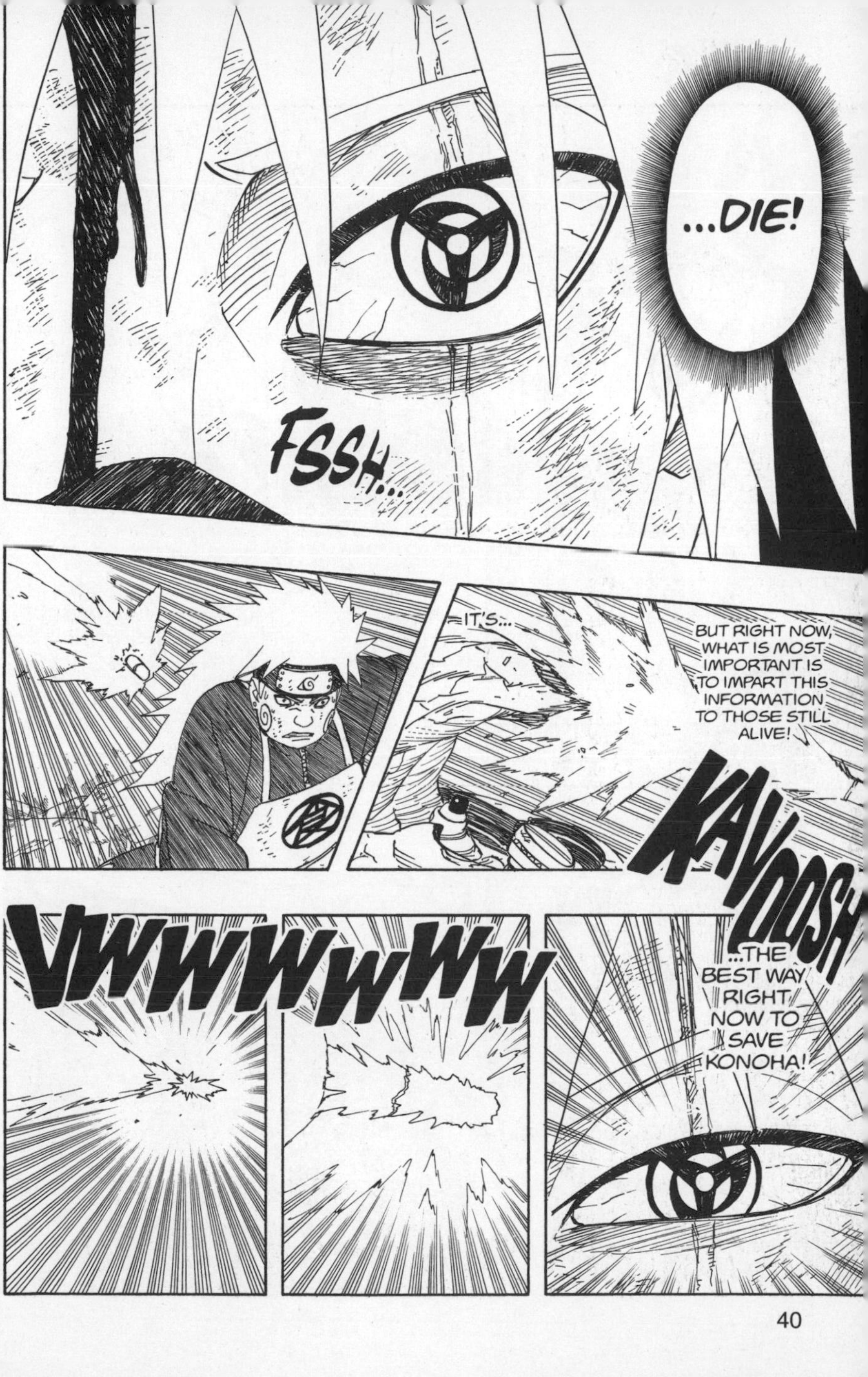
...DIE!
FSSH...
BUT RIGHT NOW, WHAT IS MOST IMPORTANT IS TO IMPART THIS INFORMATION TO THOSE STILL ALIVE!
IT'S...
KAVOOSH
...THE BEST WAY RIGHT NOW TO SAVE KONOHA!
VWWWWWWW

READ THIS WAY

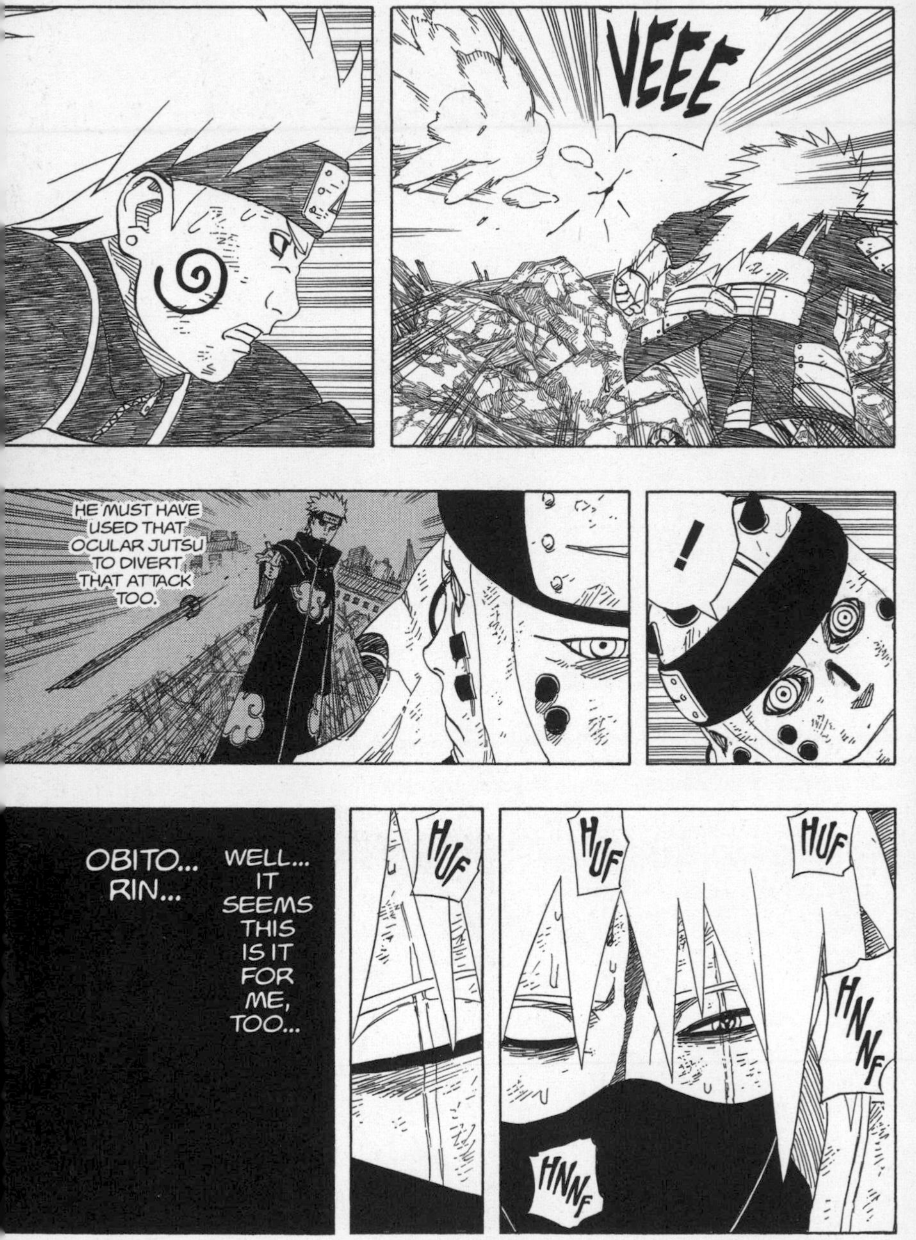
VEEE
!
HE MUST HAVE USED THAT OCULAR JUTSU TO DIVERT THAT ATTACK TOO.
HUF
HUF
HNNF
HNNF
HUF
WELL... IT SEEMS THIS IS IT FOR ME, TOO...
OBITO... RIN...

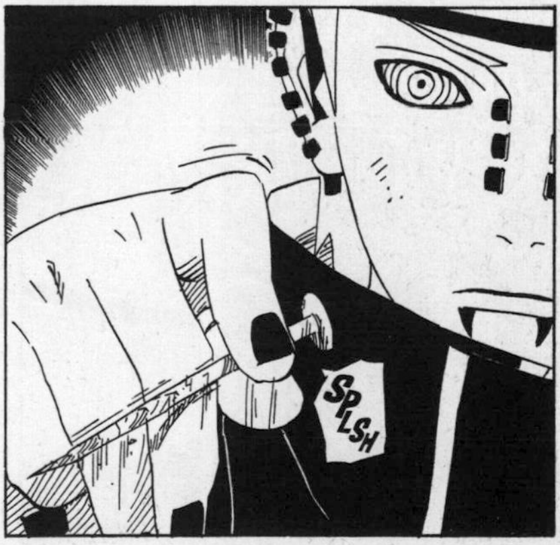
SPLSH

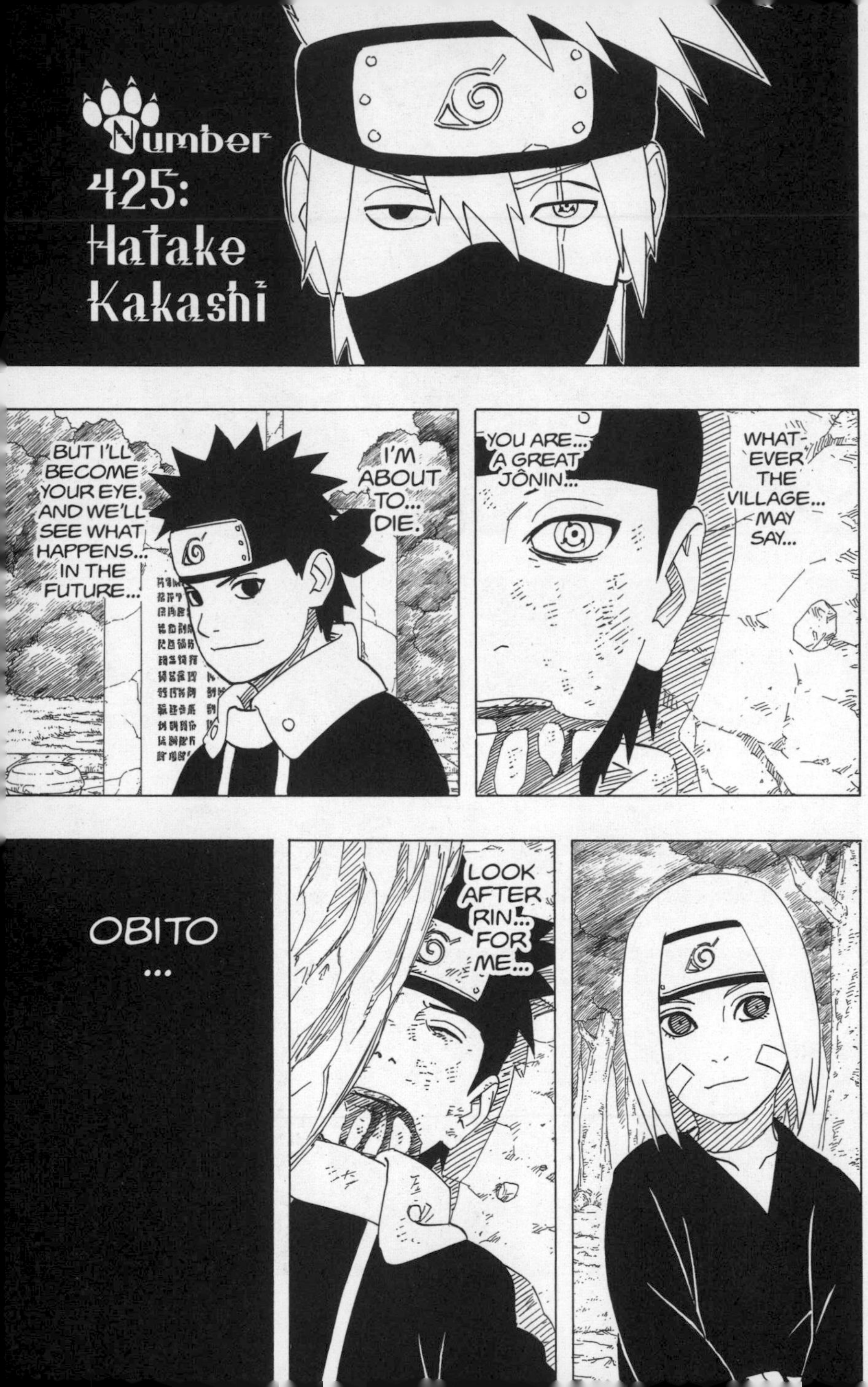
Number 425: Hatake Kakashi
WHATEVER THE VILLAGE... MAY SAY...
YOU ARE... A GREAT JÔNIN...
I'M ABOUT TO... DIE.
BUT I'LL BECOME YOUR EYE. AND WE'LL SEE WHAT HAPPENS... IN THE FUTURE...
LOOK AFTER RIN... FOR ME...
OBITO ...

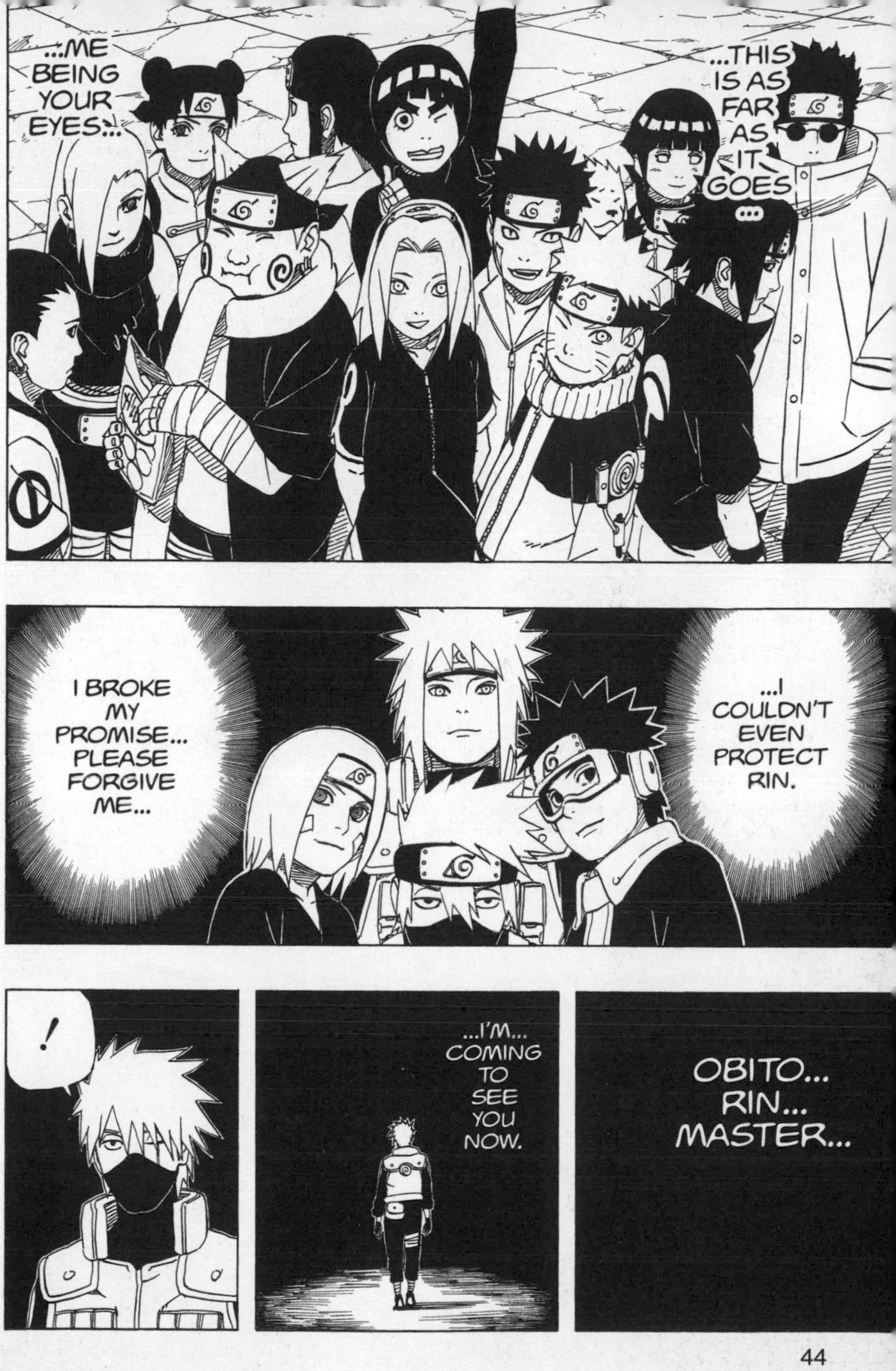
...THIS IS AS FAR AS IT GOES...
...ME BEING YOUR EYES...
...I COULDN'T EVEN PROTECT RIN.
I BROKE MY PROMISE... PLEASE FORGIVE ME...
OBITO... RIN... MASTER...
...I'M... COMING TO SEE YOU NOW.
!

READ THIS WAY

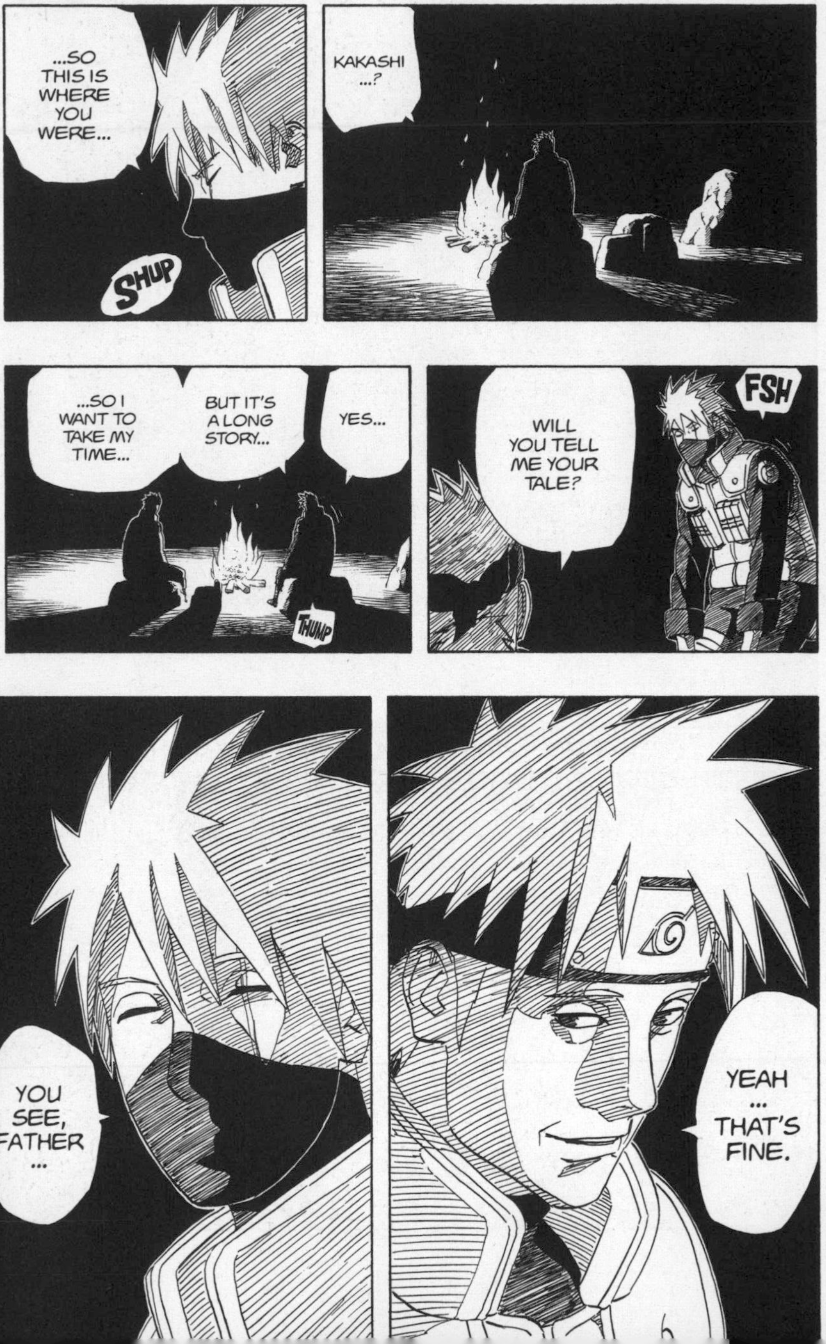
KAKASHI ...?
...SO THIS IS WHERE YOU WERE...
SHUP
FSH
WILL YOU TELL ME YOUR TALE?
YES...
BUT IT'S A LONG STORY...
...SO I WANT TO TAKE MY TIME...
THUMP
YEAH ... THAT'S FINE.
YOU SEE, FATHER ...

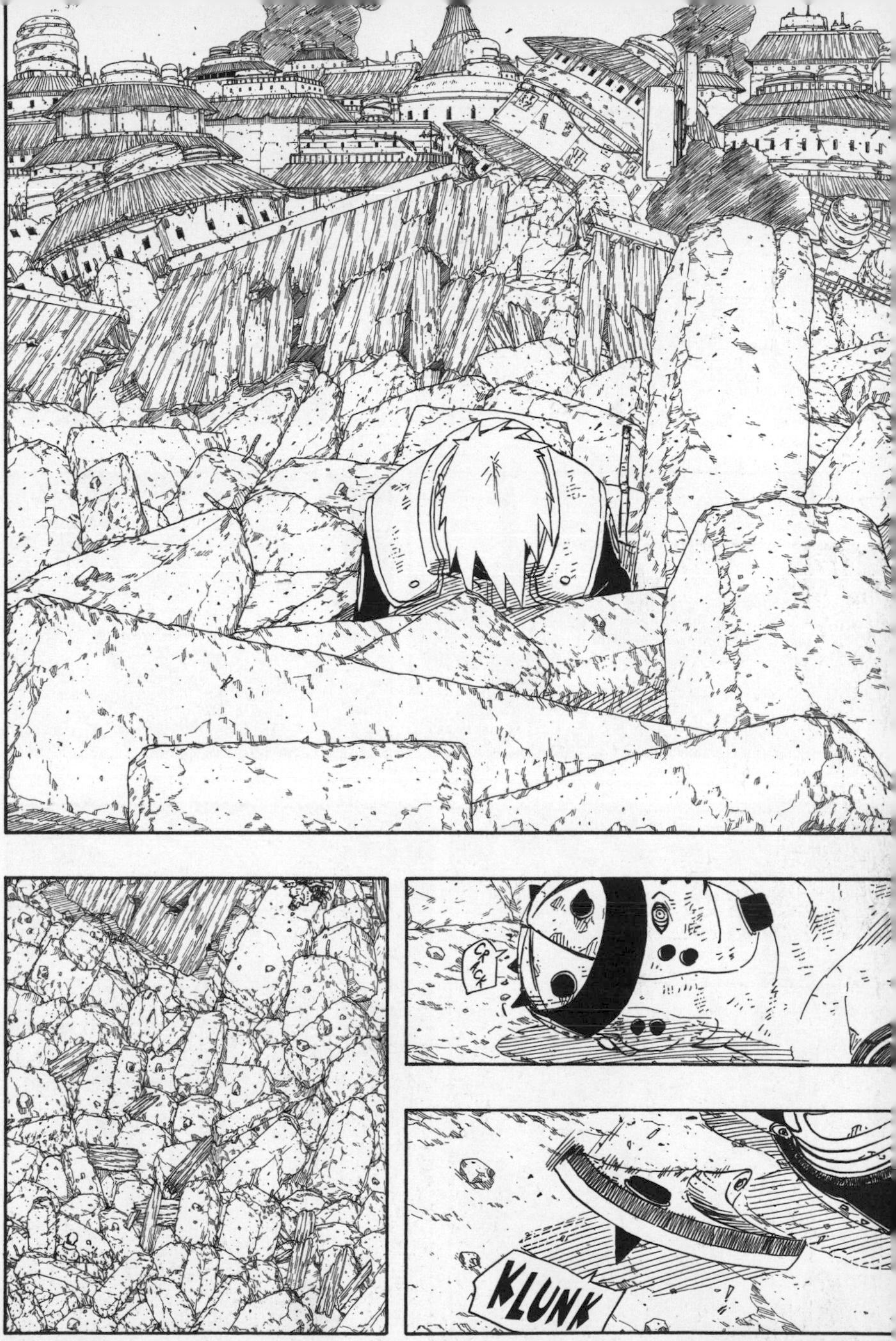
CRACK
KLUNK

READ THIS WAY

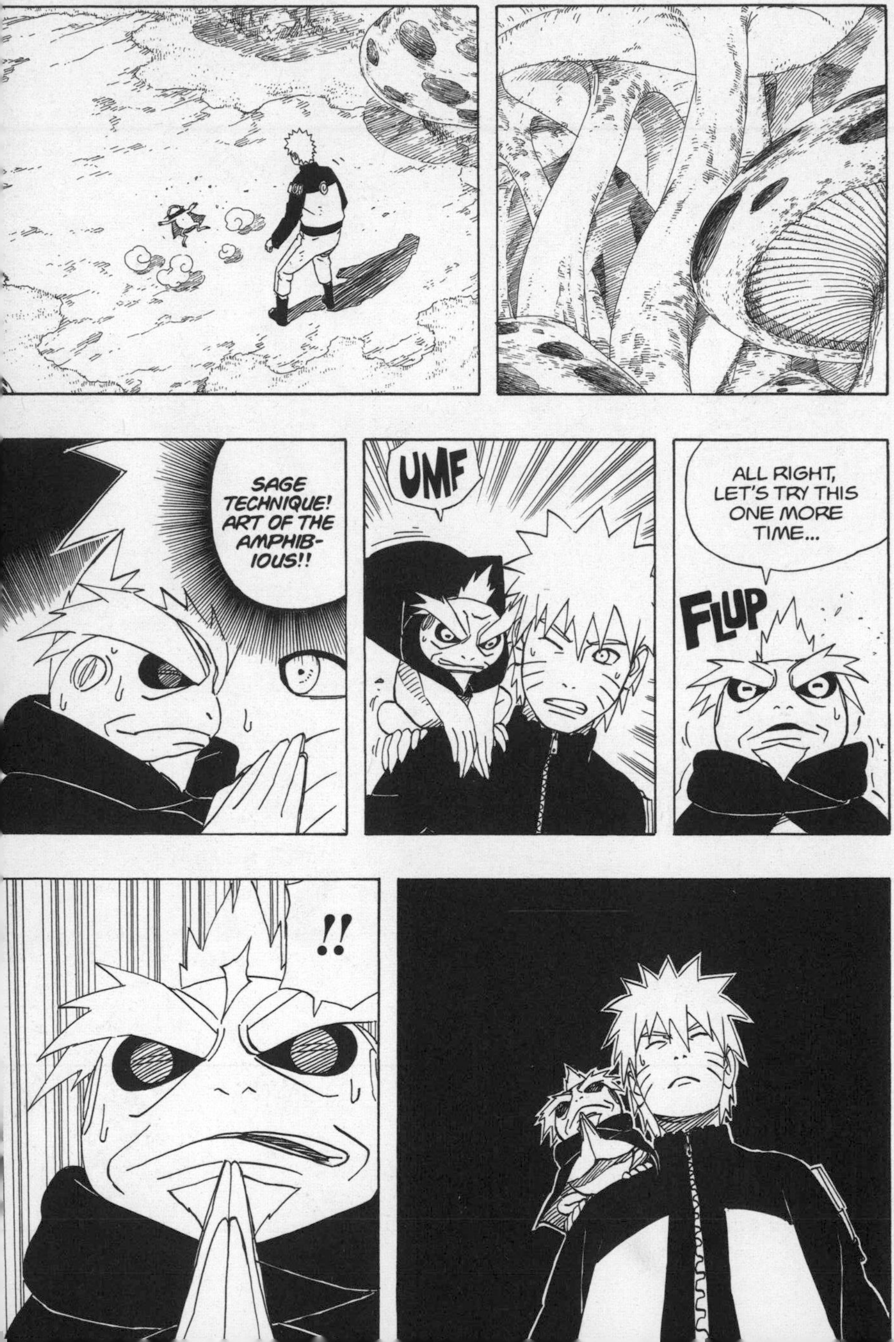
ALL RIGHT, LET'S TRY THIS ONE MORE TIME...
FLUP
UMF
SAGE TECHNIQUE! ART OF THE AMPHIB-IOUS!!
!!

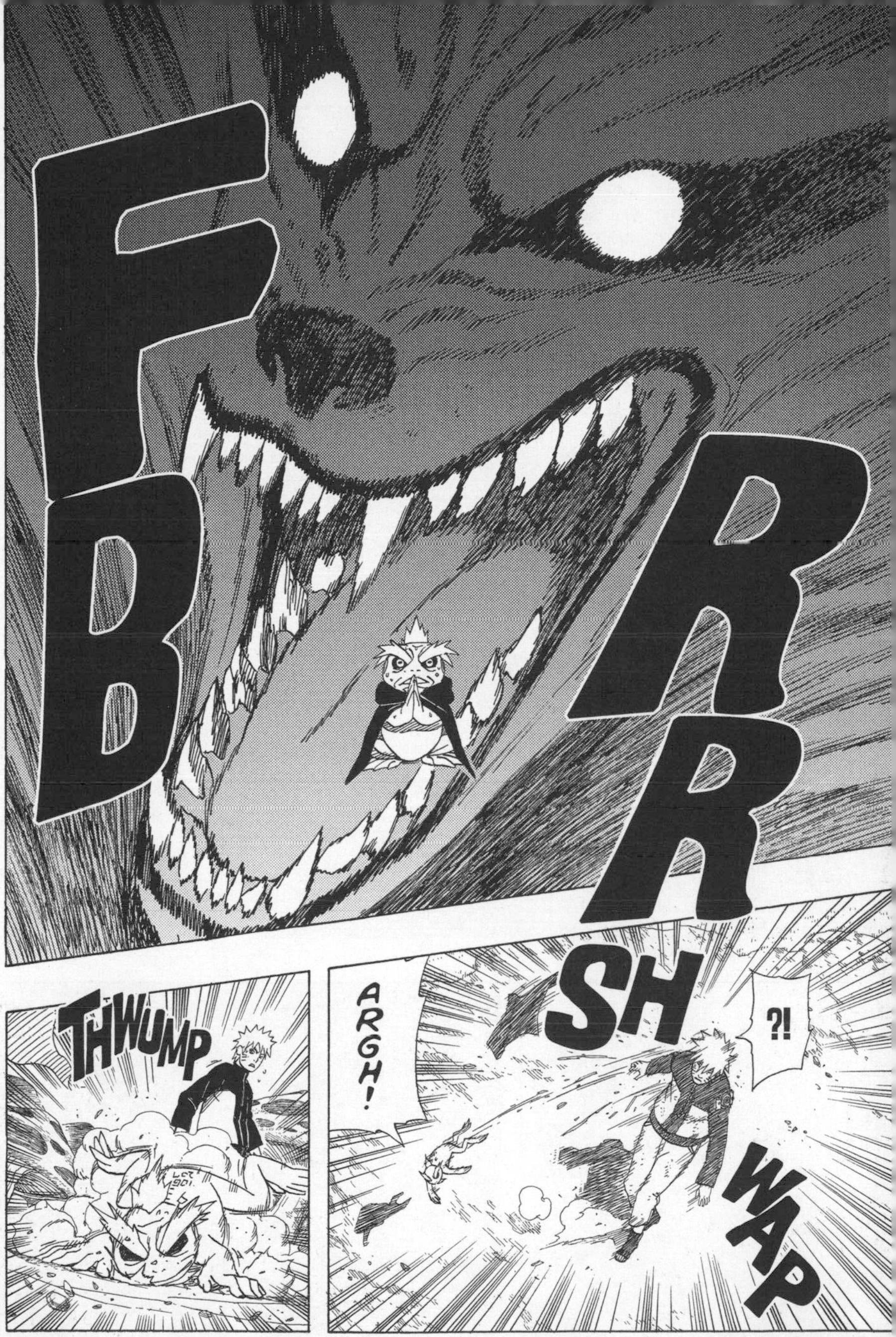
FB
RR
SH
WAP
ARGH!
?!
THWUMP

READ THIS WAY

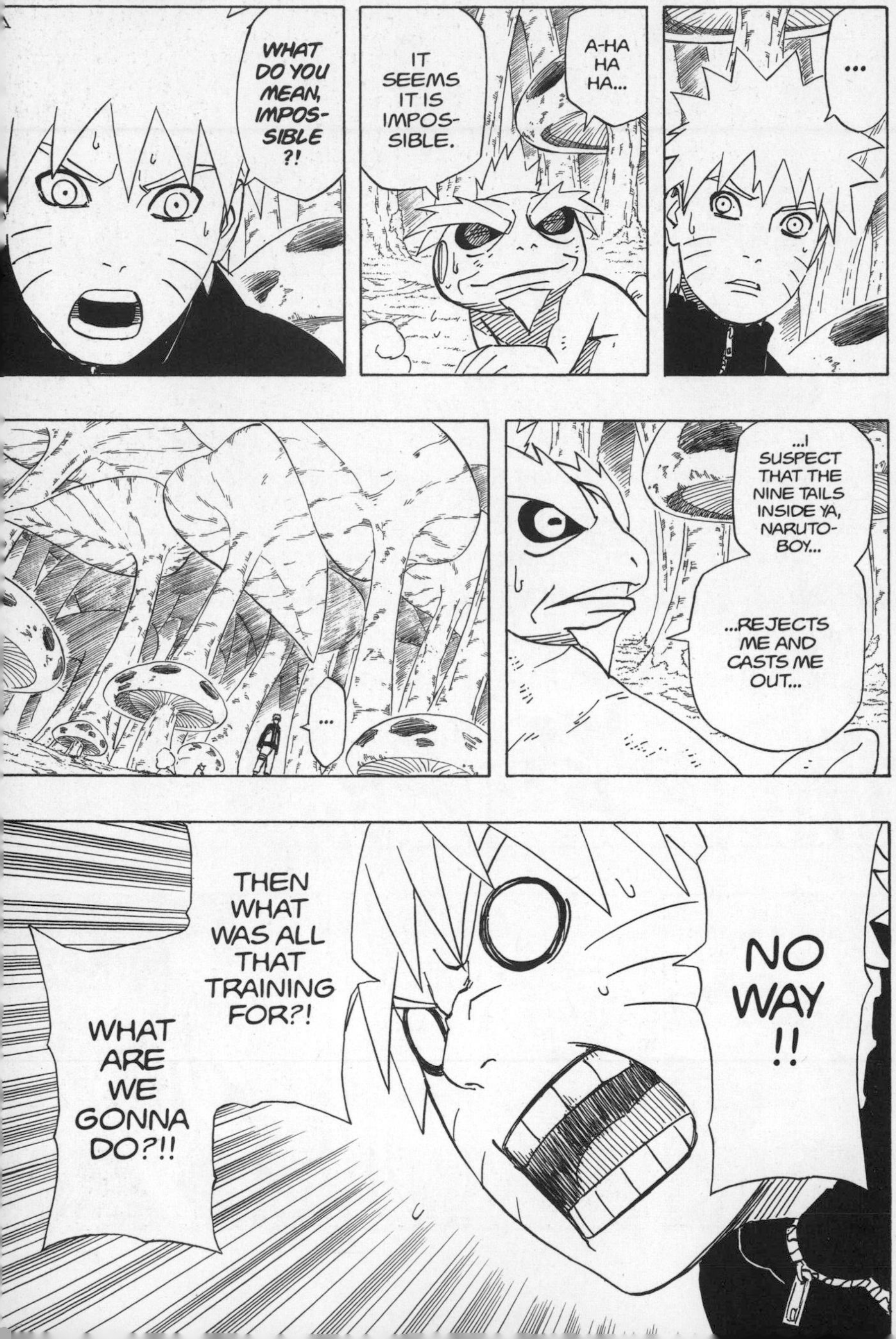
...
A-HA HA HA...
IT SEEMS IT IS IMPOSSIBLE.
WHAT DO YOU MEAN, IMPOSSIBLE?!
...I SUSPECT THAT THE NINE TAILS INSIDE YA, NARUTO-BOY...
...REJECTS ME AND CASTS ME OUT...
...
NO WAY!!
THEN WHAT WAS ALL THAT TRAINING FOR?!
WHAT ARE WE GONNA DO?!!

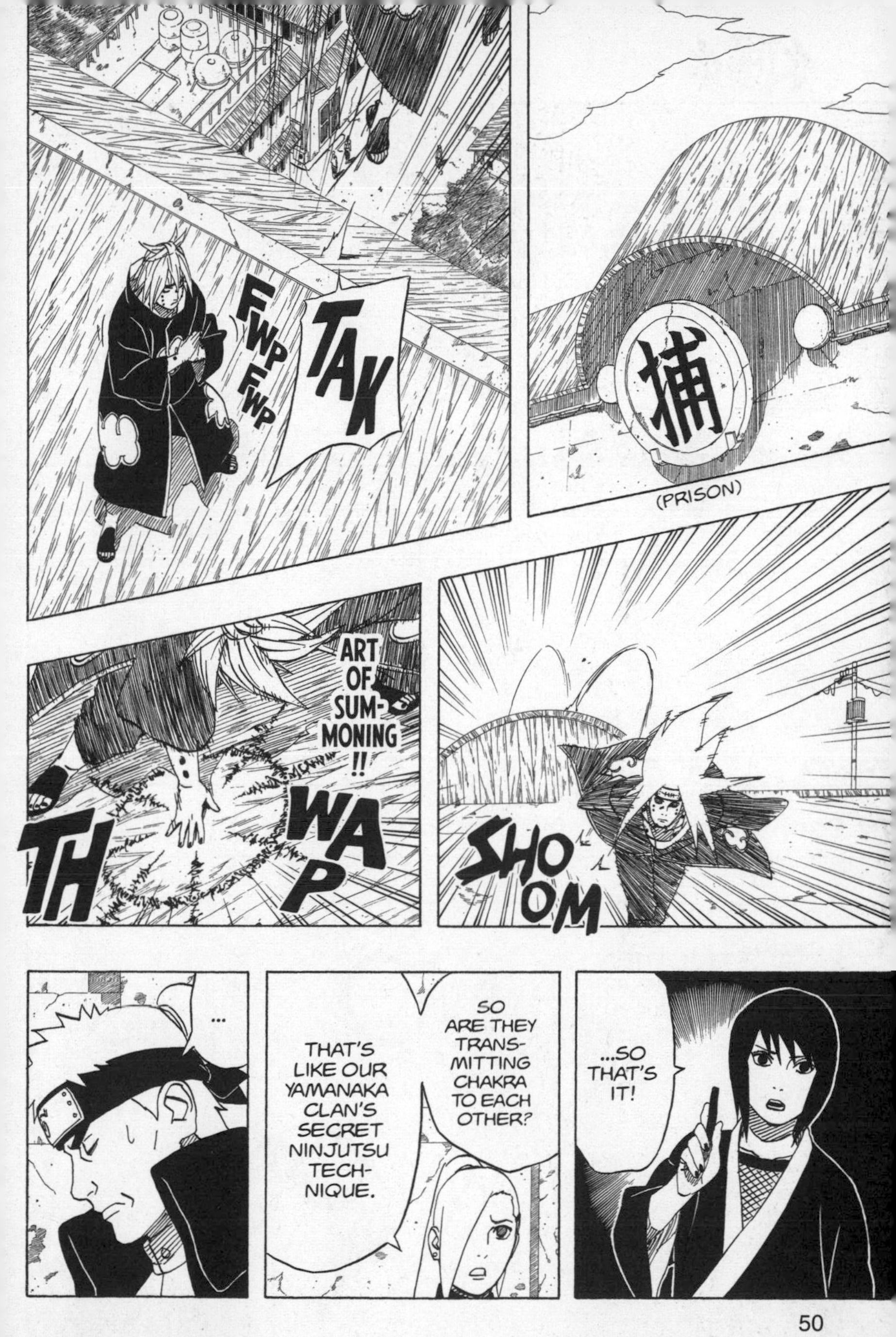
捕
(PRISON)
TAK
FWP FWP
SHO OM
ART OF SUM-MONING!!
WA P
TH
...SO THAT'S IT!
SO ARE THEY TRANS-MITTING CHAKRA TO EACH OTHER?
THAT'S LIKE OUR YAMANAKA CLAN'S SECRET NINJUTSU TECH-NIQUE.
...

READ THIS WAY

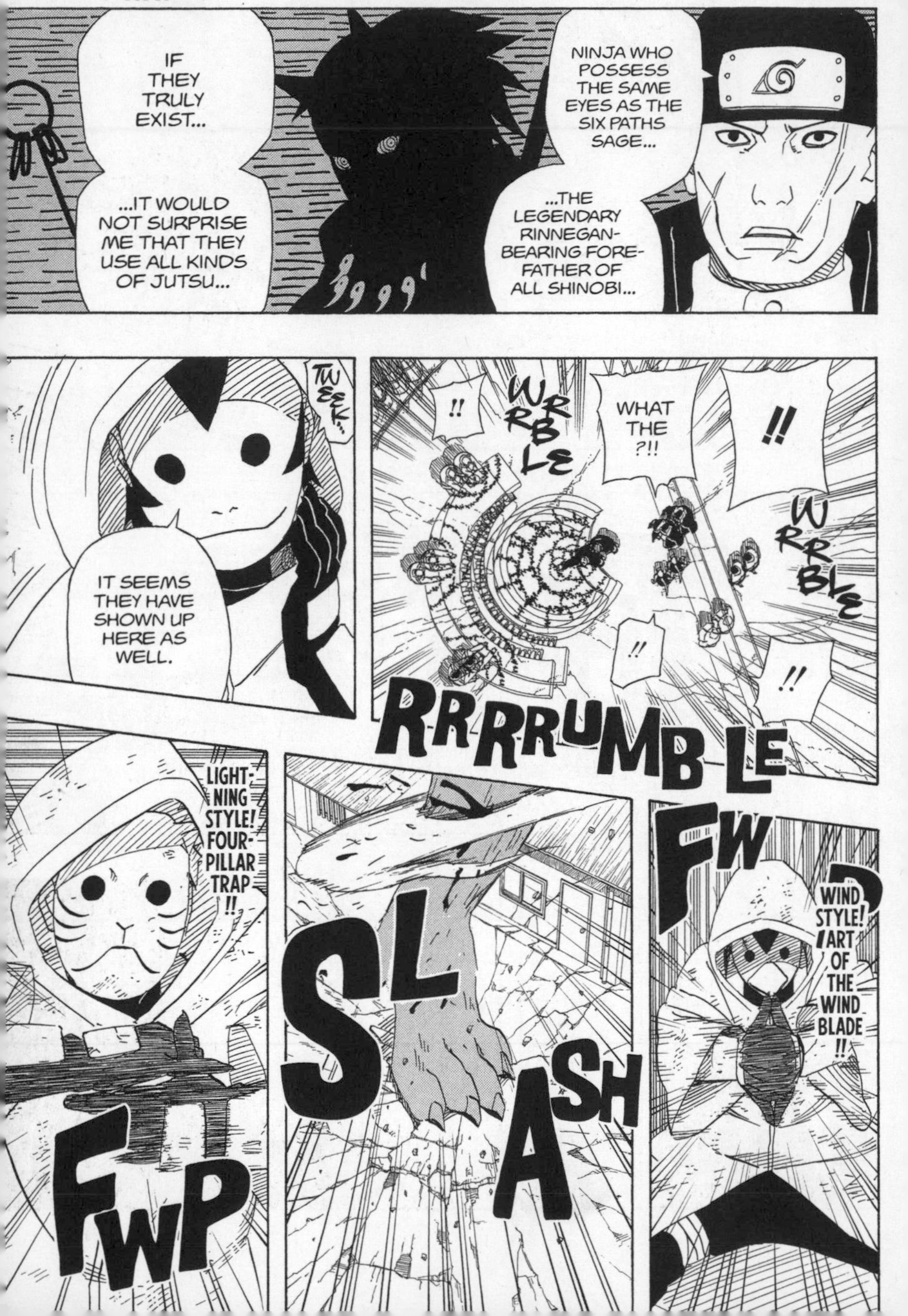
NINJA WHO POSSESS THE SAME EYES AS THE SIX PATHS SAGE...
...THE LEGENDARY RINNEGAN-BEARING FORE-FATHER OF ALL SHINOBI...
IF THEY TRULY EXIST...
...IT WOULD NOT SURPRISE ME THAT THEY USE ALL KINDS OF JUTSU...
!!
WRRBLE
WHAT THE?!!
!!
WRRBLE
!!
!!
RRRRUMBLE
TWEEK...
IT SEEMS THEY HAVE SHOWN UP HERE AS WELL.
FWD
WIND STYLE! ART OF THE WIND BLADE!!
SLASH
LIGHT-NING STYLE! FOUR-PILLAR TRAP!!
FWP

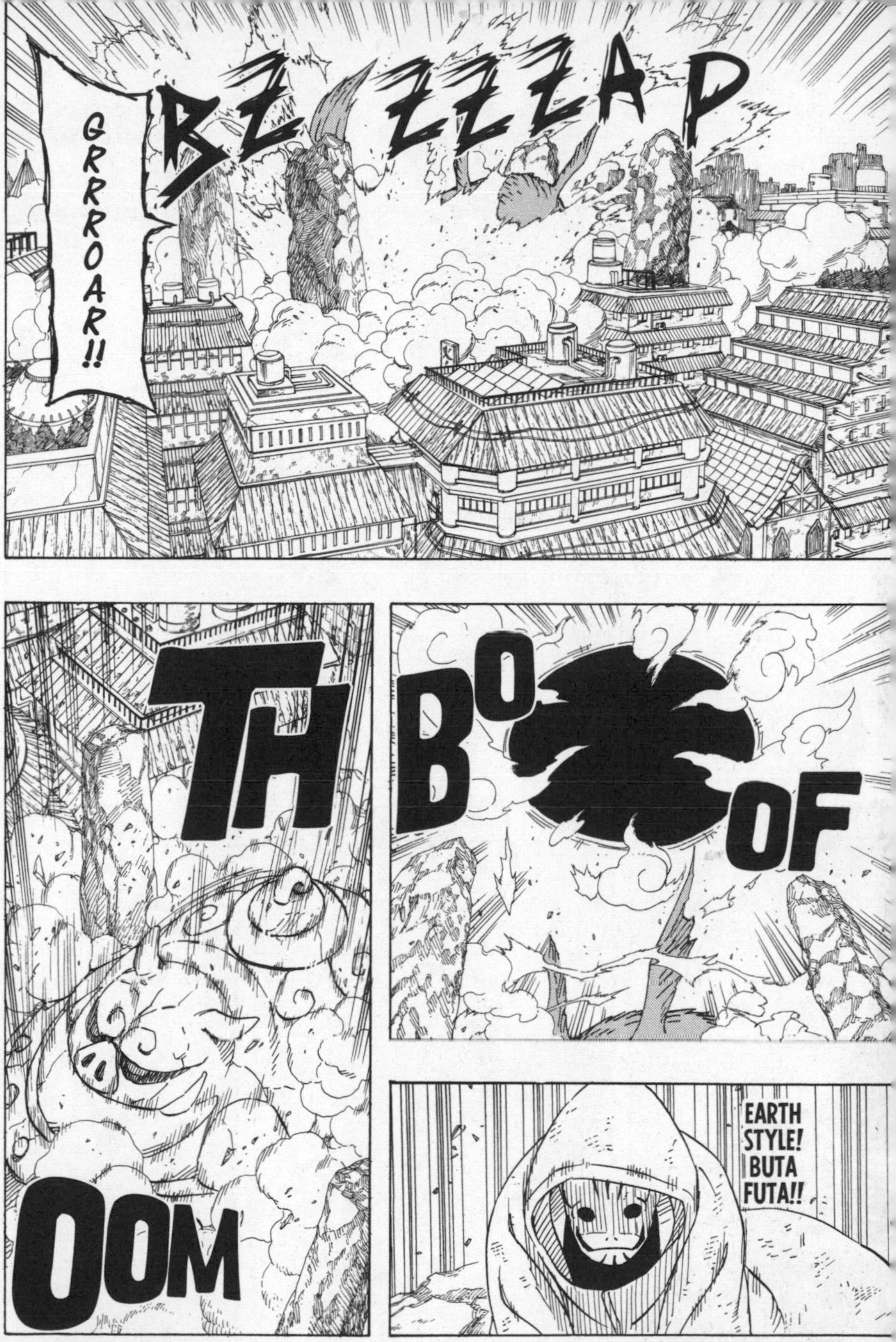
BZZZZAP
GRRROAR!!
BOOF
EARTH STYLE! BUTA FUTA!!
THOOM

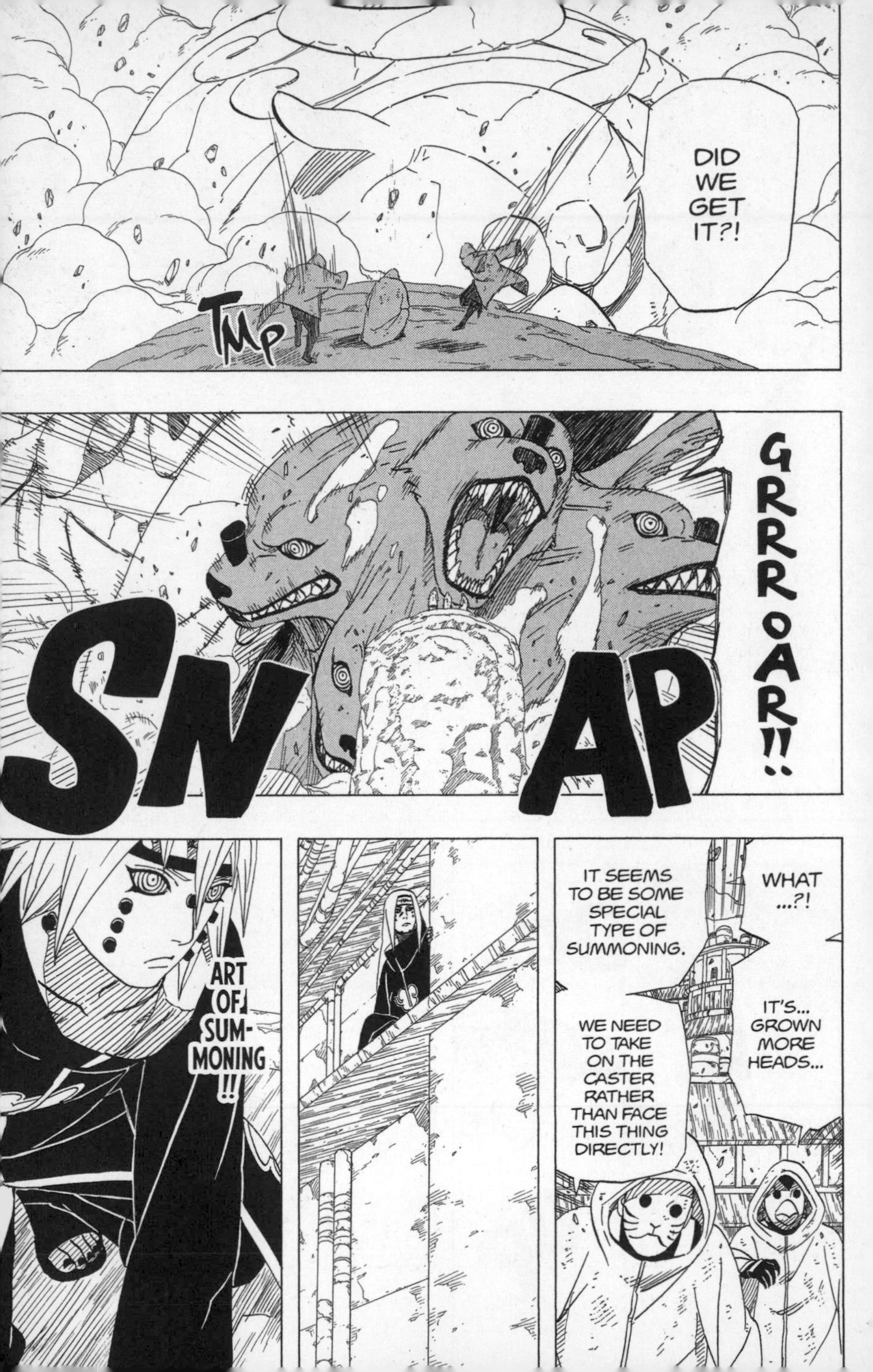
DID WE GET IT?!
TMP
GRRROAR!!
SNAP
WHAT ...?!
IT SEEMS TO BE SOME SPECIAL TYPE OF SUMMONING.
IT'S... GROWN MORE HEADS...
WE NEED TO TAKE ON THE CASTER RATHER THAN FACE THIS THING DIRECTLY!
ART OF SUM-MONING!!

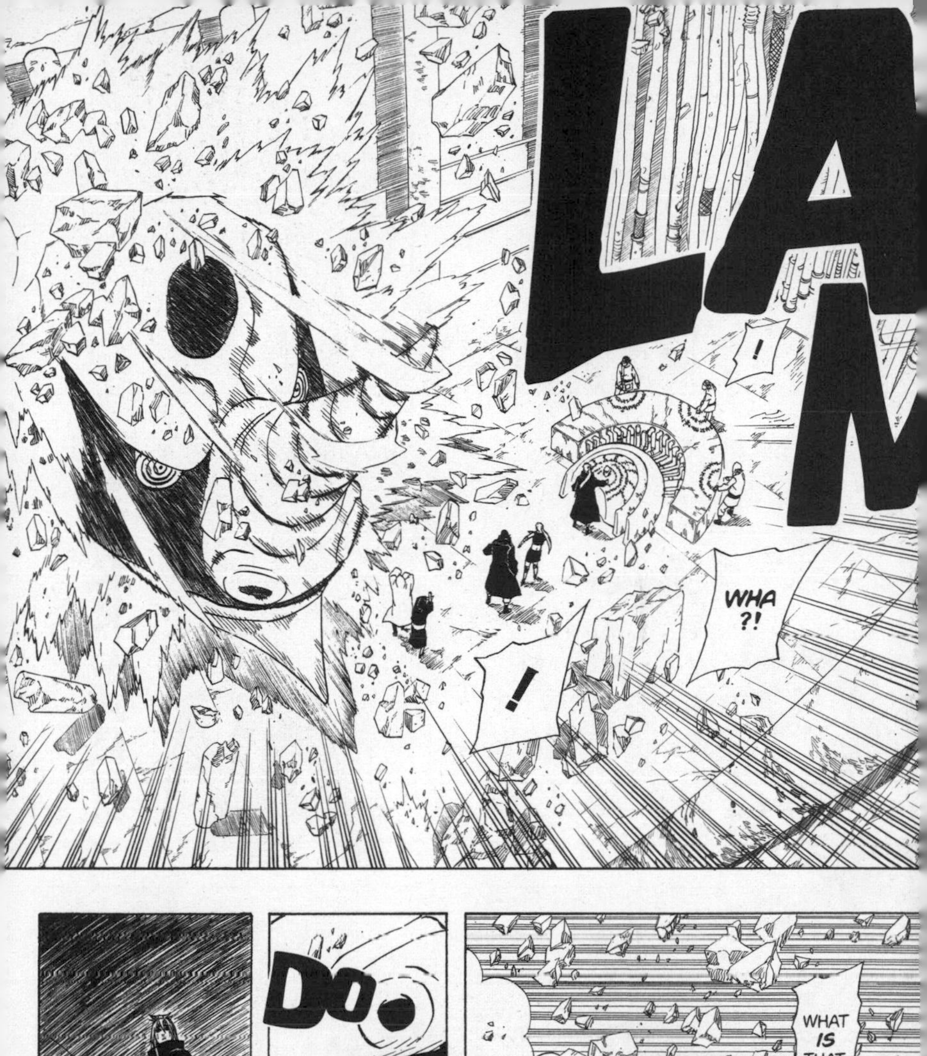
LAM
!
WHA ?!
!
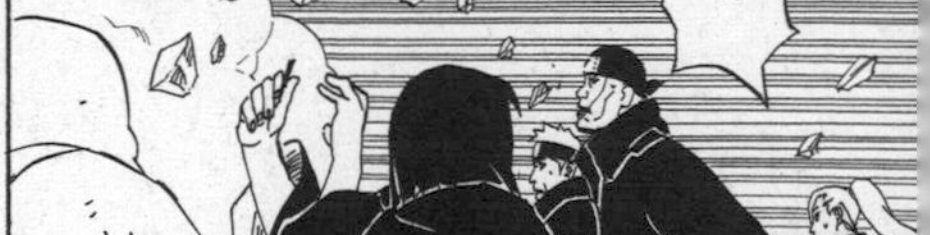
WHAT *IS* THAT ?!
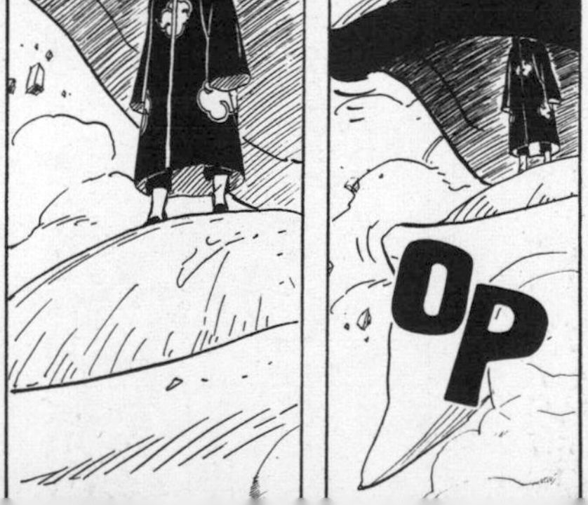
DOOOP

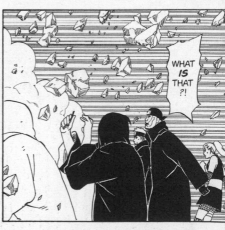

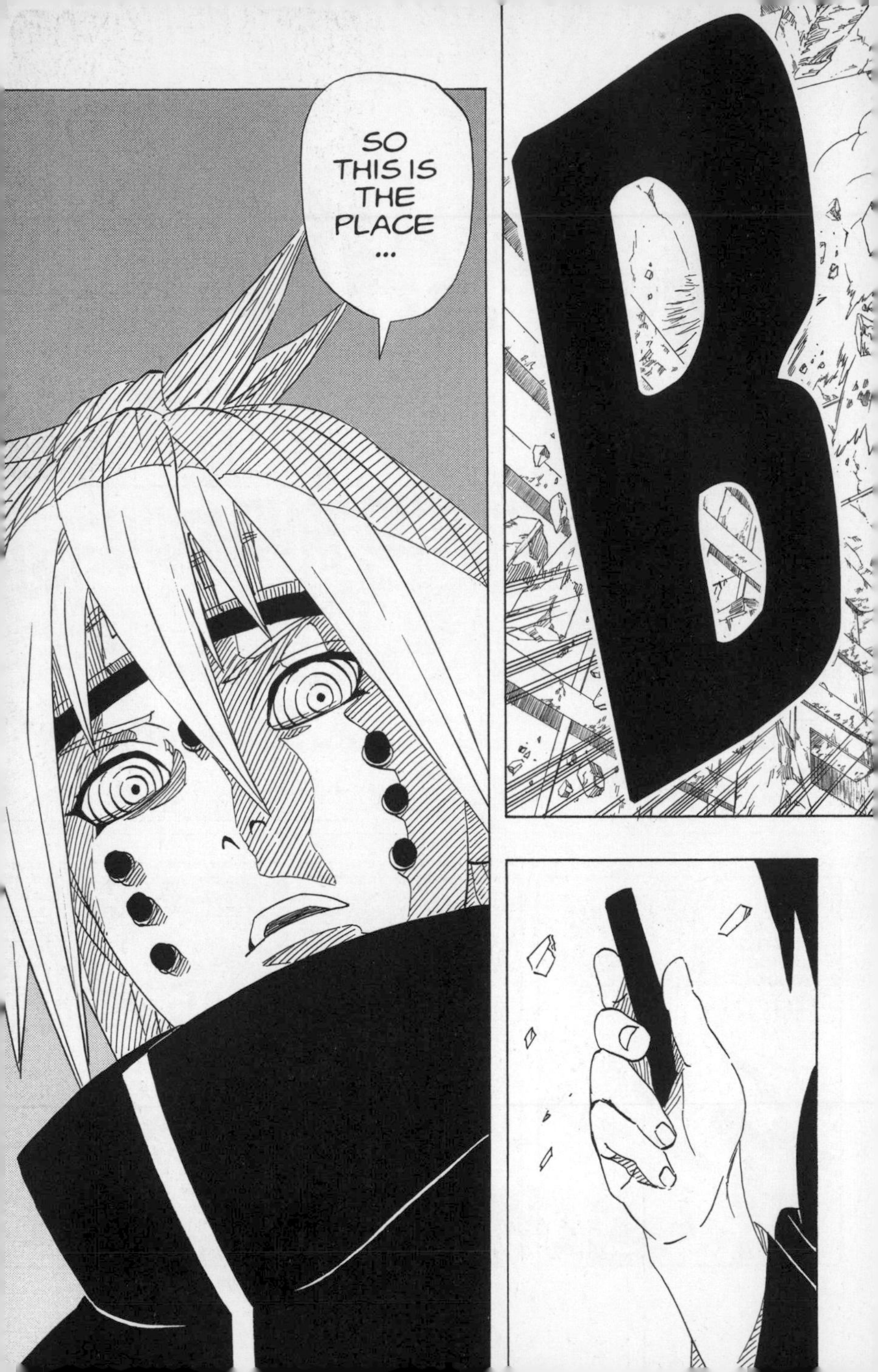
B
SO THIS IS THE PLACE ...

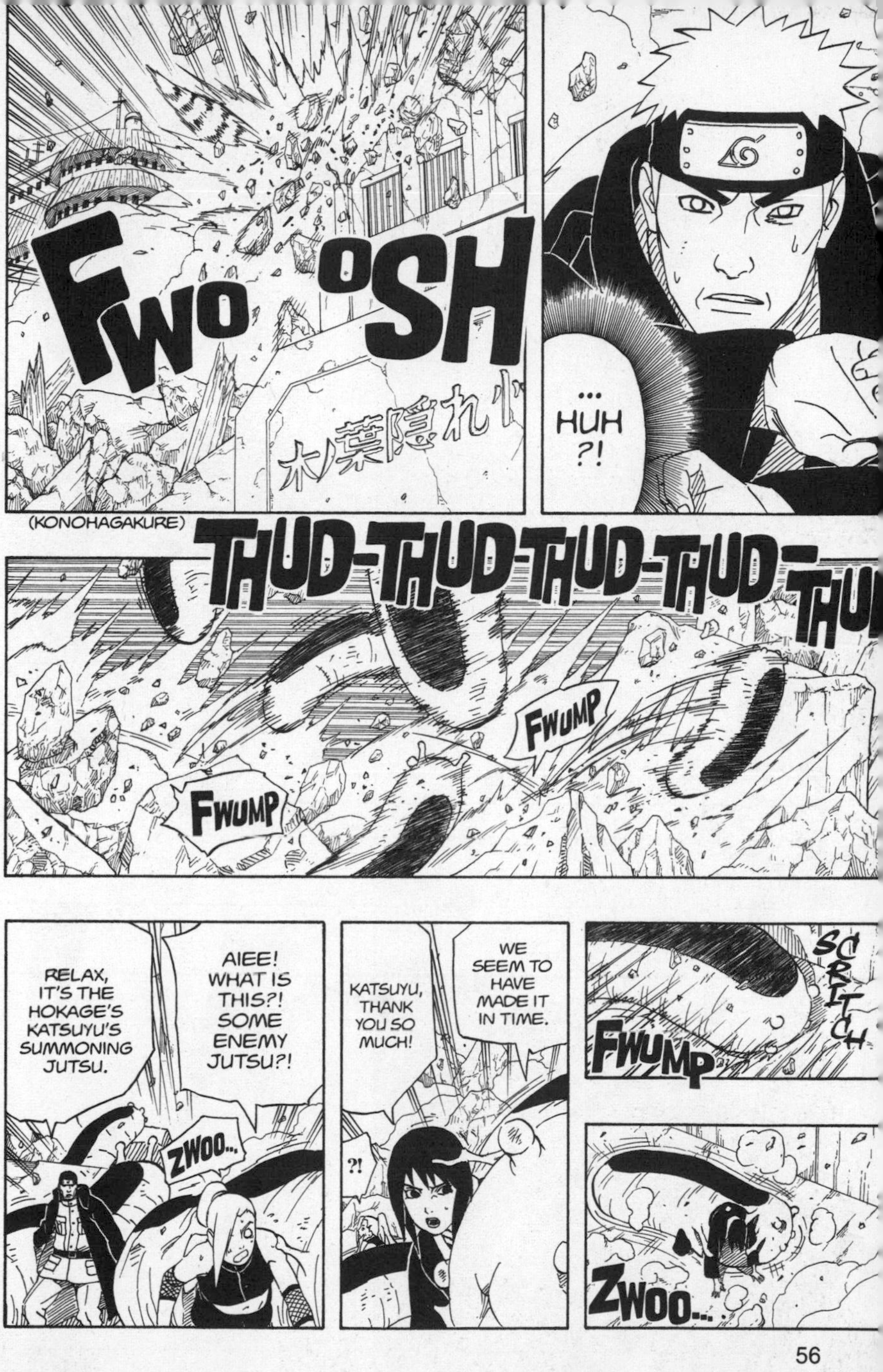
...
HUH
?!
FWOOSH
木ノ葉隠れ
(KONOHAGAKURE)
THUD-THUD-THUD-THUD-THU
FWUMP
FWUMP
SCRITCH
FWUMP
ZWOO...
WE SEEM TO HAVE MADE IT IN TIME.
KATSUYU, THANK YOU SO MUCH!
?!
AIEE! WHAT IS THIS?! SOME ENEMY JUTSU?!
RELAX, IT'S THE HOKAGE'S KATSUYU'S SUMMONING JUTSU.
ZWOO...

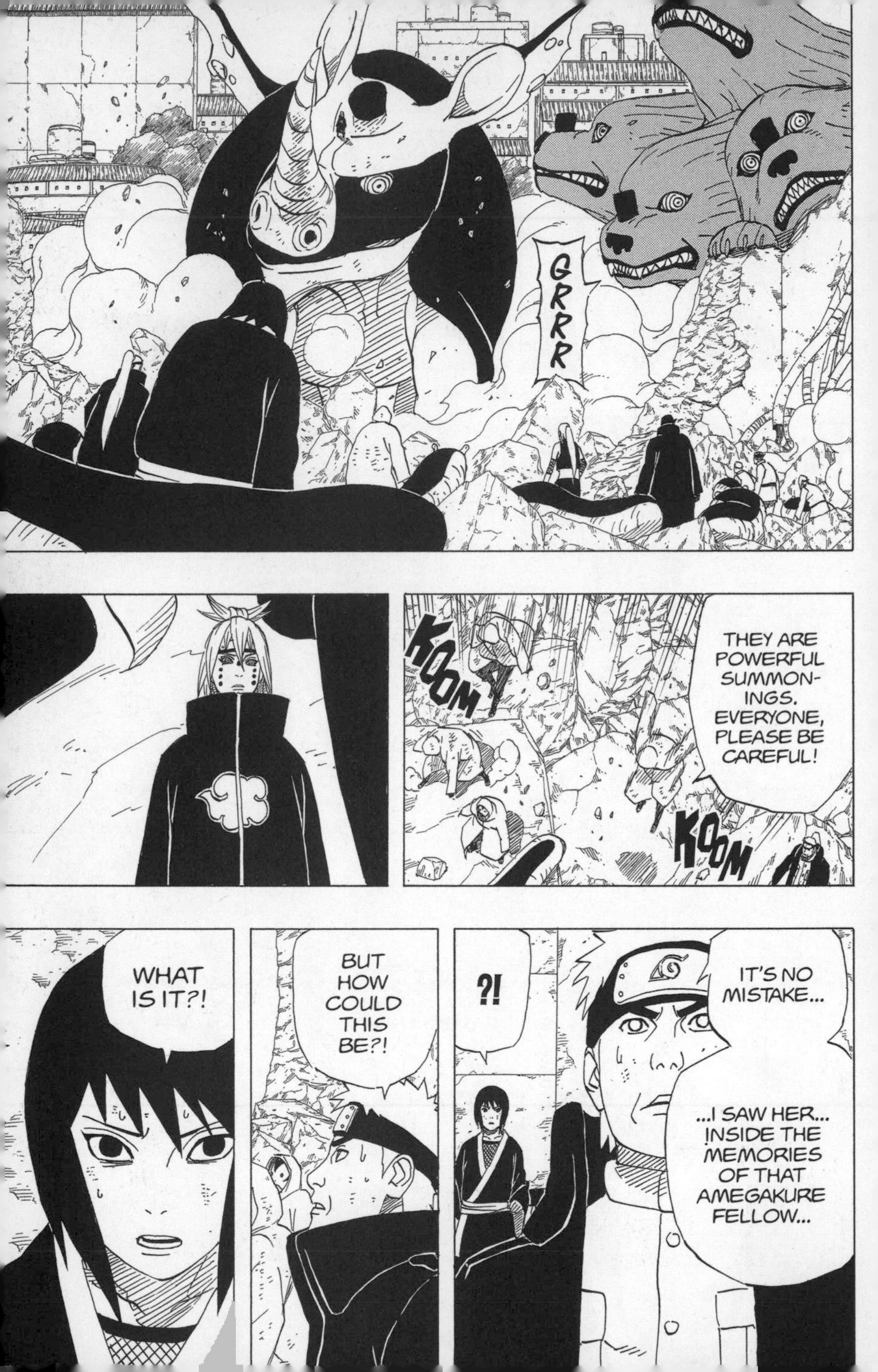
GRRR
KOOM
KOOM
THEY ARE POWERFUL SUMMONINGS. EVERYONE, PLEASE BE CAREFUL!
IT'S NO MISTAKE...
?!
...I SAW HER... INSIDE THE MEMORIES OF THAT AMEGAKURE FELLOW...
BUT HOW COULD THIS BE?!
WHAT IS IT?!

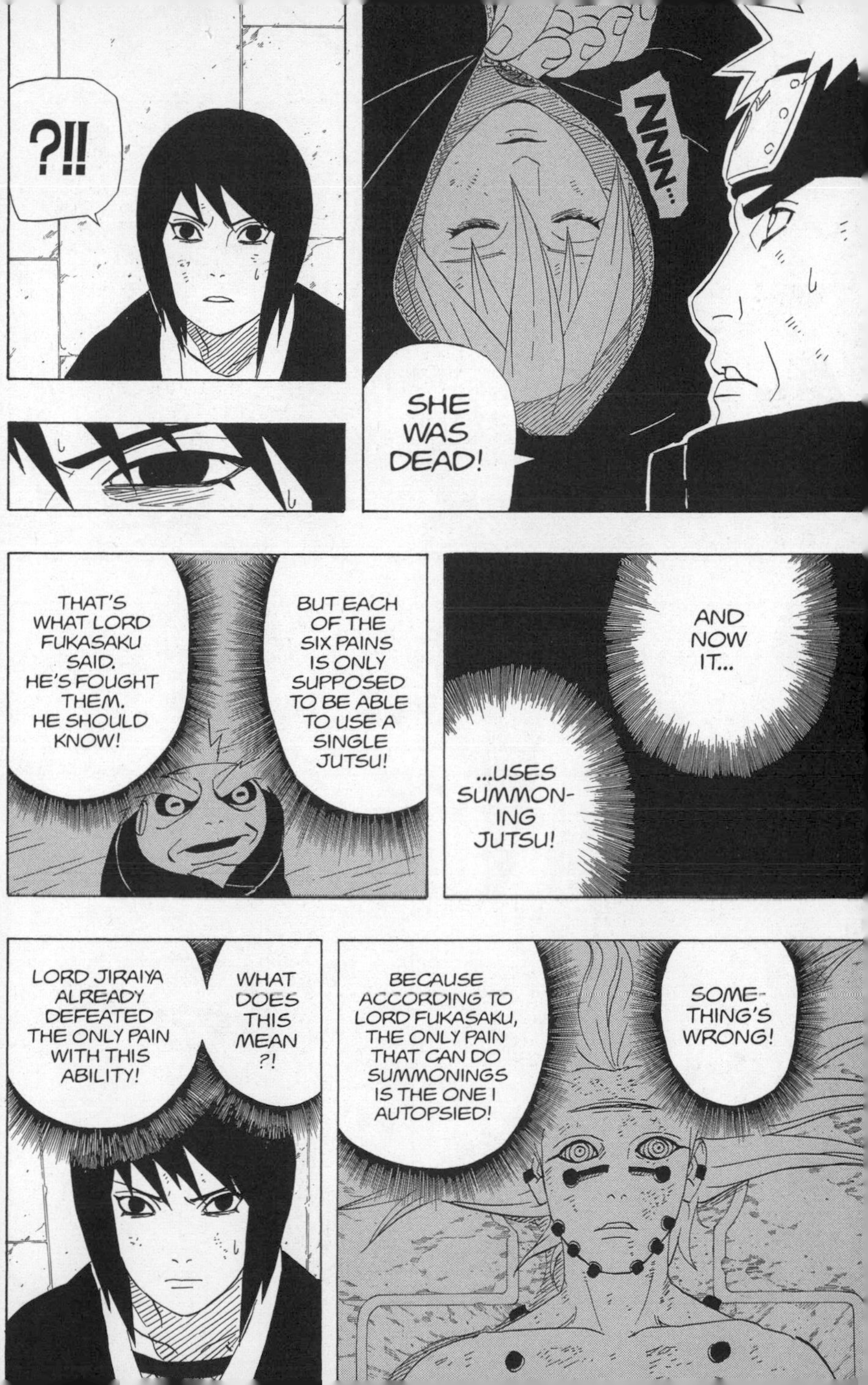
NNN...
SHE WAS DEAD!
?!!
AND NOW IT...
...USES SUMMON-ING JUTSU!
BUT EACH OF THE SIX PAINS IS ONLY SUPPOSED TO BE ABLE TO USE A SINGLE JUTSU!
THAT'S WHAT LORD FUKASAKU SAID. HE'S FOUGHT THEM. HE SHOULD KNOW!
SOME-THING'S WRONG!
BECAUSE ACCORDING TO LORD FUKASAKU, THE ONLY PAIN THAT CAN DO SUMMONINGS IS THE ONE I AUTOPSIED!
WHAT DOES THIS MEAN ?!
LORD JIRAIYA ALREADY DEFEATED THE ONLY PAIN WITH THIS ABILITY!

READ THIS WAY

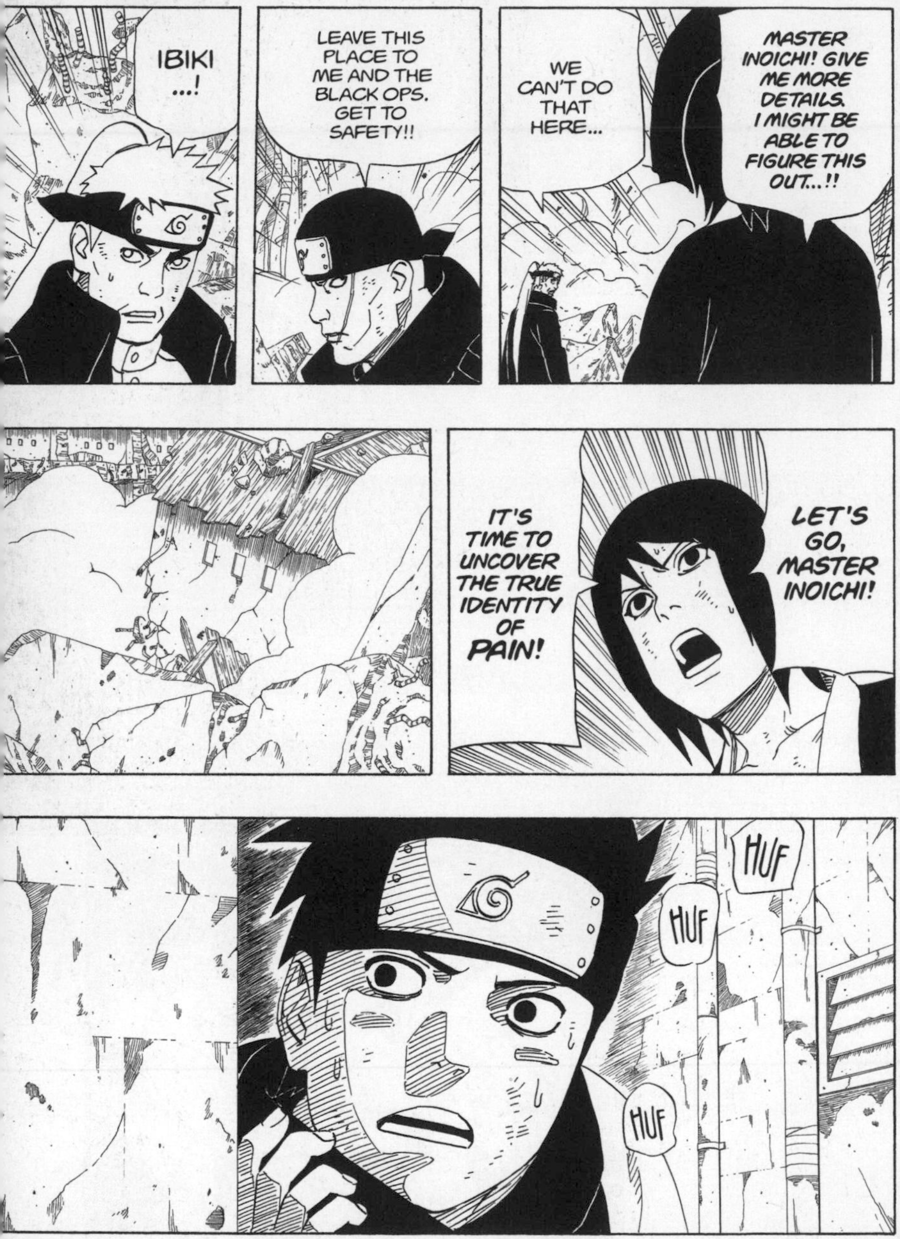

MASTER INOICHI! GIVE ME MORE DETAILS. I MIGHT BE ABLE TO FIGURE THIS OUT...!!
WE CAN'T DO THAT HERE...
LEAVE THIS PLACE TO ME AND THE BLACK OPS. GET TO SAFETY!!
IBIKI ...!
LET'S GO, MASTER INOICHI!
IT'S TIME TO UNCOVER THE TRUE IDENTITY OF PAIN!
HUF
HUF
HUF

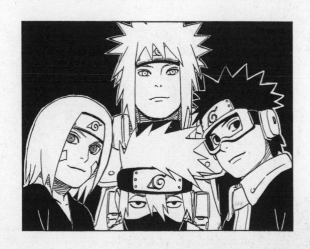

Number 426: Naruto & Konoha!!

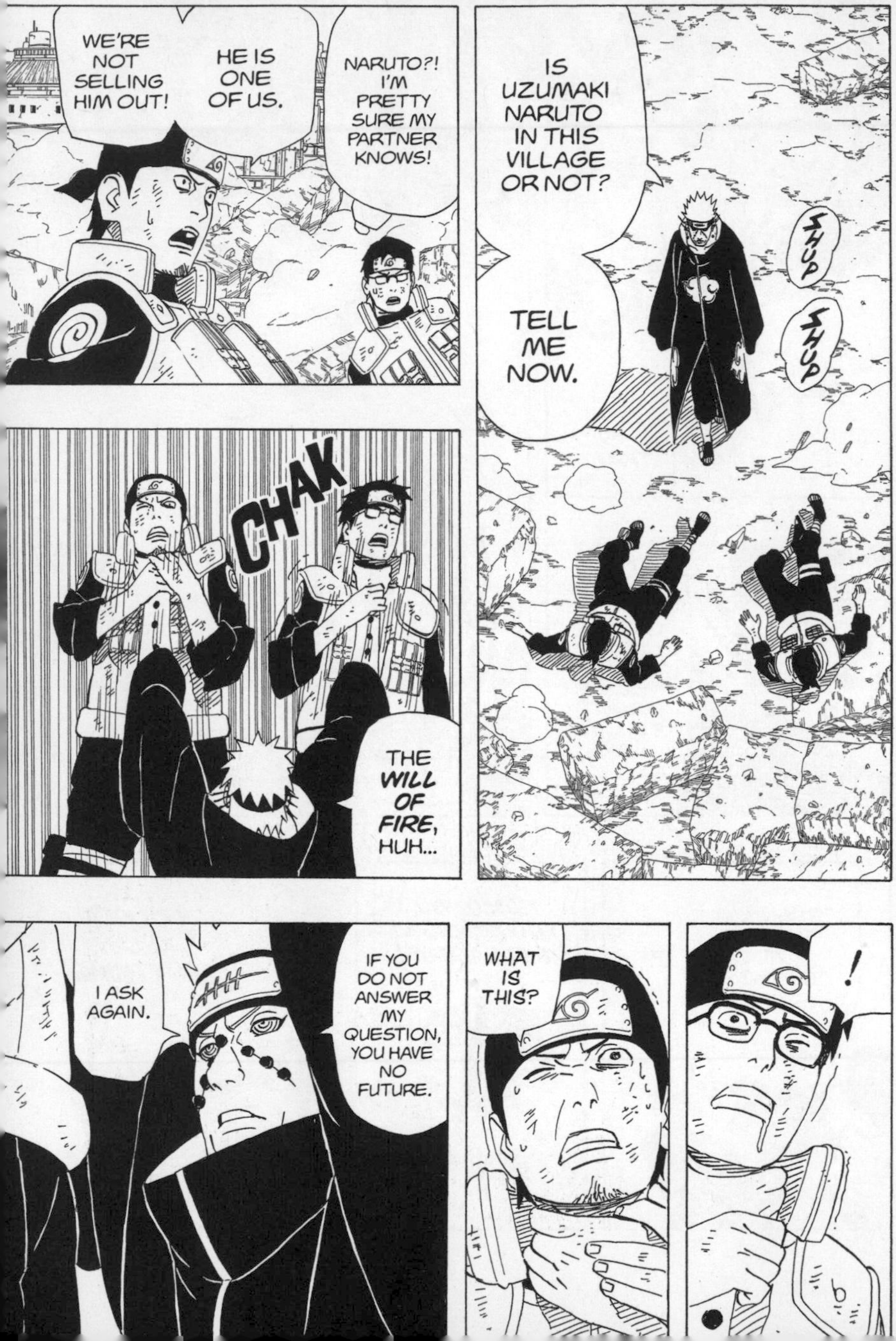
IS UZUMAKI NARUTO IN THIS VILLAGE OR NOT?
TELL ME NOW.
SHUP
SHUP
NARUTO?! I'M PRETTY SURE MY PARTNER KNOWS!
HE IS ONE OF US.
WE'RE NOT SELLING HIM OUT!
CHAK
THE WILL OF FIRE, HUH...
!
WHAT IS THIS?
IF YOU DO NOT ANSWER MY QUESTION, YOU HAVE NO FUTURE.
I ASK AGAIN.

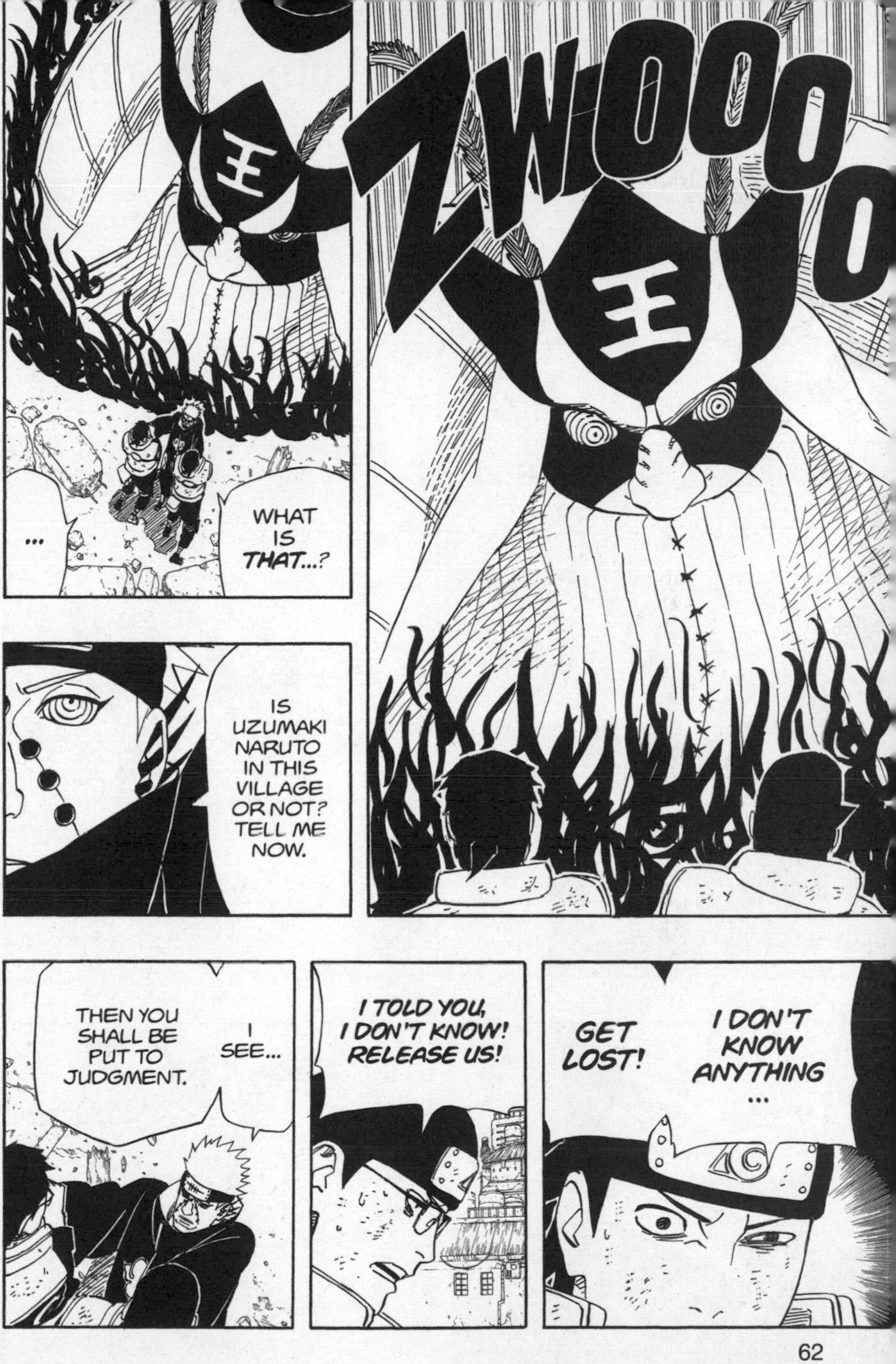
ZWOOOOO
WHAT IS THAT...?
...
IS UZUMAKI NARUTO IN THIS VILLAGE OR NOT? TELL ME NOW.
I DON'T KNOW ANYTHING ...
GET LOST!
I TOLD YOU, I DON'T KNOW! RELEASE US!
I SEE...
THEN YOU SHALL BE PUT TO JUDGMENT.

READ THIS WAY

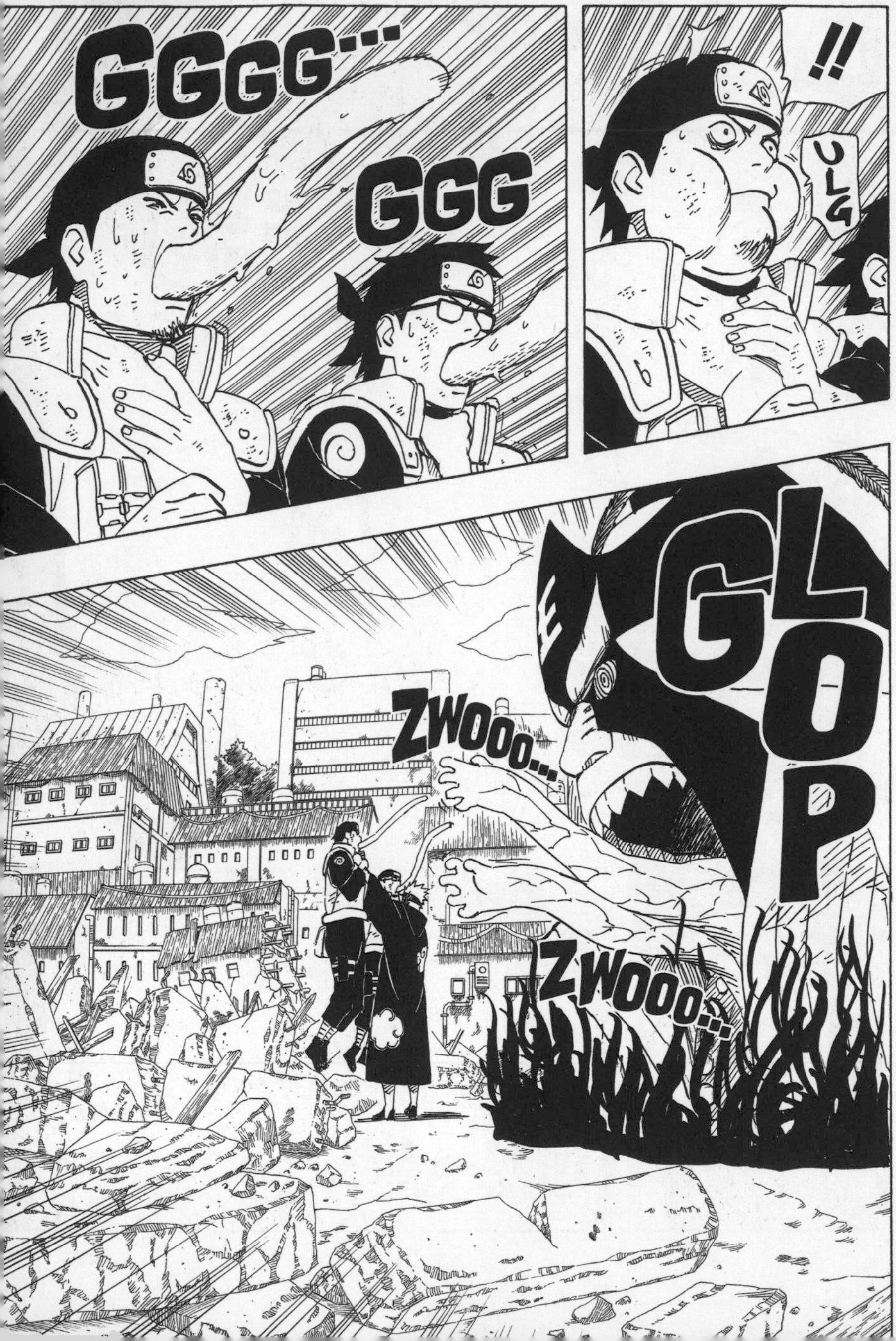
!!
ULG
GGGG...
GGG
GLOP
ZWOOO...
ZWOOO...

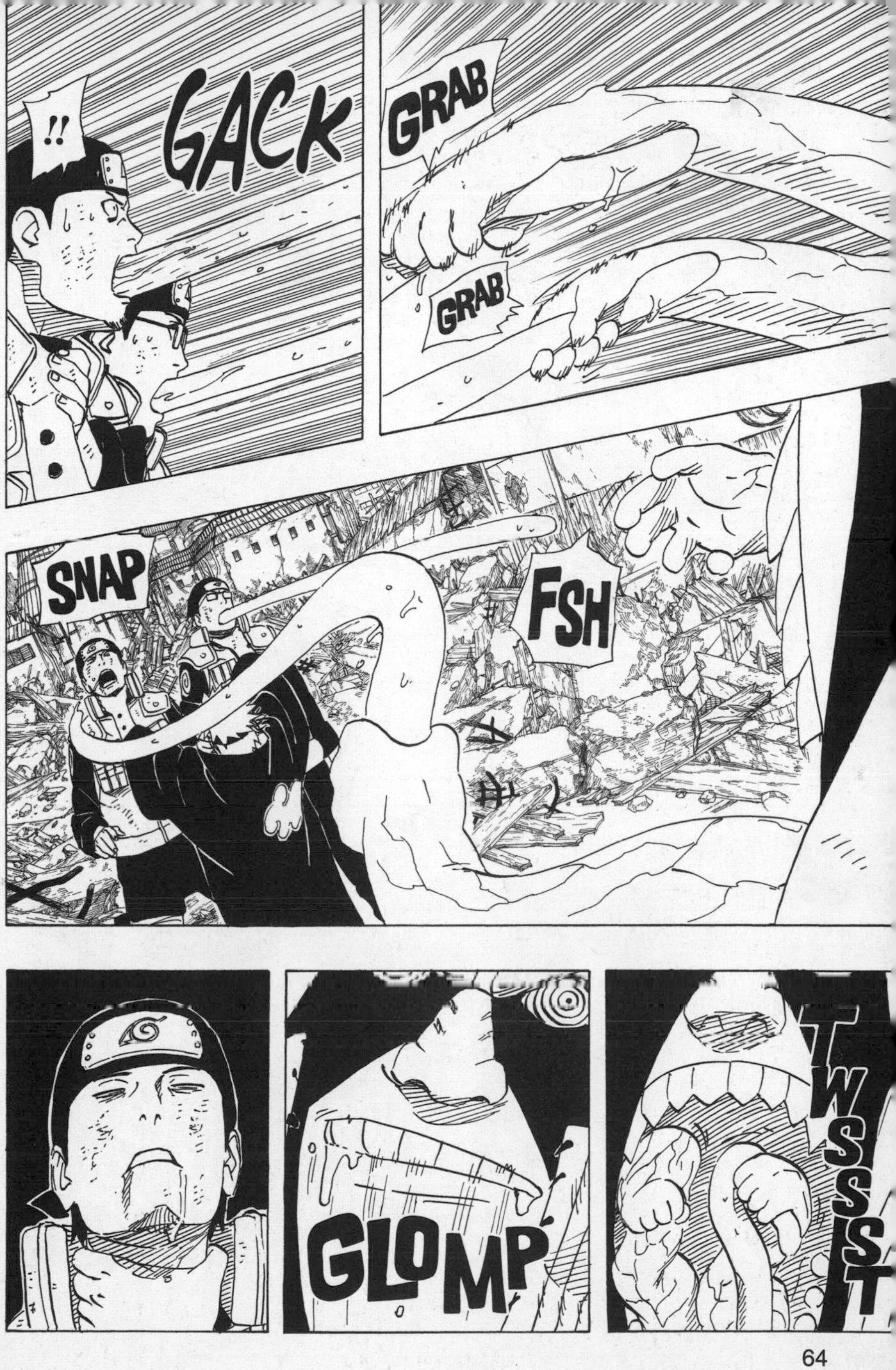
GRAB
GRAB
!!
GACK
FSH
SNAP
TWSSST
GLOMP

READ THIS WAY

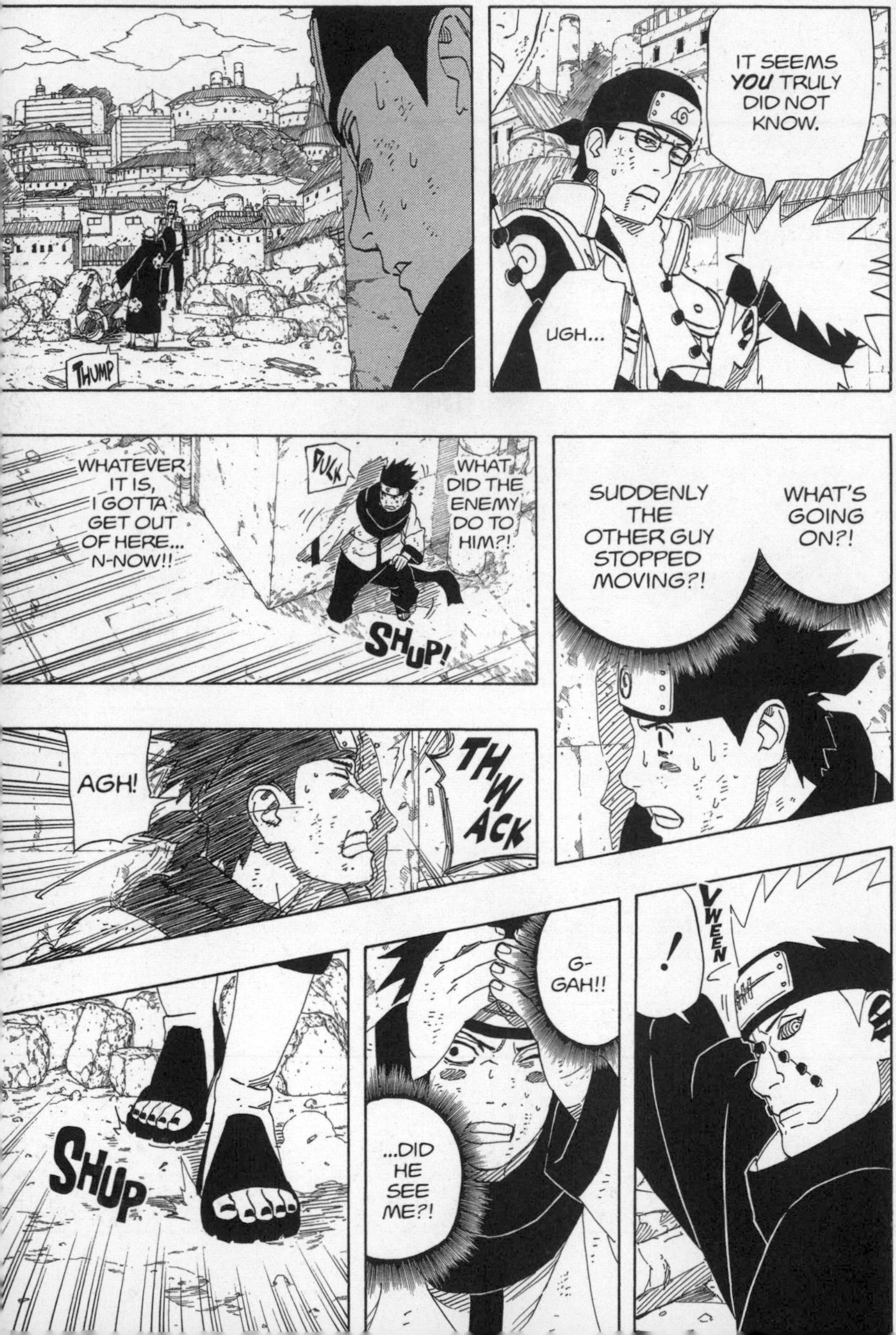
IT SEEMS YOU TRULY DID NOT KNOW.
UGH...
THUMP
WHAT'S GOING ON?!
SUDDENLY THE OTHER GUY STOPPED MOVING?!
WHAT DID THE ENEMY DO TO HIM?!
DUCK
WHATEVER IT IS, I GOTTA GET OUT OF HERE... N-NOW!!
SHUP!
THWACK
AGH!
VWEEN
!
G-GAH!!
...DID HE SEE ME?!
SHUP

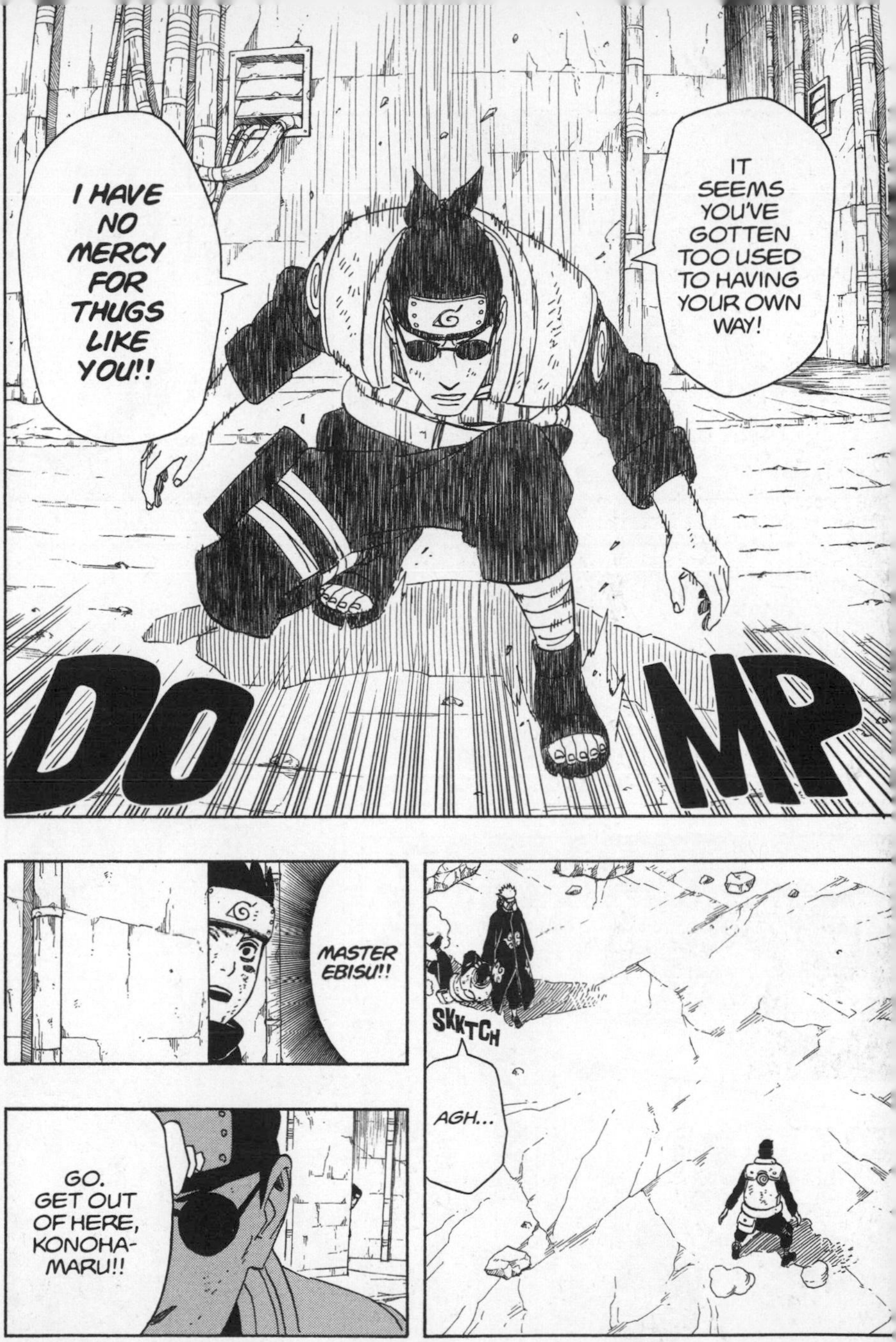
IT SEEMS YOU'VE GOTTEN TOO USED TO HAVING YOUR OWN WAY!
I HAVE NO MERCY FOR THUGS LIKE YOU!!
DOMP
SKKTCH
AGH...
MASTER EBISU!!
GO. GET OUT OF HERE, KONOHA-MARU!!

READ THIS WAY

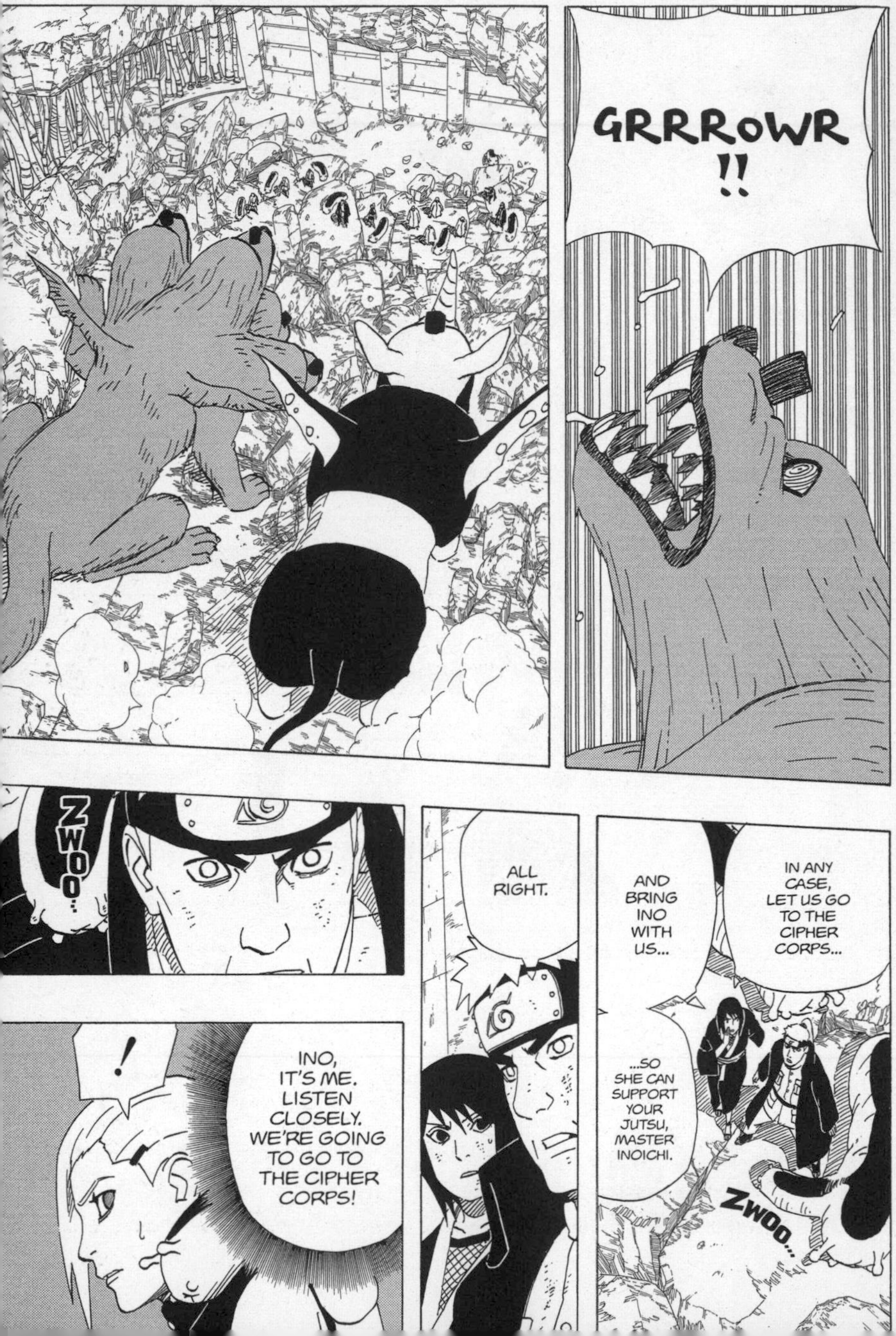
GRRROWR !!
IN ANY CASE, LET US GO TO THE CIPHER CORPS...
AND BRING INO WITH US...
...SO SHE CAN SUPPORT YOUR JUTSU, MASTER INOICHI.
ZWOO...
ALL RIGHT.
ZWOO...
!
INO, IT'S ME. LISTEN CLOSELY. WE'RE GOING TO GO TO THE CIPHER CORPS!

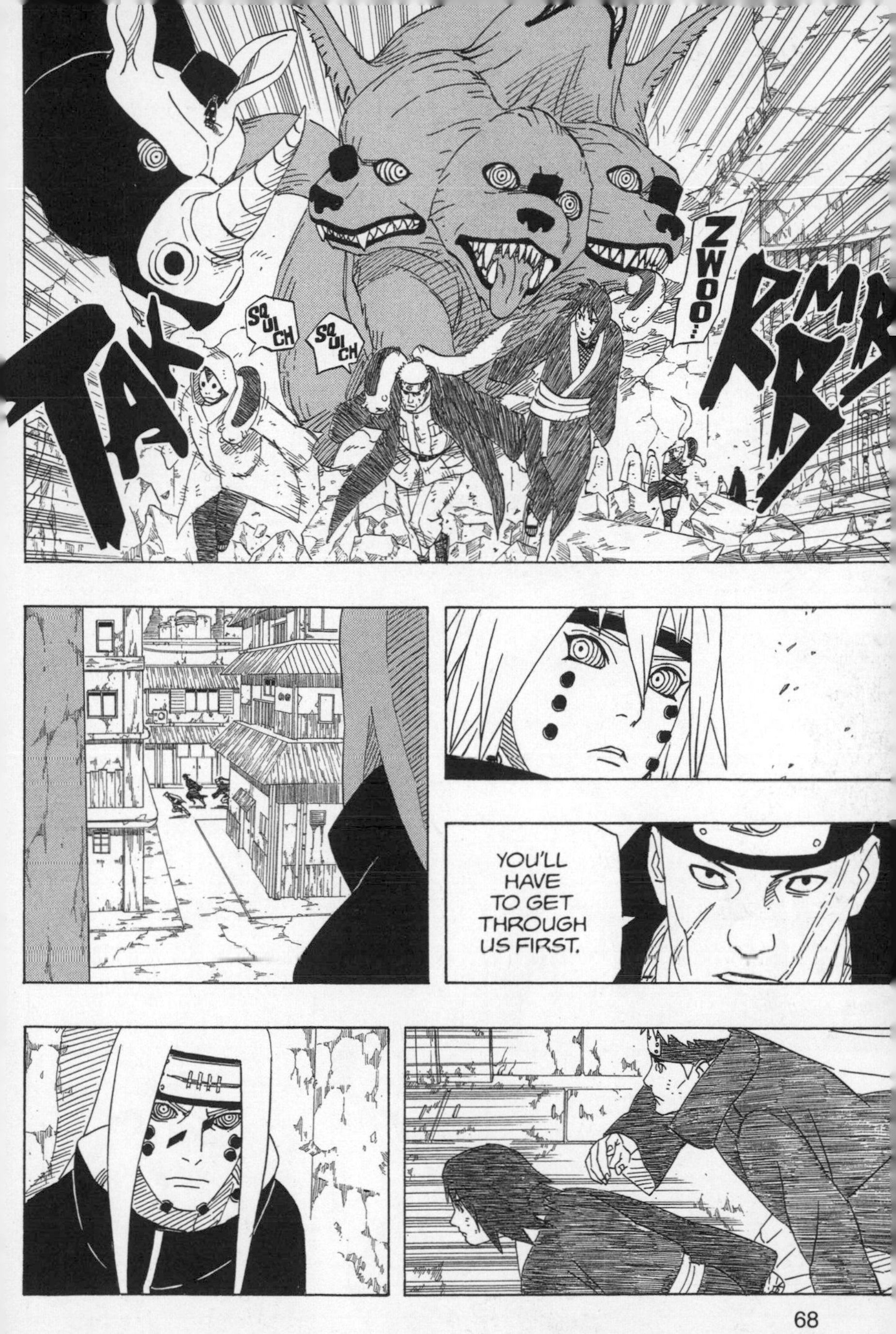
ZWOO...
SQUICH
SQUICH
TAK
YOU'LL HAVE TO GET THROUGH US FIRST.

READ THIS WAY

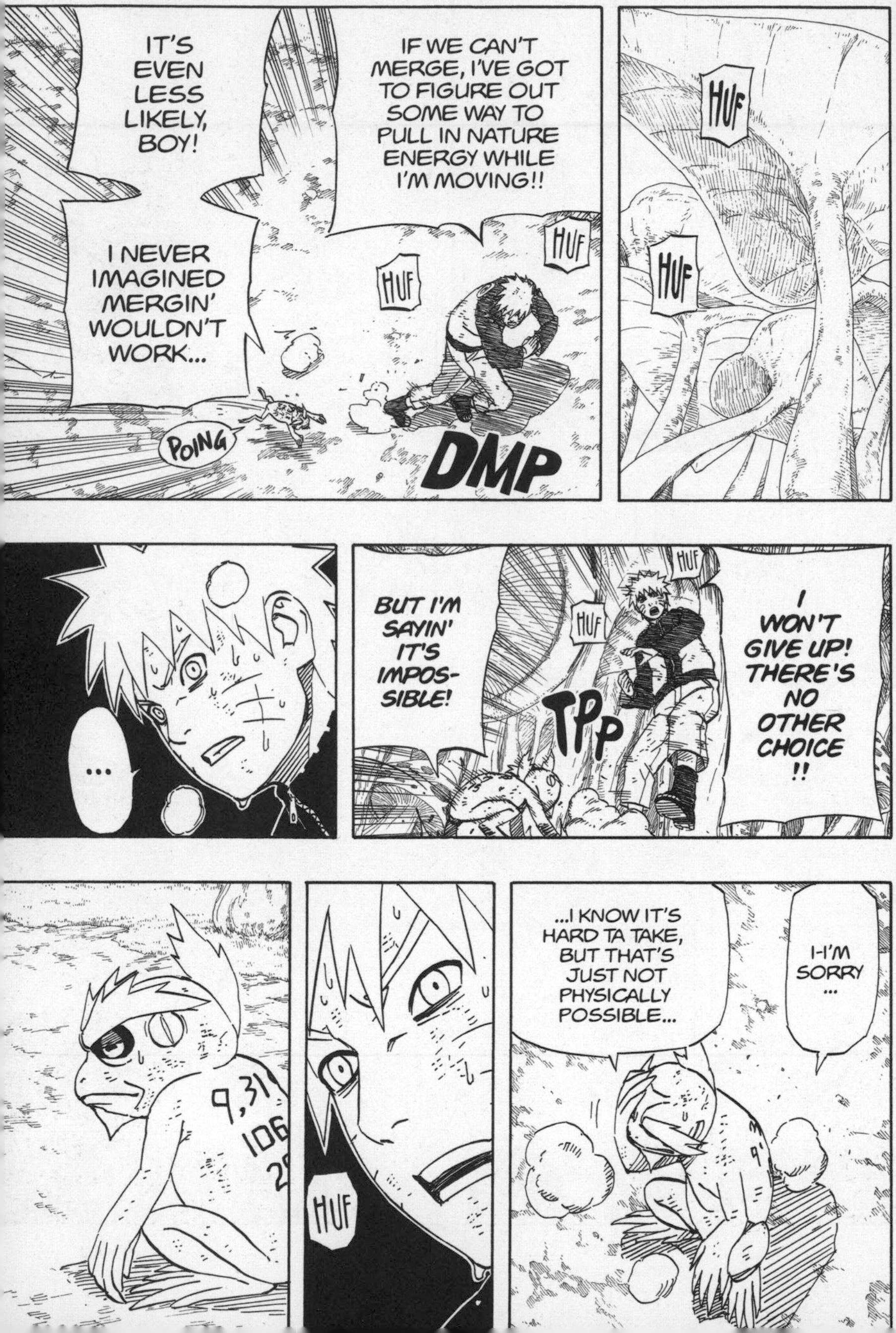
HUF
HUF
IF WE CAN'T MERGE, I'VE GOT TO FIGURE OUT SOME WAY TO PULL IN NATURE ENERGY WHILE I'M MOVING!!
IT'S EVEN LESS LIKELY, BOY!
HUF
HUF
I NEVER IMAGINED MERGIN' WOULDN'T WORK...
DMP
POING
I WON'T GIVE UP! THERE'S NO OTHER CHOICE !!
HUF
HUF
BUT I'M SAYIN' IT'S IMPOSSIBLE!
TPP
...
I-I'M SORRY ...
...I KNOW IT'S HARD TA TAKE, BUT THAT'S JUST NOT PHYSICALLY POSSIBLE...
HUF

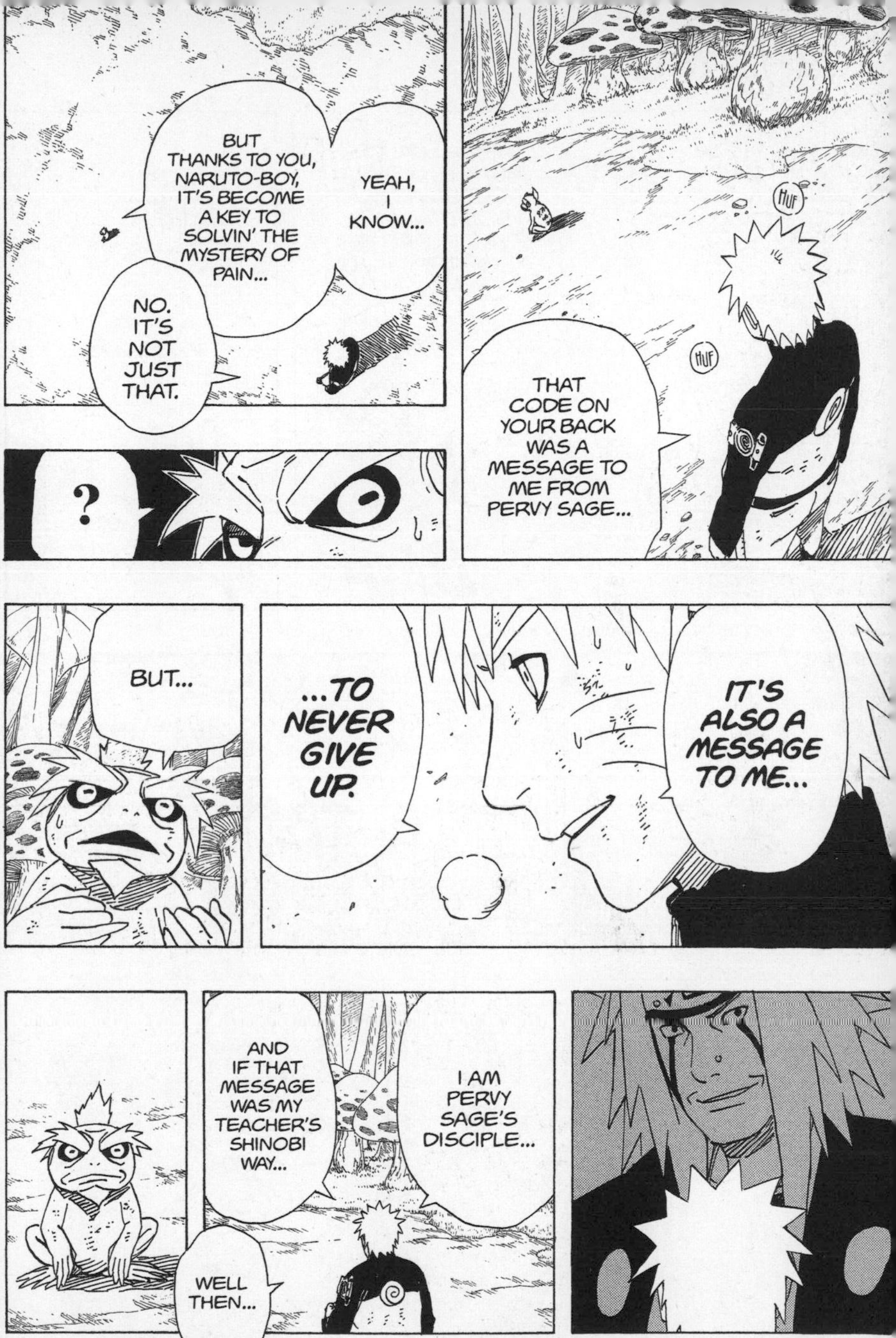
HUF
HUF
THAT CODE ON YOUR BACK WAS A MESSAGE TO ME FROM PERVY SAGE...
BUT THANKS TO YOU, NARUTO-BOY, IT'S BECOME A KEY TO SOLVIN' THE MYSTERY OF PAIN...
YEAH, I KNOW...
NO. IT'S NOT JUST THAT.
?
IT'S ALSO A MESSAGE TO ME...
...TO NEVER GIVE UP.
BUT...
I AM PERVY SAGE'S DISCIPLE...
AND IF THAT MESSAGE WAS MY TEACHER'S SHINOBI WAY...
WELL THEN...

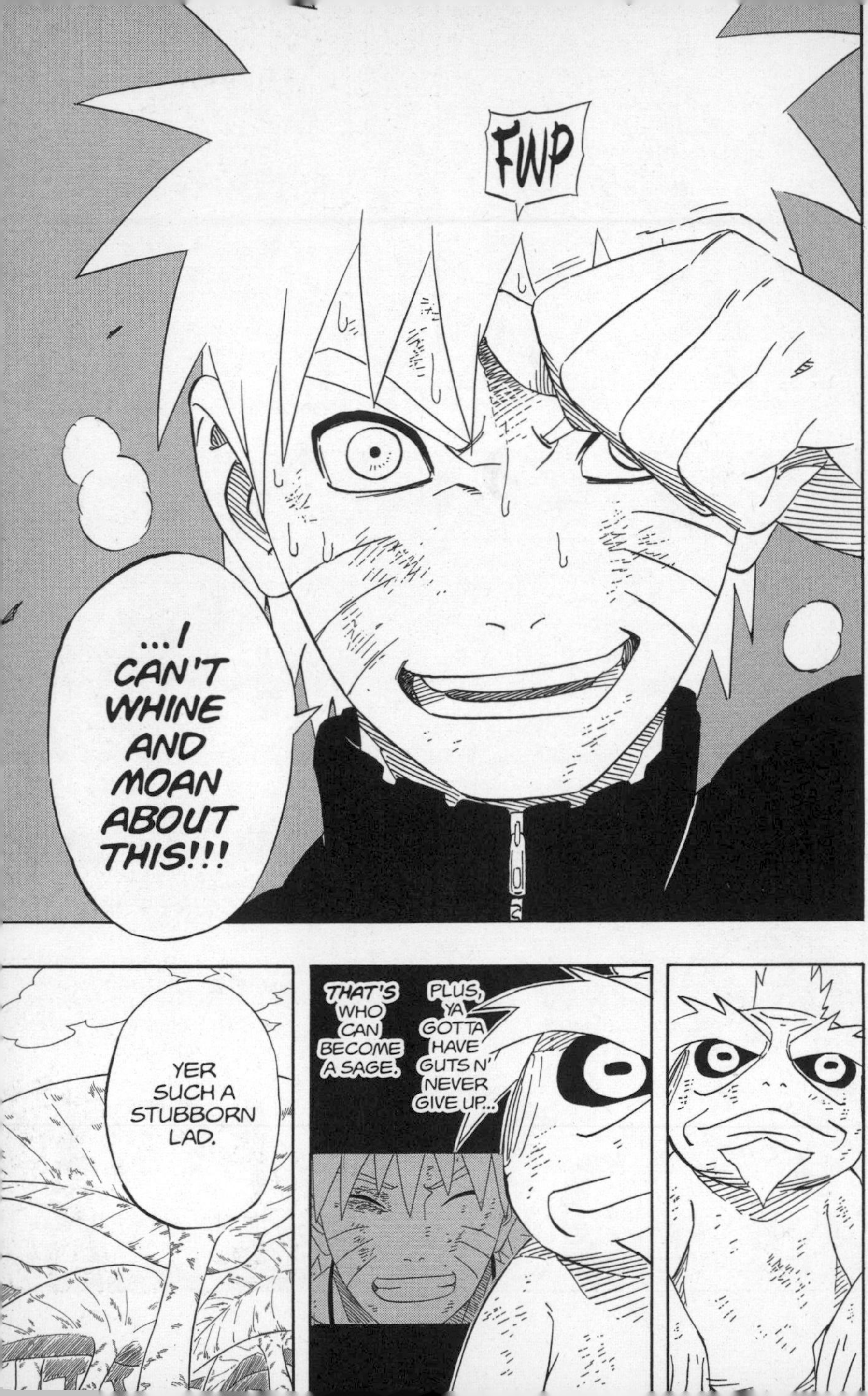
FWP
...I CAN'T WHINE AND MOAN ABOUT THIS!!!
PLUS, YA GOTTA HAVE GUTS N' NEVER GIVE UP...
THAT'S WHO CAN BECOME A SAGE.
YER SUCH A STUBBORN LAD.

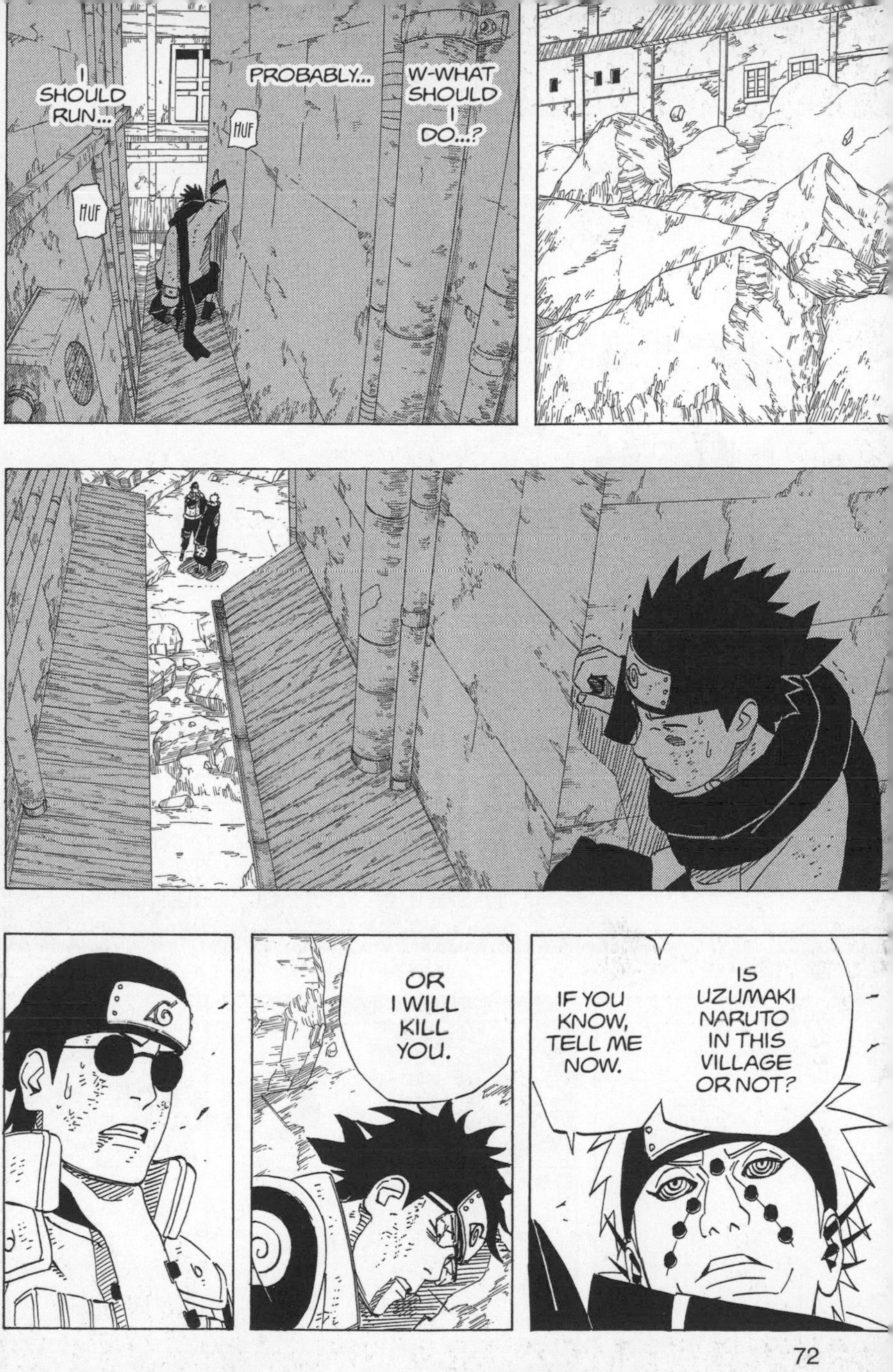
W-WHAT SHOULD I DO...?
PROBABLY...
HUF
I SHOULD RUN...
HUF
IS UZUMAKI NARUTO IN THIS VILLAGE OR NOT?
IF YOU KNOW, TELL ME NOW.
OR I WILL KILL YOU.

READ THIS WAY

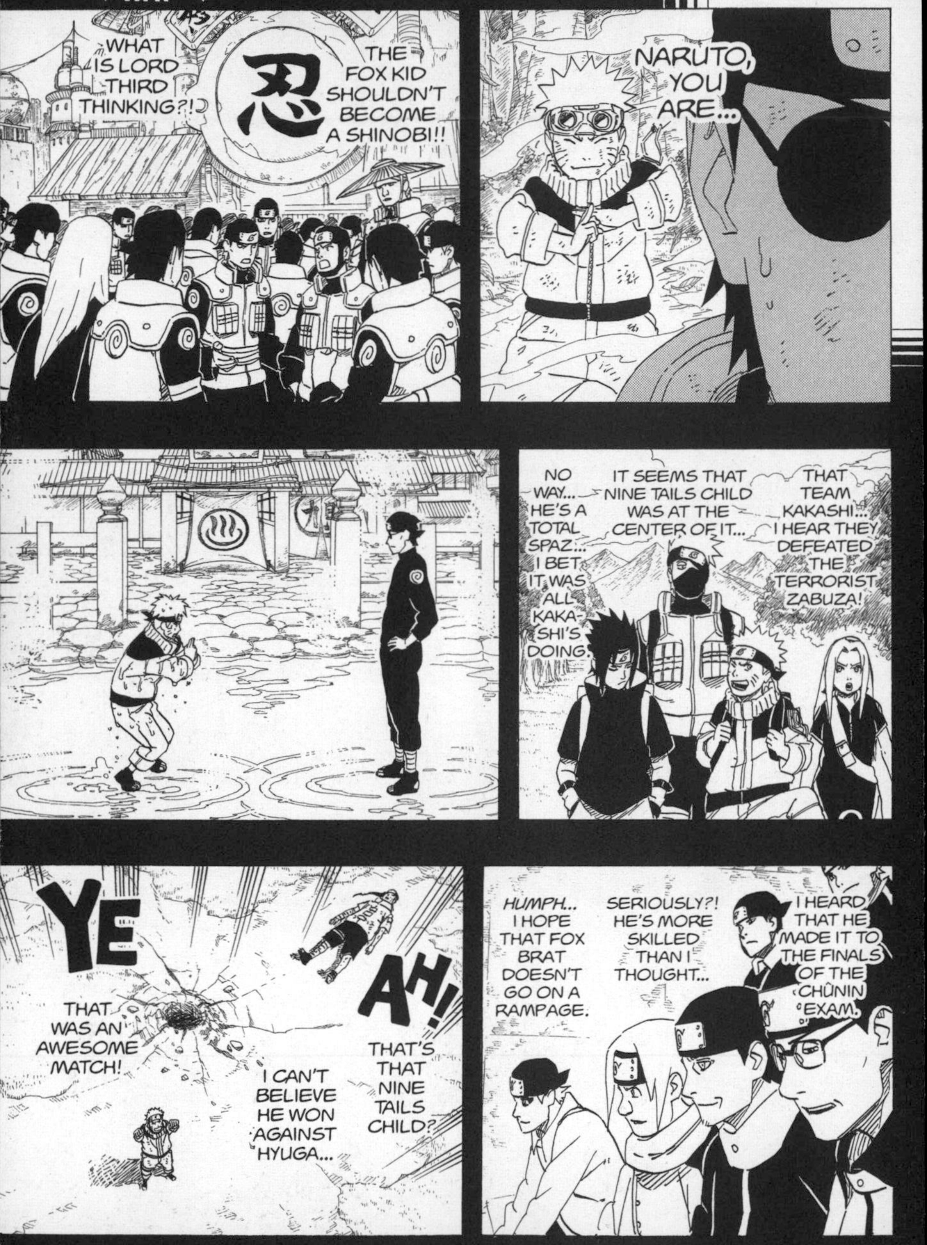

NARUTO, YOU ARE...
THE FOX KID SHOULDN'T BECOME A SHINOBI!!
忍
WHAT IS LORD THIRD THINKING?!
THAT TEAM KAKASHI... I HEAR THEY DEFEATED THE TERRORIST ZABUZA!
IT SEEMS THAT NINE TAILS CHILD WAS AT THE CENTER OF IT...
NO WAY... HE'S A TOTAL SPAZ... I BET IT WAS ALL KAKASHI'S DOING.
I HEARD THAT HE MADE IT TO THE FINALS OF THE CHÛNIN EXAM.
SERIOUSLY?! HE'S MORE SKILLED THAN I THOUGHT...
HUMPH... I HOPE THAT FOX BRAT DOESN'T GO ON A RAMPAGE.
YEAH!
THAT'S THAT NINE TAILS CHILD?
I CAN'T BELIEVE HE WON AGAINST HYUGA...
THAT WAS AN AWESOME MATCH!

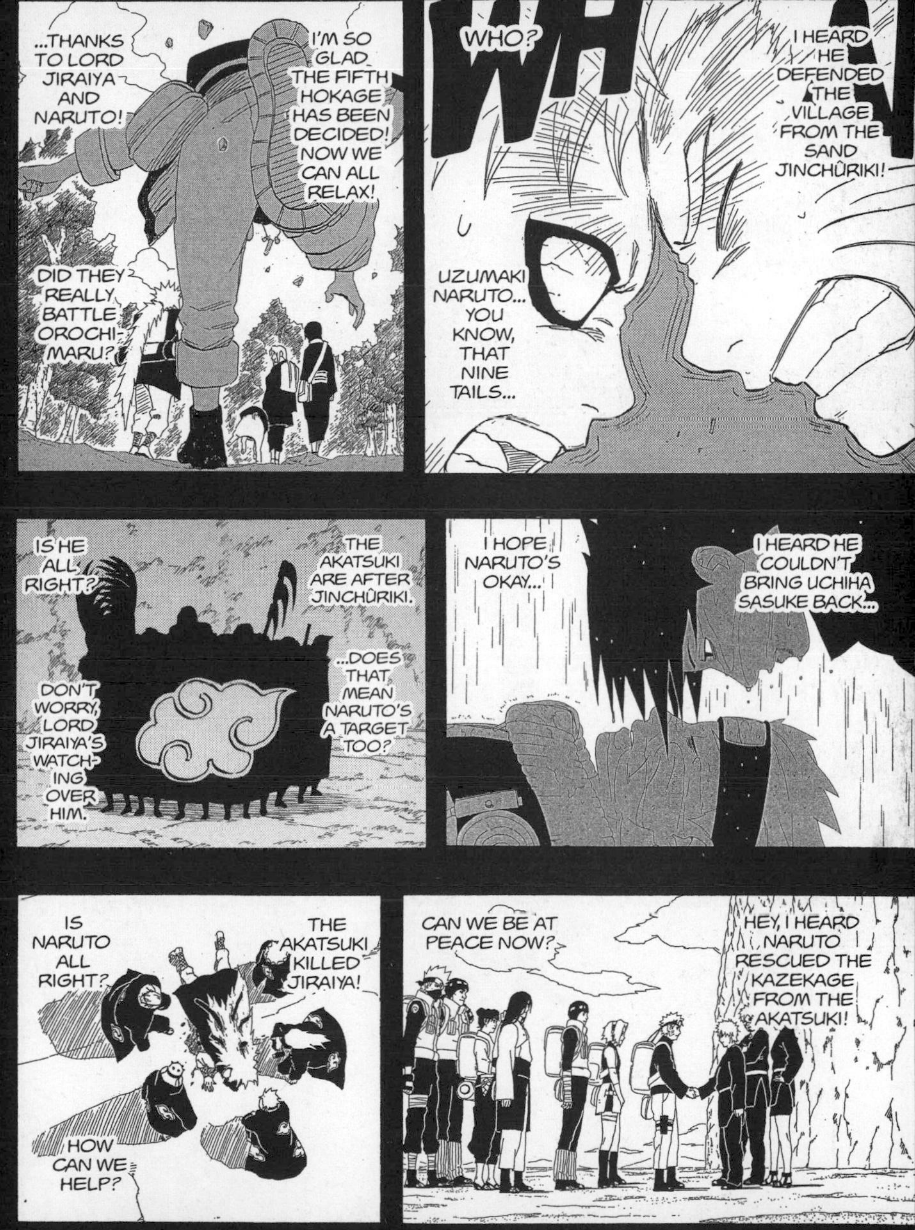
I HEARD HE DEFENDED THE VILLAGE FROM THE SAND JINCHÛRIKI!
WHO?
UZUMAKI NARUTO... YOU KNOW, THAT NINE TAILS...
I'M SO GLAD THE FIFTH HOKAGE HAS BEEN DECIDED! NOW WE CAN ALL RELAX!
...THANKS TO LORD JIRAIYA AND NARUTO!
DID THEY REALLY BATTLE OROCHIMARU?
I HEARD HE COULDN'T BRING UCHIHA SASUKE BACK...
I HOPE NARUTO'S OKAY...
THE AKATSUKI ARE AFTER JINCHÛRIKI.
IS HE ALL RIGHT?
...DOES THAT MEAN NARUTO'S A TARGET TOO?
DON'T WORRY, LORD JIRAIYA'S WATCHING OVER HIM.
HEY, I HEARD NARUTO RESCUED THE KAZEKAGE FROM THE AKATSUKI!
CAN WE BE AT PEACE NOW?
THE AKATSUKI KILLED JIRAIYA!
IS NARUTO ALL RIGHT?
HOW CAN WE HELP?

READ THIS WAY

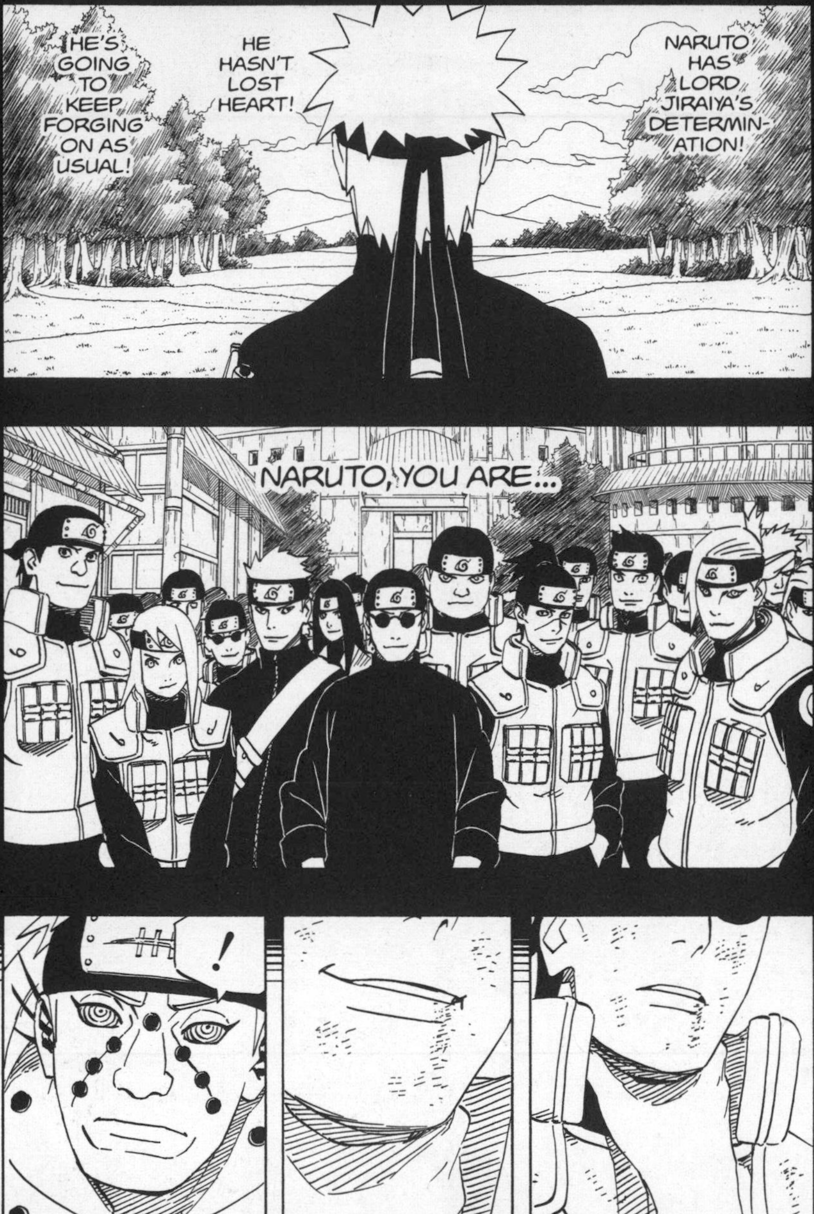
NARUTO HAS LORD JIRAIYA'S DETERMIN-ATION!
HE HASN'T LOST HEART!
HE'S GOING TO KEEP FORGING ON AS USUAL!
NARUTO, YOU ARE...
!

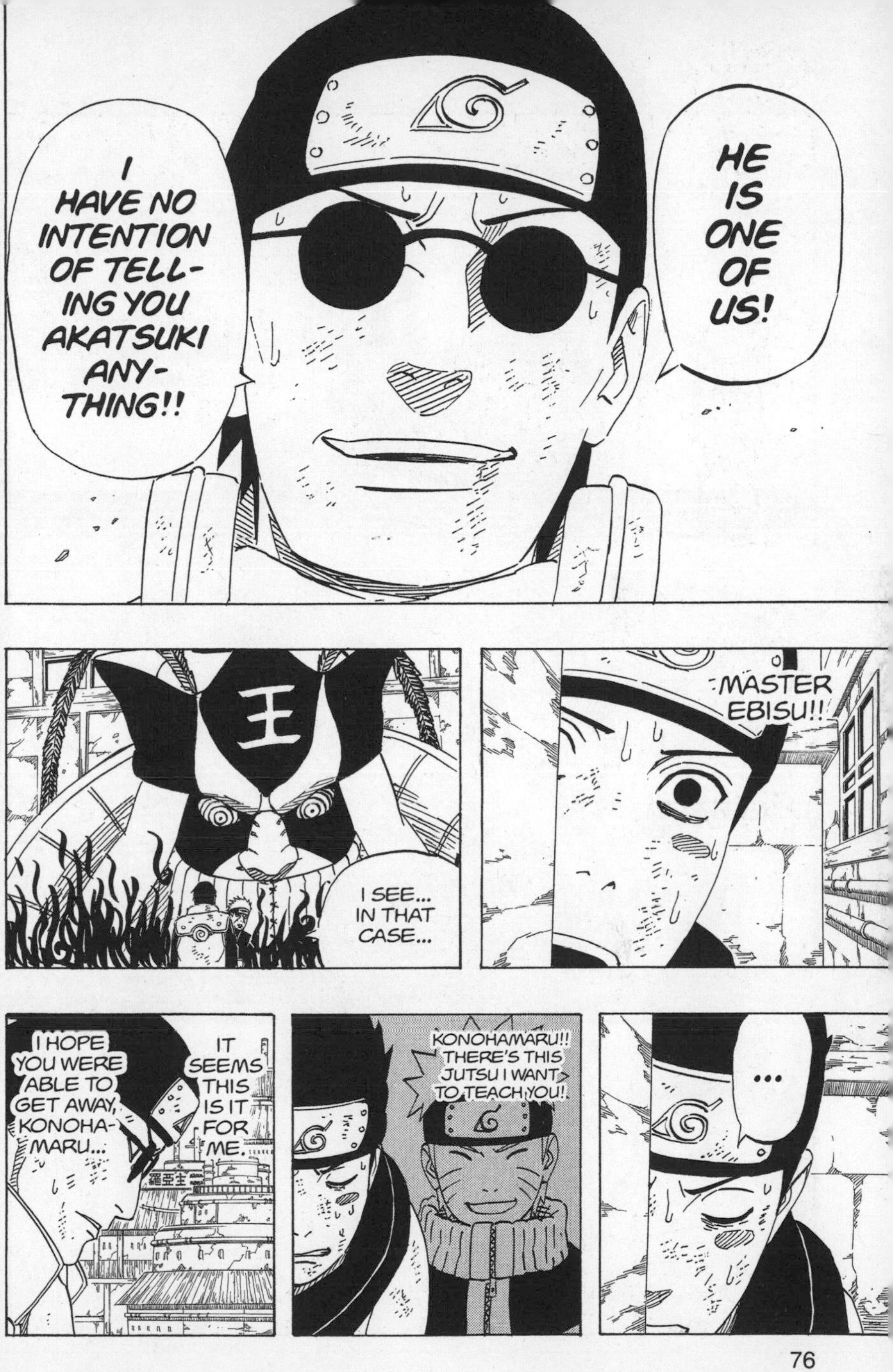
HE IS ONE OF US!
I HAVE NO INTENTION OF TELLING YOU AKATSUKI ANYTHING!!
MASTER EBISU!!
I SEE... IN THAT CASE...
...
KONOHAMARU!! THERE'S THIS JUTSU I WANT TO TEACH YOU!
IT SEEMS THIS IS IT FOR ME.
I HOPE YOU WERE ABLE TO GET AWAY, KONOHAMARU...

READ THIS WAY

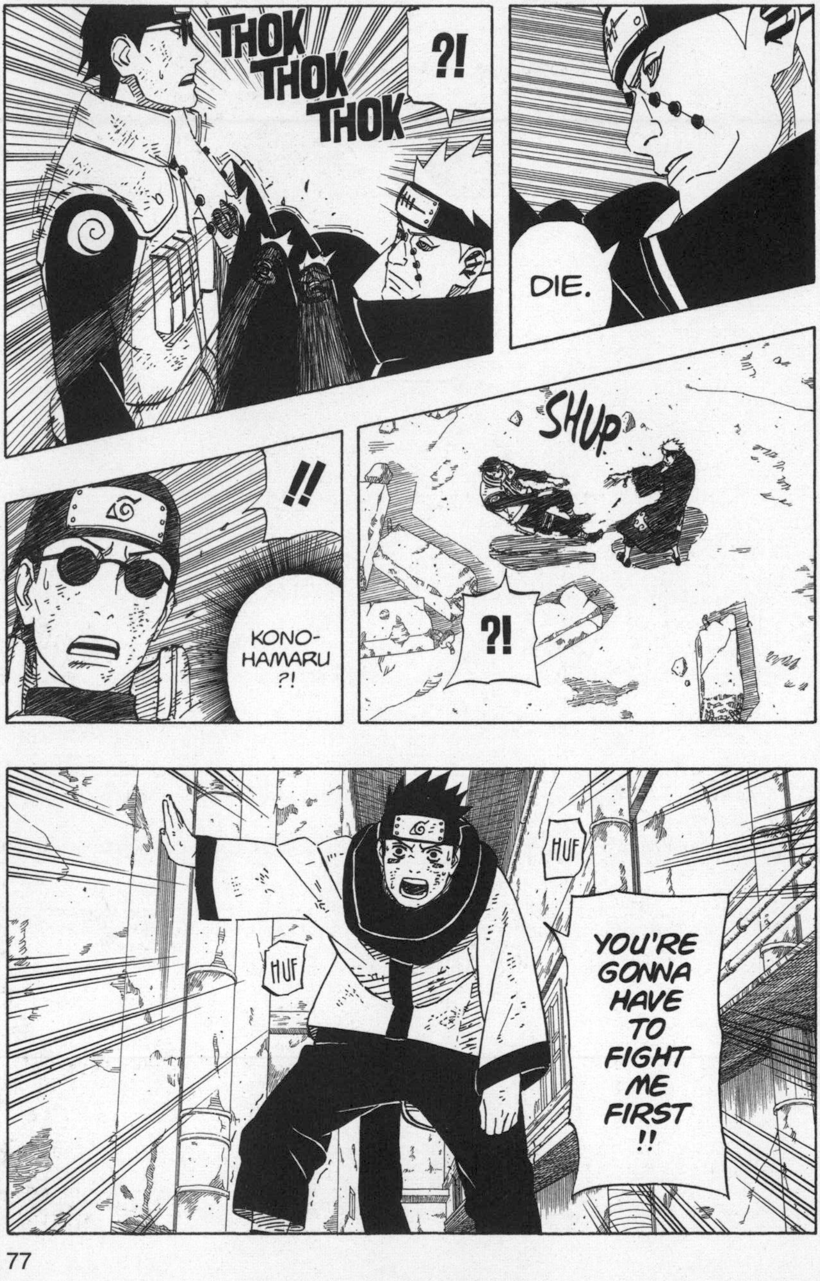
DIE.
THOK THOK THOK
?!
SHUP
?!
!!
KONO-HAMARU ?!
HUF
HUF
YOU'RE GONNA HAVE TO FIGHT ME FIRST !!

NARUTO

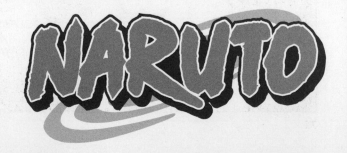

Number 427: Reunion

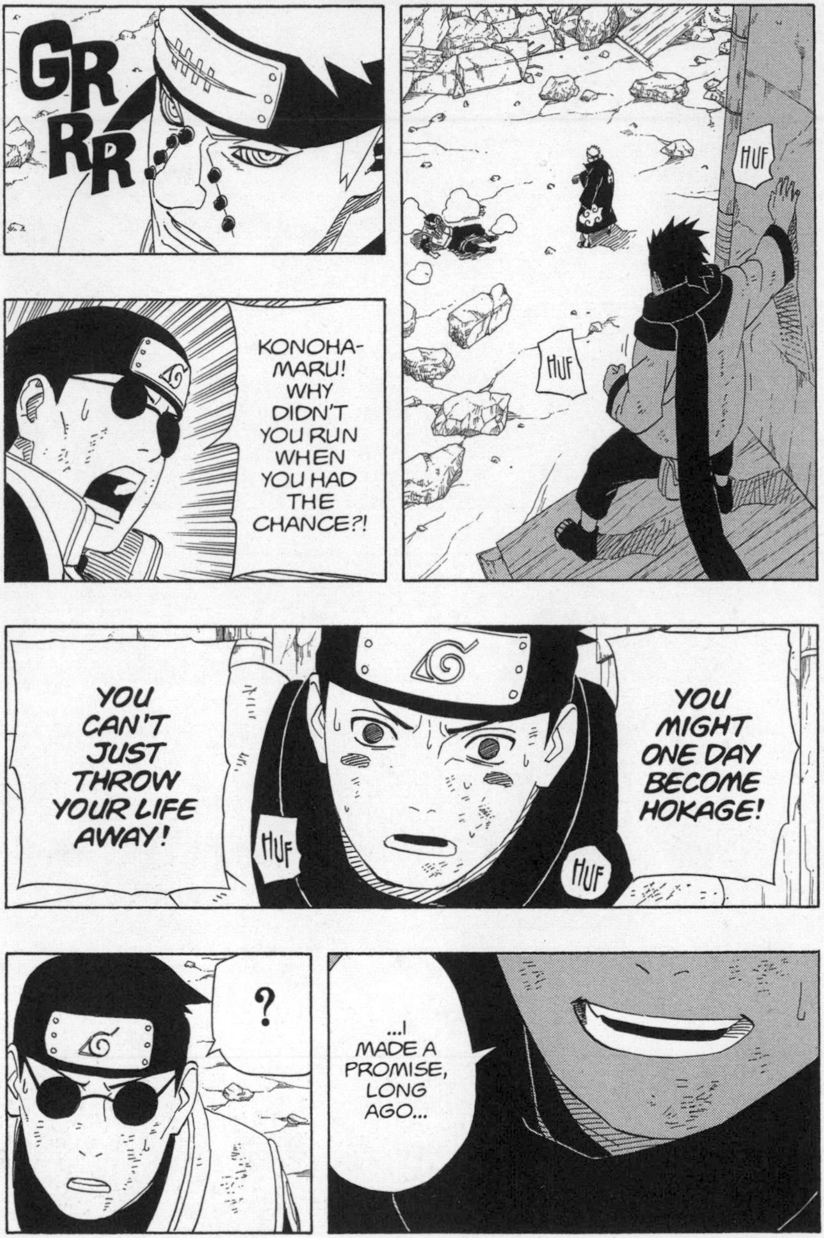
HUF
HUF
GRRR
KONOHAMARU! WHY DIDN'T YOU RUN WHEN YOU HAD THE CHANCE?!
YOU MIGHT ONE DAY BECOME HOKAGE!
HUF
YOU CAN'T JUST THROW YOUR LIFE AWAY!
HUF
...I MADE A PROMISE, LONG AGO...
?

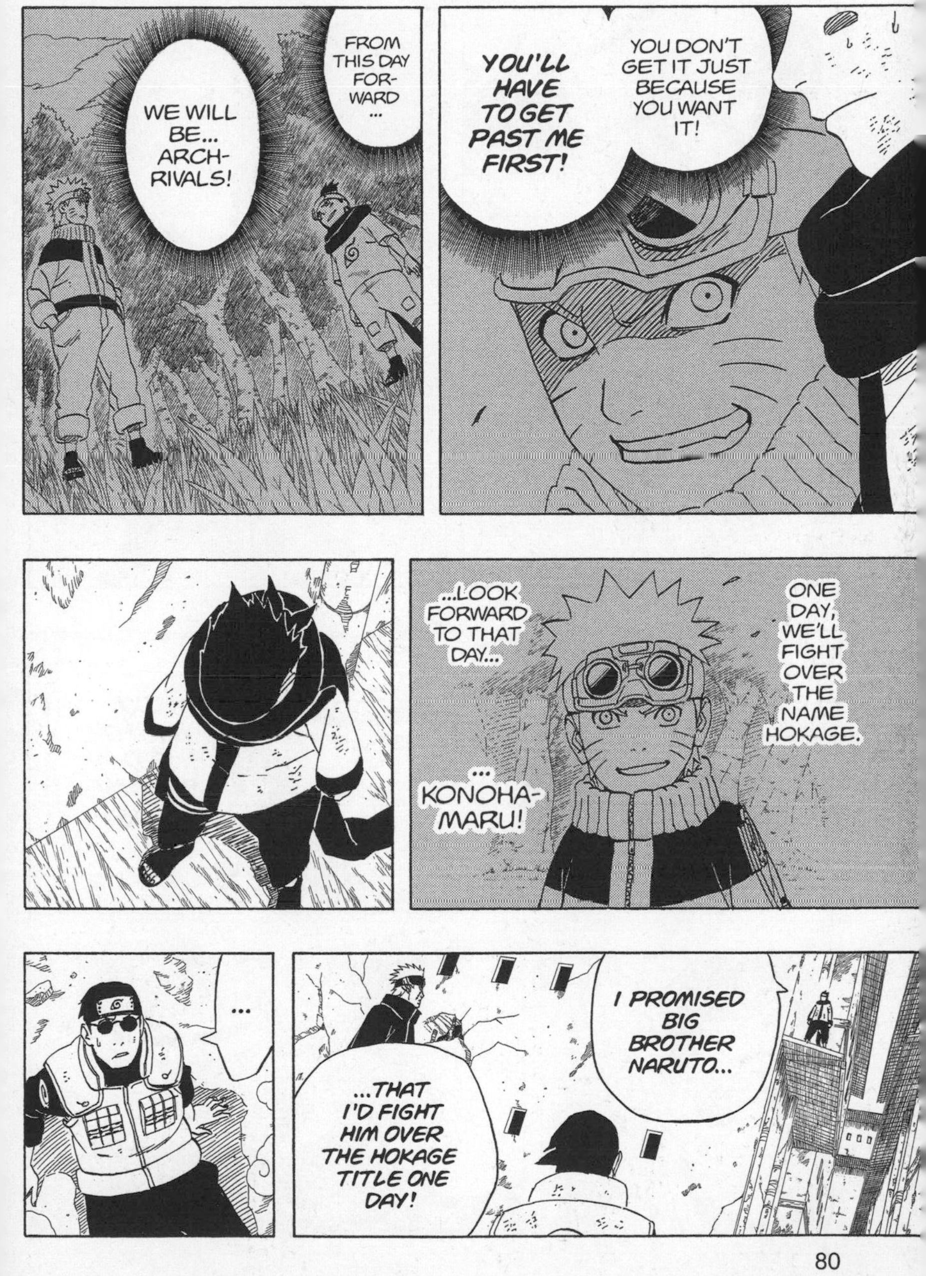
YOU DON'T GET IT JUST BECAUSE YOU WANT IT!
YOU'LL HAVE TO GET PAST ME FIRST!
FROM THIS DAY FORWARD ...
WE WILL BE... ARCH-RIVALS!
ONE DAY, WE'LL FIGHT OVER THE NAME HOKAGE.
...LOOK FORWARD TO THAT DAY...
... KONOHAMARU!
I PROMISED BIG BROTHER NARUTO...
...THAT I'D FIGHT HIM OVER THE HOKAGE TITLE ONE DAY!
...

READ THIS WAY

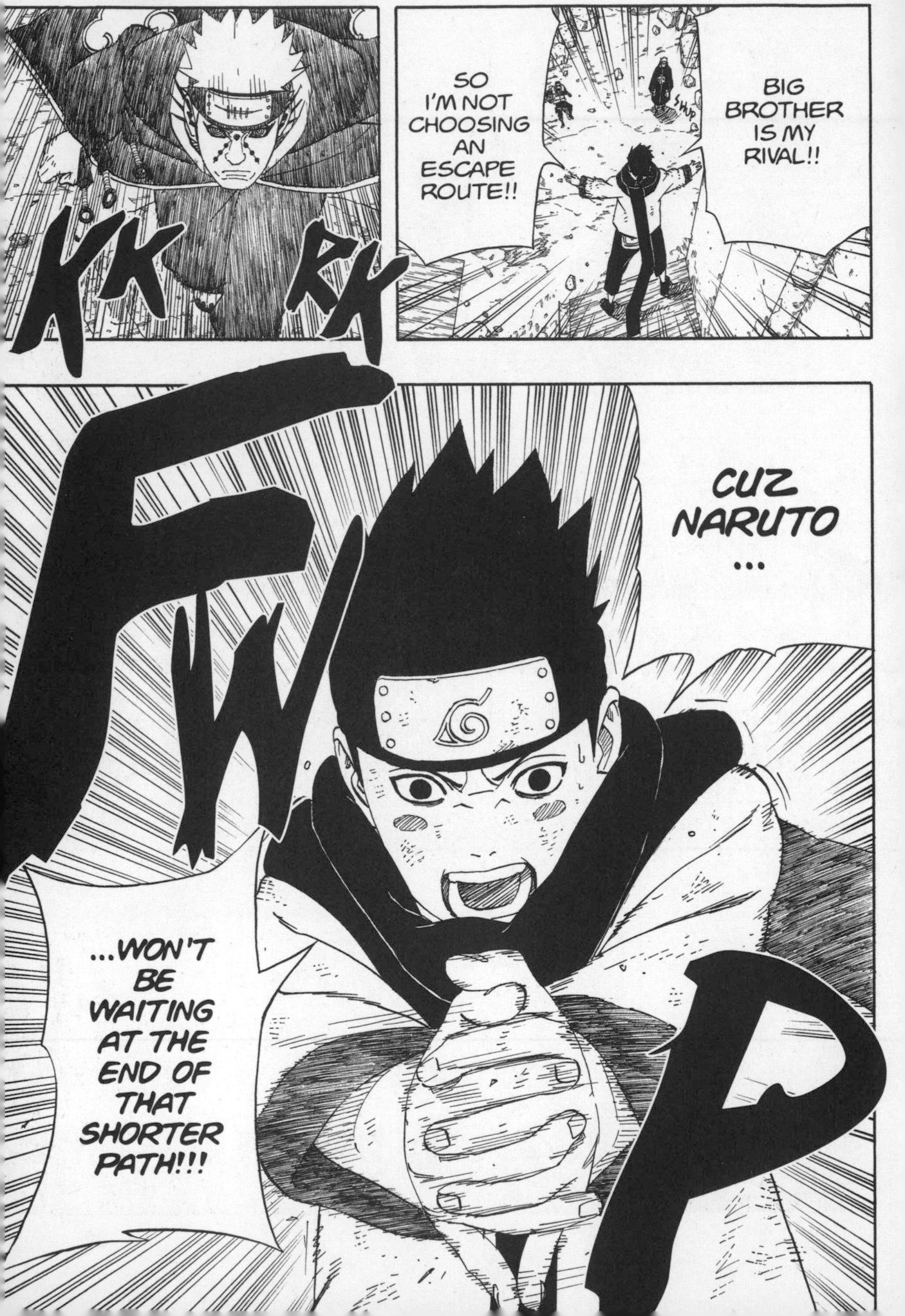
BIG BROTHER IS MY RIVAL!!
SO I'M NOT CHOOSING AN ESCAPE ROUTE!!
KKRK
CUZ NARUTO ...
...WON'T BE WAITING AT THE END OF THAT SHORTER PATH!!!
FWP

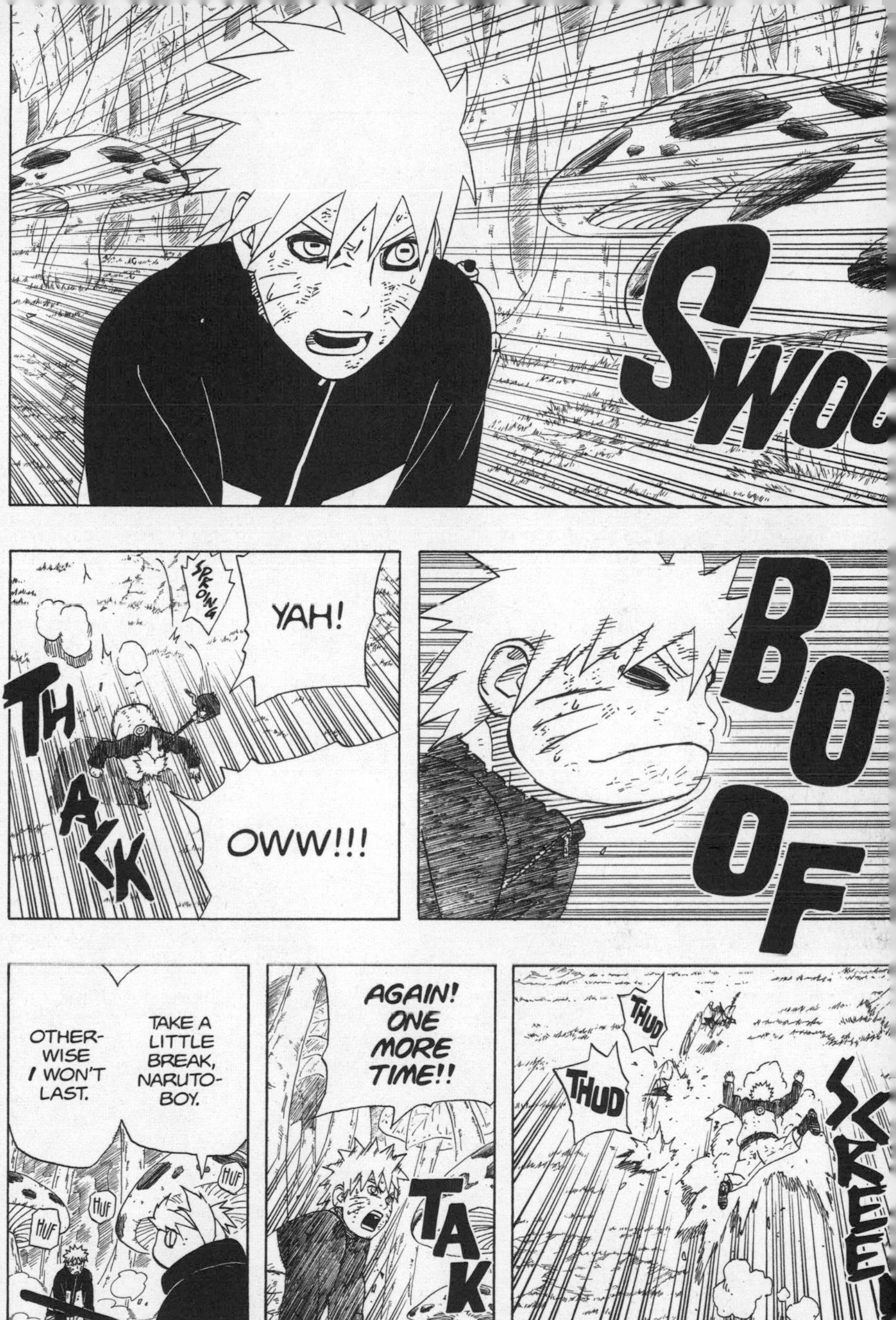
SWOO
BOOF
SPROING
YAH!
THACK
OWW!!!
THUD
THUD
SKREE!
AGAIN! ONE MORE TIME!!
TAK
TAKE A LITTLE BREAK, NARUTO-BOY.
OTHER-WISE I WON'T LAST.
HUF
HUF
HUF

READ THIS WAY

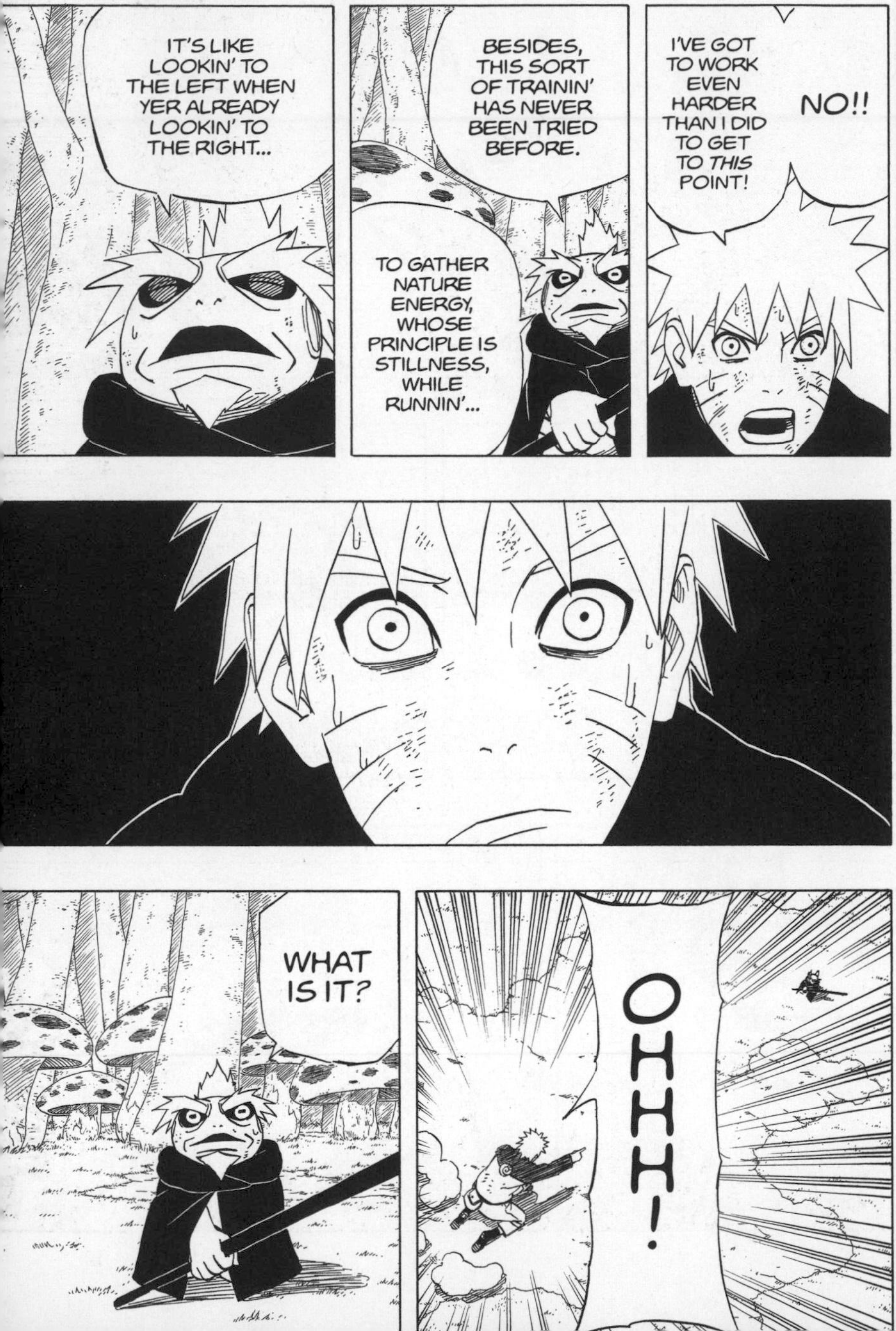
NO!!
I'VE GOT TO WORK EVEN HARDER THAN I DID TO GET TO *THIS* POINT!
BESIDES, THIS SORT OF TRAININ' HAS NEVER BEEN TRIED BEFORE.
TO GATHER NATURE ENERGY, WHOSE PRINCIPLE IS STILLNESS, WHILE RUNNIN'...
IT'S LIKE LOOKIN' TO THE LEFT WHEN YER ALREADY LOOKIN' TO THE RIGHT...
OHHH!
WHAT IS IT?

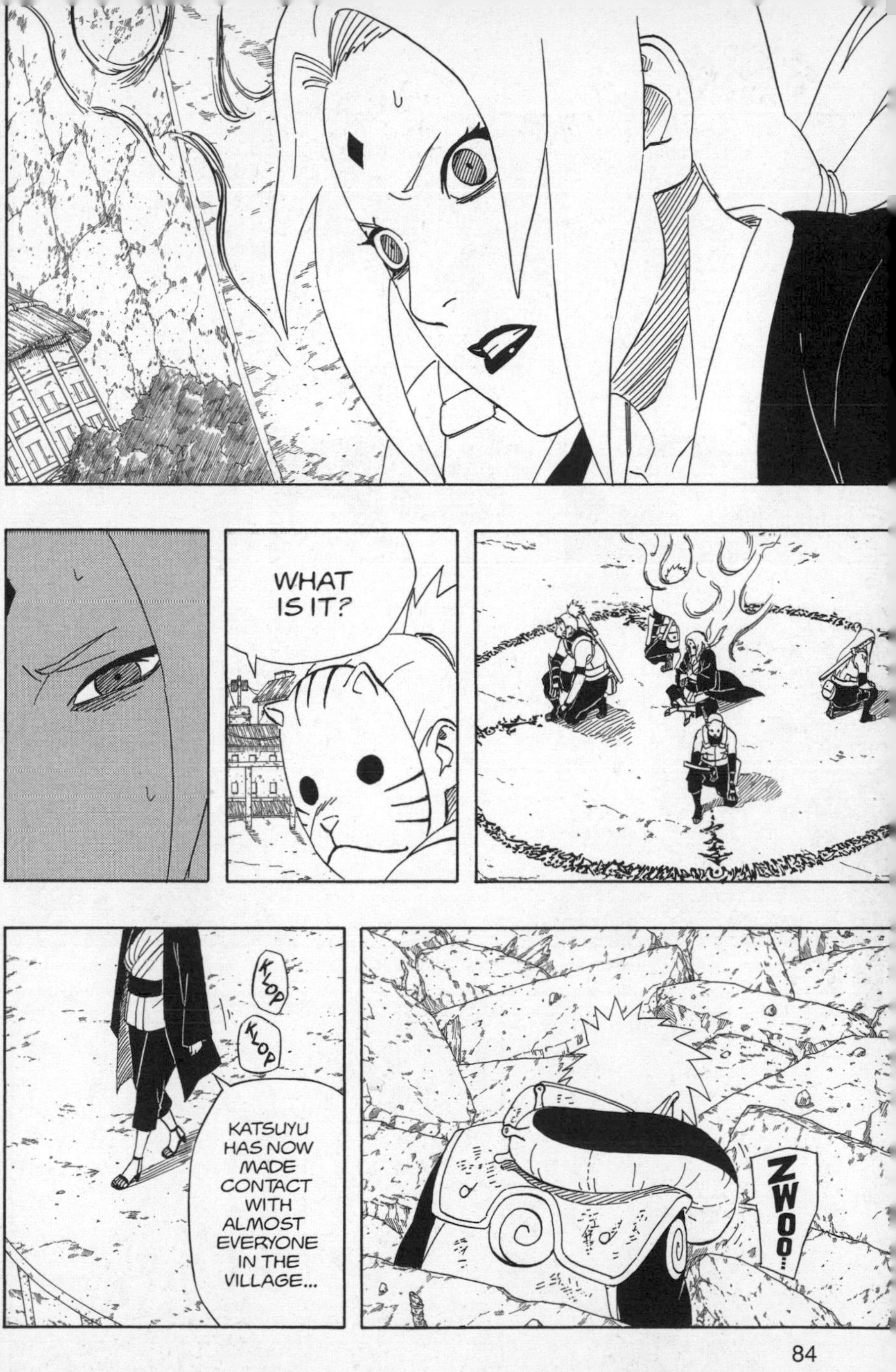
WHAT IS IT?
ZWOO...
KLOP
KLOP
KATSUYU HAS NOW MADE CONTACT WITH ALMOST EVERYONE IN THE VILLAGE...

READ THIS WAY

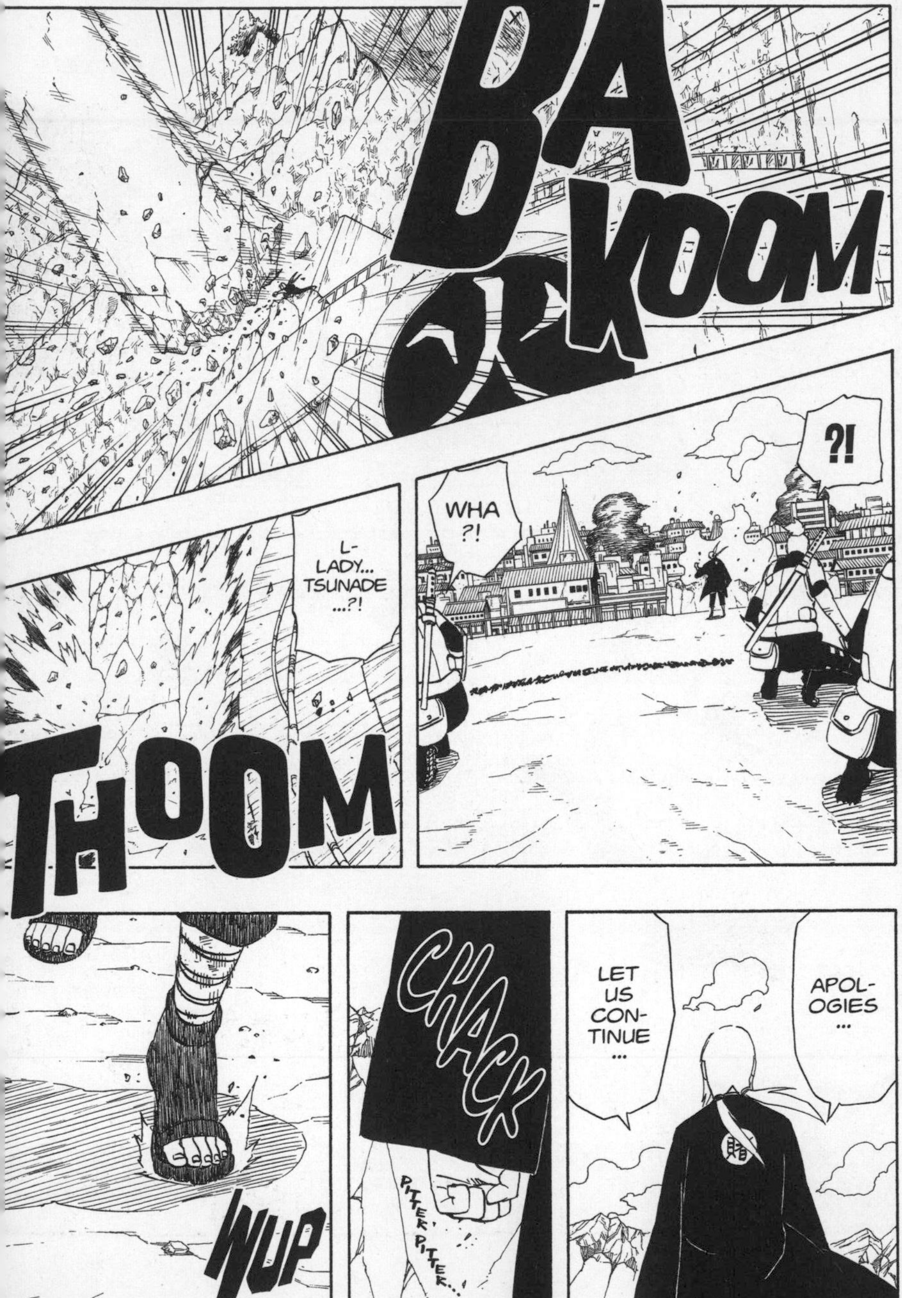
BA-KOOM
?!
WHA ?!
L-LADY... TSUNADE ...?!
THOOM
APOLOGIES ...
LET US CONTINUE ...
CHACK
PITTER PITTER...!
WUP

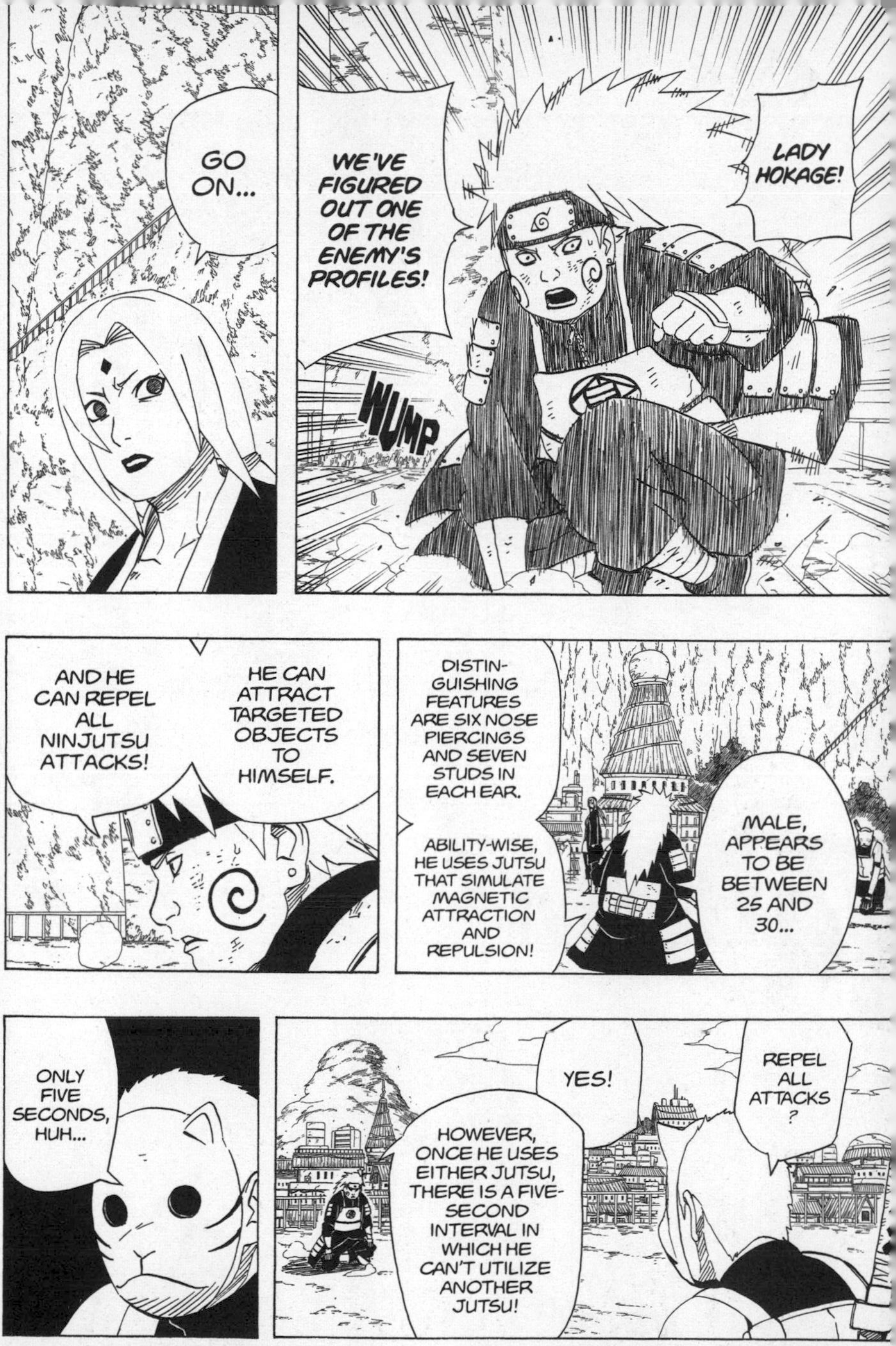
LADY HOKAGE!
WE'VE FIGURED OUT ONE OF THE ENEMY'S PROFILES!
WUMP
GO ON...
MALE, APPEARS TO BE BETWEEN 25 AND 30...
DISTIN-GUISHING FEATURES ARE SIX NOSE PIERCINGS AND SEVEN STUDS IN EACH EAR.
ABILITY-WISE, HE USES JUTSU THAT SIMULATE MAGNETIC ATTRACTION AND REPULSION!
HE CAN ATTRACT TARGETED OBJECTS TO HIMSELF.
AND HE CAN REPEL ALL NINJUTSU ATTACKS!
REPEL ALL ATTACKS?
YES!
HOWEVER, ONCE HE USES EITHER JUTSU, THERE IS A FIVE-SECOND INTERVAL IN WHICH HE CAN'T UTILIZE ANOTHER JUTSU!
ONLY FIVE SECONDS, HUH...

READ THIS WAY

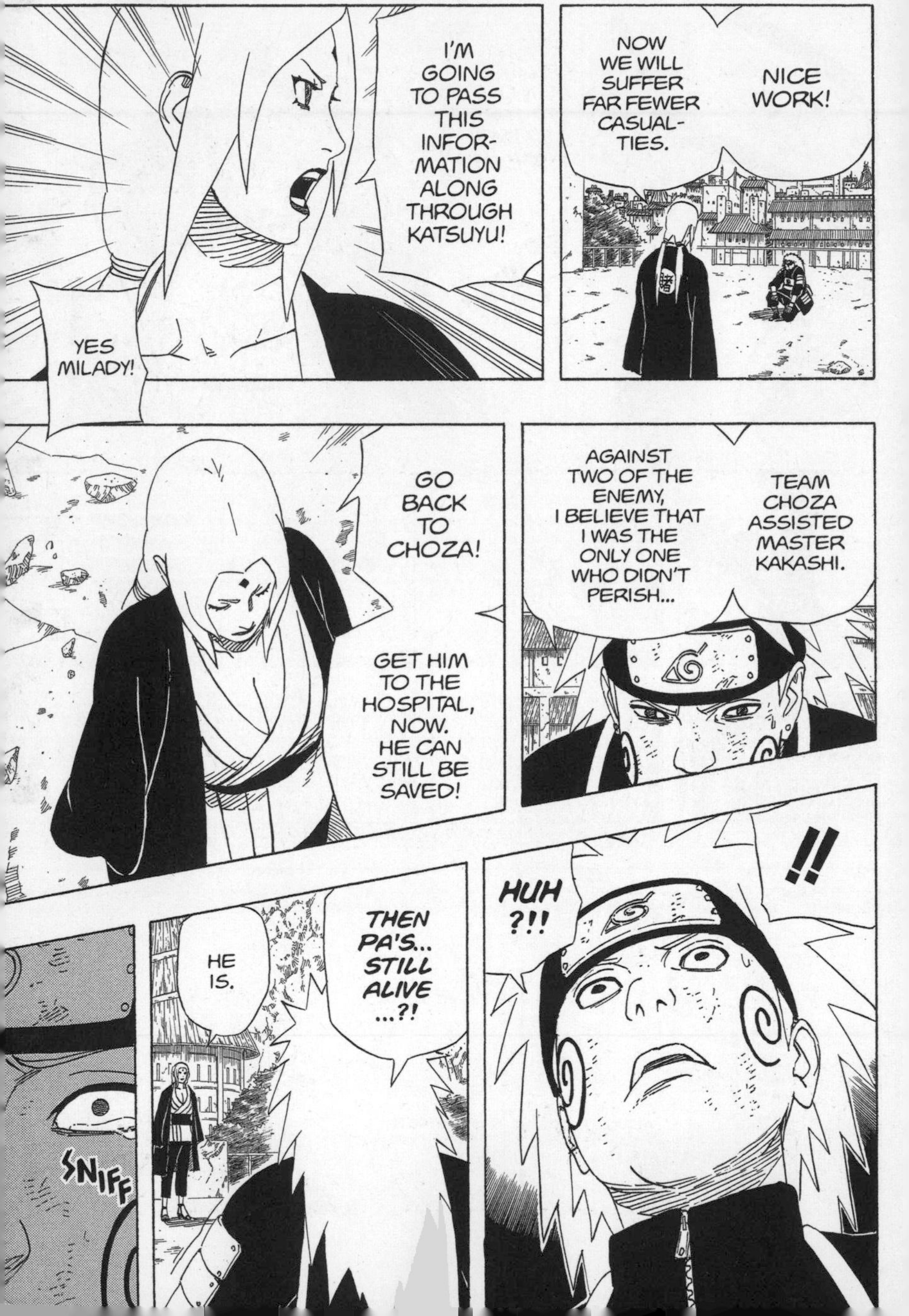
NICE WORK!
NOW WE WILL SUFFER FAR FEWER CASUAL-TIES.
I'M GOING TO PASS THIS INFOR-MATION ALONG THROUGH KATSUYU!
YES MILADY!
TEAM CHOZA ASSISTED MASTER KAKASHI.
AGAINST TWO OF THE ENEMY, I BELIEVE THAT I WAS THE ONLY ONE WHO DIDN'T PERISH...
GO BACK TO CHOZA!
GET HIM TO THE HOSPITAL, NOW. HE CAN STILL BE SAVED!
!!
HUH ?!!
THEN PA'S... STILL ALIVE ...?!
HE IS.
SNIFF

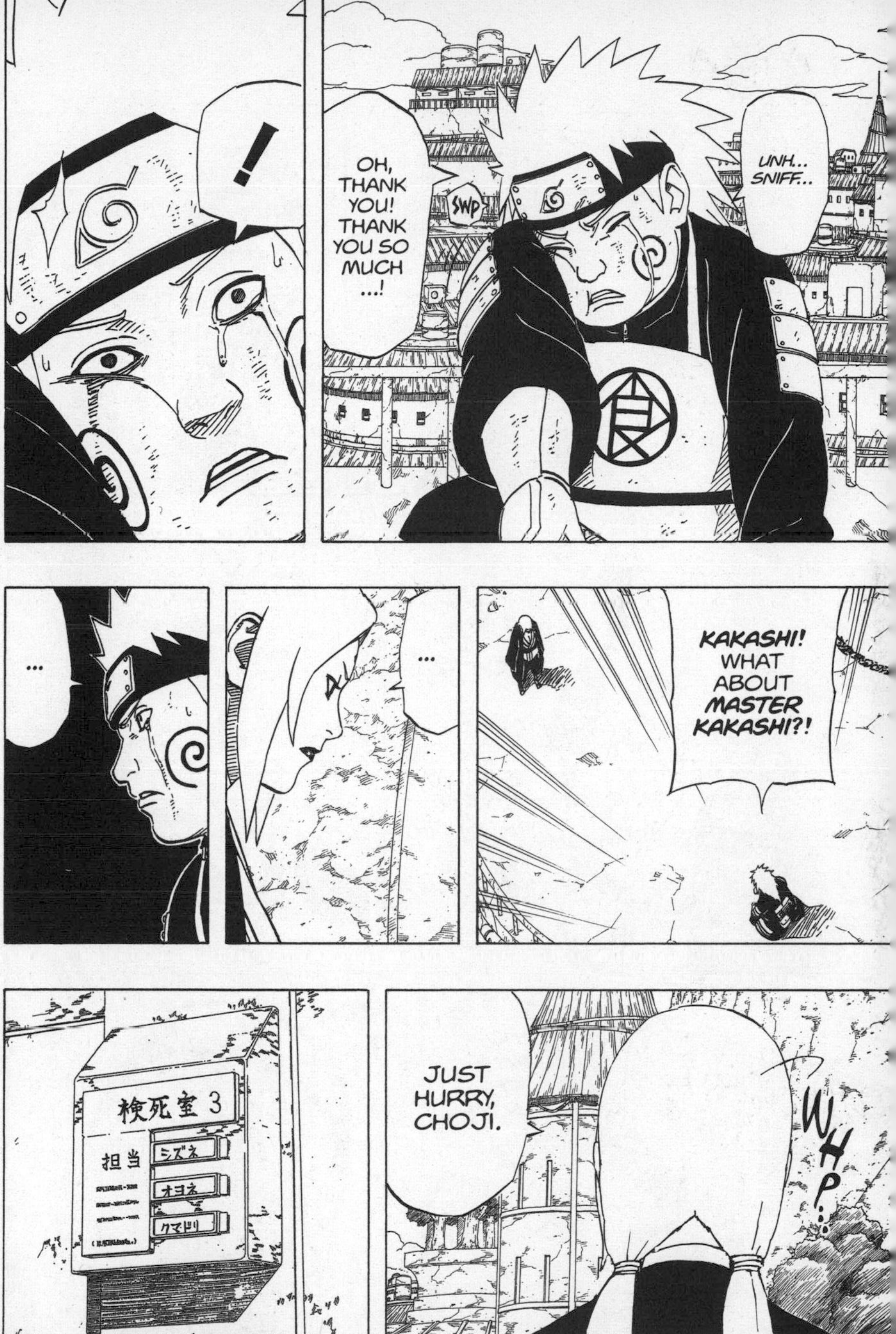
UNH... SNIFF...
OH, THANK YOU! THANK YOU SO MUCH ...!
SWP
!
KAKASHI! WHAT ABOUT MASTER KAKASHI?!
...
...
JUST HURRY, CHOJI.
WHP...
検死室 3
担当
シズネ
オヨネ
クマドリ

(AUTOPSY ROOM 3)

READ THIS WAY

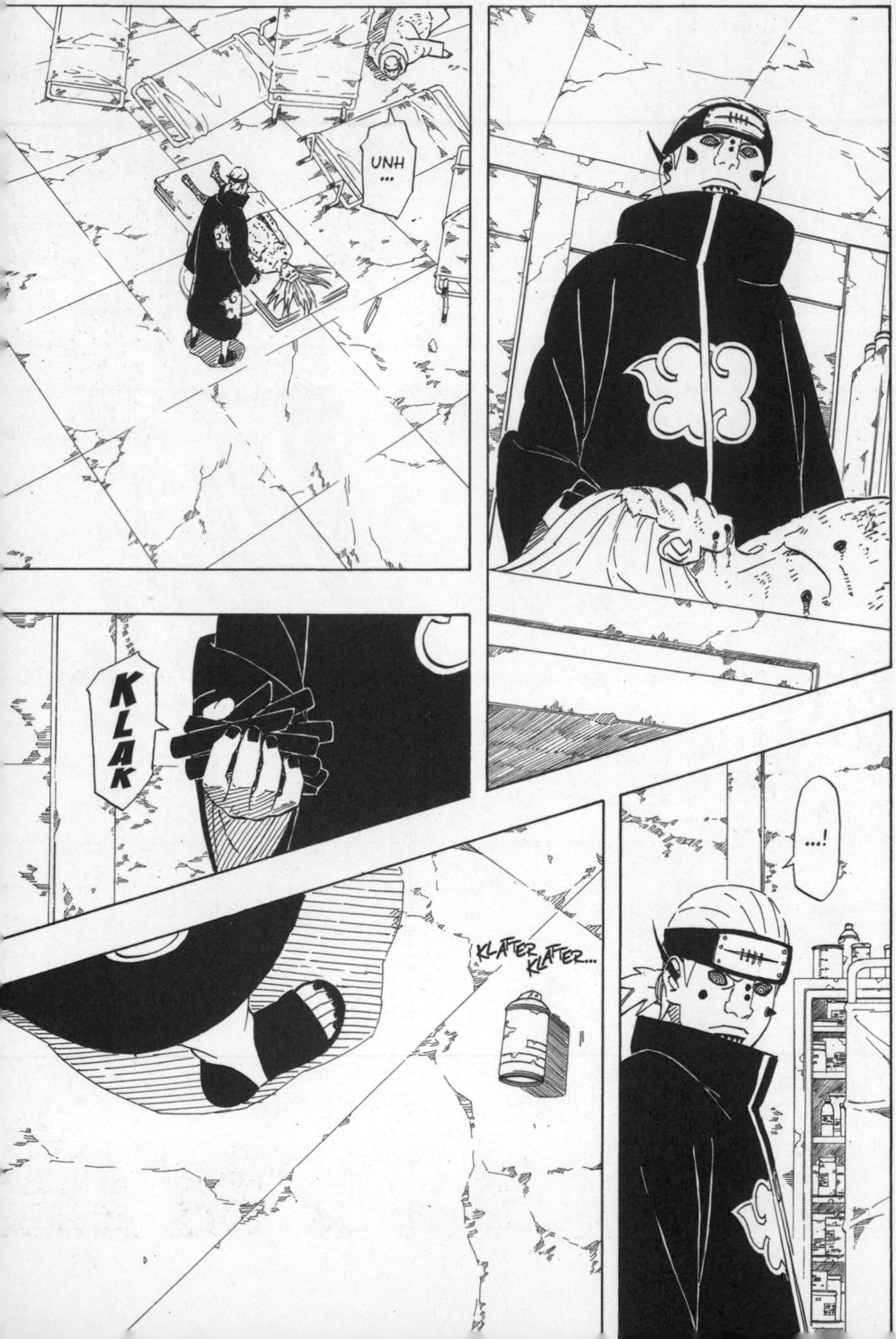
UNH ...
KLAK
...!
KLATTER KLATTER...

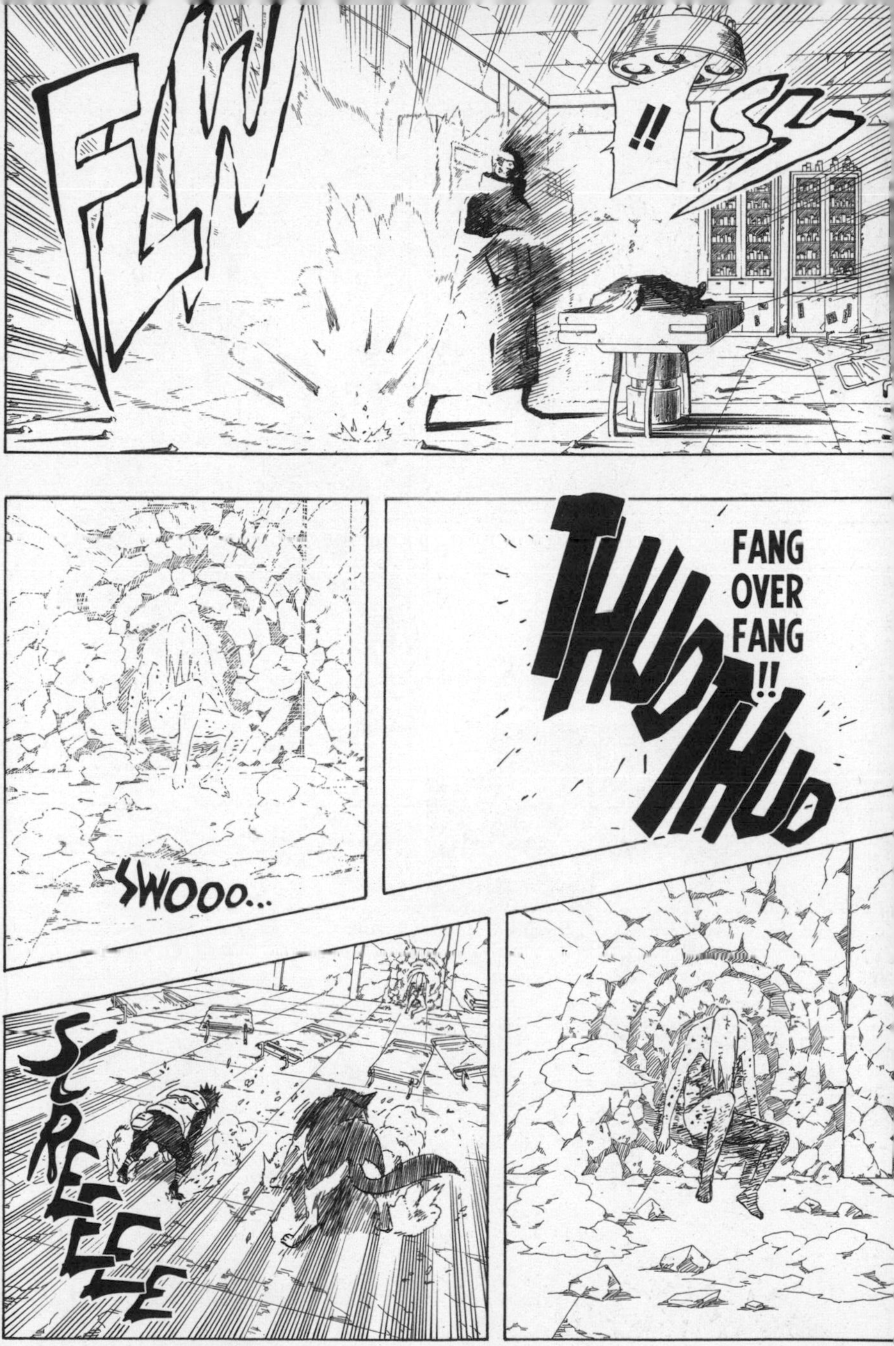
!!
FANG OVER FANG!!
THUD THUD
SWOOO...
SCREEEE

READ THIS WAY

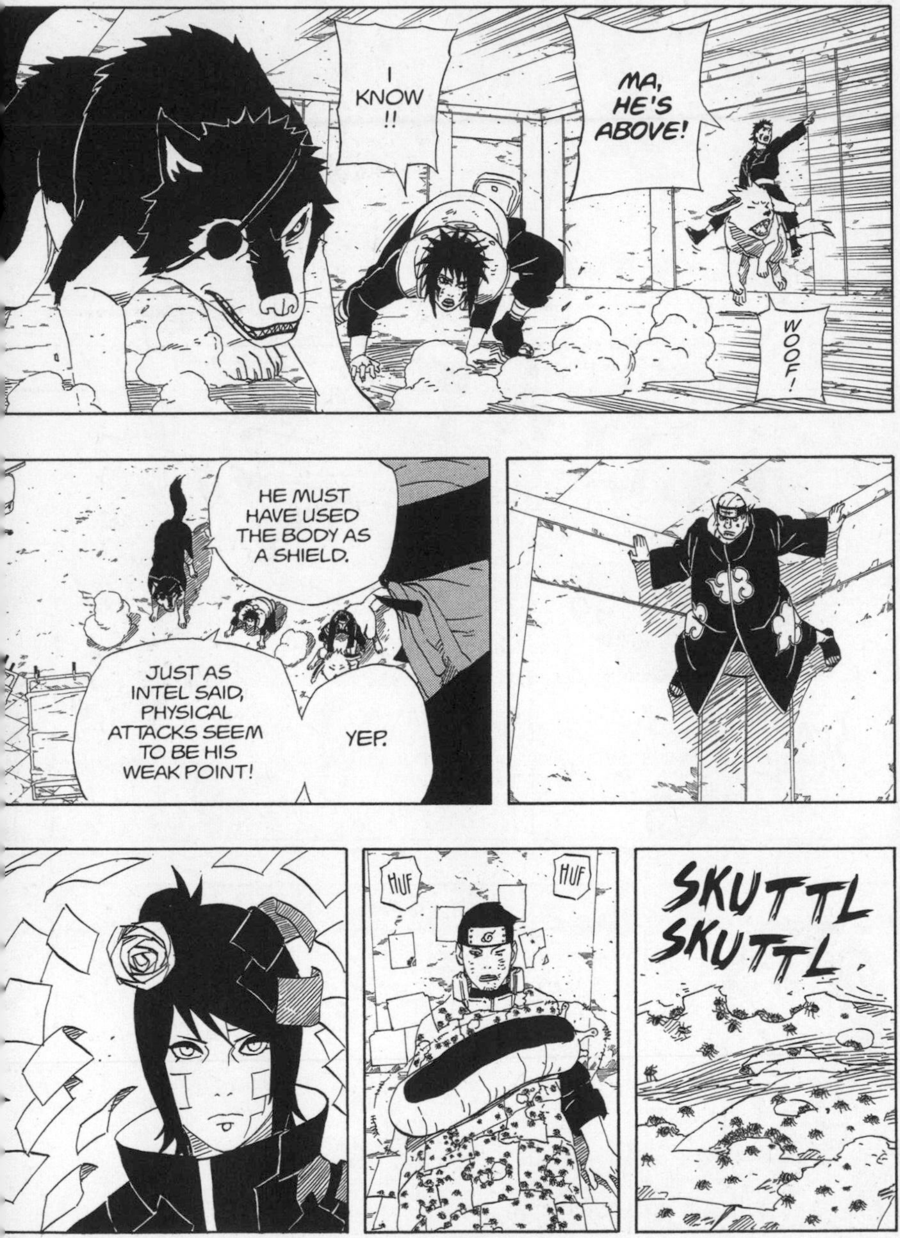
MA, HE'S ABOVE!
WOOF!
I KNOW!!
HE MUST HAVE USED THE BODY AS A SHIELD.
JUST AS INTEL SAID, PHYSICAL ATTACKS SEEM TO BE HIS WEAK POINT!
YEP.
SKUTTL SKUTTL
HUF
HUF

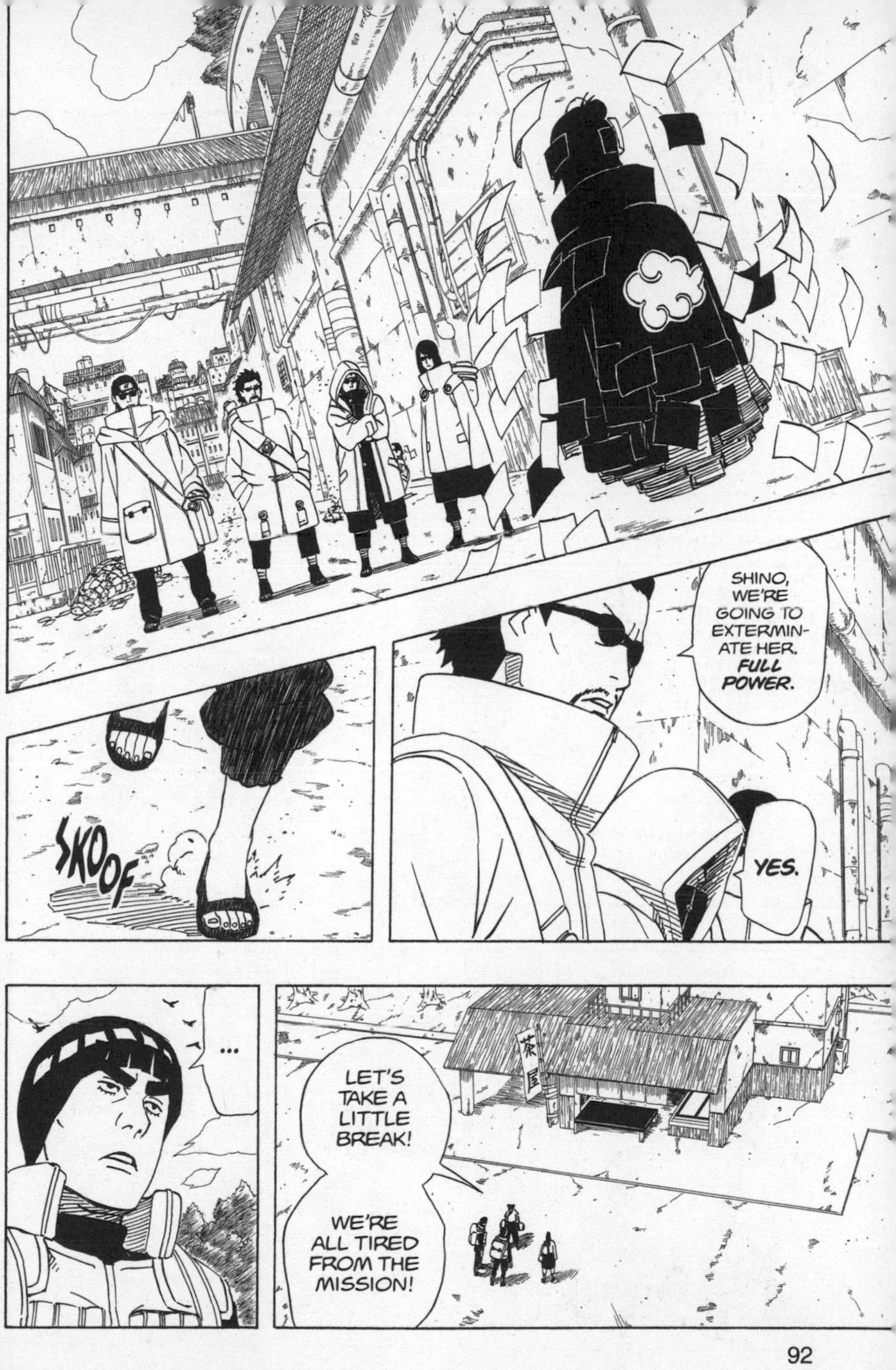
SHINO, WE'RE GOING TO EXTERMINATE HER. **FULL POWER.**
YES.
SKOOF
茶屋
LET'S TAKE A LITTLE BREAK!
WE'RE ALL TIRED FROM THE MISSION!
...

READ THIS WAY

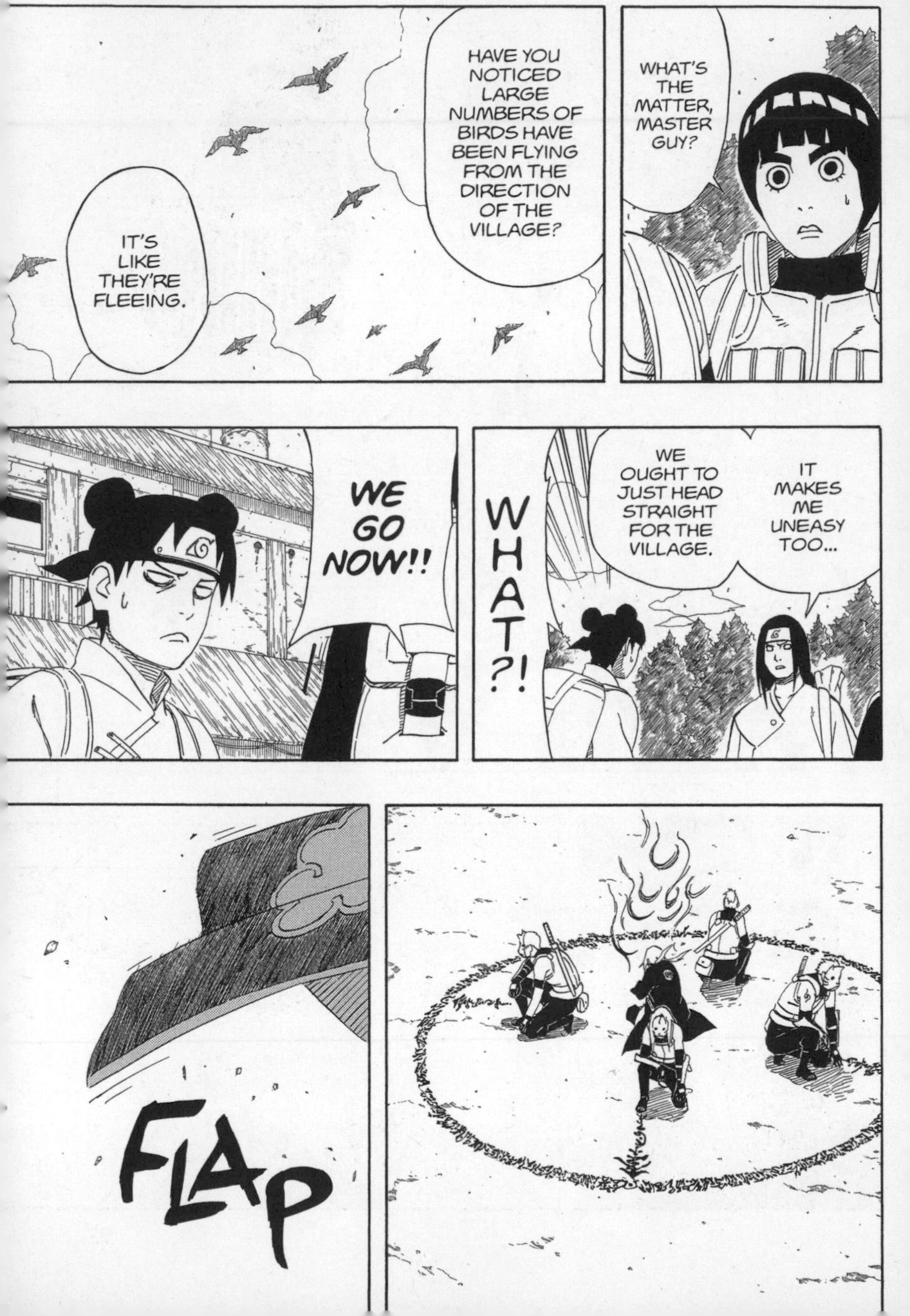
WHAT'S THE MATTER, MASTER GUY?
HAVE YOU NOTICED LARGE NUMBERS OF BIRDS HAVE BEEN FLYING FROM THE DIRECTION OF THE VILLAGE?
IT'S LIKE THEY'RE FLEEING.
IT MAKES ME UNEASY TOO...
WE OUGHT TO JUST HEAD STRAIGHT FOR THE VILLAGE.
WHAT?!
WE GO NOW!!
FLAP

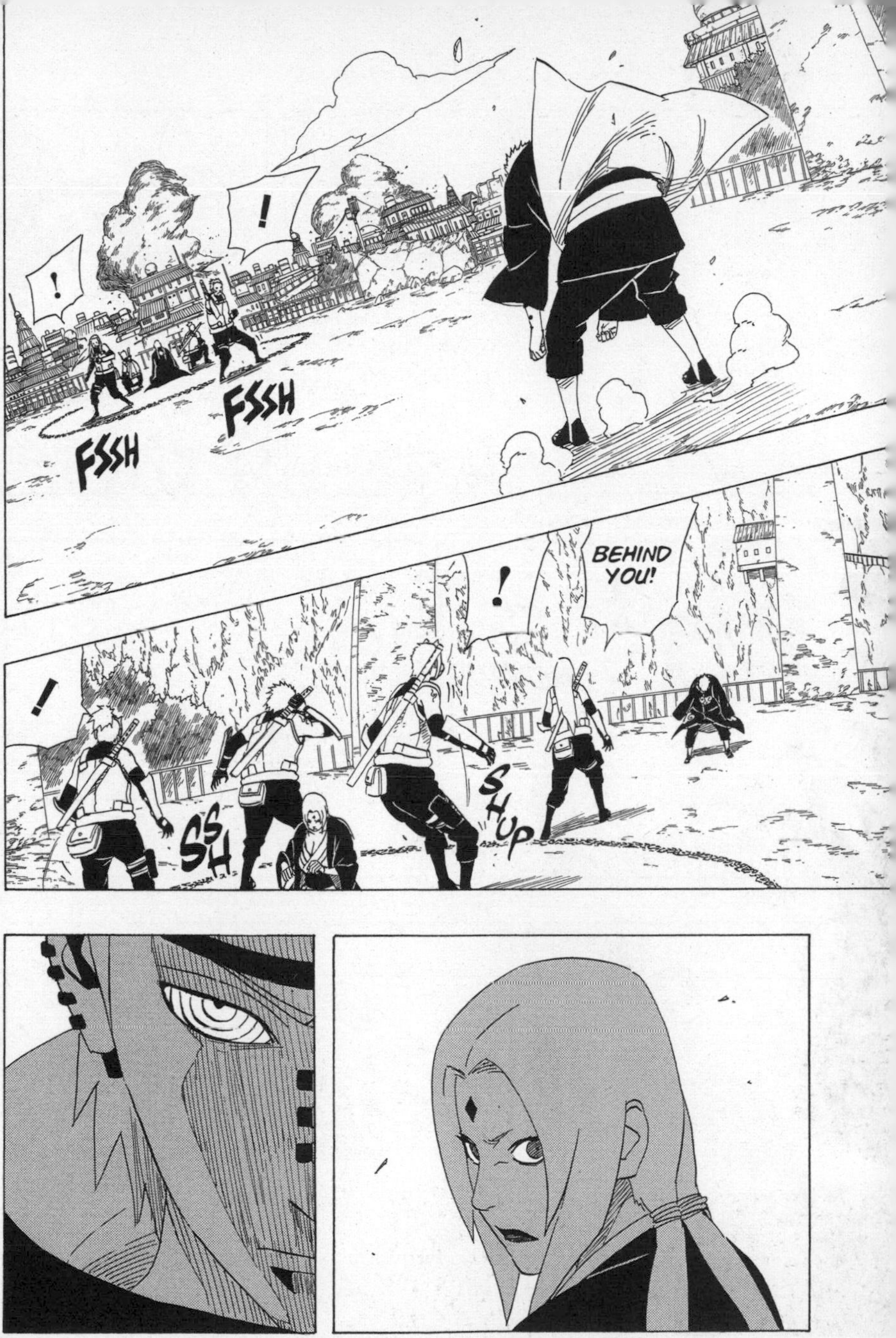
!
!
FSSH
FSSH
BEHIND YOU!
!
!
SHUP
SSH

READ THIS WAY

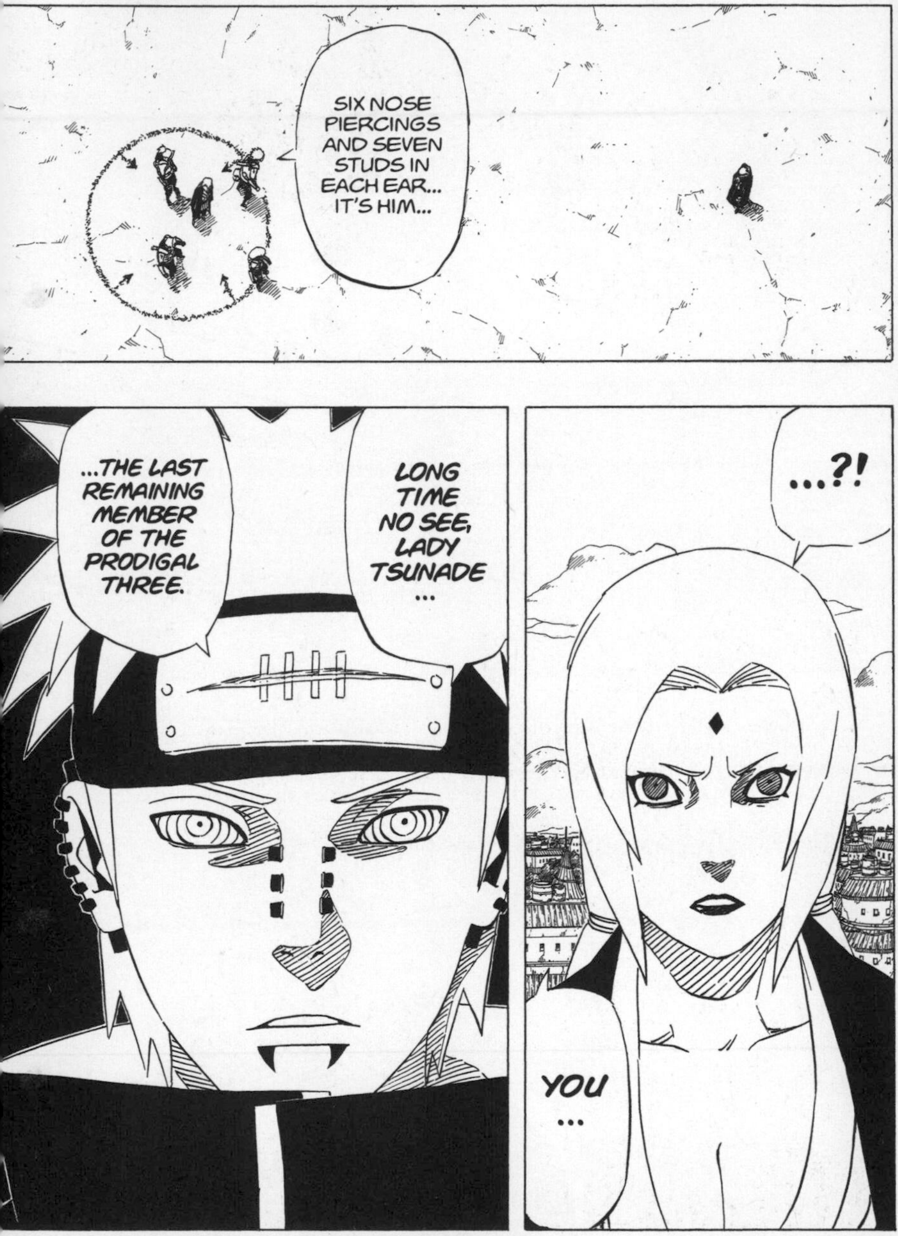
SIX NOSE PIERCINGS AND SEVEN STUDS IN EACH EAR... IT'S HIM...
...?!
YOU ...
LONG TIME NO SEE, LADY TSUNADE ...
...THE LAST REMAINING MEMBER OF THE PRODIGAL THREE.

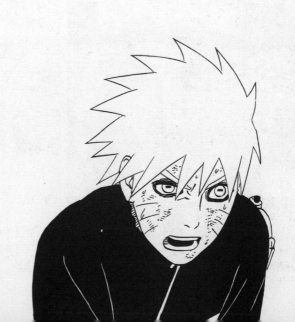

Number 428: Discourse

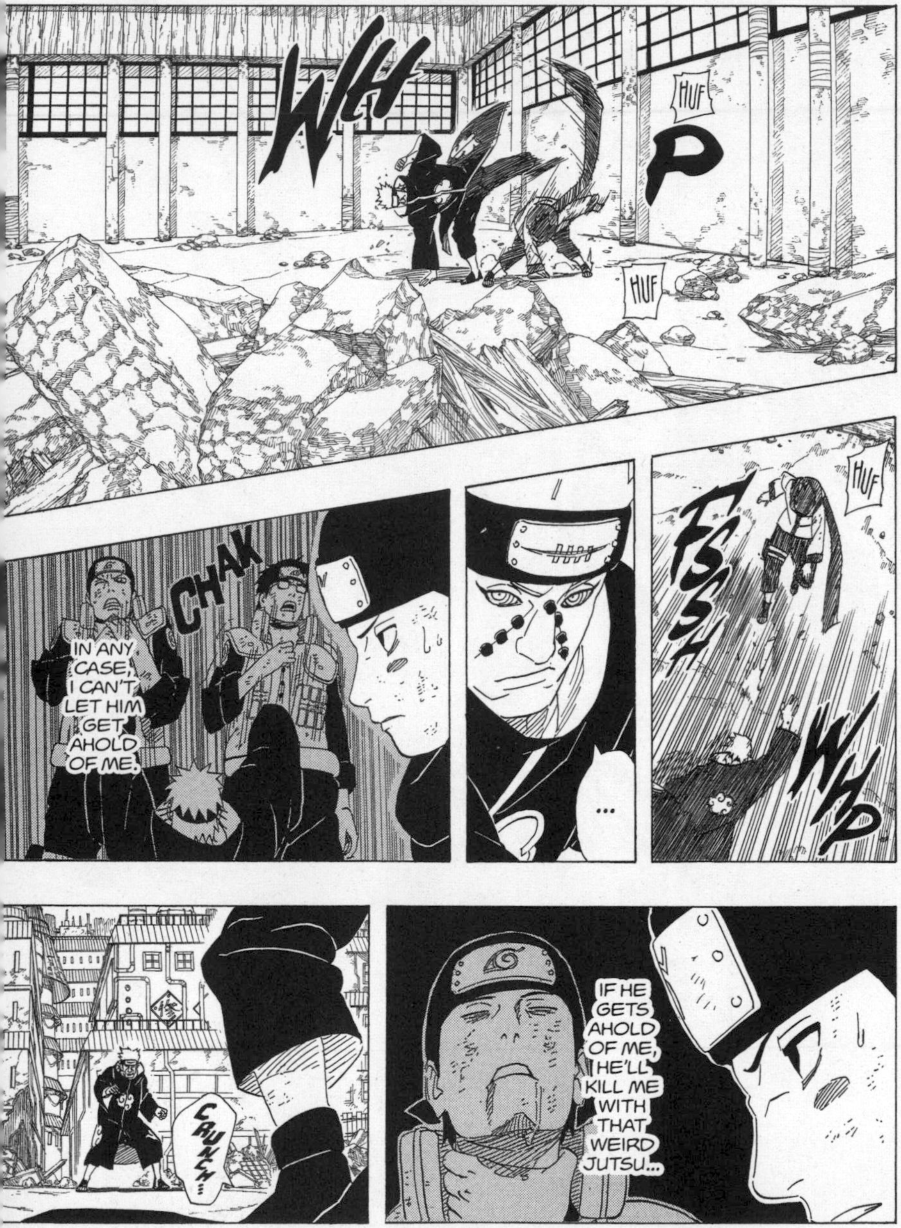
WHP
HUF
HUF
HUF
FSSH
WHP
...
CHAK
IN ANY CASE, I CAN'T LET HIM GET AHOLD OF ME.
IF HE GETS AHOLD OF ME, HE'LL KILL ME WITH THAT WEIRD JUTSU...
CRUNCH

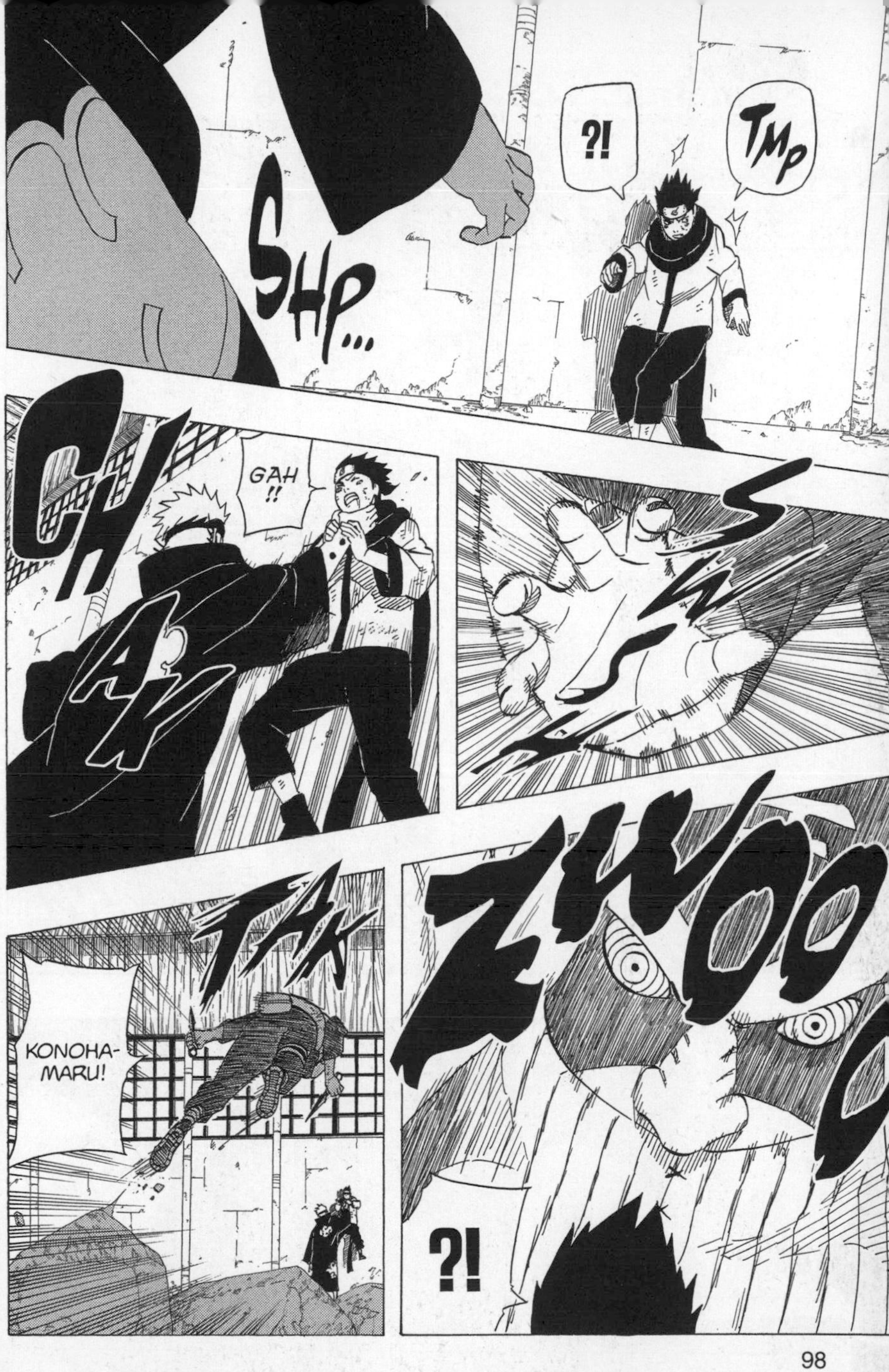
TMP
?!
SHP...
GAH!!
CHAK
ZWOOO
?!
KONOHAMARU!

READ THIS WAY

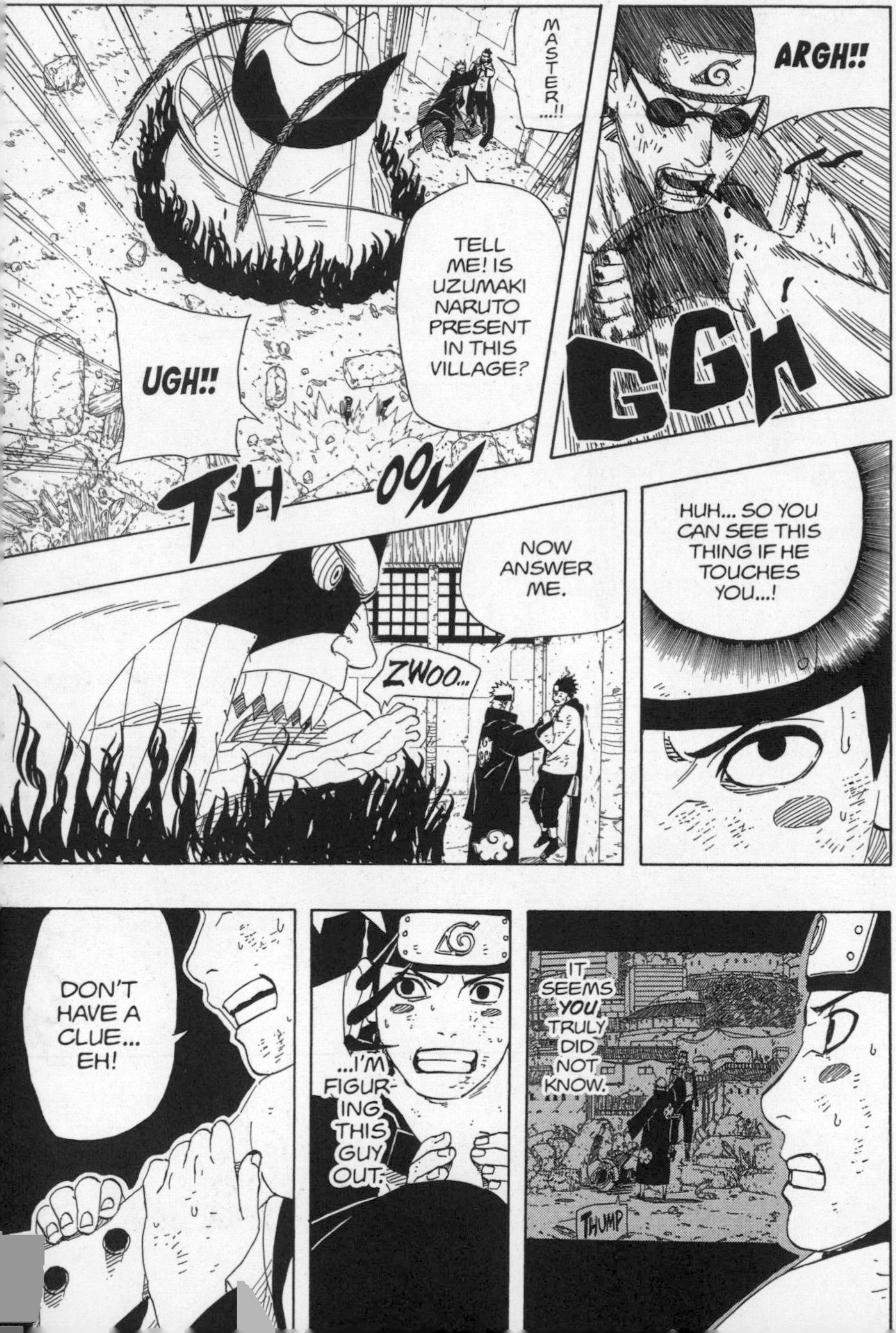
ARGH!!
GGH
MASTER...!!
TELL ME! IS UZUMAKI NARUTO PRESENT IN THIS VILLAGE?
UGH!!
THOOM
HUH... SO YOU CAN SEE THIS THING IF HE TOUCHES YOU...!
NOW ANSWER ME.
ZWOO...
IT SEEMS YOU TRULY DID NOT KNOW.
THUMP
...I'M FIGURING THIS GUY OUT.
DON'T HAVE A CLUE... EH!

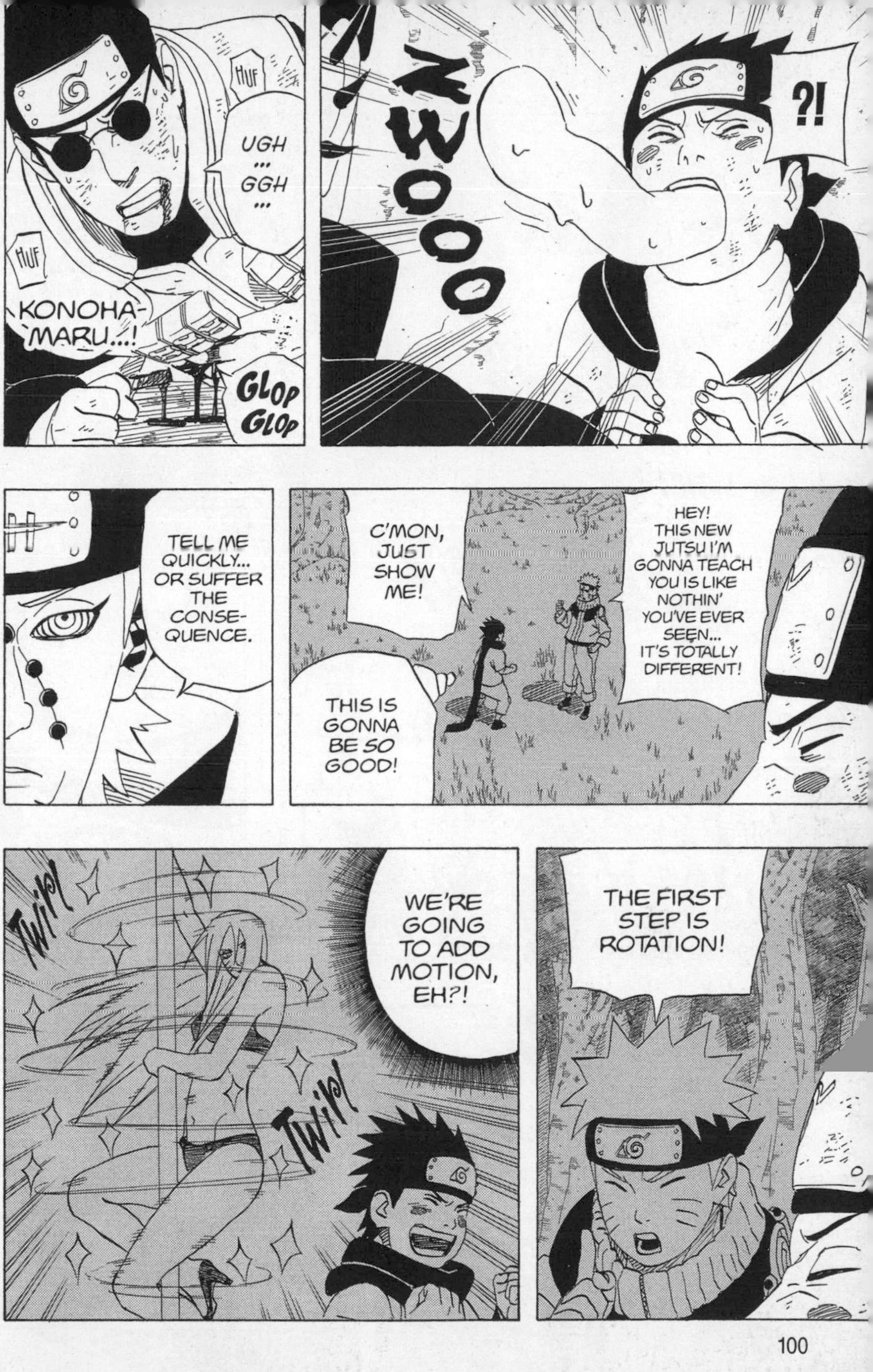
?!
ZWOOO
HUF
UGH ... GGH ...
HUF
KONOHA-MARU...!
GLOP GLOP
HEY! THIS NEW JUTSU I'M GONNA TEACH YOU IS LIKE NOTHIN' YOU'VE EVER SEEN... IT'S TOTALLY DIFFERENT!
C'MON, JUST SHOW ME!
THIS IS GONNA BE SO GOOD!
TELL ME QUICKLY... OR SUFFER THE CONSE-QUENCE.
THE FIRST STEP IS ROTATION!
WE'RE GOING TO ADD MOTION, EH?!
TWIRL
TWIRL

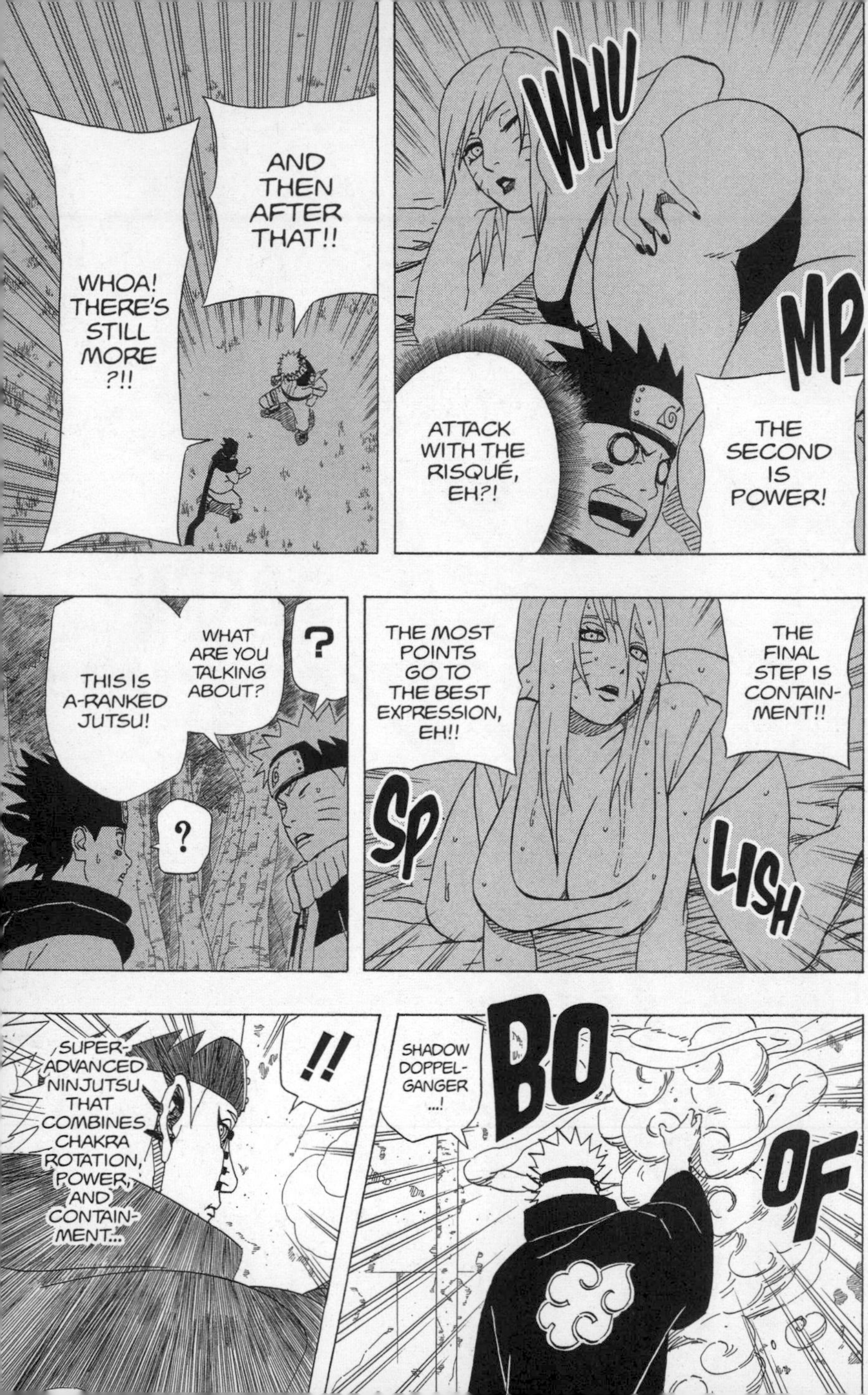
WHU
MP
THE SECOND IS POWER!
ATTACK WITH THE RISQUÉ, EH?!
AND THEN AFTER THAT!!
WHOA! THERE'S STILL MORE ?!!
THE FINAL STEP IS CONTAIN-MENT!!
THE MOST POINTS GO TO THE BEST EXPRESSION, EH!!
SP
LISH
?
WHAT ARE YOU TALKING ABOUT?
THIS IS A-RANKED JUTSU!
?
BO
OF
SHADOW DOPPEL-GANGER ...!
!!
SUPER-ADVANCED NINJUTSU THAT COMBINES CHAKRA ROTATION, POWER, AND CONTAIN-MENT...

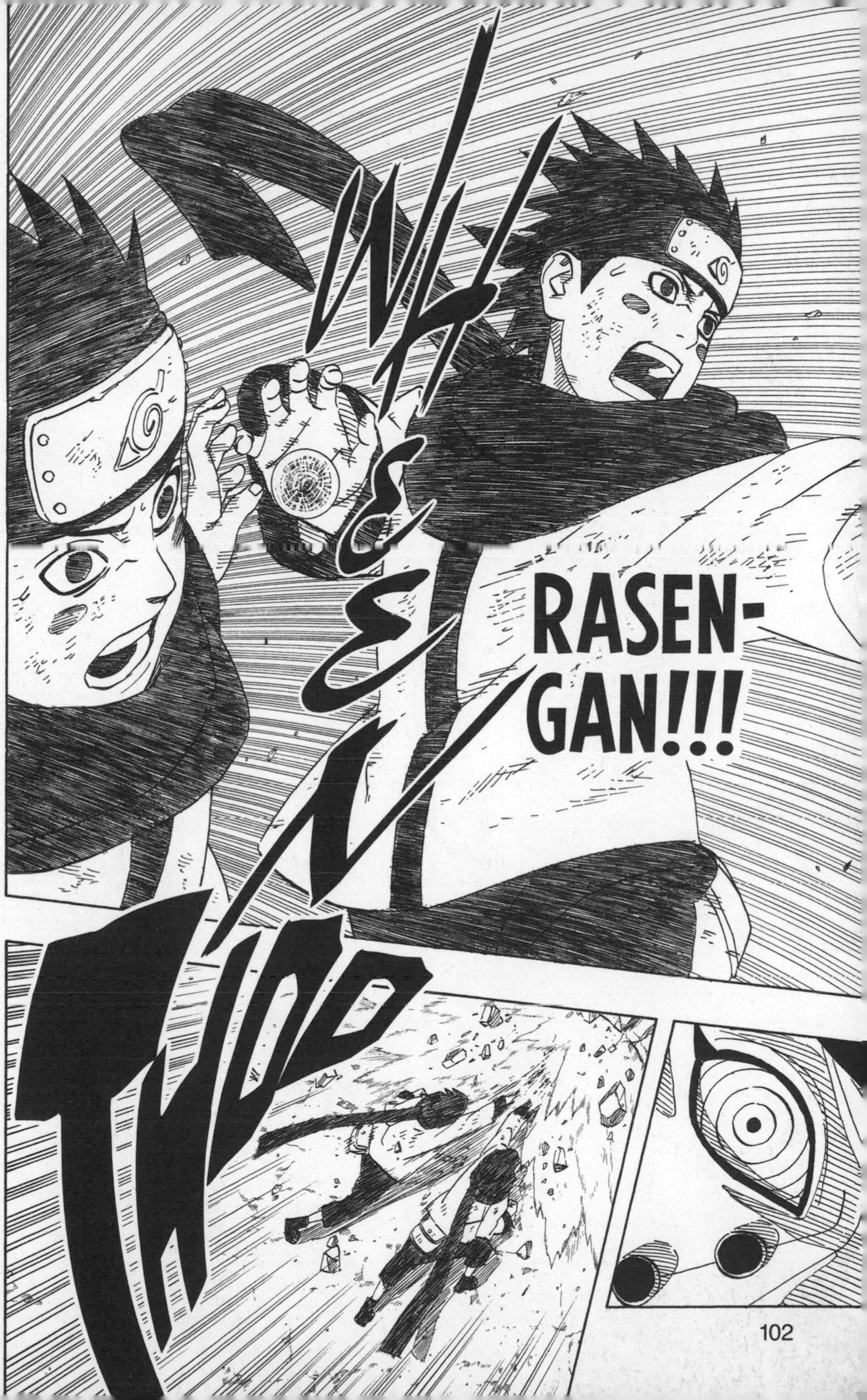
RASEN-GAN!!!

READ THIS WAY

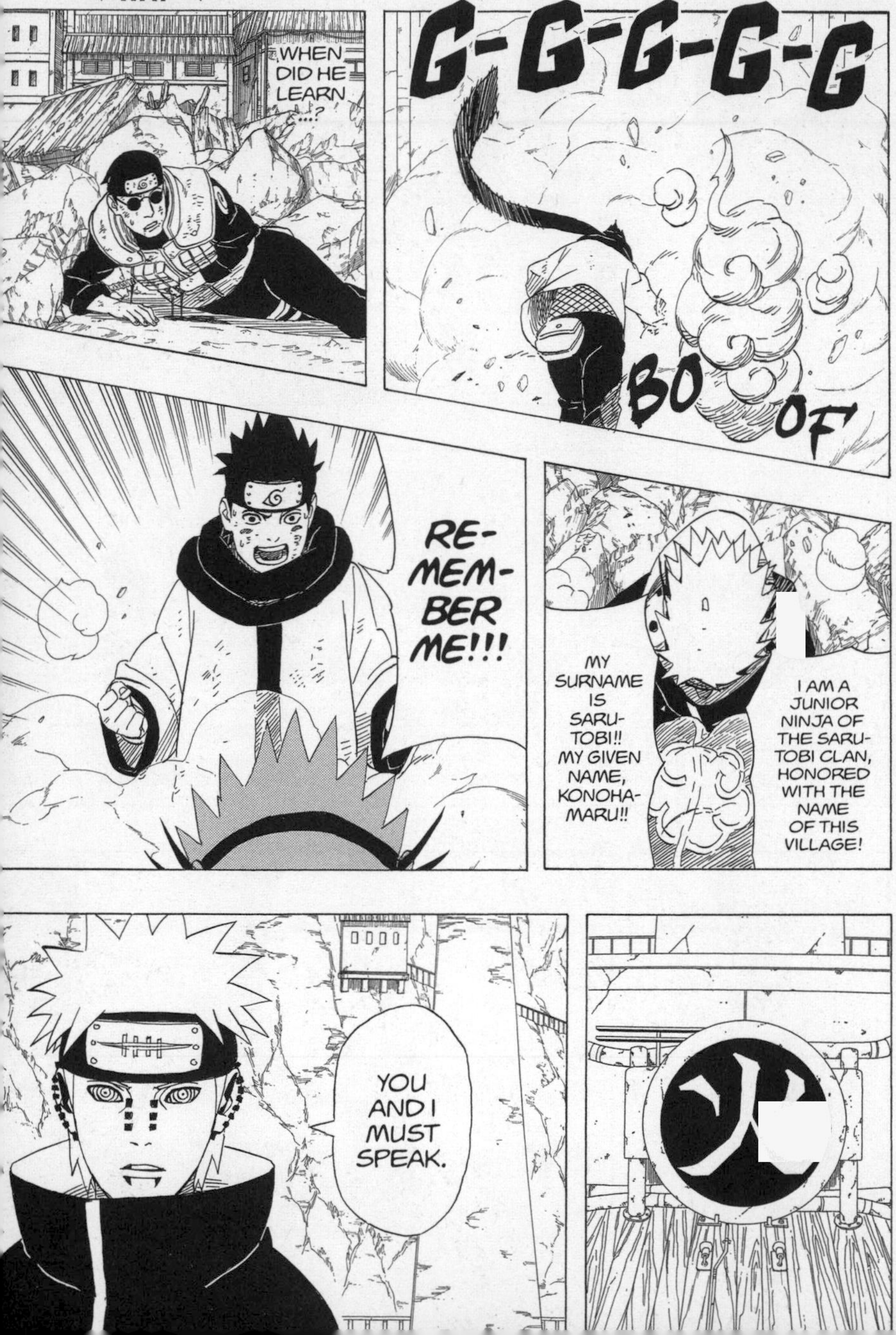
G-G-G-G-G
BOOF
WHEN DID HE LEARN ...?
MY SURNAME IS SARUTOBI!! MY GIVEN NAME, KONOHAMARU!!
I AM A JUNIOR NINJA OF THE SARUTOBI CLAN, HONORED WITH THE NAME OF THIS VILLAGE!
REMEMBER ME!!!
YOU AND I MUST SPEAK.

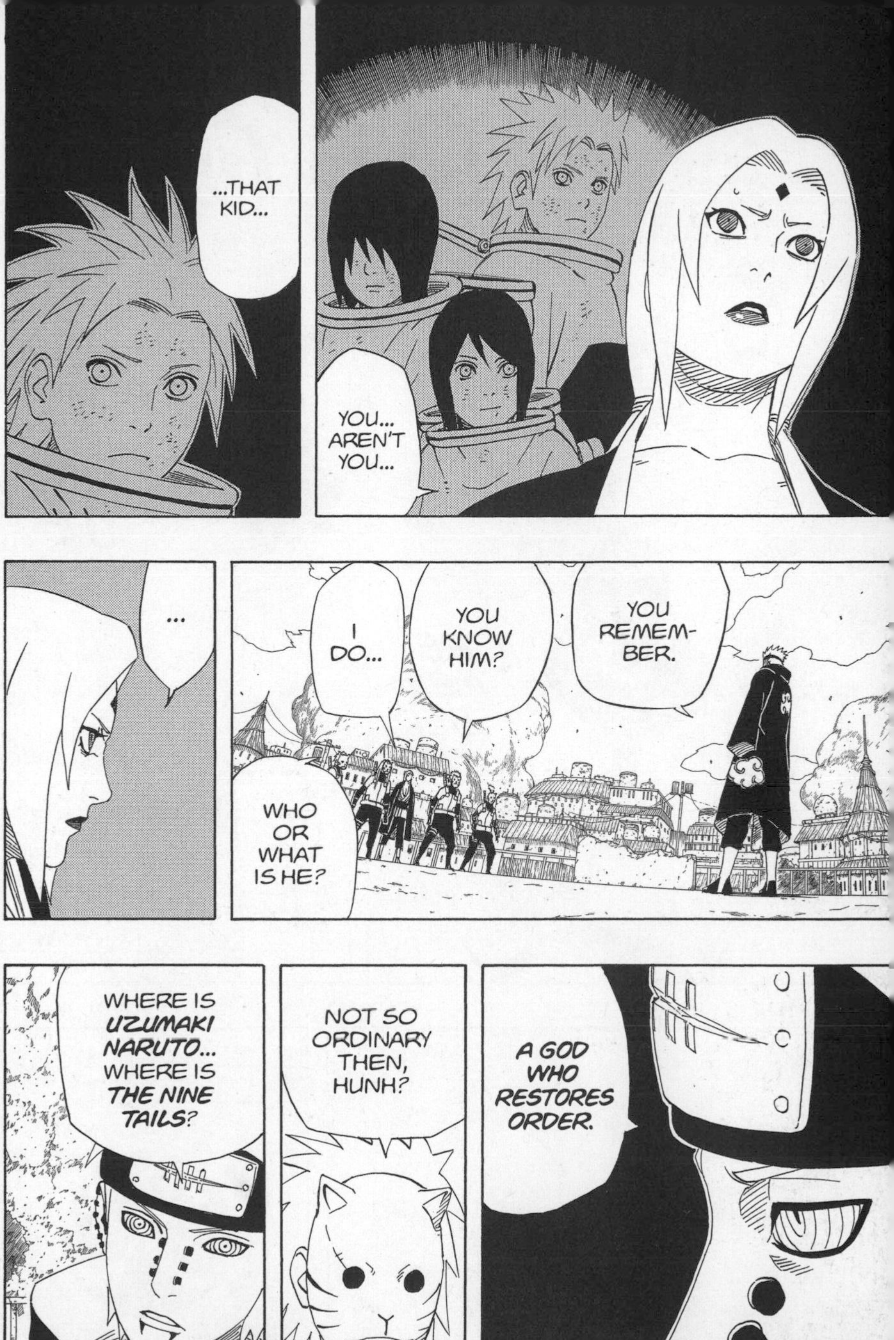
YOU... AREN'T YOU...
...THAT KID...
YOU REMEM-BER.
YOU KNOW HIM?
I DO...
WHO OR WHAT IS HE?
...
A GOD WHO RESTORES ORDER.
NOT SO ORDINARY THEN, HUNH?
WHERE IS UZUMAKI NARUTO... WHERE IS THE NINE TAILS?

READ THIS WAY

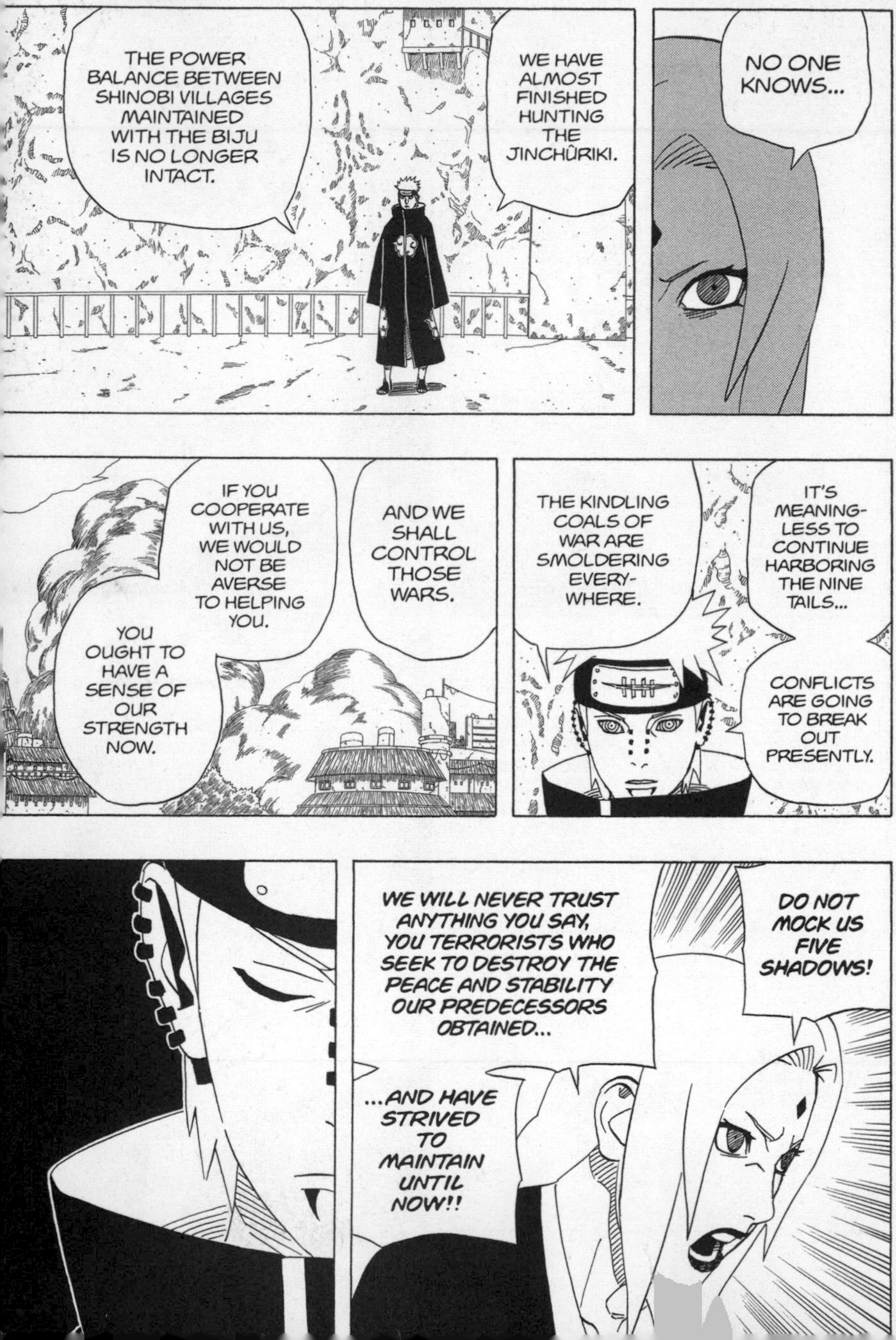
NO ONE KNOWS...
WE HAVE ALMOST FINISHED HUNTING THE JINCHŪRIKI.
THE POWER BALANCE BETWEEN SHINOBI VILLAGES MAINTAINED WITH THE BIJU IS NO LONGER INTACT.
IT'S MEANING-LESS TO CONTINUE HARBORING THE NINE TAILS...
THE KINDLING COALS OF WAR ARE SMOLDERING EVERY-WHERE.
CONFLICTS ARE GOING TO BREAK OUT PRESENTLY.
AND WE SHALL CONTROL THOSE WARS.
IF YOU COOPERATE WITH US, WE WOULD NOT BE AVERSE TO HELPING YOU.
YOU OUGHT TO HAVE A SENSE OF OUR STRENGTH NOW.
DO NOT MOCK US FIVE SHADOWS!
WE WILL NEVER TRUST ANYTHING YOU SAY, YOU TERRORISTS WHO SEEK TO DESTROY THE PEACE AND STABILITY OUR PREDECESSORS OBTAINED...
...AND HAVE STRIVED TO MAINTAIN UNTIL NOW!!

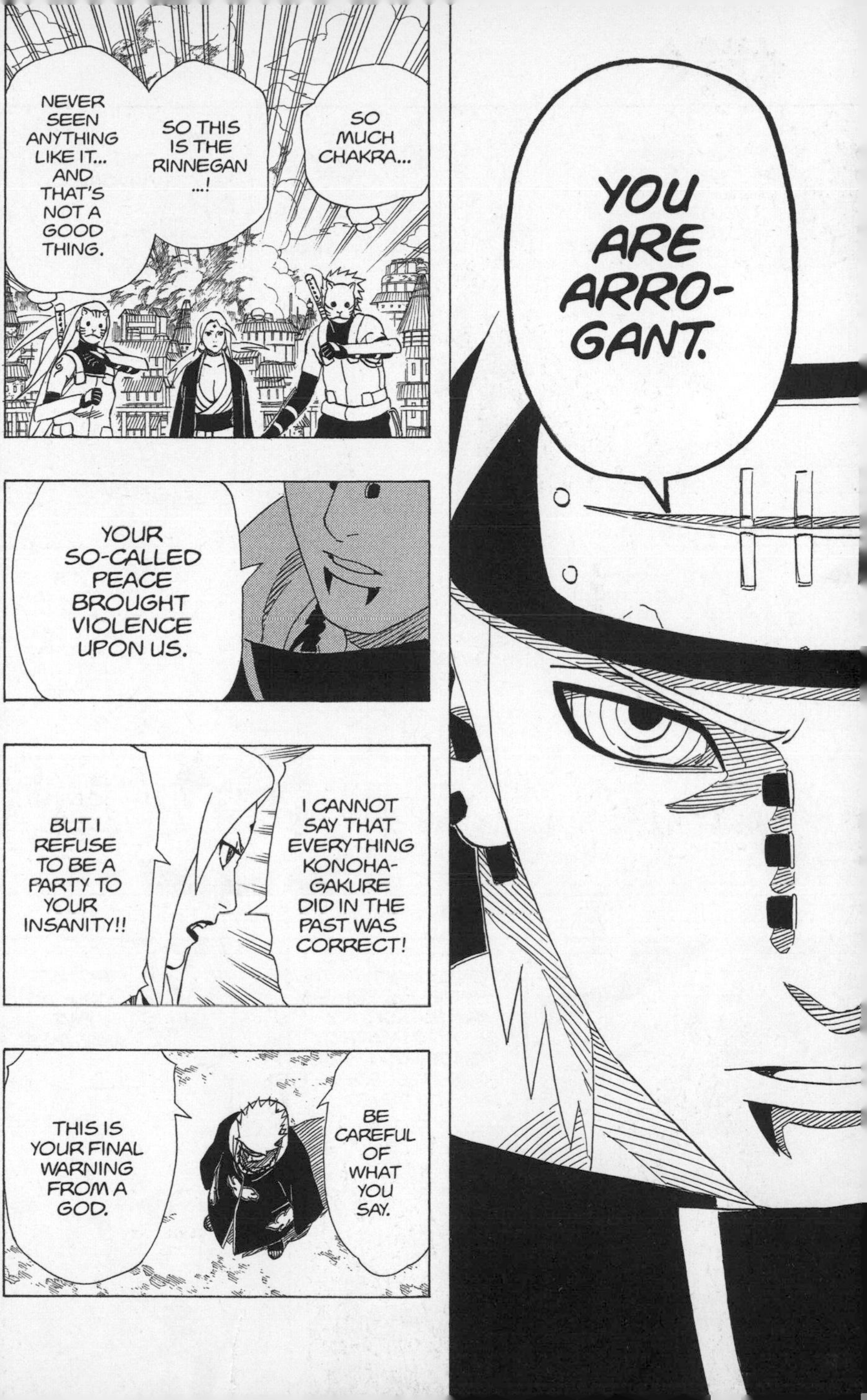
YOU ARE ARRO-GANT.
SO MUCH CHAKRA...
SO THIS IS THE RINNEGAN ...!
NEVER SEEN ANYTHING LIKE IT... AND THAT'S NOT A GOOD THING.
YOUR SO-CALLED PEACE BROUGHT VIOLENCE UPON US.
I CANNOT SAY THAT EVERYTHING KONOHA-GAKURE DID IN THE PAST WAS CORRECT!
BUT I REFUSE TO BE A PARTY TO YOUR INSANITY!!
BE CAREFUL OF WHAT YOU SAY.
THIS IS YOUR FINAL WARNING FROM A GOD.

READ THIS WAY

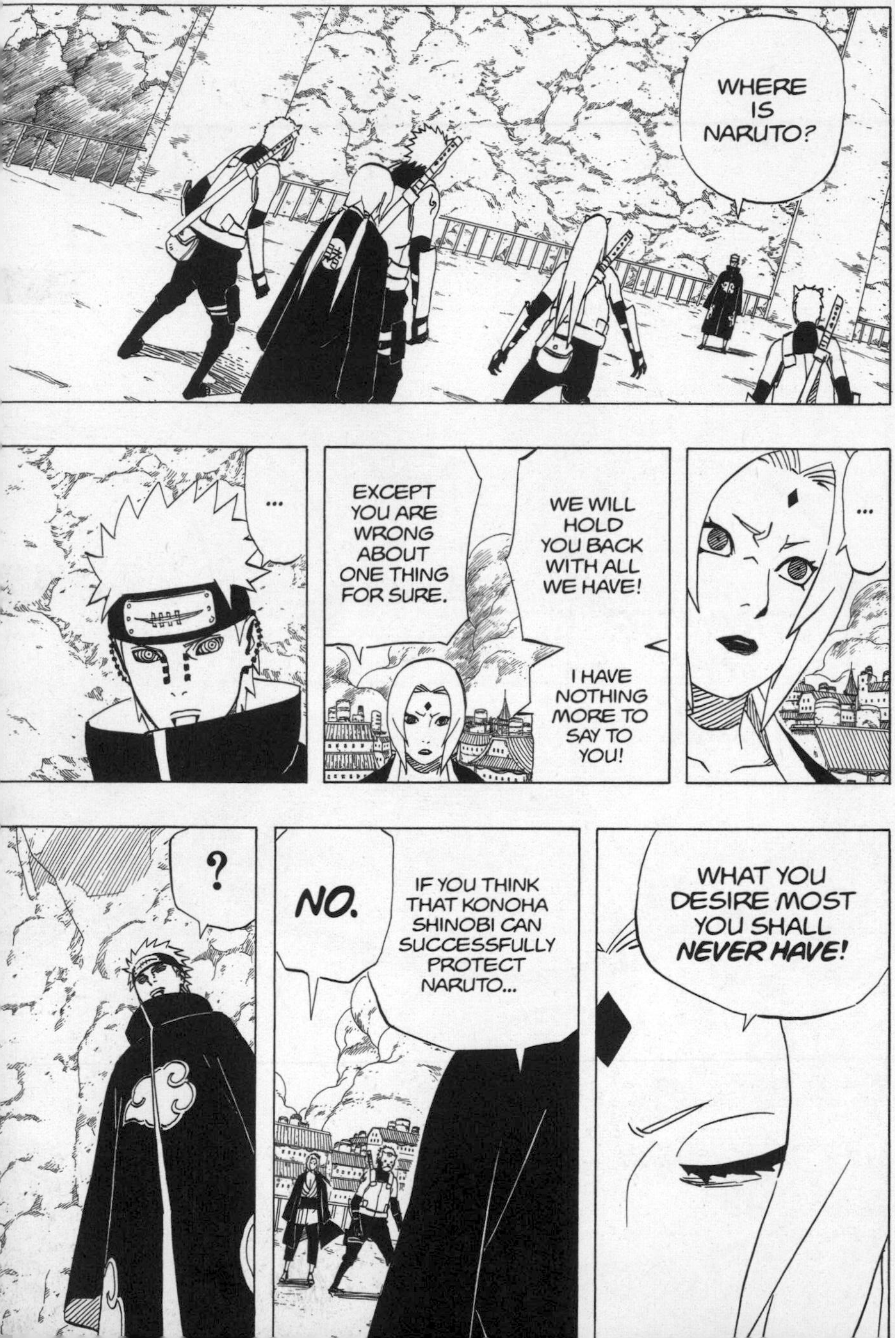
WHERE IS NARUTO?
...
WE WILL HOLD YOU BACK WITH ALL WE HAVE!
I HAVE NOTHING MORE TO SAY TO YOU!
EXCEPT YOU ARE WRONG ABOUT ONE THING FOR SURE.
...
WHAT YOU DESIRE MOST YOU SHALL **NEVER HAVE!**
IF YOU THINK THAT KONOHA SHINOBI CAN SUCCESSFULLY PROTECT NARUTO...
NO.
?

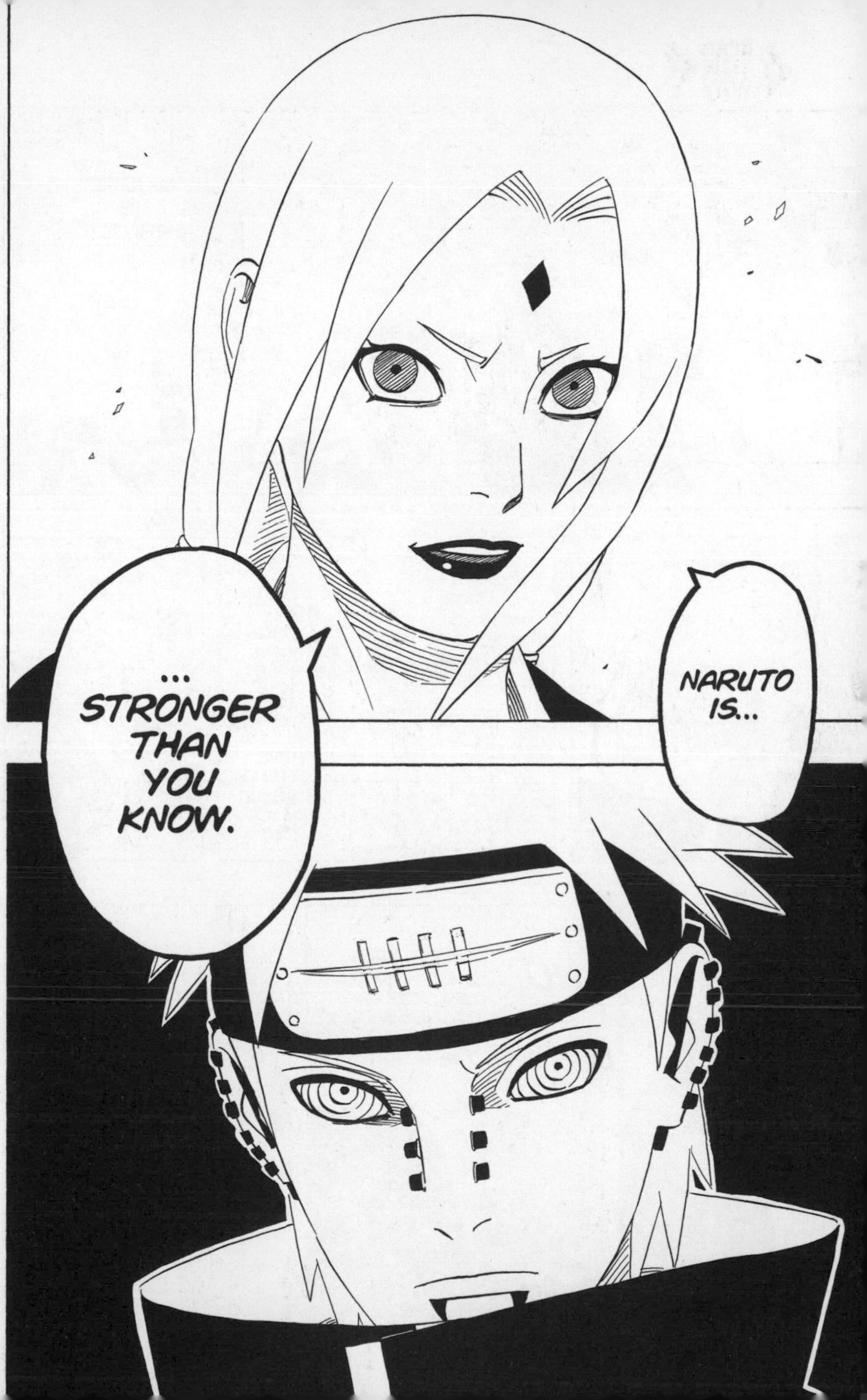
NARUTO IS...
... STRONGER THAN YOU KNOW.

READ THIS WAY

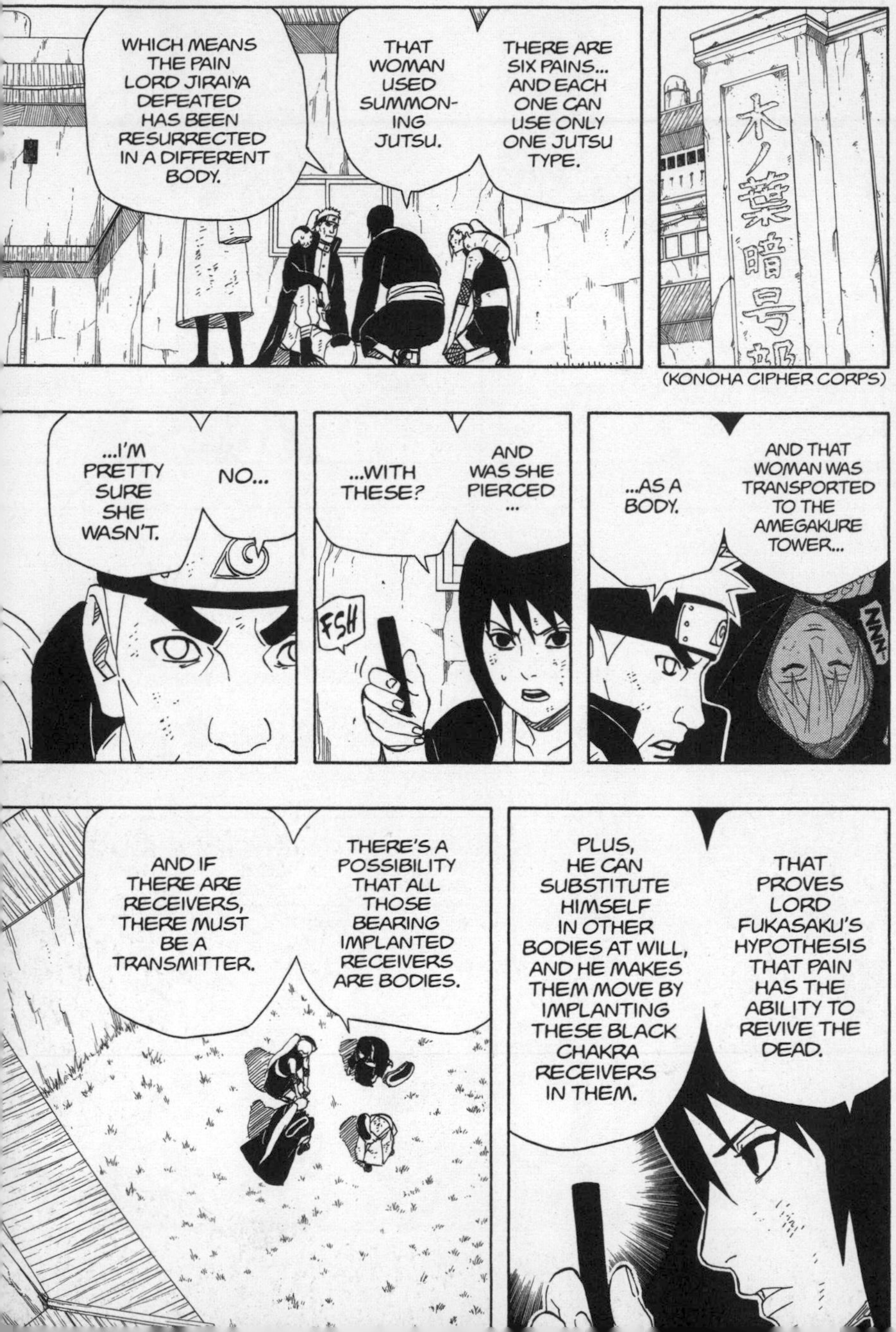
木ノ葉暗号部
(KONOHA CIPHER CORPS)
THERE ARE SIX PAINS... AND EACH ONE CAN USE ONLY ONE JUTSU TYPE.
THAT WOMAN USED SUMMON-ING JUTSU.
WHICH MEANS THE PAIN LORD JIRAIYA DEFEATED HAS BEEN RESURRECTED IN A DIFFERENT BODY.
AND THAT WOMAN WAS TRANSPORTED TO THE AMEGAKURE TOWER...
...AS A BODY.
NNN
AND WAS SHE PIERCED ...
...WITH THESE?
FSH
NO...
...I'M PRETTY SURE SHE WASN'T.
THAT PROVES LORD FUKASAKU'S HYPOTHESIS THAT PAIN HAS THE ABILITY TO REVIVE THE DEAD.
PLUS, HE CAN SUBSTITUTE HIMSELF IN OTHER BODIES AT WILL, AND HE MAKES THEM MOVE BY IMPLANTING THESE BLACK CHAKRA RECEIVERS IN THEM.
THERE'S A POSSIBILITY THAT ALL THOSE BEARING IMPLANTED RECEIVERS ARE BODIES.
AND IF THERE ARE RECEIVERS, THERE MUST BE A TRANSMITTER.

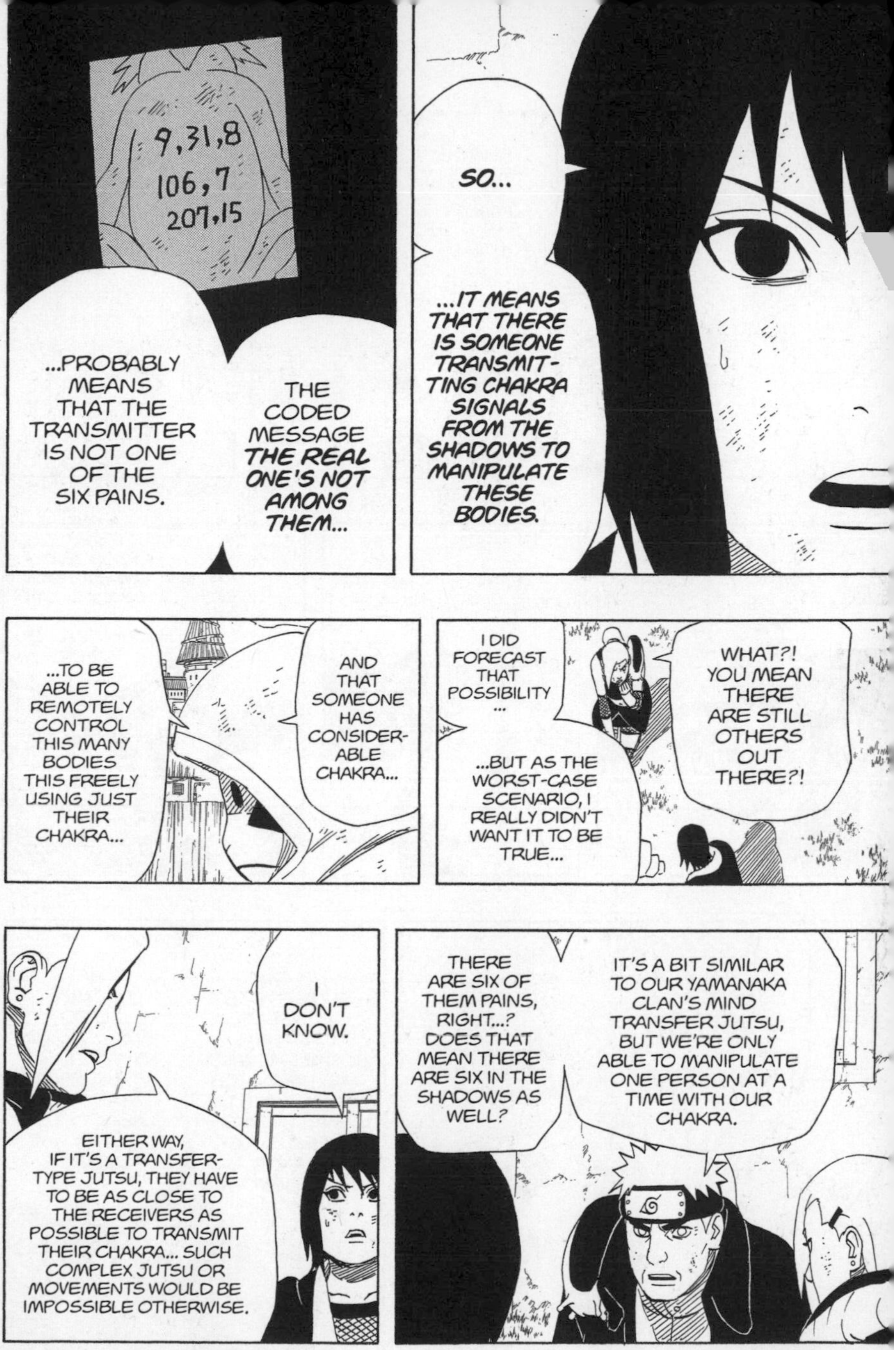
SO...
...IT MEANS THAT THERE IS SOMEONE TRANSMITTING CHAKRA SIGNALS FROM THE SHADOWS TO MANIPULATE THESE BODIES.
9,31,8
106,7
207,15
THE CODED MESSAGE THE REAL ONE'S NOT AMONG THEM...
...PROBABLY MEANS THAT THE TRANSMITTER IS NOT ONE OF THE SIX PAINS.
WHAT?! YOU MEAN THERE ARE STILL OTHERS OUT THERE?!
I DID FORECAST THAT POSSIBILITY...
...BUT AS THE WORST-CASE SCENARIO, I REALLY DIDN'T WANT IT TO BE TRUE...
AND THAT SOMEONE HAS CONSIDERABLE CHAKRA...
...TO BE ABLE TO REMOTELY CONTROL THIS MANY BODIES THIS FREELY USING JUST THEIR CHAKRA...
IT'S A BIT SIMILAR TO OUR YAMANAKA CLAN'S MIND TRANSFER JUTSU, BUT WE'RE ONLY ABLE TO MANIPULATE ONE PERSON AT A TIME WITH OUR CHAKRA.
THERE ARE SIX OF THEM PAINS, RIGHT...? DOES THAT MEAN THERE ARE SIX IN THE SHADOWS AS WELL?
I DON'T KNOW.
EITHER WAY, IF IT'S A TRANSFER-TYPE JUTSU, THEY HAVE TO BE AS CLOSE TO THE RECEIVERS AS POSSIBLE TO TRANSMIT THEIR CHAKRA... SUCH COMPLEX JUTSU OR MOVEMENTS WOULD BE IMPOSSIBLE OTHERWISE.

READ THIS WAY

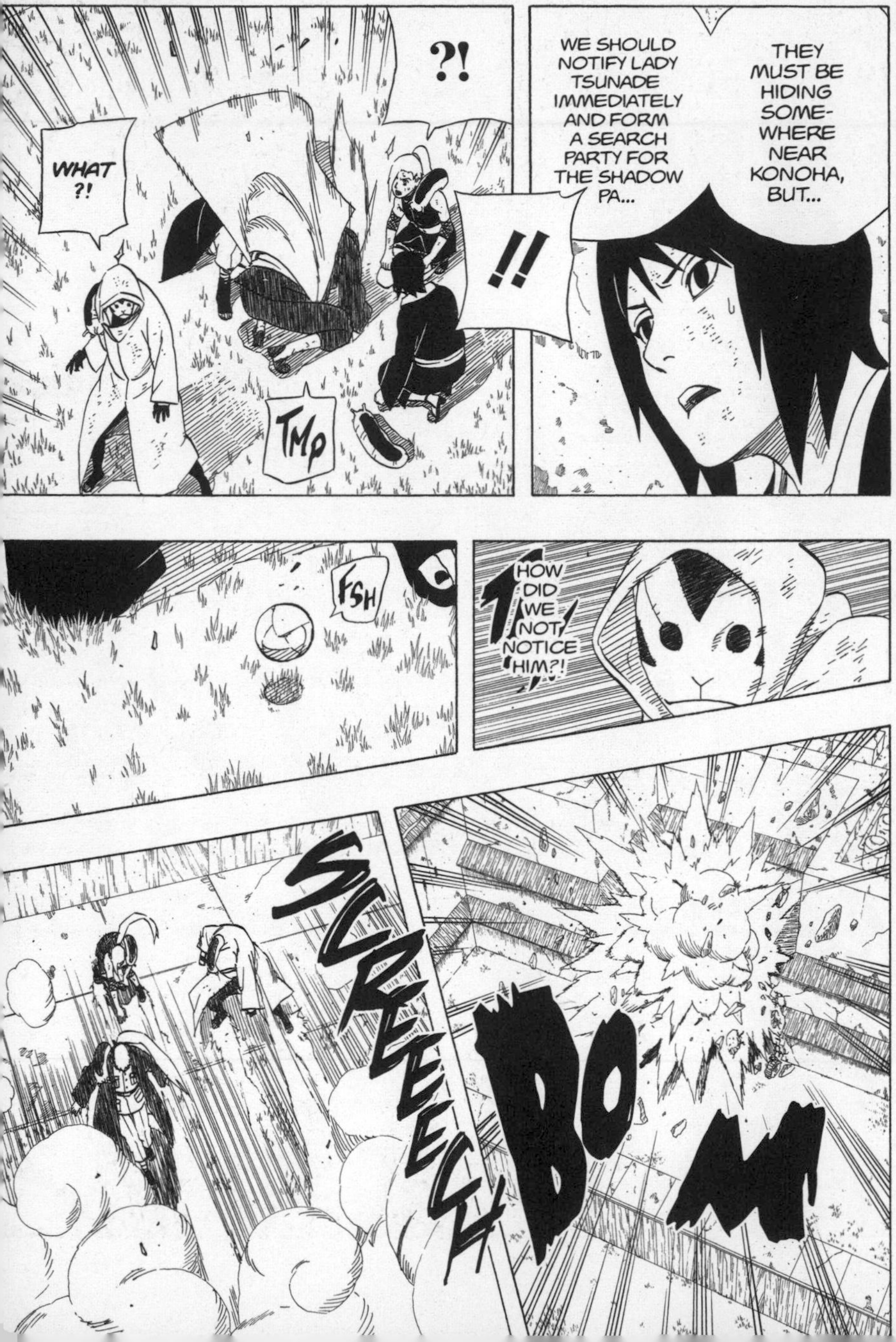
THEY MUST BE HIDING SOME-WHERE NEAR KONOHA, BUT...
WE SHOULD NOTIFY LADY TSUNADE IMMEDIATELY AND FORM A SEARCH PARTY FOR THE SHADOW PA...
!!
?!
WHAT ?!
TMP
HOW DID WE NOT NOTICE HIM?!
FSH
BOOM
SCREEEECH

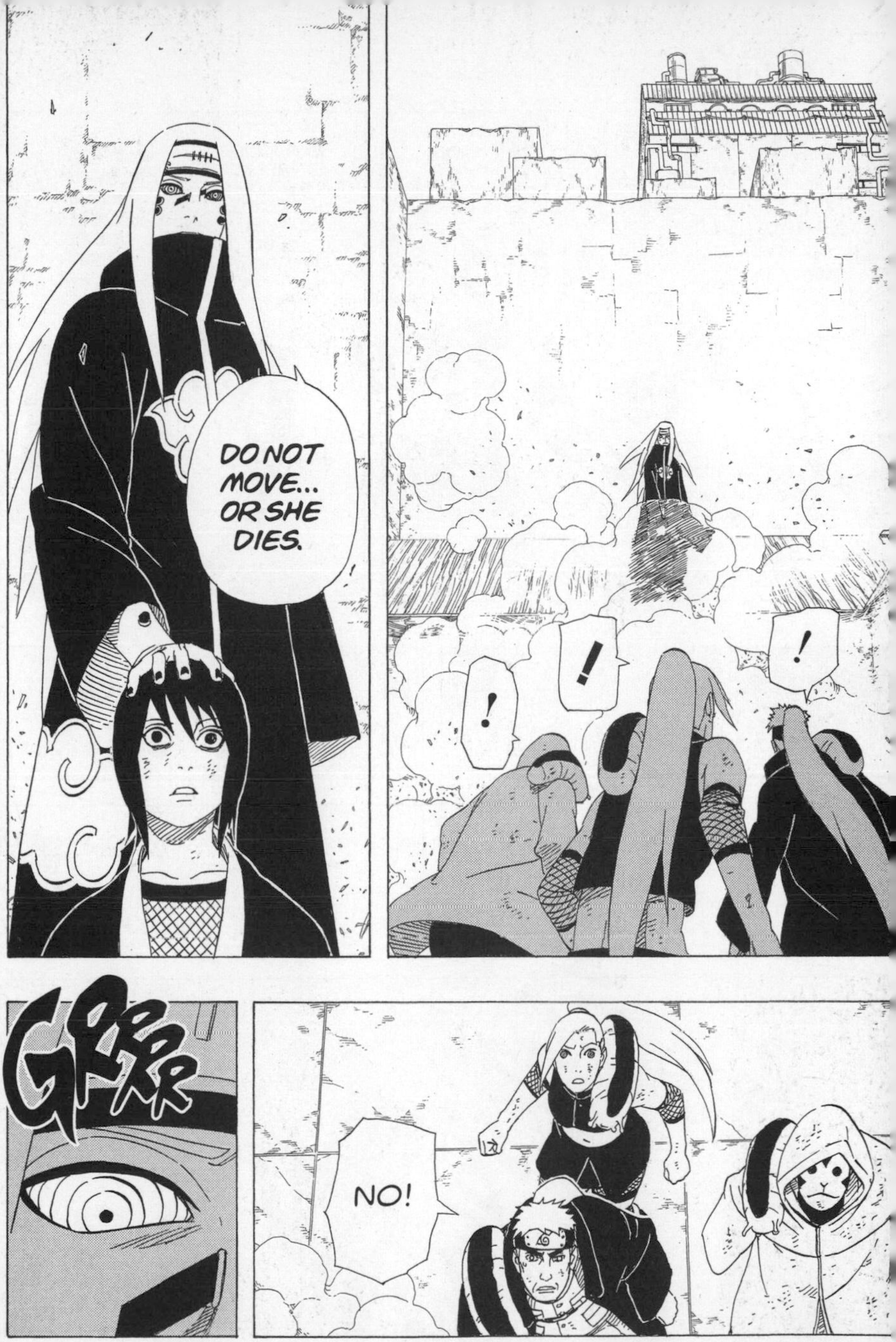
!
!
!
DO NOT MOVE... OR SHE DIES.
NO!
GRRRR

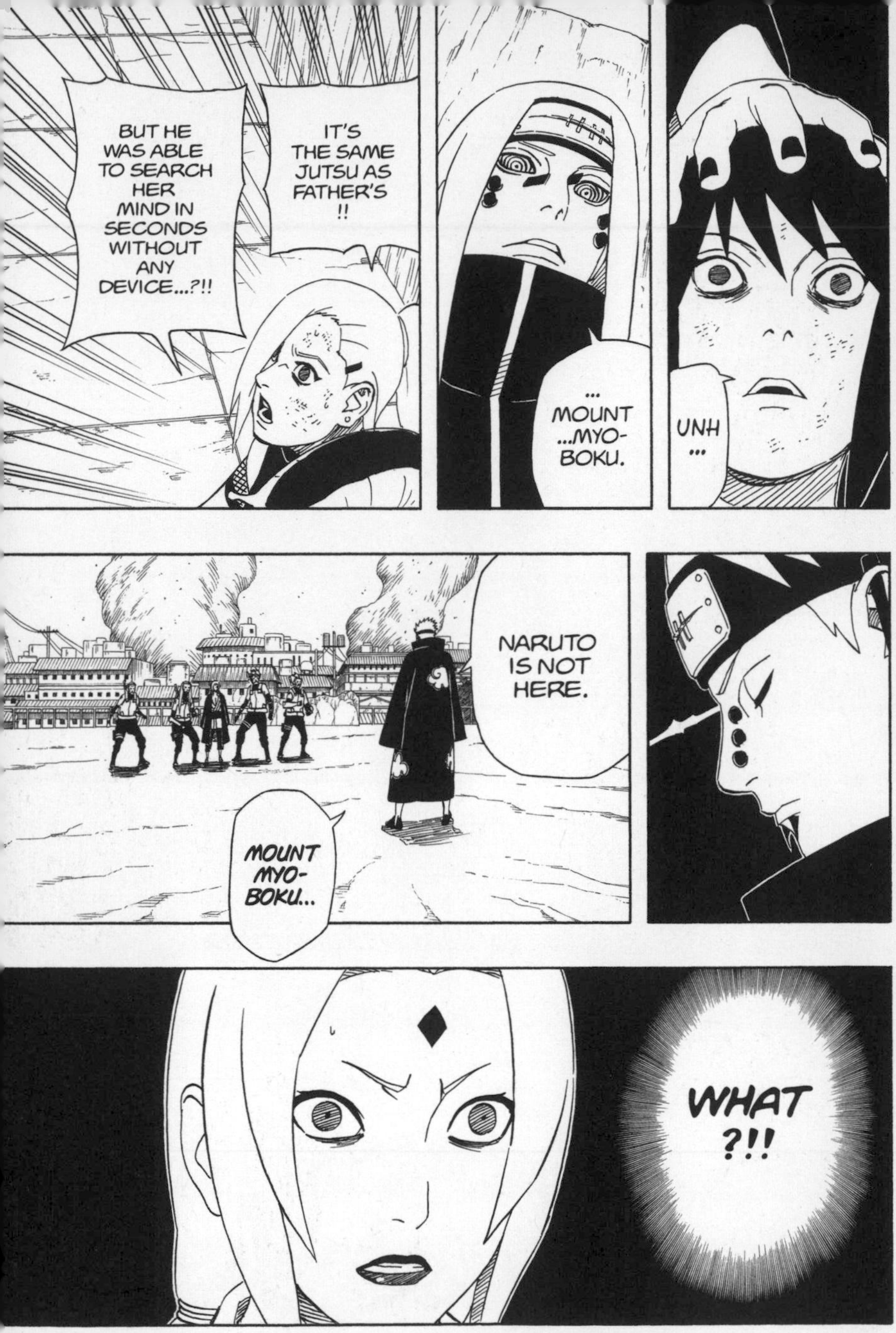
UNH ...
... MOUNT ...MYO-BOKU.
IT'S THE SAME JUTSU AS FATHER'S !!
BUT HE WAS ABLE TO SEARCH HER MIND IN SECONDS WITHOUT ANY DEVICE...?!!
NARUTO IS NOT HERE.
MOUNT MYO-BOKU...
WHAT ?!!

NARUTO

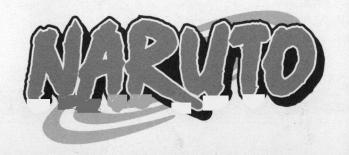

Number 429: Know Pain

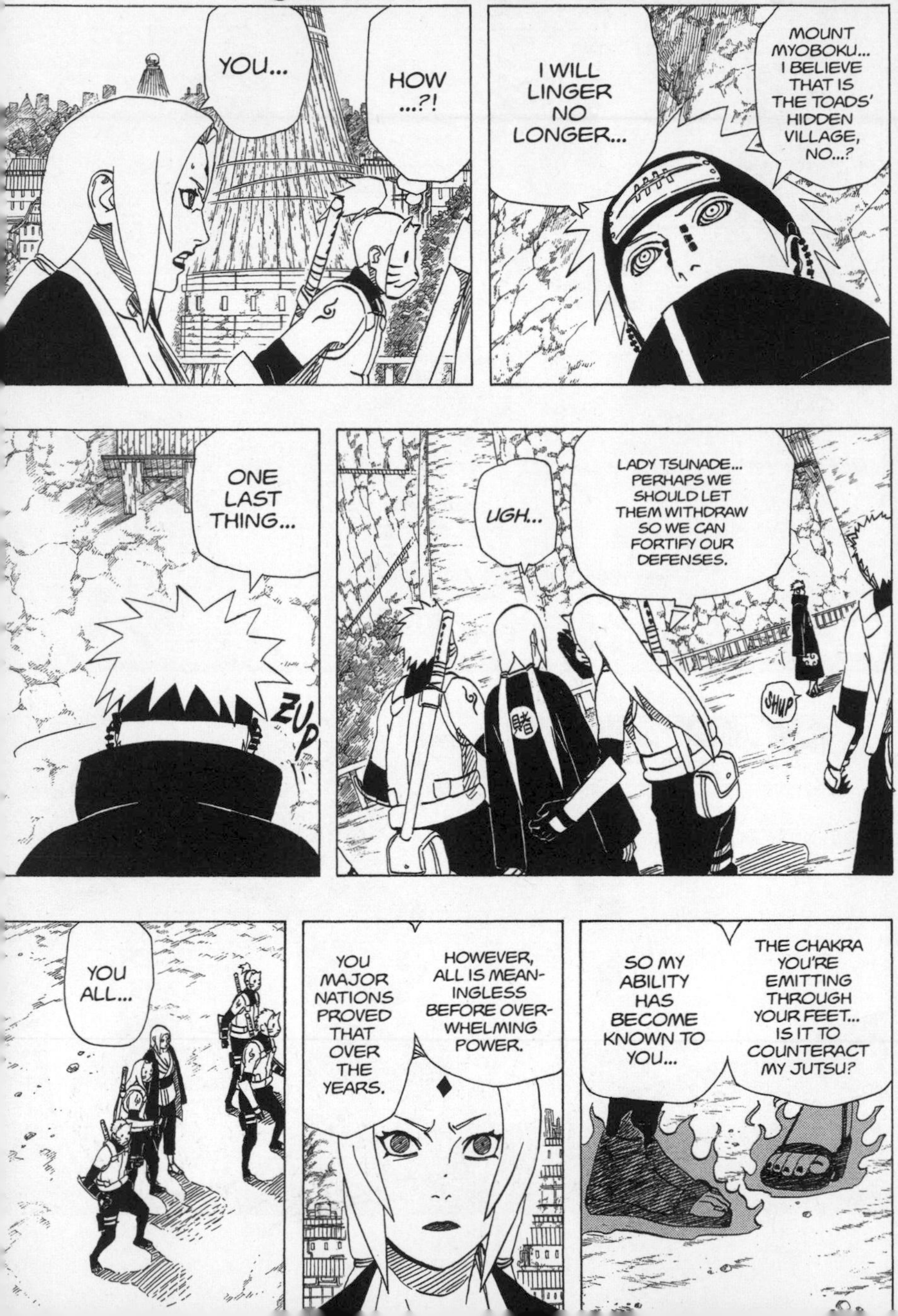

MOUNT MYOBOKU... I BELIEVE THAT IS THE TOADS' HIDDEN VILLAGE, NO...?
I WILL LINGER NO LONGER...
YOU...
HOW ...?!
LADY TSUNADE... PERHAPS WE SHOULD LET THEM WITHDRAW SO WE CAN FORTIFY OUR DEFENSES.
UGH...
SHUP
ONE LAST THING...
ZUP
THE CHAKRA YOU'RE EMITTING THROUGH YOUR FEET... IS IT TO COUNTERACT MY JUTSU?
SO MY ABILITY HAS BECOME KNOWN TO YOU...
HOWEVER, ALL IS MEANINGLESS BEFORE OVERWHELMING POWER.
YOU MAJOR NATIONS PROVED THAT OVER THE YEARS.
YOU ALL...

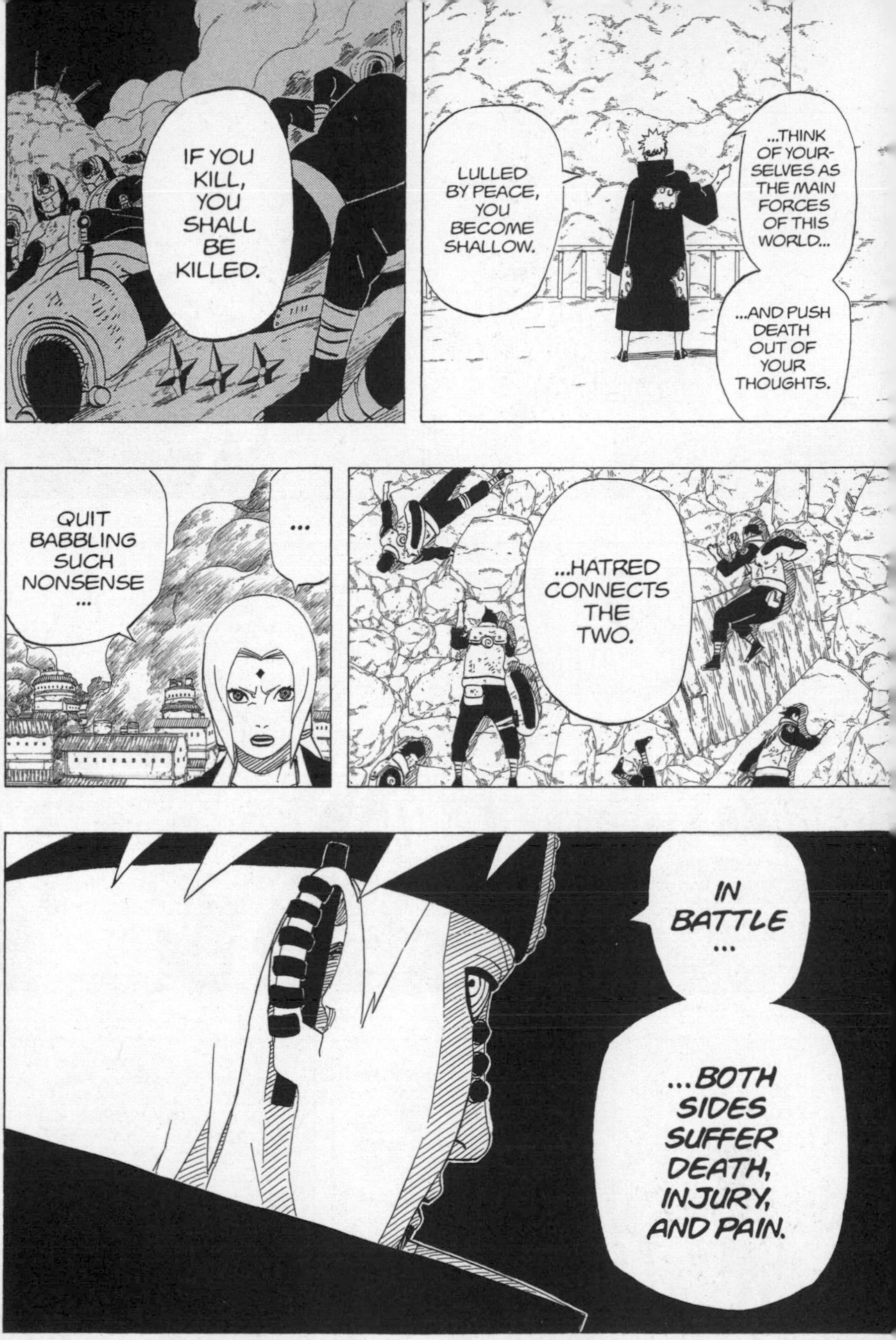
...THINK OF YOURSELVES AS THE MAIN FORCES OF THIS WORLD...
...AND PUSH DEATH OUT OF YOUR THOUGHTS.
LULLED BY PEACE, YOU BECOME SHALLOW.
IF YOU KILL, YOU SHALL BE KILLED.
...HATRED CONNECTS THE TWO.
...
QUIT BABBLING SUCH NONSENSE ...
IN BATTLE ...
...BOTH SIDES SUFFER DEATH, INJURY, AND PAIN.

READ THIS WAY

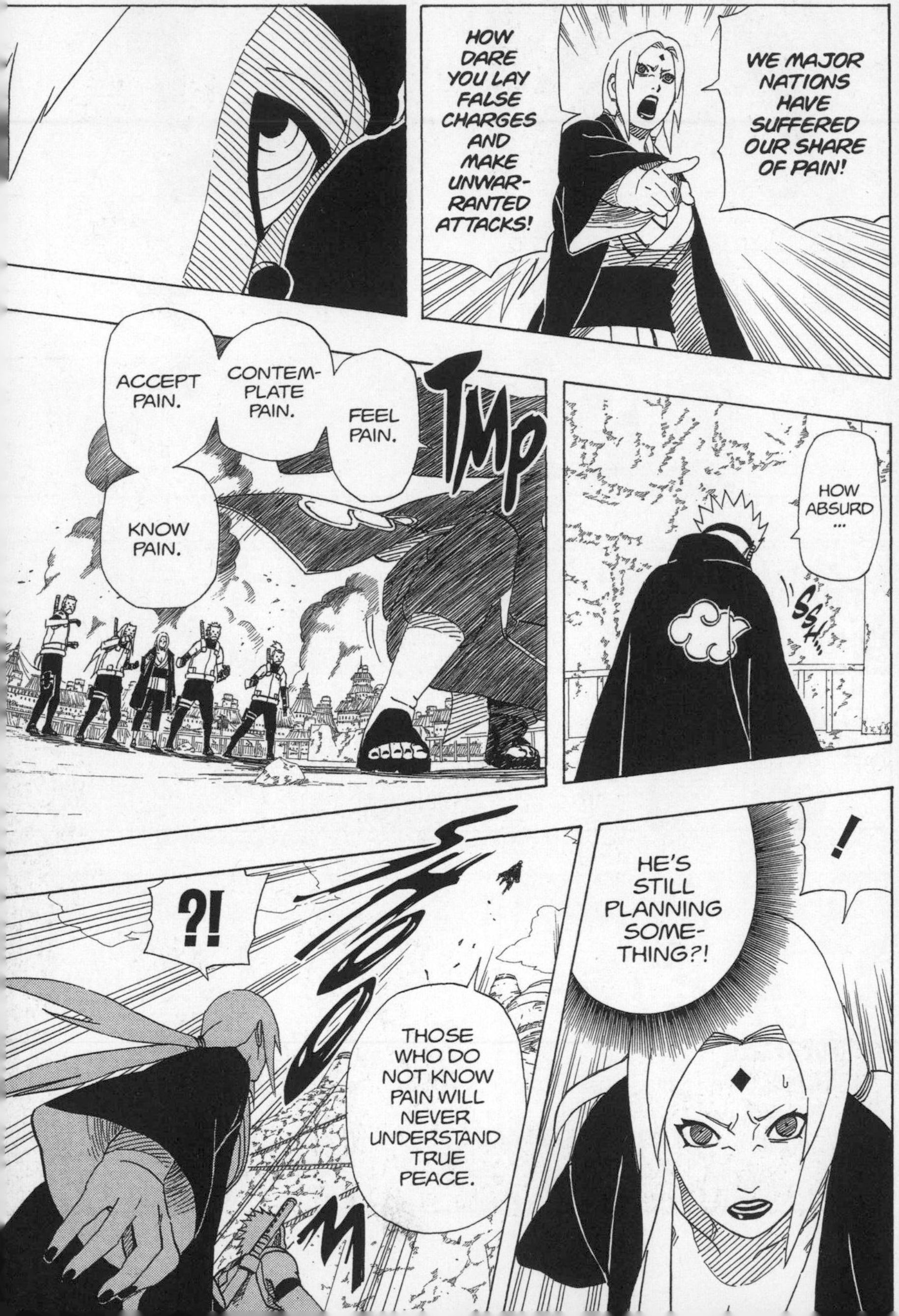
WE MAJOR NATIONS HAVE SUFFERED OUR SHARE OF PAIN!
HOW DARE YOU LAY FALSE CHARGES AND MAKE UNWAR-RANTED ATTACKS!
HOW ABSURD ...
SSH...
TMP
FEEL PAIN.
CONTEM-PLATE PAIN.
ACCEPT PAIN.
KNOW PAIN.
!
HE'S STILL PLANNING SOME-THING?!
THOSE WHO DO NOT KNOW PAIN WILL NEVER UNDERSTAND TRUE PEACE.
?!

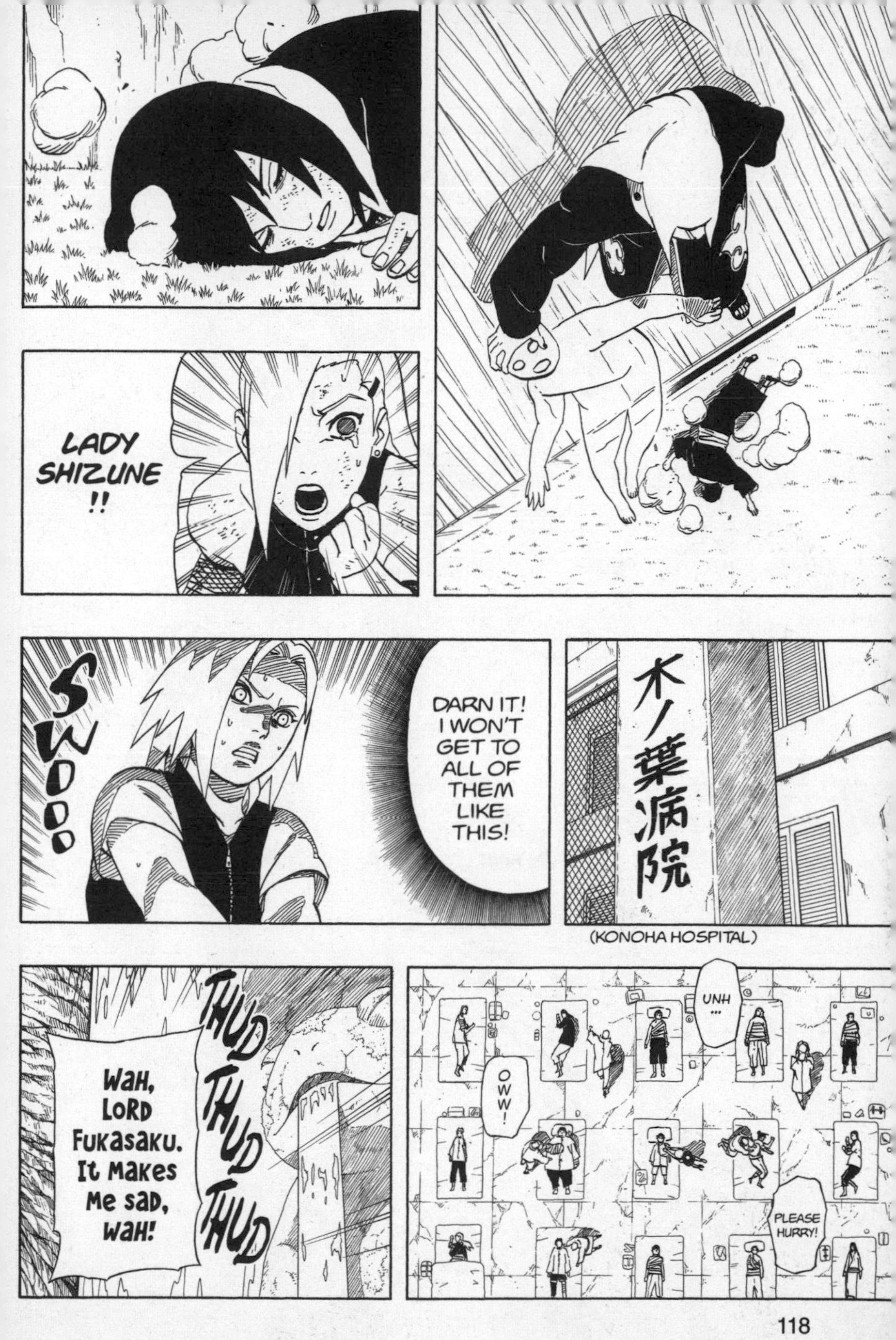
LADY SHIZUNE !!
木ノ葉病院
(KONOHA HOSPITAL)
DARN IT! I WON'T GET TO ALL OF THEM LIKE THIS!
SWOOO
UNH ...
OWW!
PLEASE HURRY!
THUD THUD THUD
Wah, Lord Fukasaku. It Makes Me sad, wah!

READ THIS WAY

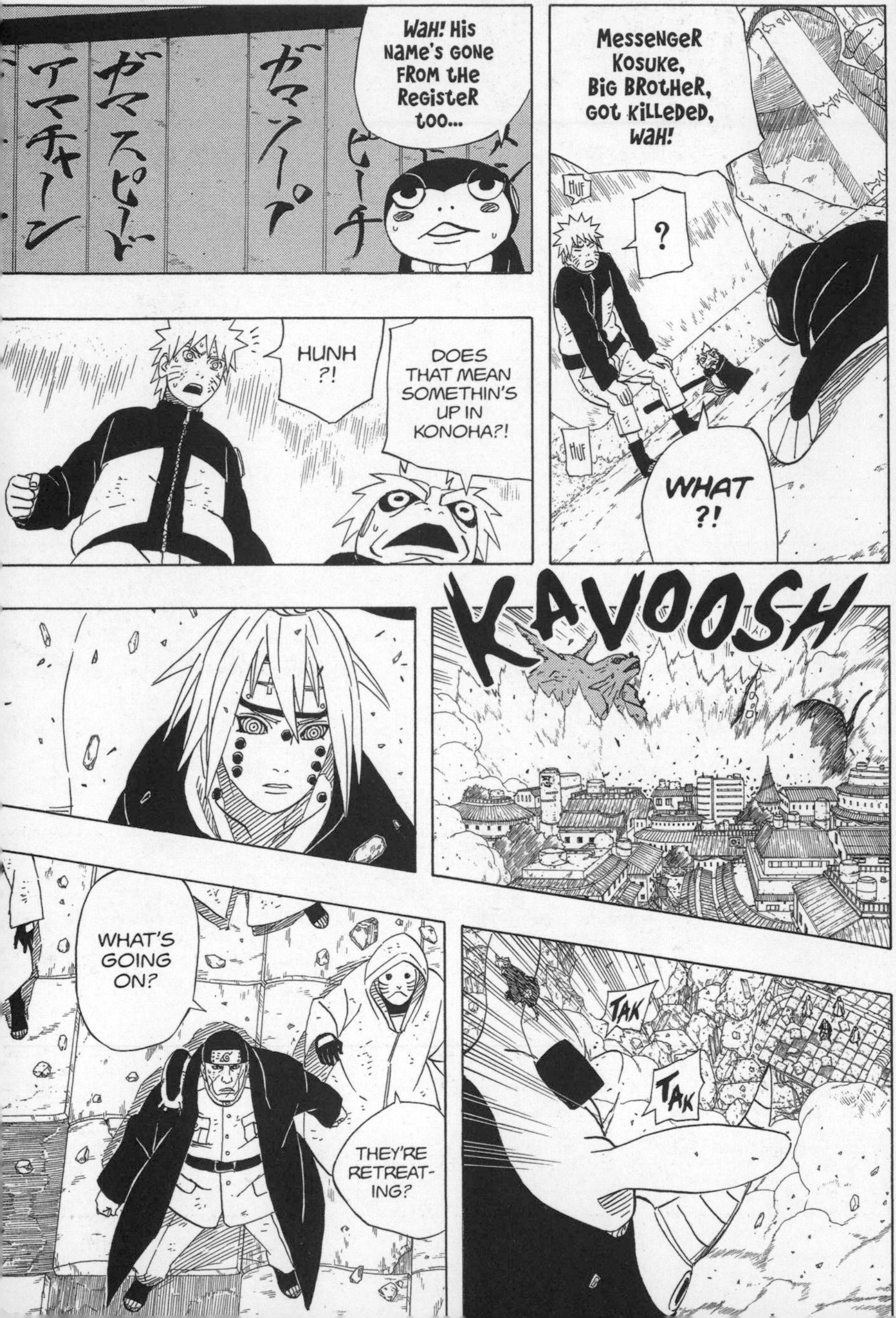
Messenger Kosuke, Big Brother, got killeded, wah!
HUF
?
HUF
WHAT?!
Wah! His name's gone from the Register too...
ピーチ
ガマスピード
アマチャーン
HUNH?!
DOES THAT MEAN SOMETHIN'S UP IN KONOHA?!
KAVOOSH
TAK
TAK
WHAT'S GOING ON?
THEY'RE RETREATING?

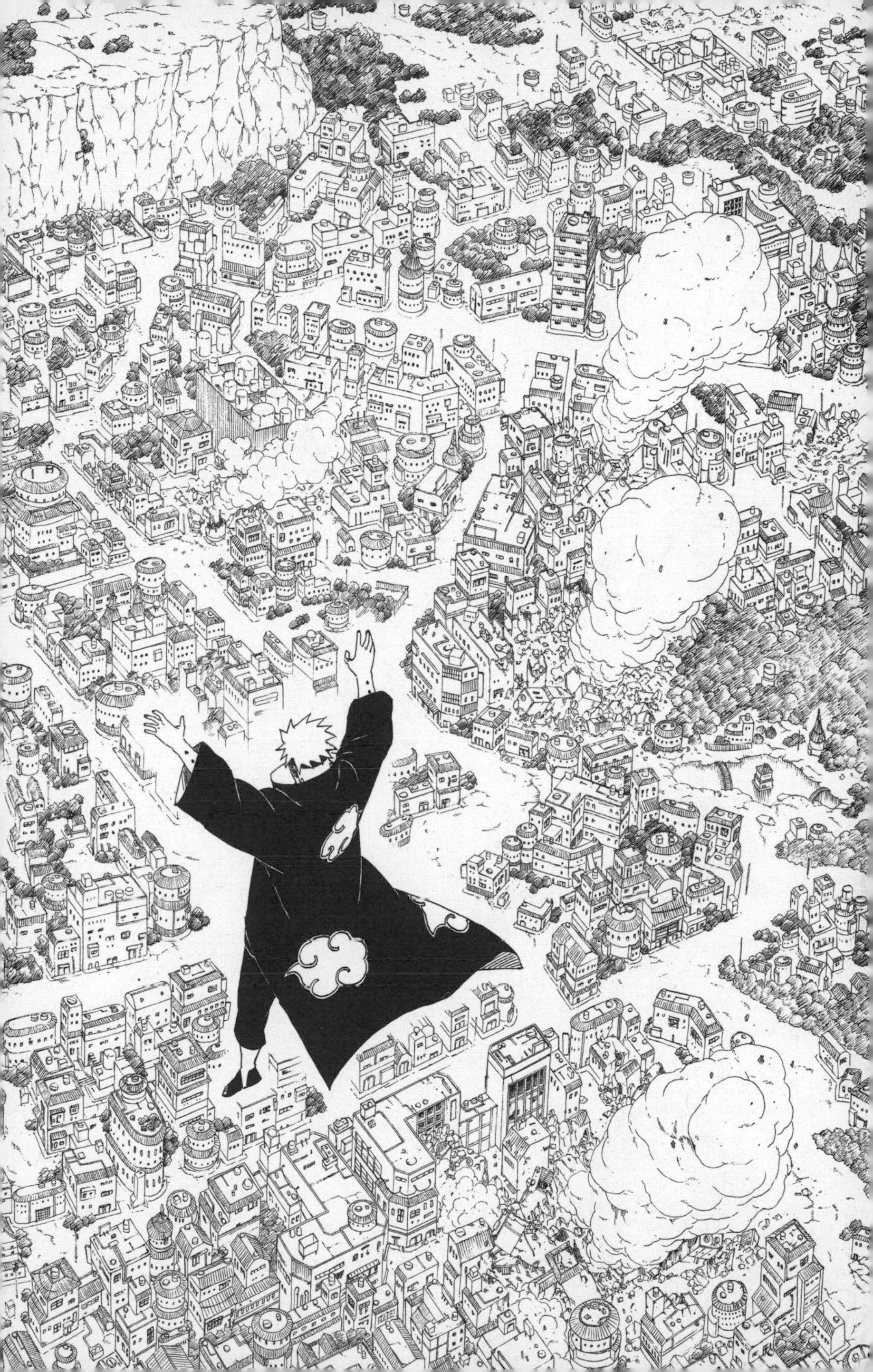

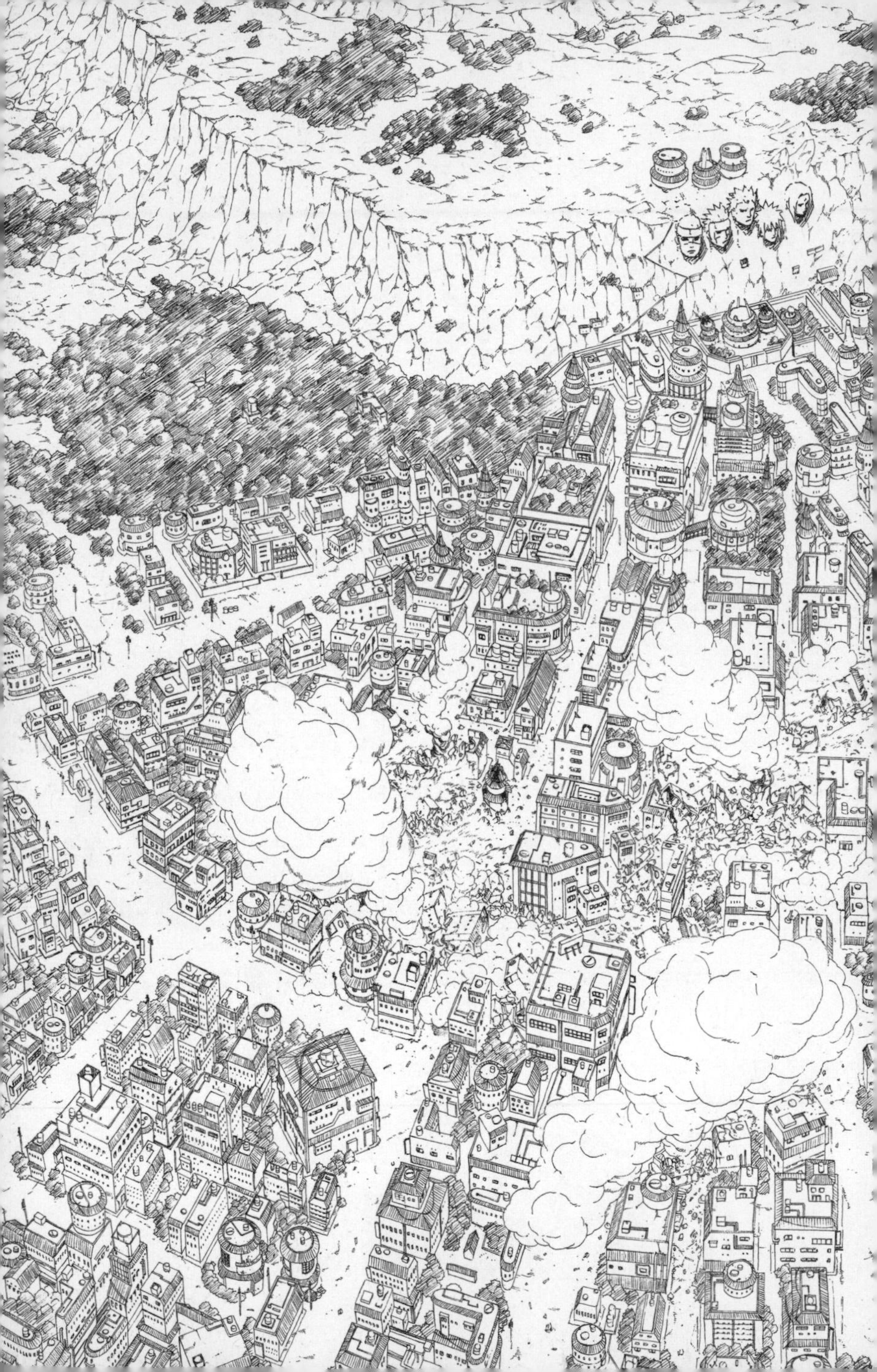

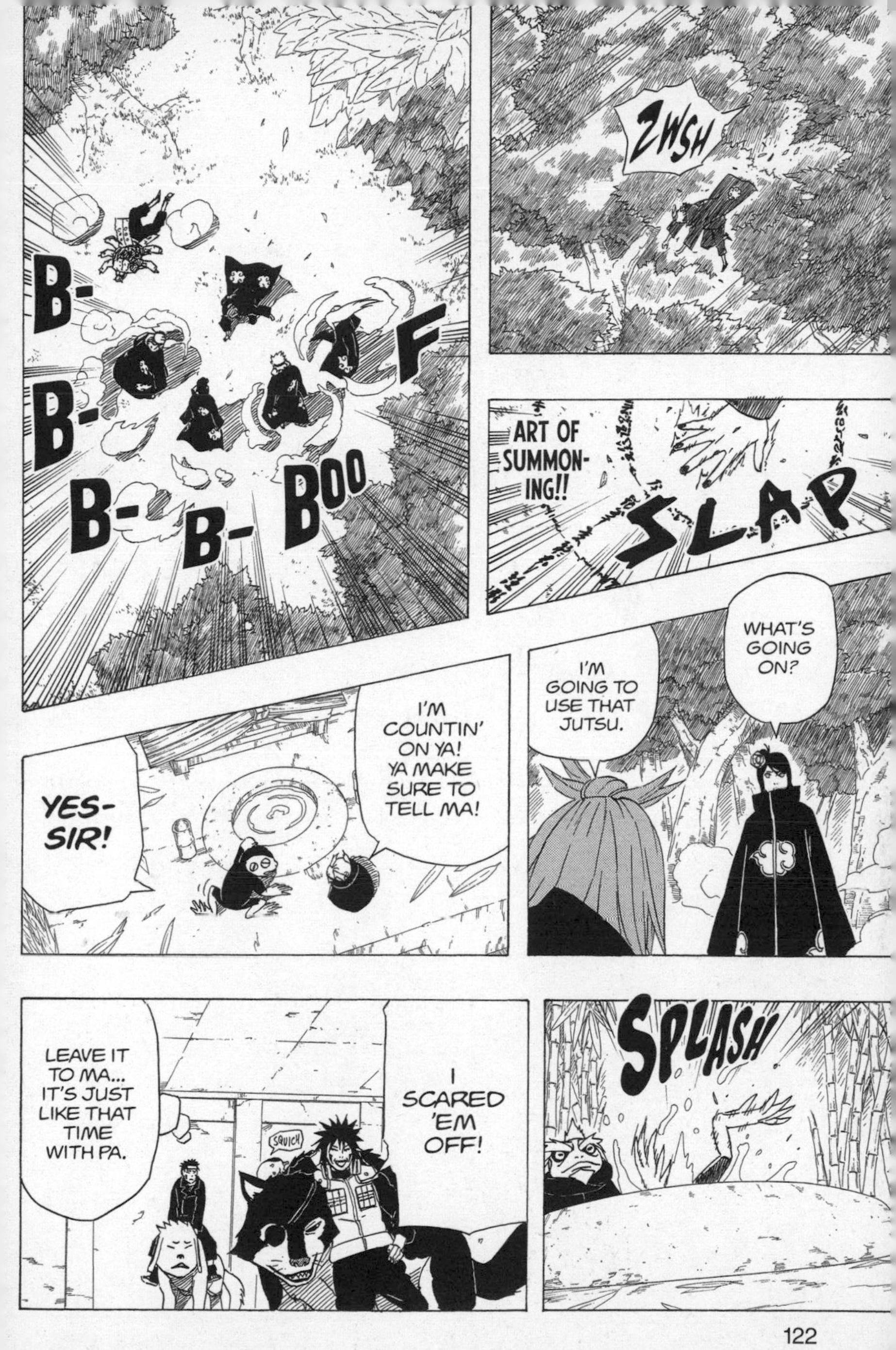
ZWSH
ART OF SUMMONING!!
SLAP
B-B-B-B-BOOF
WHAT'S GOING ON?
I'M GOING TO USE THAT JUTSU.
I'M COUNTIN' ON YA! YA MAKE SURE TO TELL MA!
YES-SIR!
SPLASH
I SCARED 'EM OFF!
SQUICH
LEAVE IT TO MA... IT'S JUST LIKE THAT TIME WITH PA.

READ THIS WAY

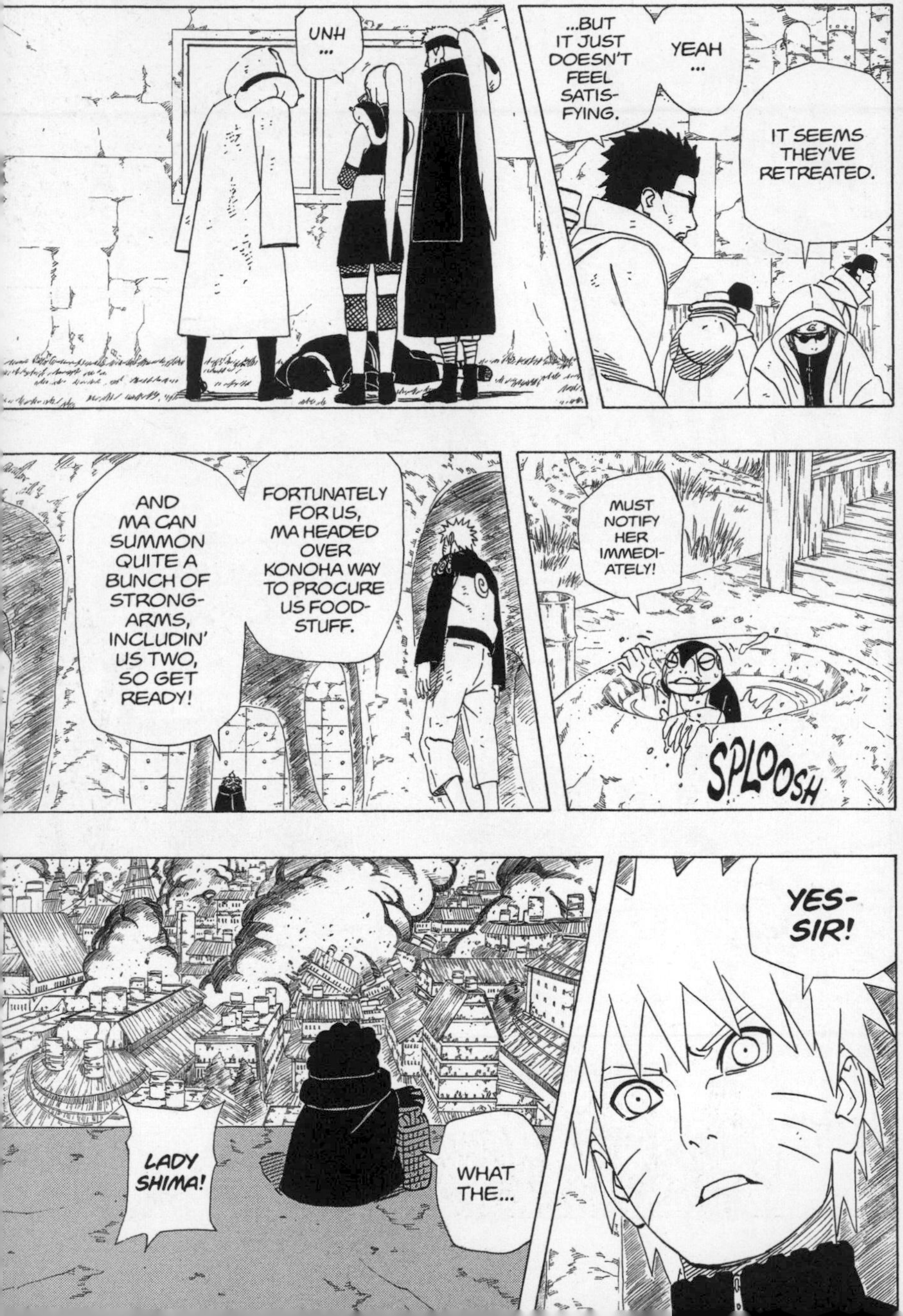
IT SEEMS THEY'VE RETREATED.
YEAH...
...BUT IT JUST DOESN'T FEEL SATIS-FYING.
UNH...
MUST NOTIFY HER IMMEDI-ATELY!
SPLOOSH
FORTUNATELY FOR US, MA HEADED OVER KONOHA WAY TO PROCURE US FOOD-STUFF.
AND MA CAN SUMMON QUITE A BUNCH OF STRONG-ARMS, INCLUDIN' US TWO, SO GET READY!
YES-SIR!
WHAT THE...
LADY SHIMA!

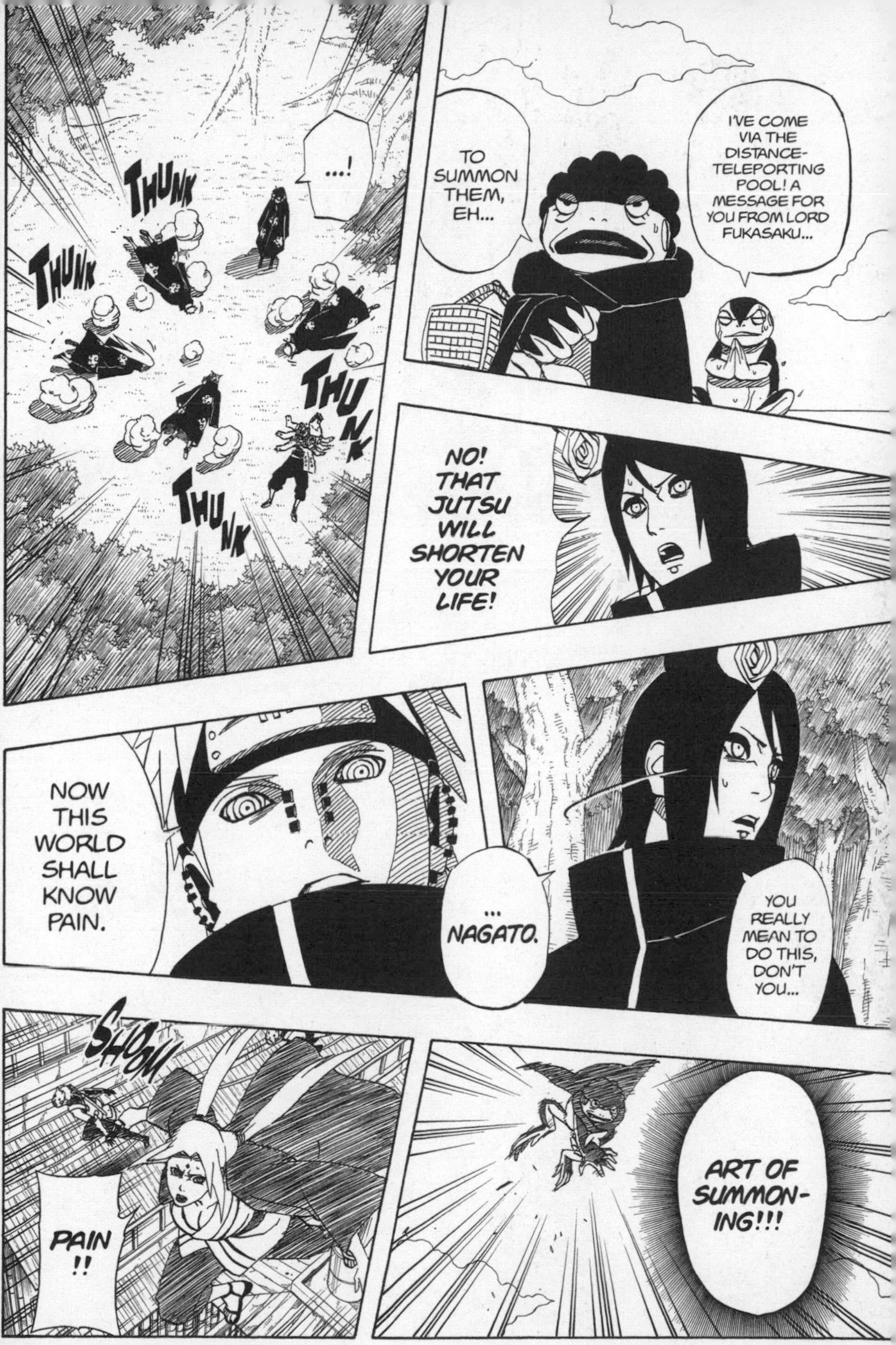
I'VE COME VIA THE DISTANCE-TELEPORTING POOL! A MESSAGE FOR YOU FROM LORD FUKASAKU...
TO SUMMON THEM, EH...
NO! THAT JUTSU WILL SHORTEN YOUR LIFE!
...!
THUNK
THUNK
THUNK
THUNK
YOU REALLY MEAN TO DO THIS, DON'T YOU...
... NAGATO.
NOW THIS WORLD SHALL KNOW PAIN.
ART OF SUMMONING!!!
SHOOM
PAIN !!

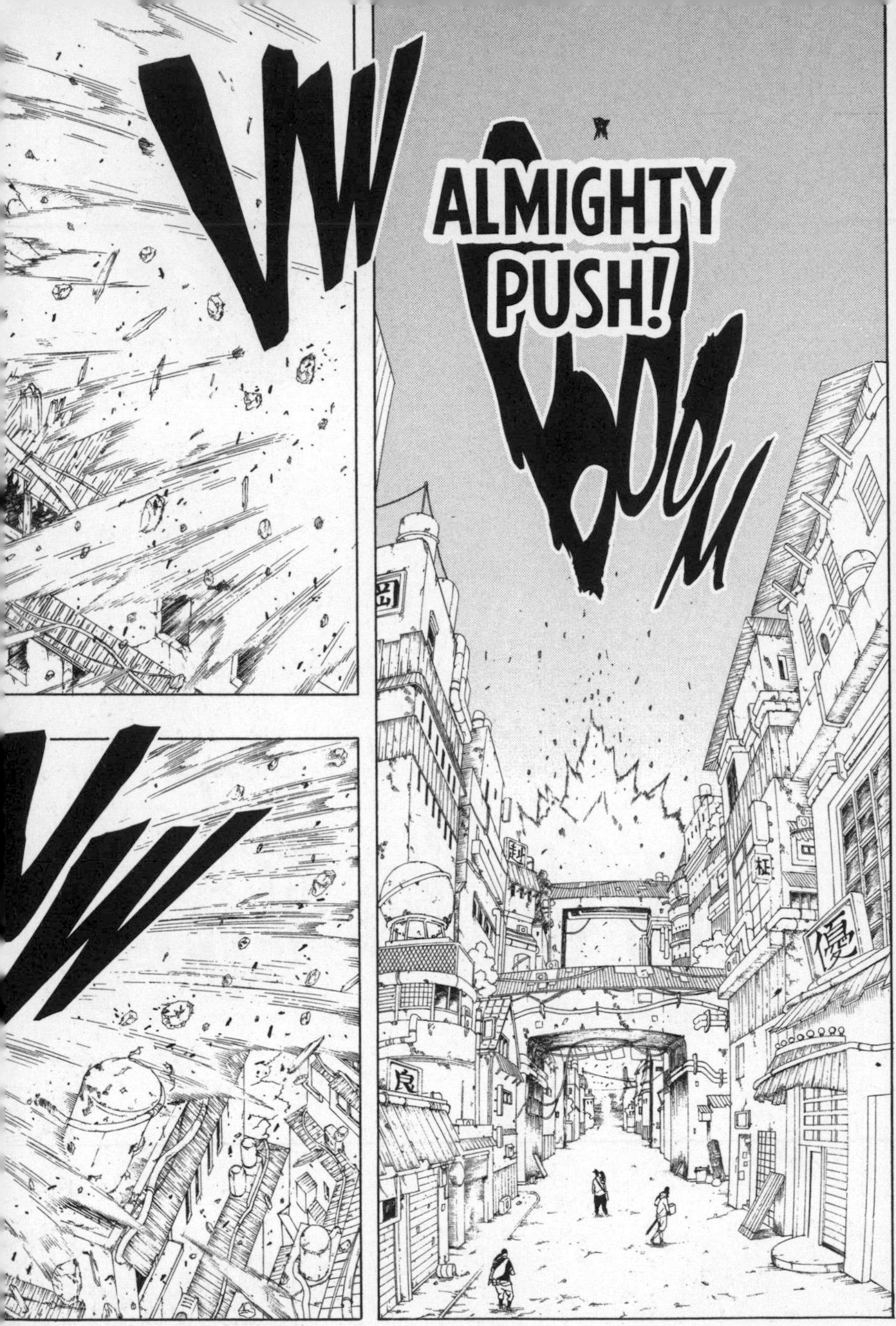
ALMIGHTY PUSH!

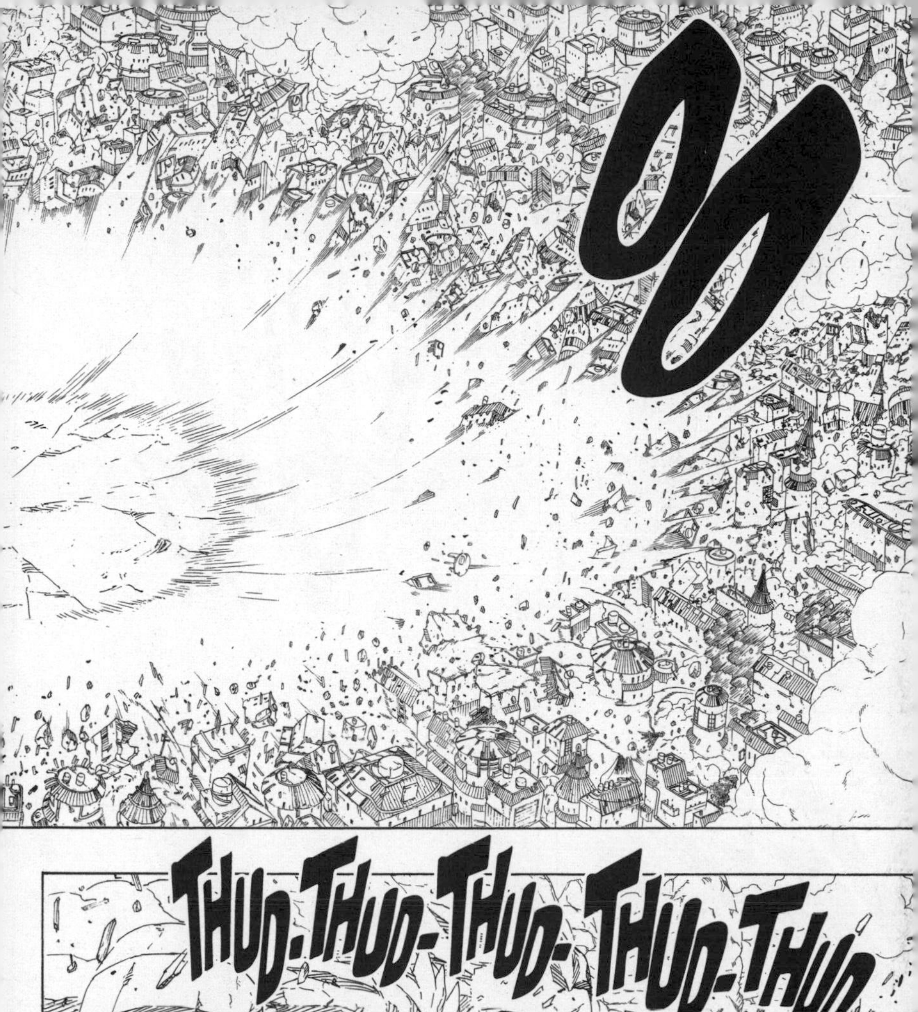

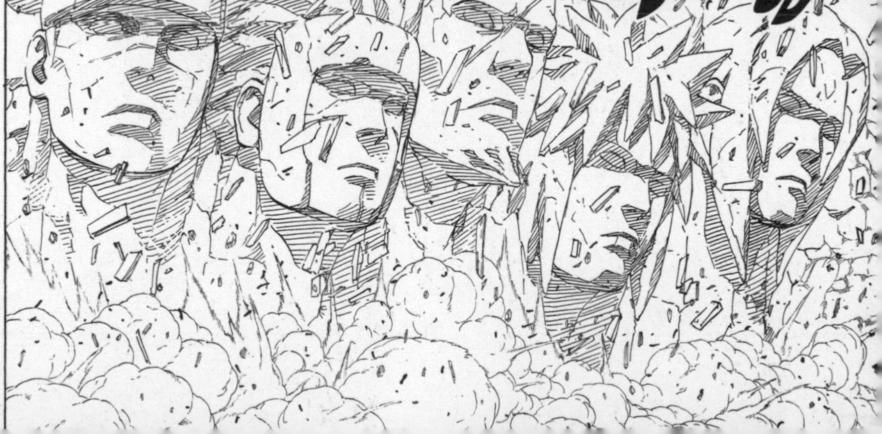
THUD-THUD-THUD-THUD-THUD

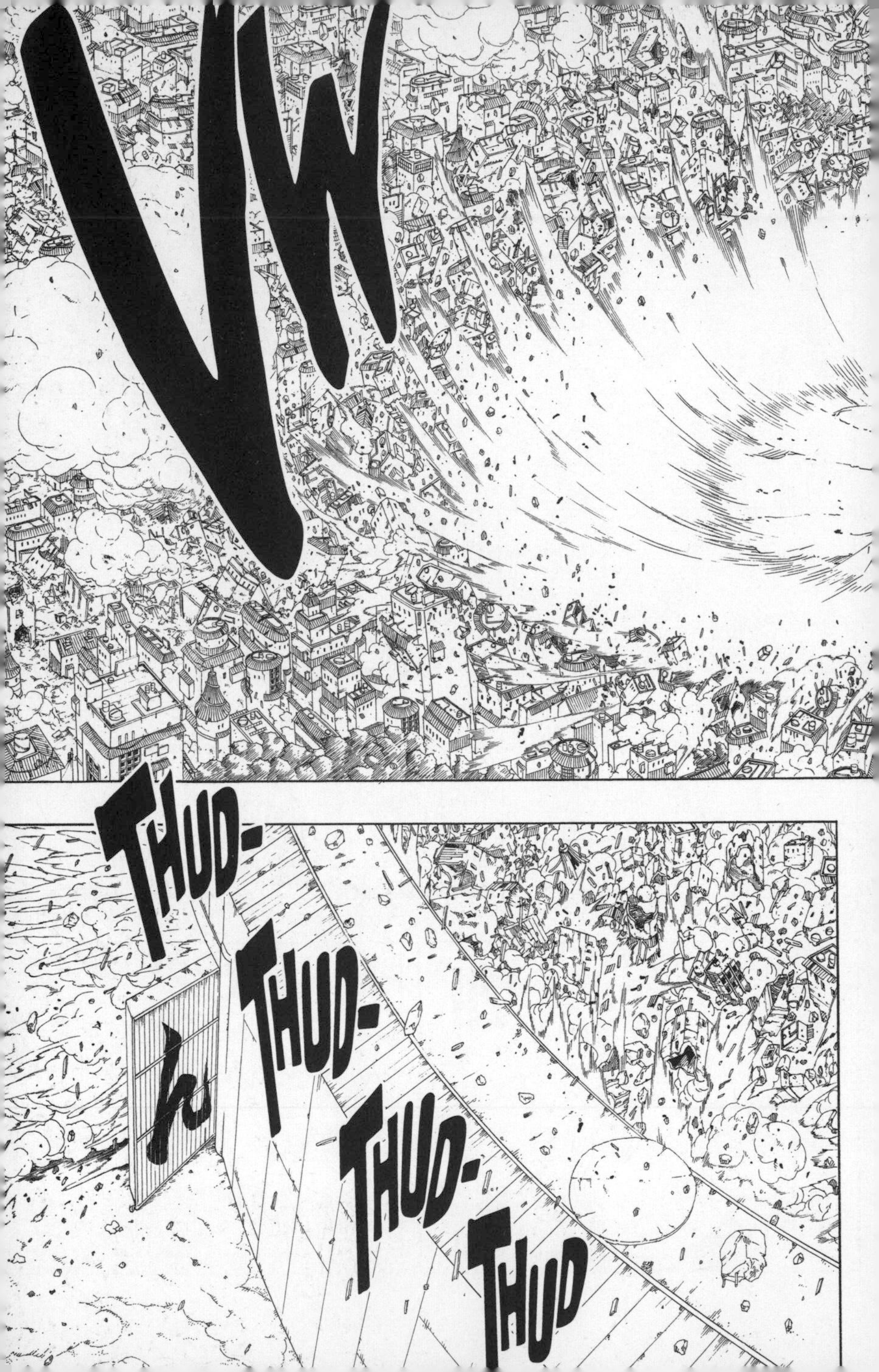
THUD-
THUD-
THUD-
THUD

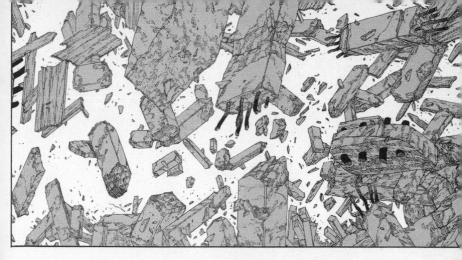

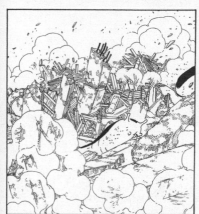

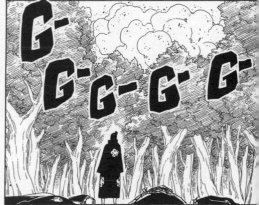

G- G- G- G- G-

?!!

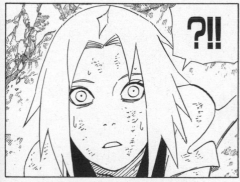

HACK!!

COUGH!!

ZWOOO...

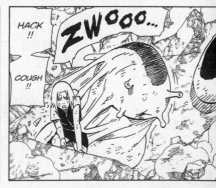

READ THIS WAY

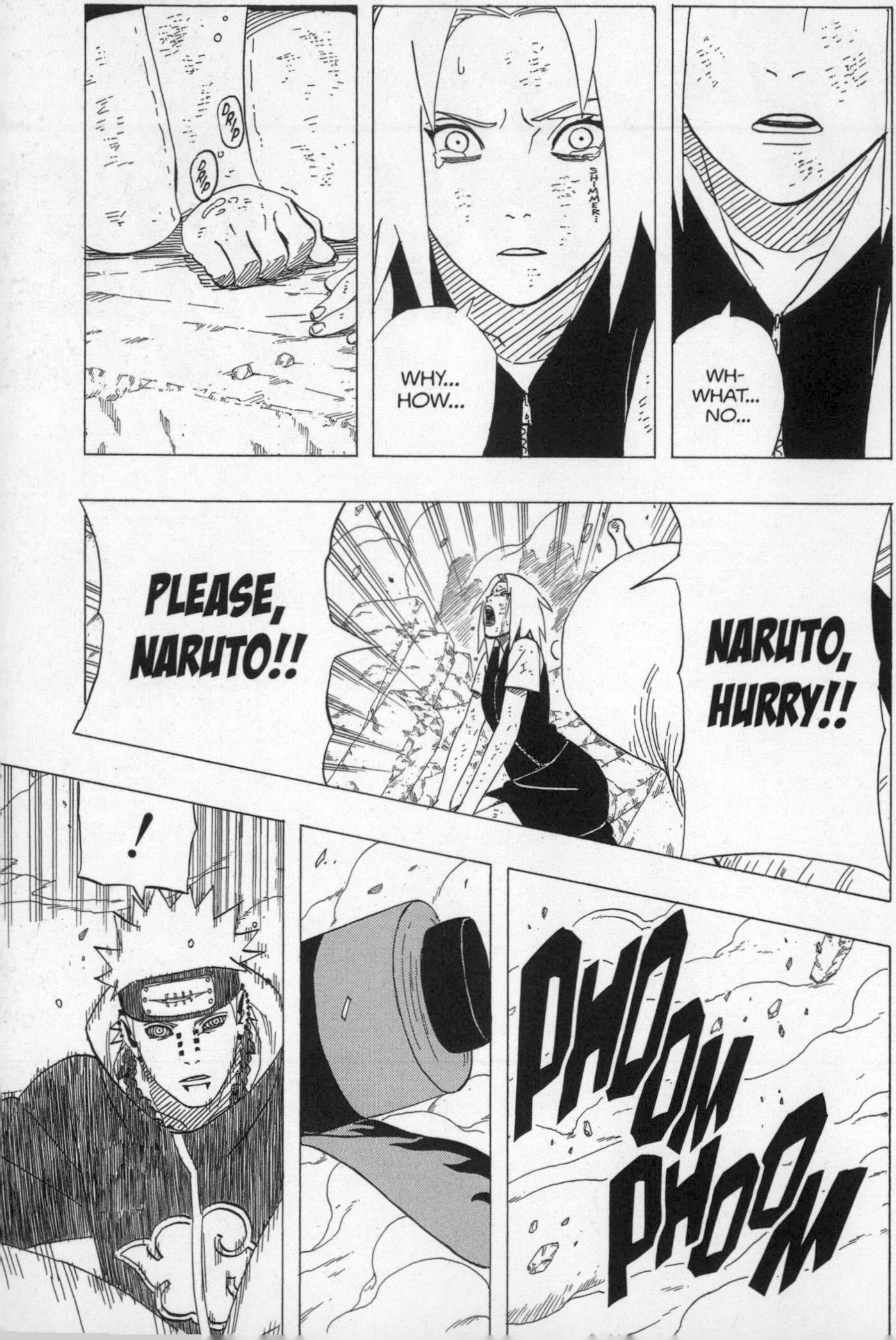

WH-
WHAT...
NO...
WHY...
HOW...
SHIMMER
DRIP
DRIP
NARUTO, HURRY!!
PLEASE, NARUTO!!
PHOOM
PHOOM
!

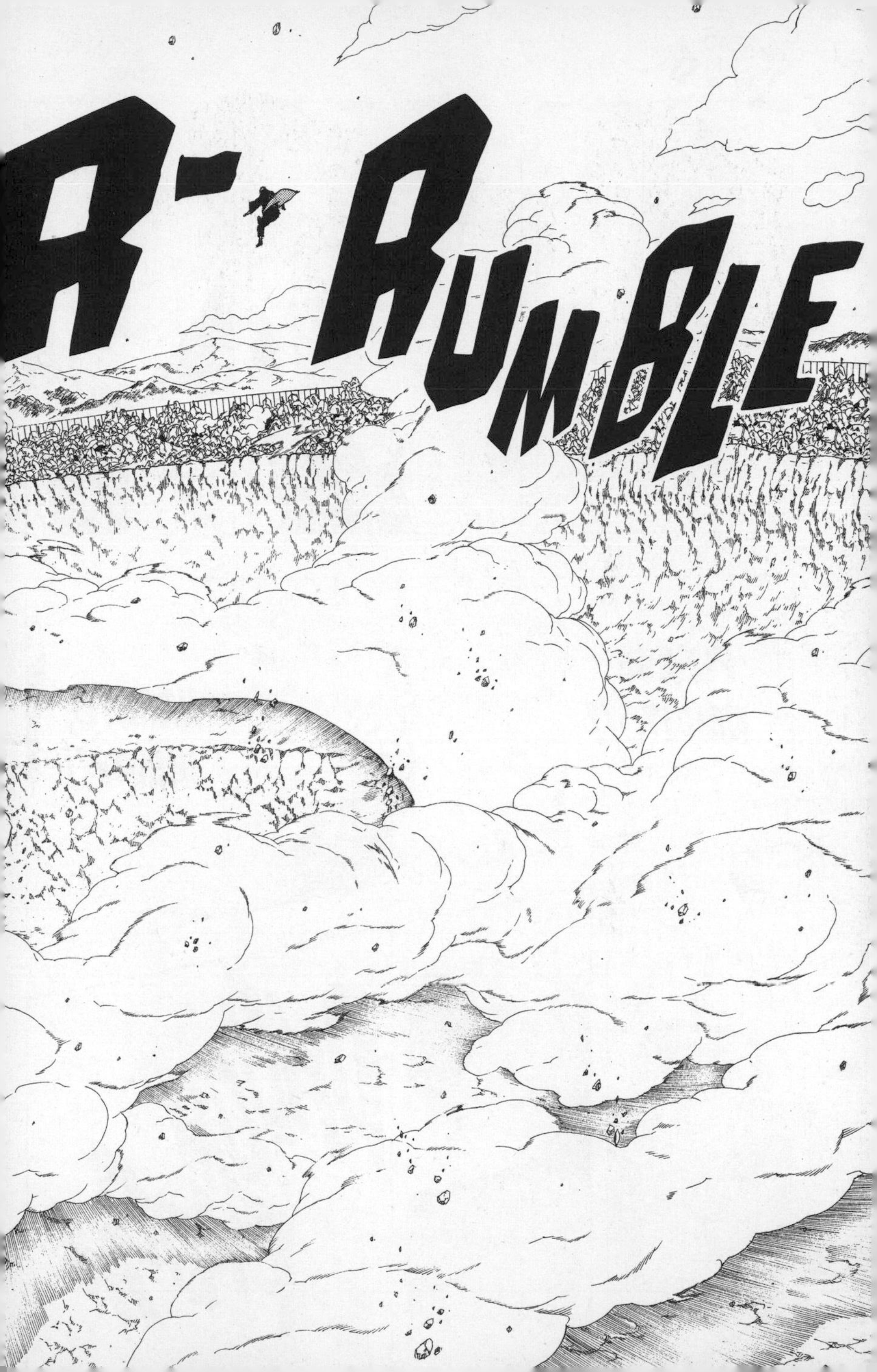
R-RUMBLE

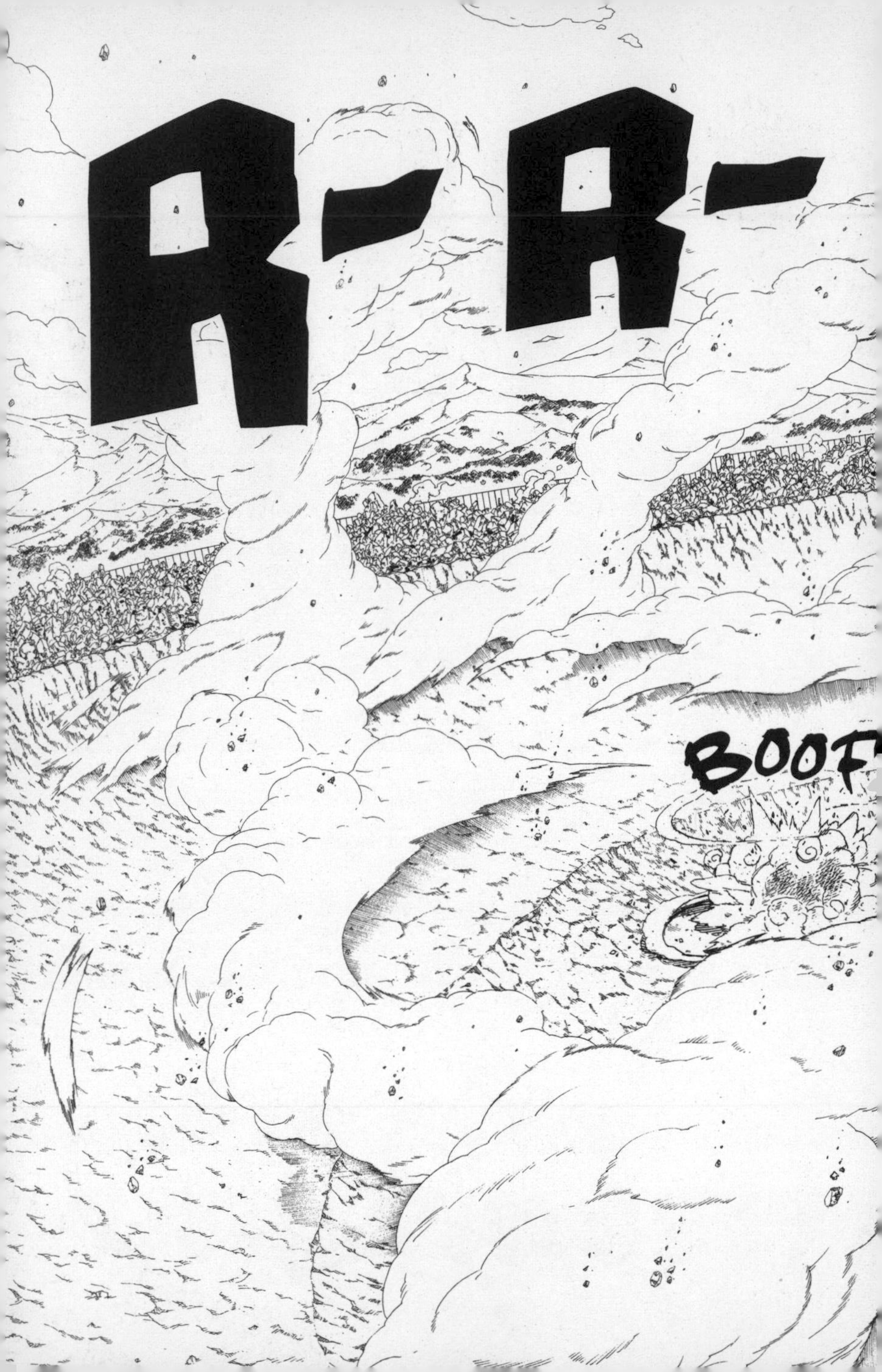
R-R-
BOOF

NARUTO

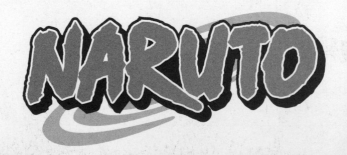

Number 430: Naruto Returns!!

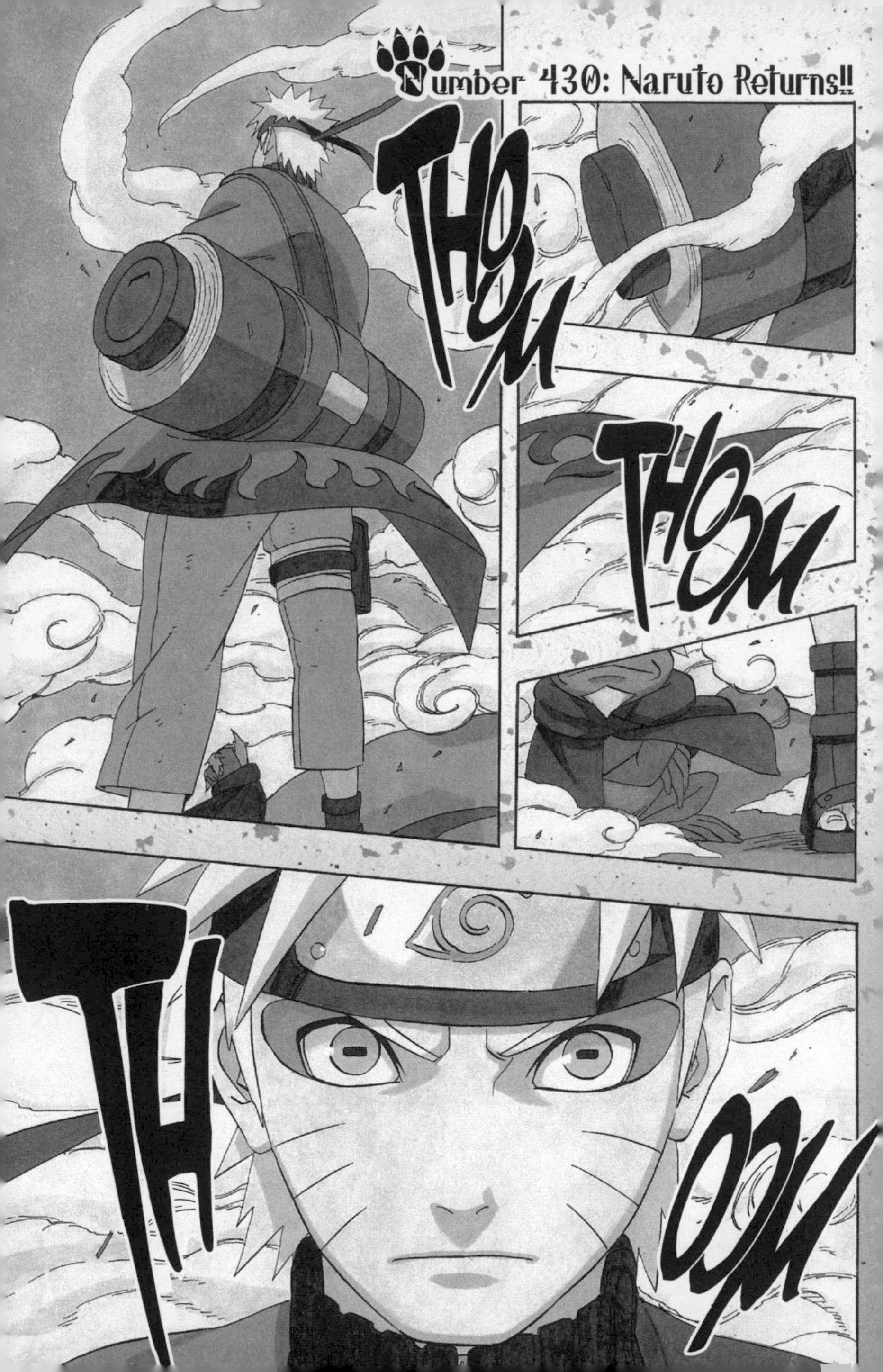
THOOM
THOOM
THOOM

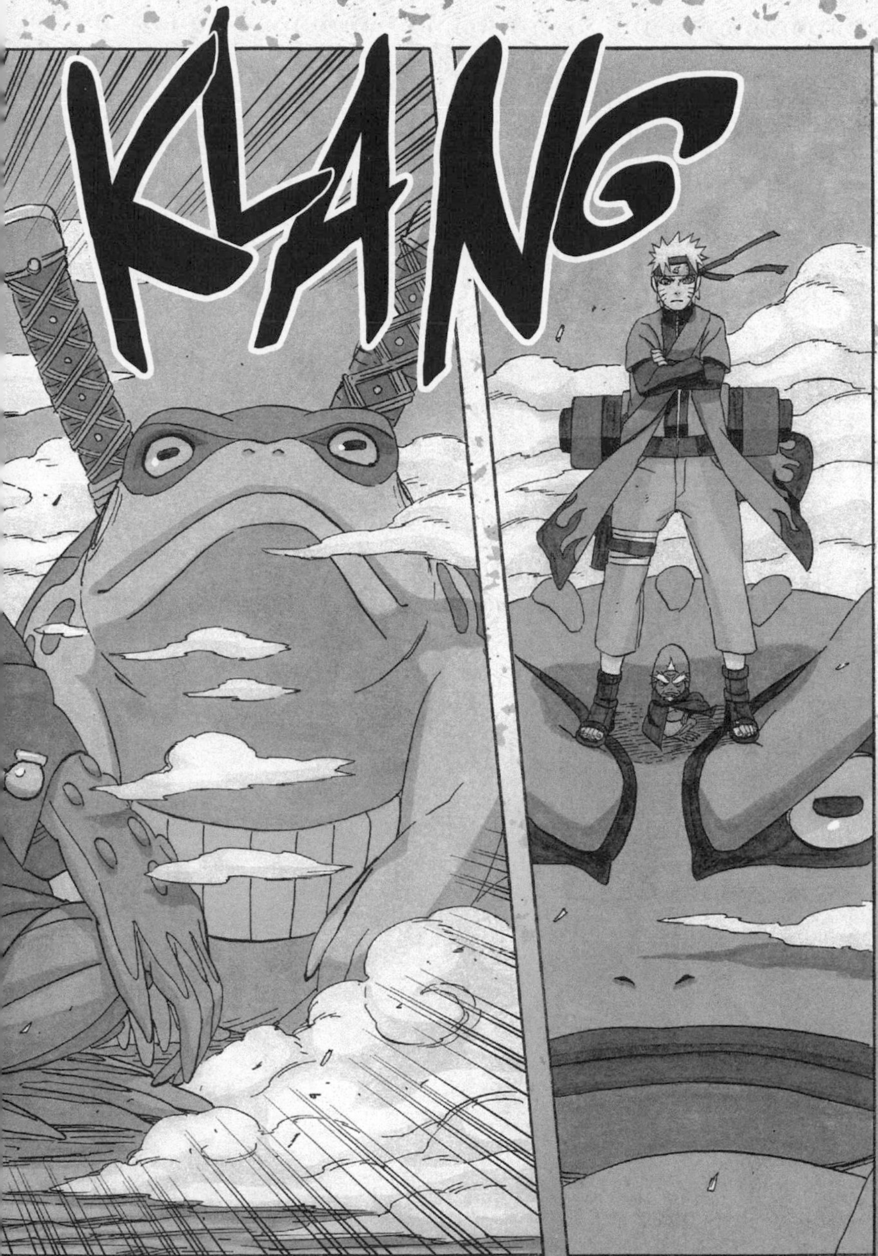
KLANG

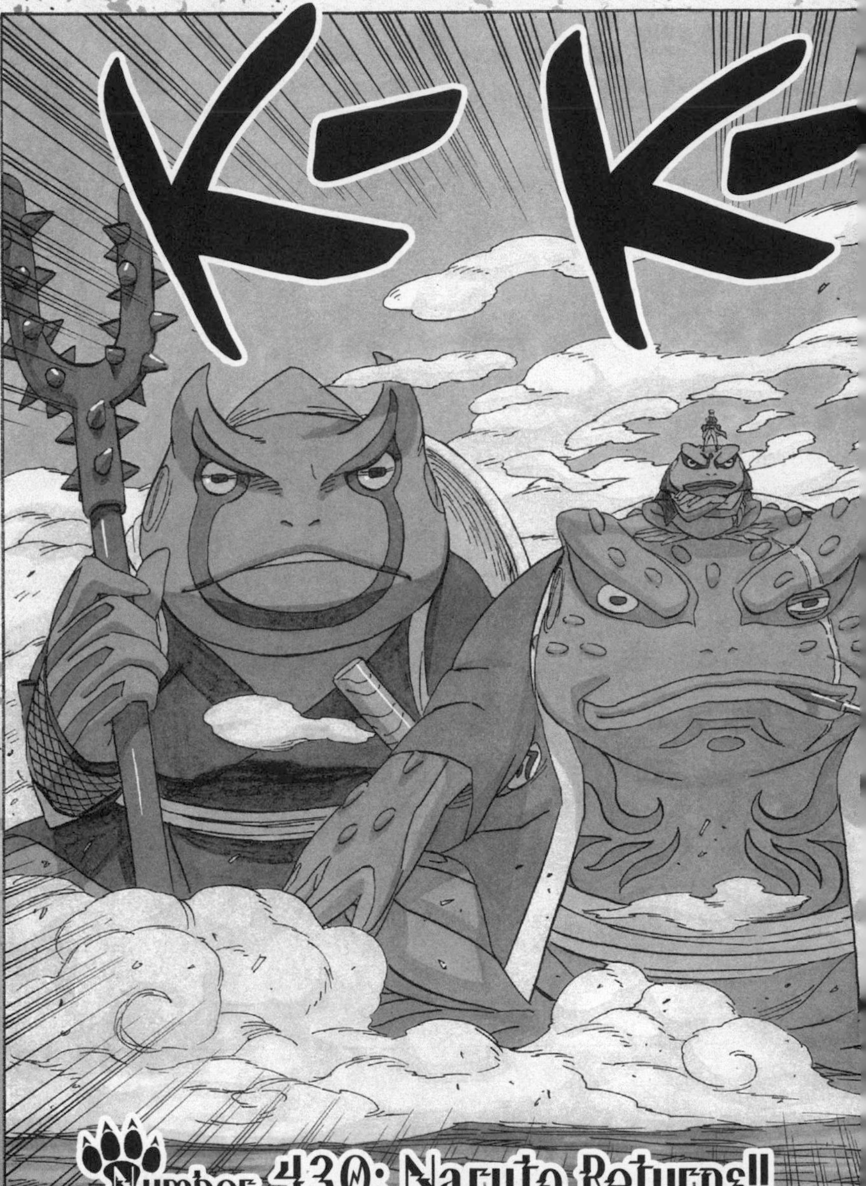
K-K
Number 430: Naruto Returns!!

NARUTO

火

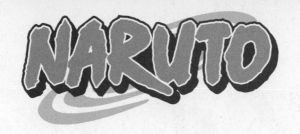

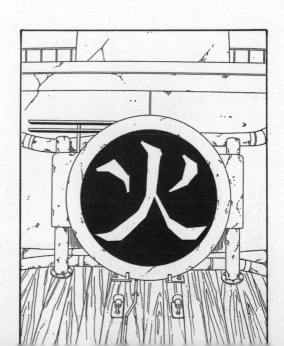

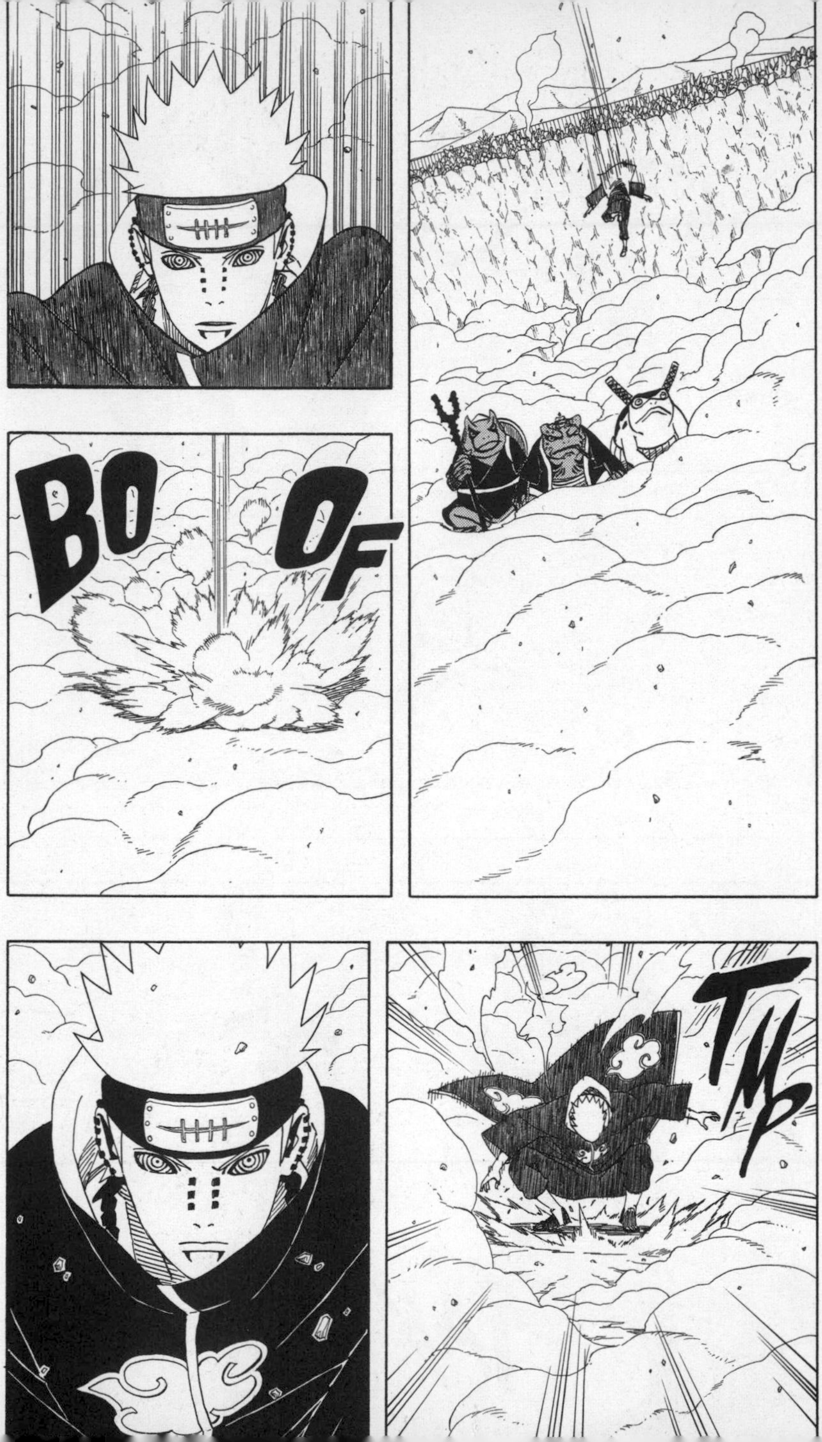
BOOF
TMP

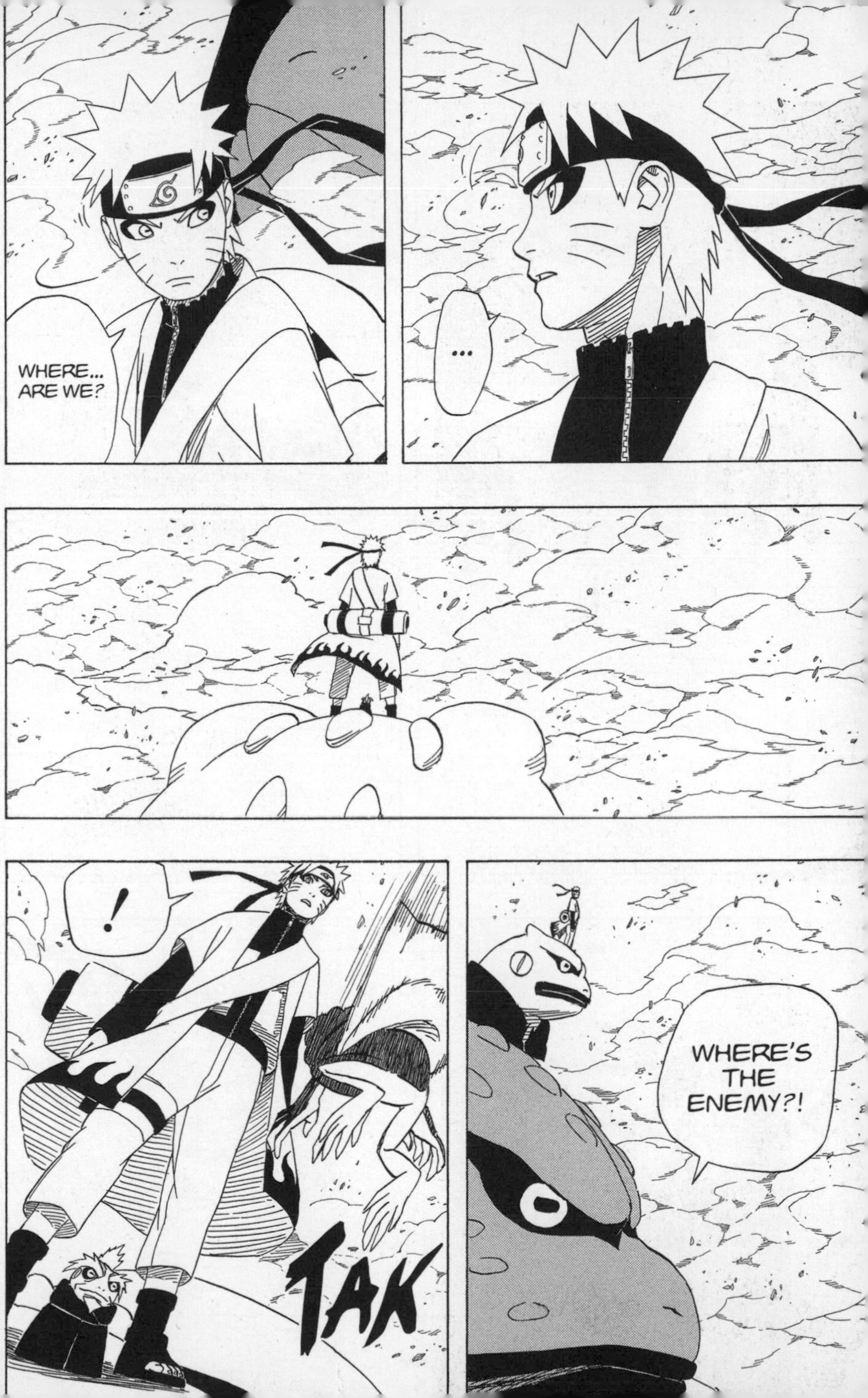
...
WHERE... ARE WE?
WHERE'S THE ENEMY?!
!
TAK

READ THIS WAY

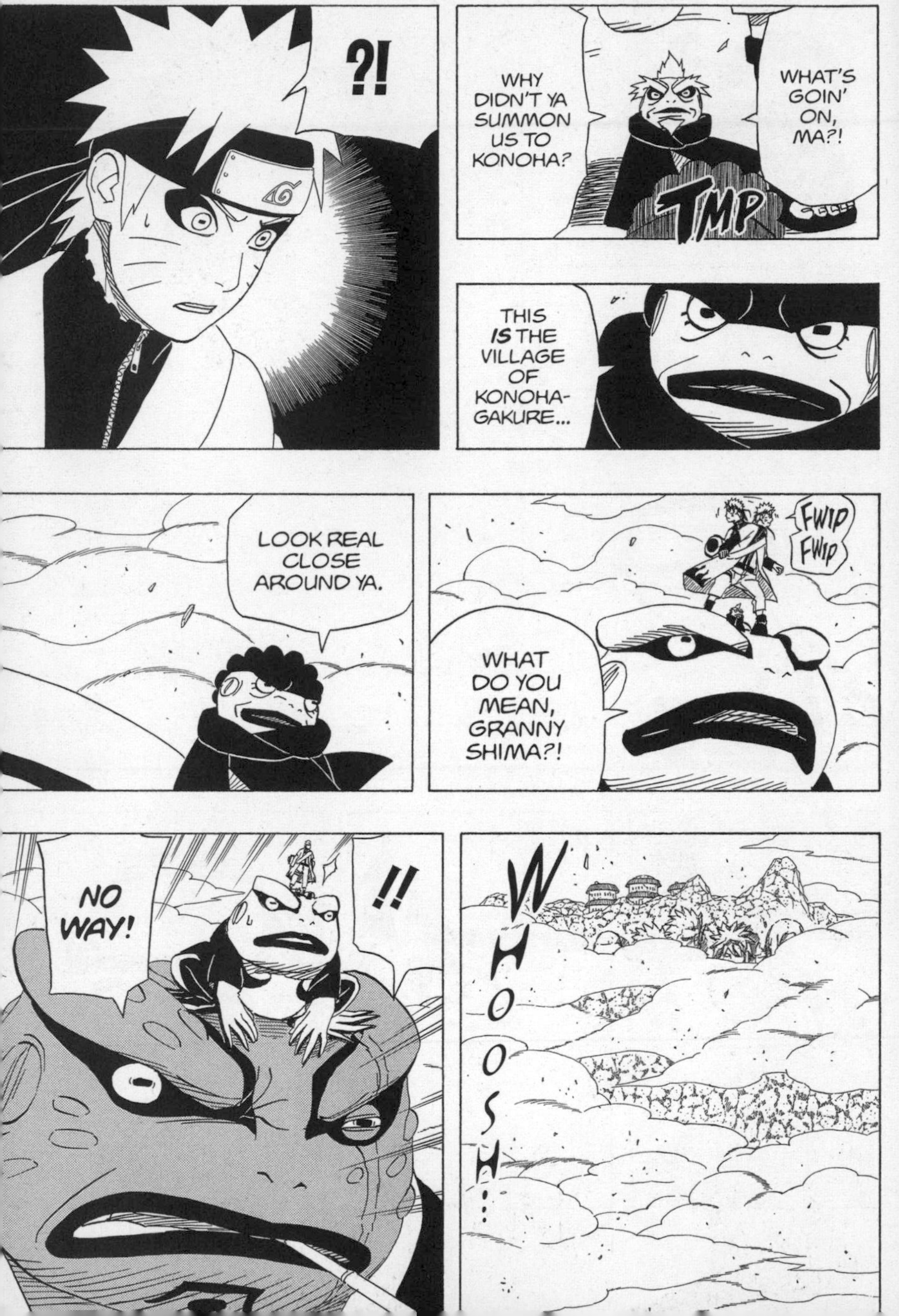
WHAT'S GOIN' ON, MA?!
WHY DIDN'T YA SUMMON US TO KONOHA?
TMP
THIS *IS* THE VILLAGE OF KONOHA-GAKURE...
?!
FWIP FWIP
WHAT DO YOU MEAN, GRANNY SHIMA?!
LOOK REAL CLOSE AROUND YA.
WHOOOSH...
!!
NO WAY!

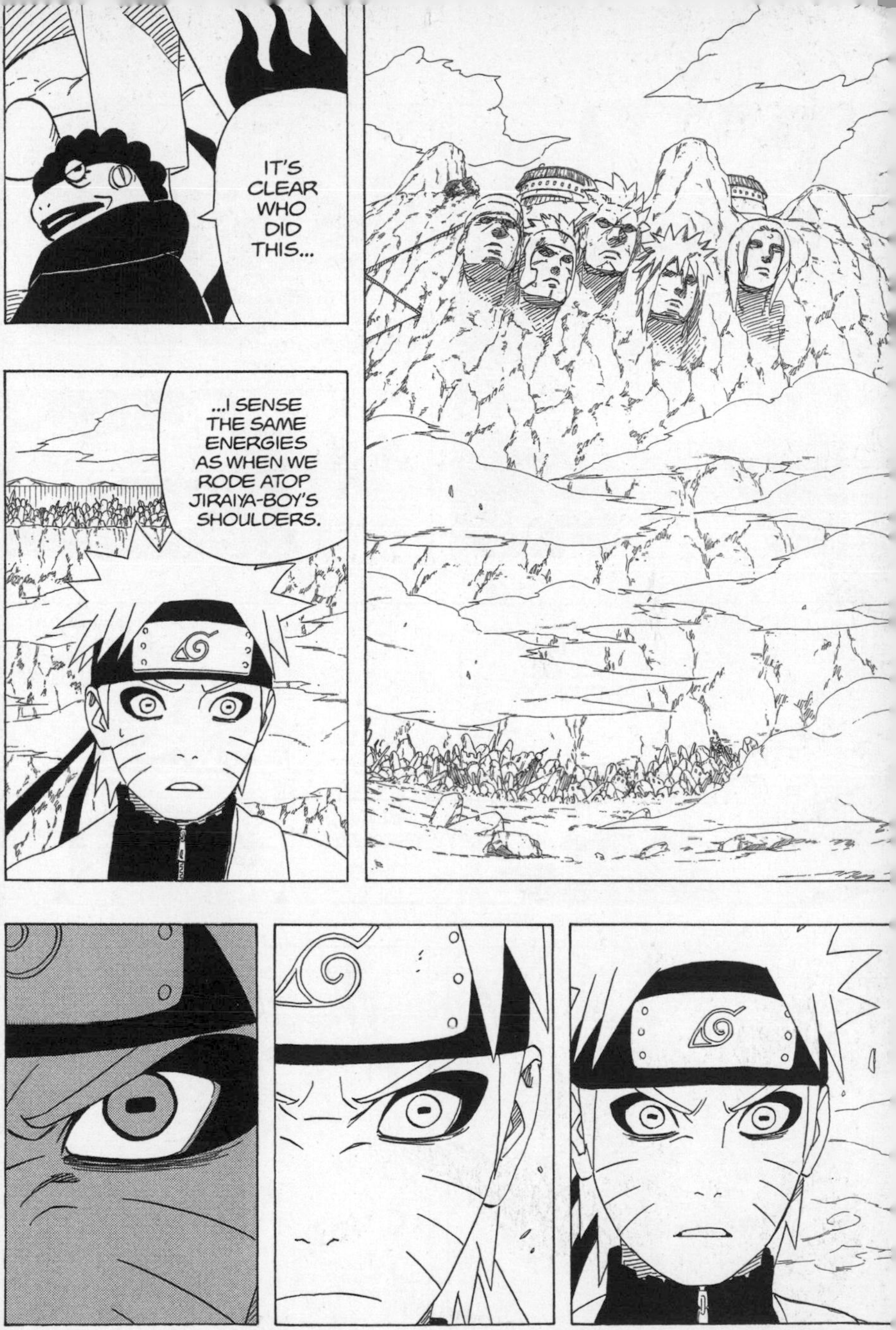
IT'S CLEAR WHO DID THIS...
...I SENSE THE SAME ENERGIES AS WHEN WE RODE ATOP JIRAIYA-BOY'S SHOULDERS.

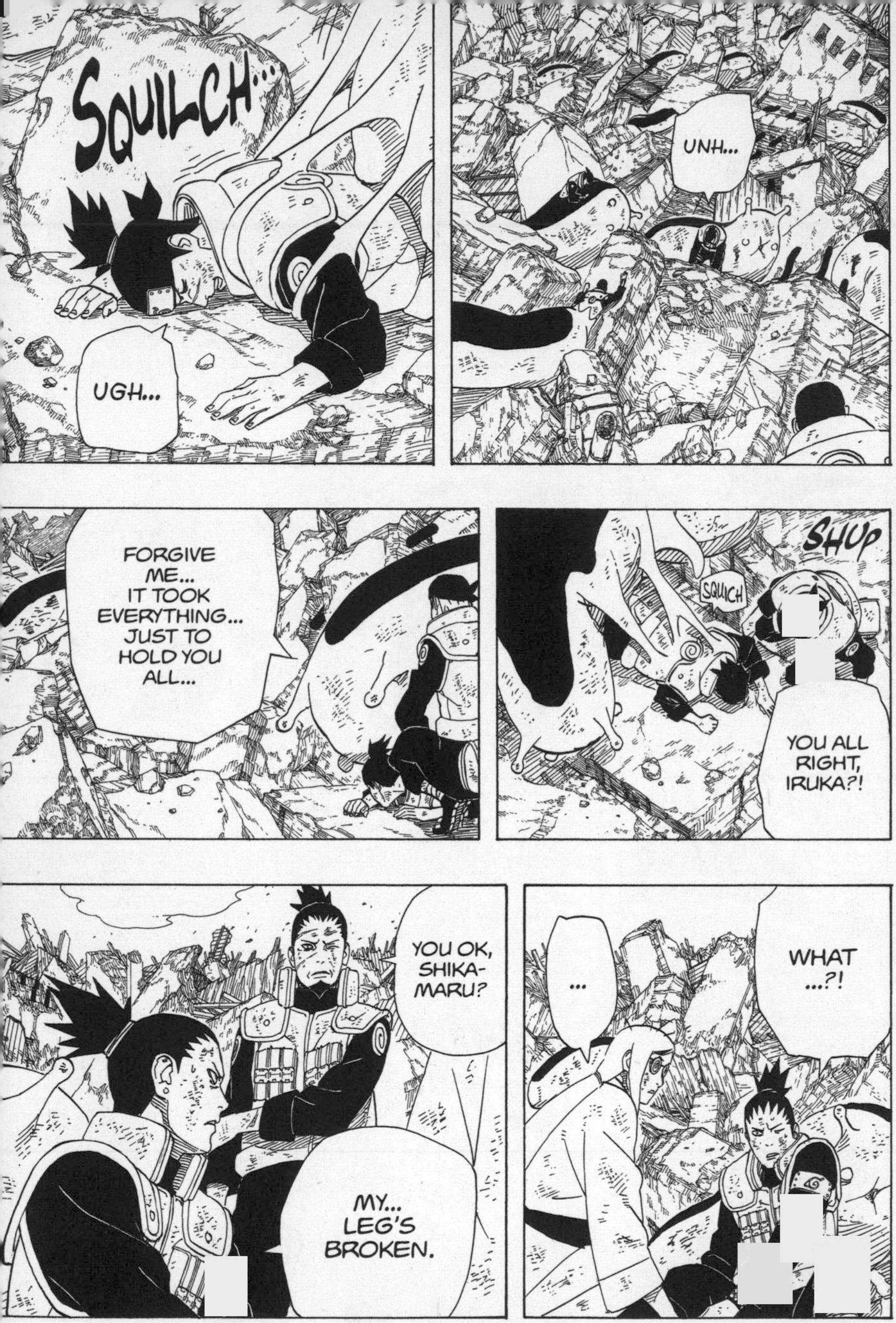
UNH...
SQUILCH...
UGH...
SHUP
SQUICH
YOU ALL RIGHT, IRUKA?!
FORGIVE ME... IT TOOK EVERYTHING... JUST TO HOLD YOU ALL...
WHAT ...?!
...
YOU OK, SHIKA-MARU?
MY... LEG'S BROKEN.

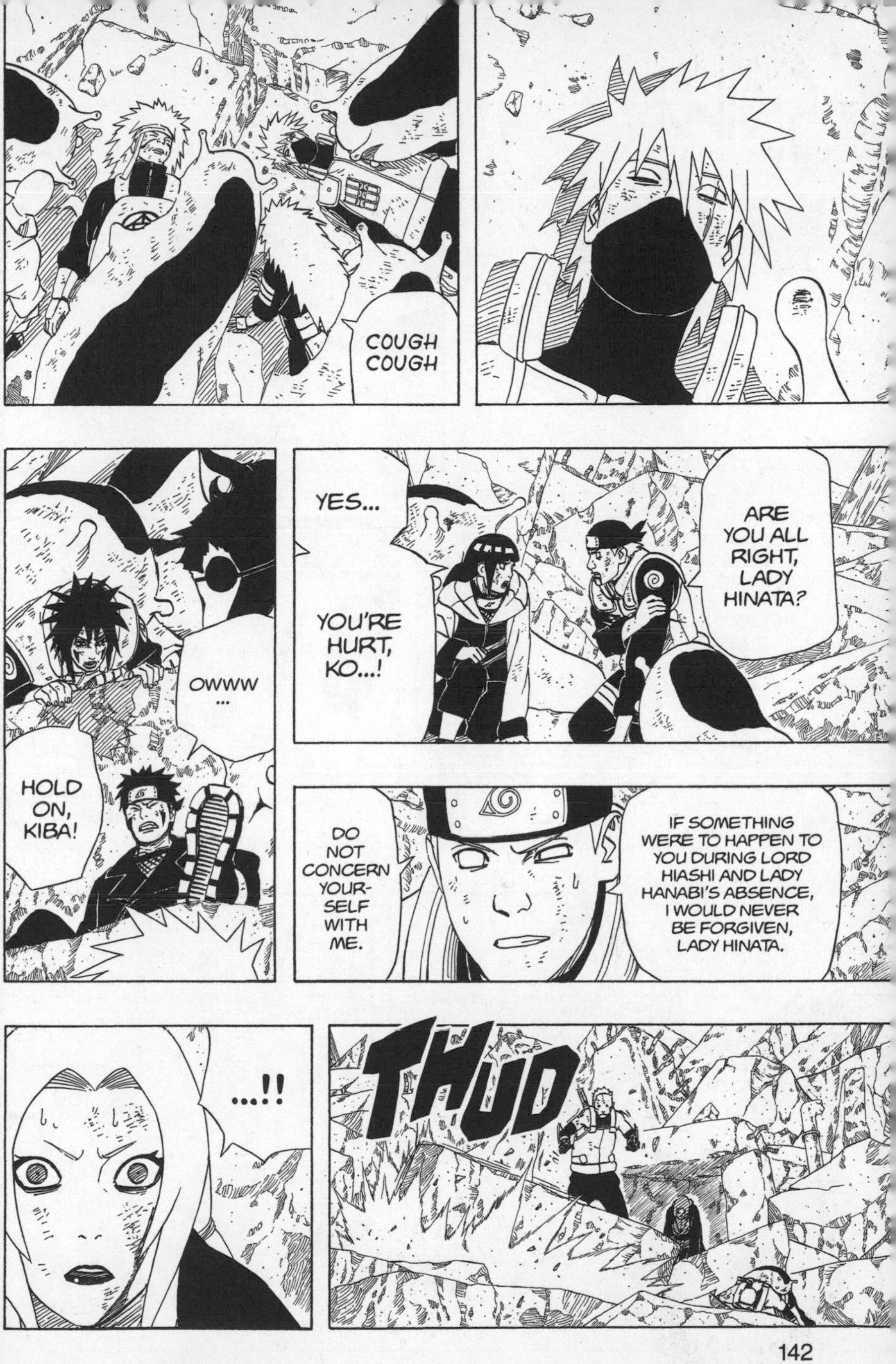
COUGH COUGH
ARE YOU ALL RIGHT, LADY HINATA?
YES...
YOU'RE HURT, KO...!
IF SOMETHING WERE TO HAPPEN TO YOU DURING LORD HIASHI AND LADY HANABI'S ABSENCE, I WOULD NEVER BE FORGIVEN, LADY HINATA.
DO NOT CONCERN YOUR-SELF WITH ME.
OWWW...
HOLD ON, KIBA!
THUD
...!!

READ THIS WAY

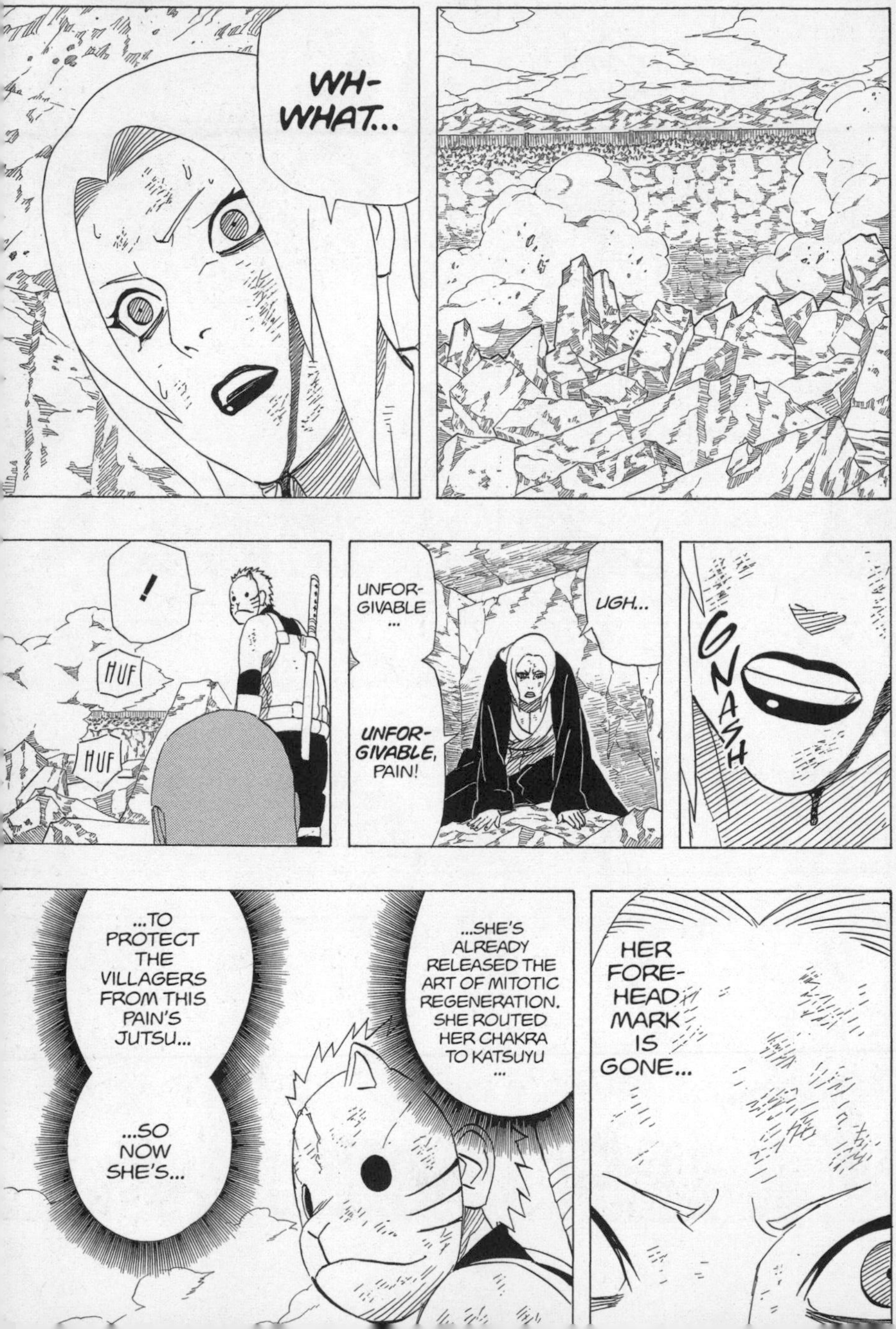

WH-WHAT...
GNASH
UGH...
UNFORGIVABLE...
UNFORGIVABLE, PAIN!
!
HUF
HUF
HER FOREHEAD MARK IS GONE...
...SHE'S ALREADY RELEASED THE ART OF MITOTIC REGENERATION. SHE ROUTED HER CHAKRA TO KATSUYU...
...TO PROTECT THE VILLAGERS FROM THIS PAIN'S JUTSU...
...SO NOW SHE'S...

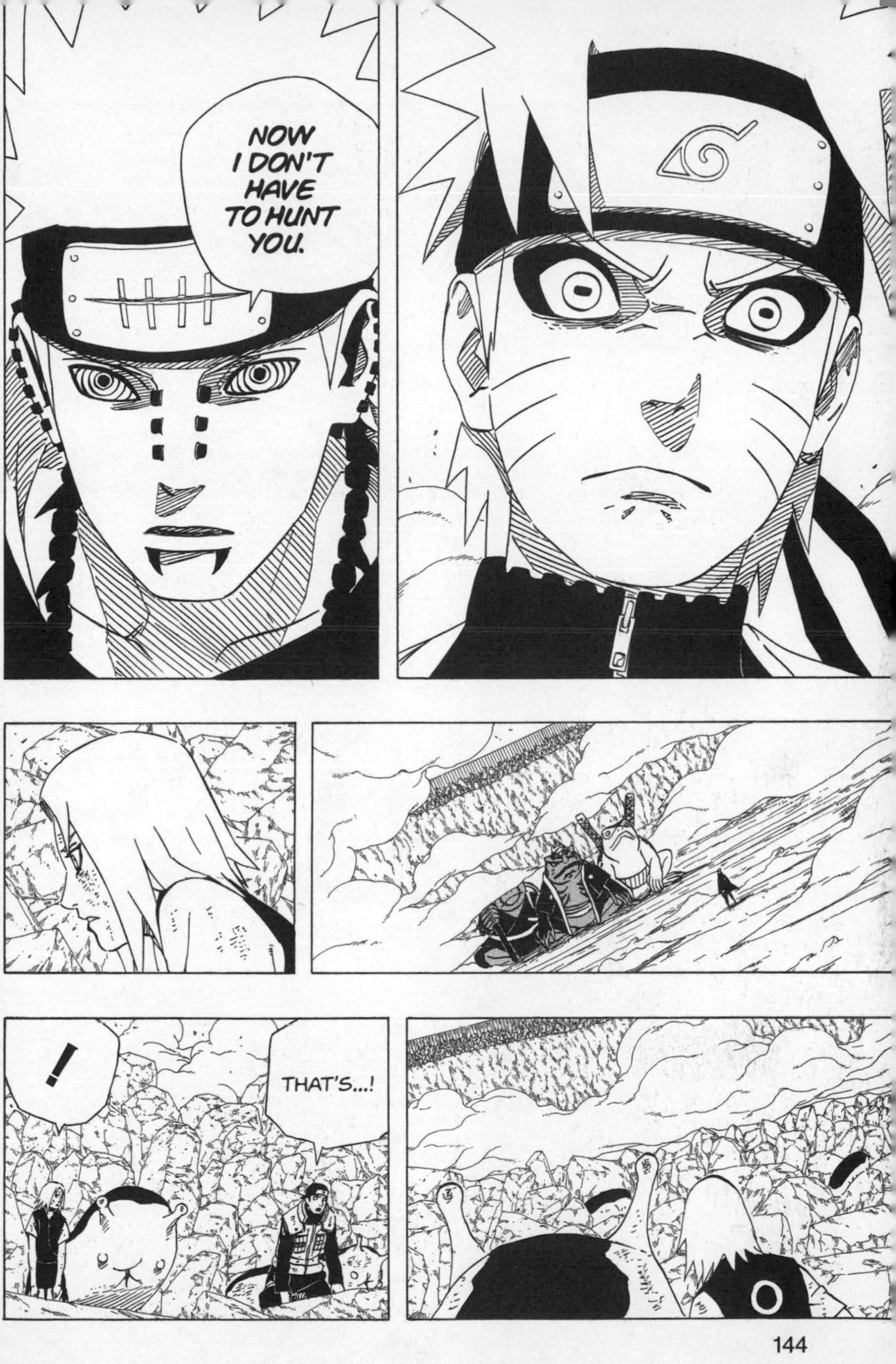
NOW I DON'T HAVE TO HUNT YOU.
THAT'S...!
!

READ THIS WAY

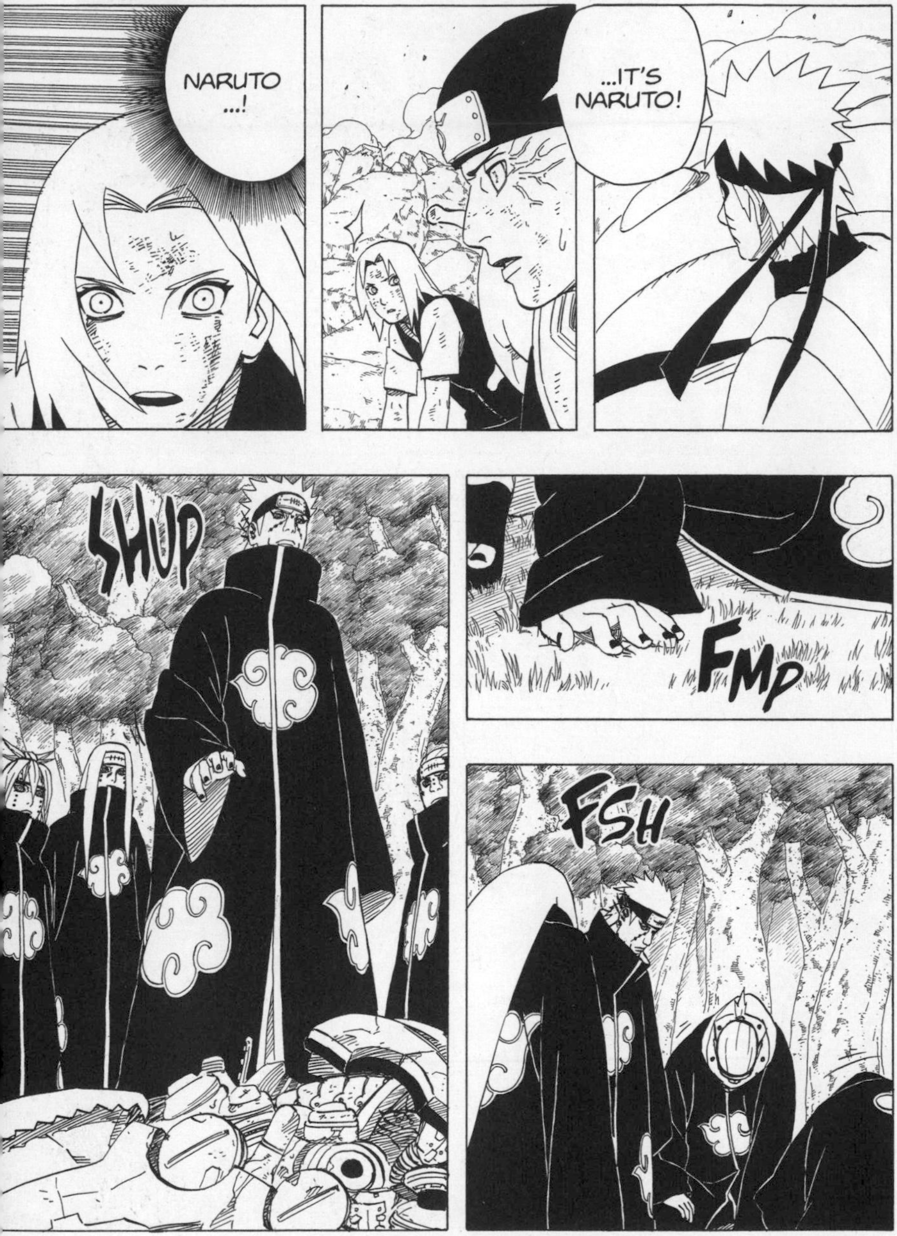
...IT'S NARUTO!
NARUTO ...!
FMP
FSH
SHUP

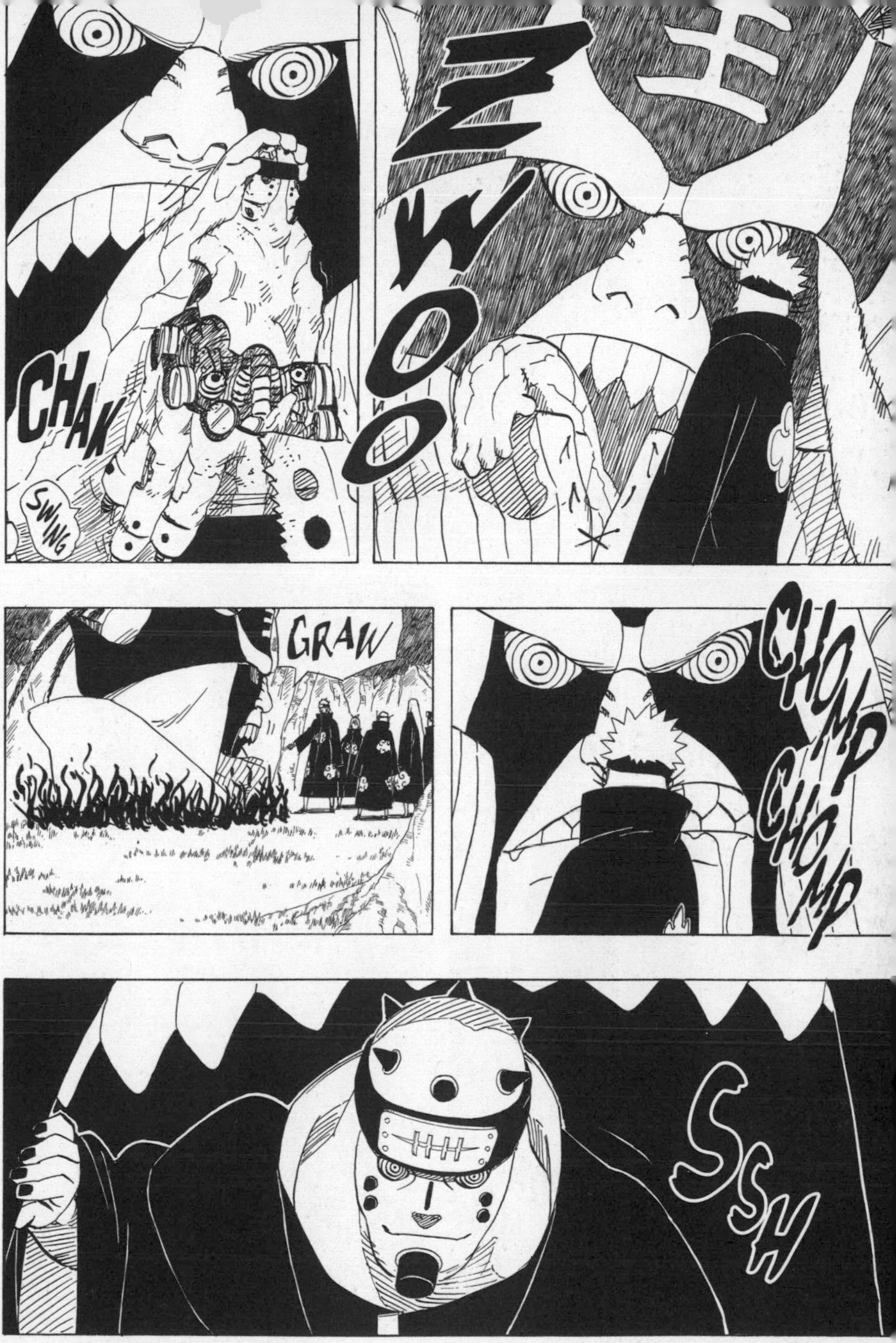
CHAK
SWING
CHOMP
CHOMP
CHOMP
GRAW
SSH

READ THIS WAY

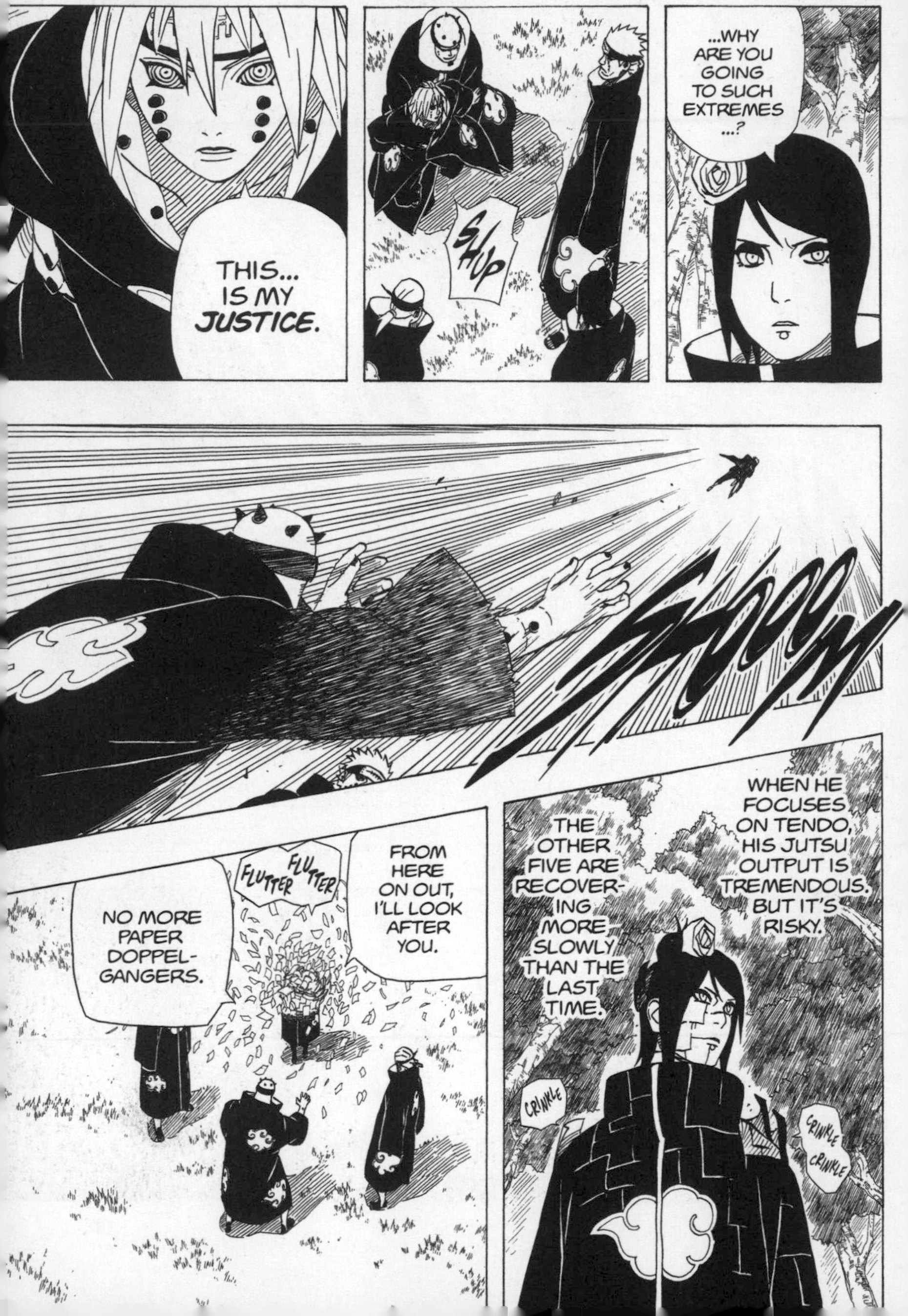
...WHY ARE YOU GOING TO SUCH EXTREMES ...?
SHUP
THIS... IS MY JUSTICE.
WHEN HE FOCUSES ON TENDO, HIS JUTSU OUTPUT IS TREMENDOUS. BUT IT'S RISKY.
THE OTHER FIVE ARE RECOVER-ING MORE SLOWLY THAN THE LAST TIME.
CRINKLE
CRINKLE
CRINKLE
FROM HERE ON OUT, I'LL LOOK AFTER YOU.
FLUTTER FLUTTER
NO MORE PAPER DOPPEL-GANGERS.

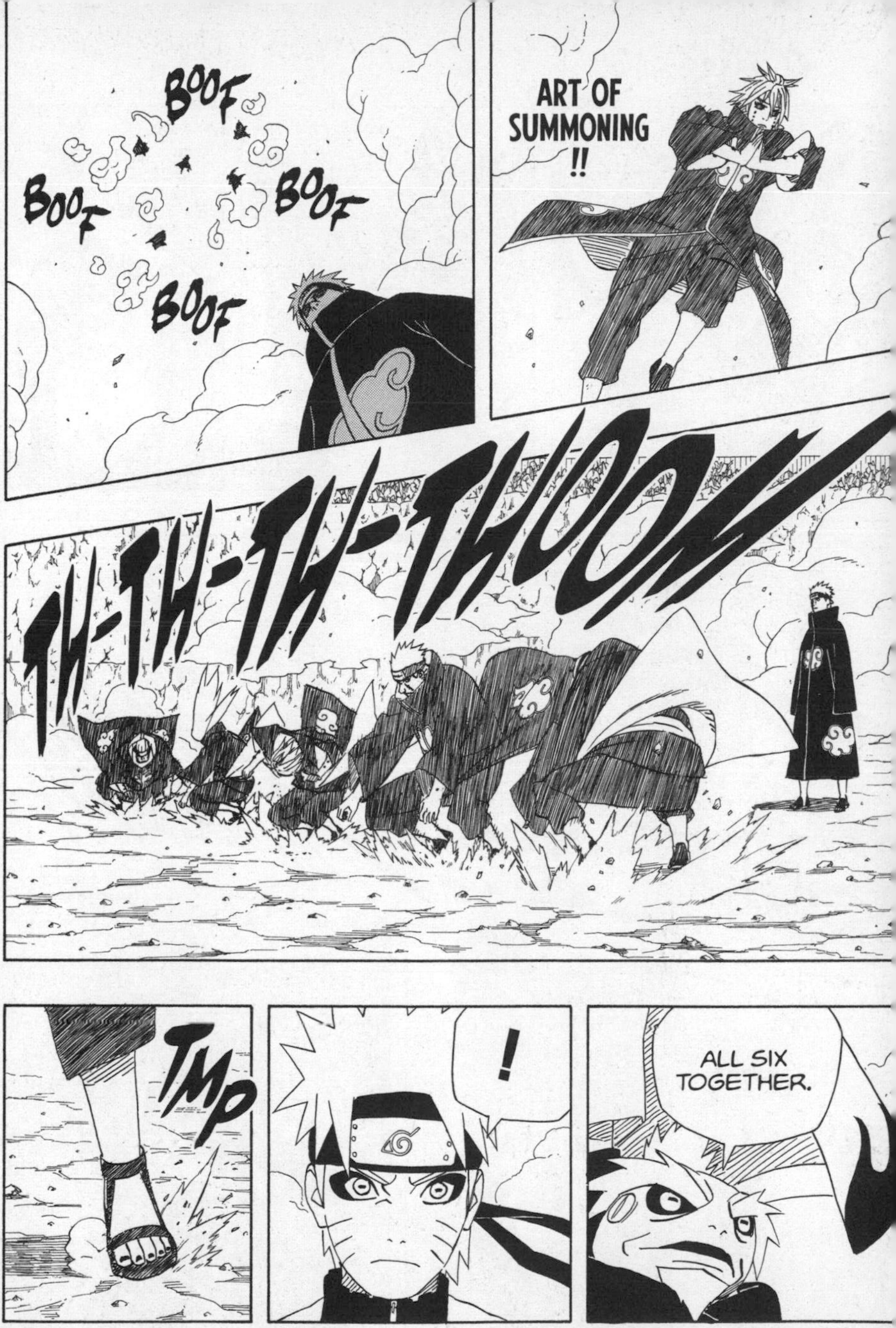
ART OF SUMMONING !!
BOOF
BOOF
BOOF
BOOF
TH-TH-TH-THOOM
ALL SIX TOGETHER.
!
TMP

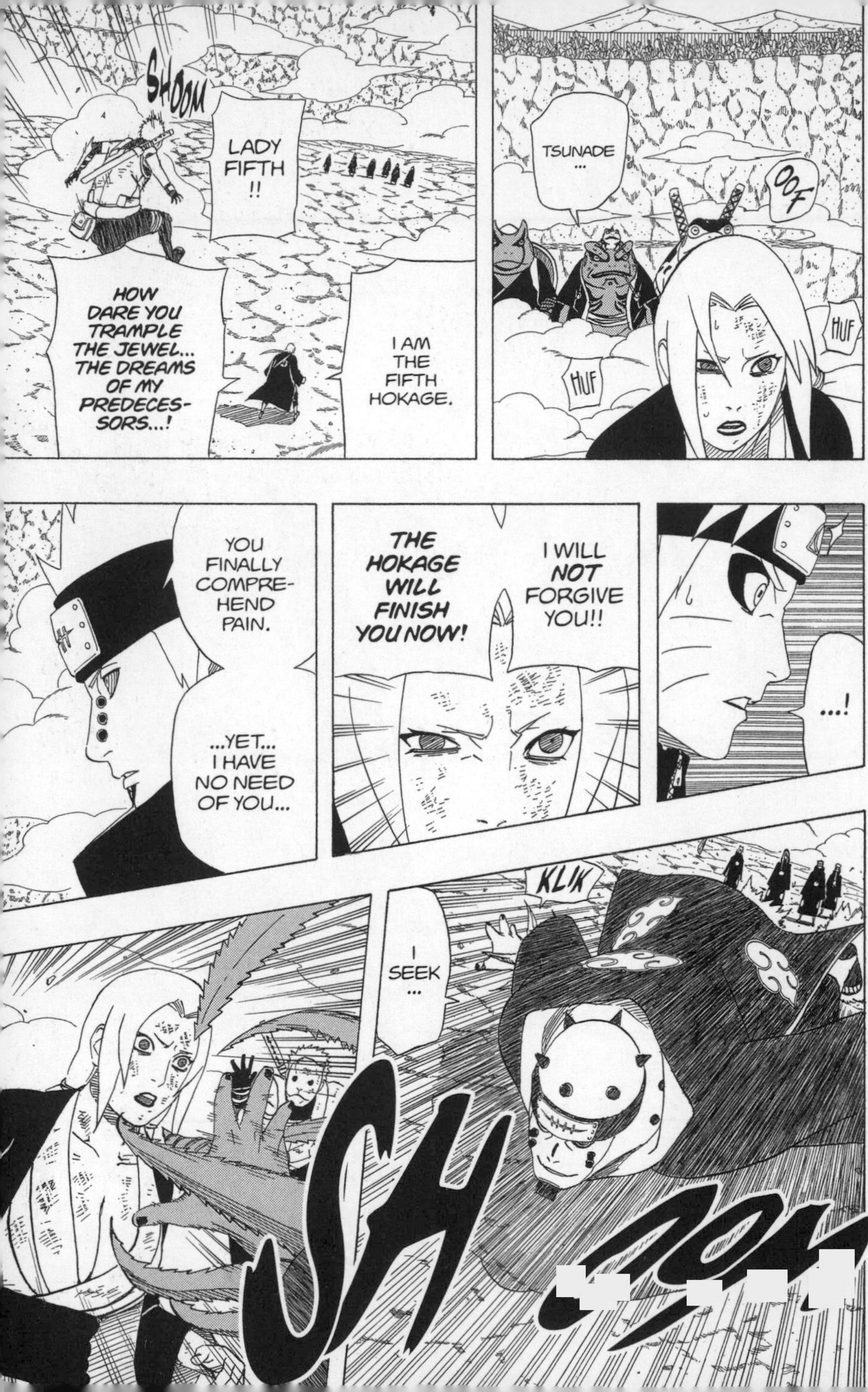
TSUNADE ...
OOF
HUF
HUF
LADY FIFTH !!
SHOOM
I AM THE FIFTH HOKAGE.
HOW DARE YOU TRAMPLE THE JEWEL... THE DREAMS OF MY PREDECES-SORS...!
...!
I WILL NOT FORGIVE YOU!!
THE HOKAGE WILL FINISH YOU NOW!
YOU FINALLY COMPRE-HEND PAIN.
...YET... I HAVE NO NEED OF YOU...
KLIK
I SEEK ...

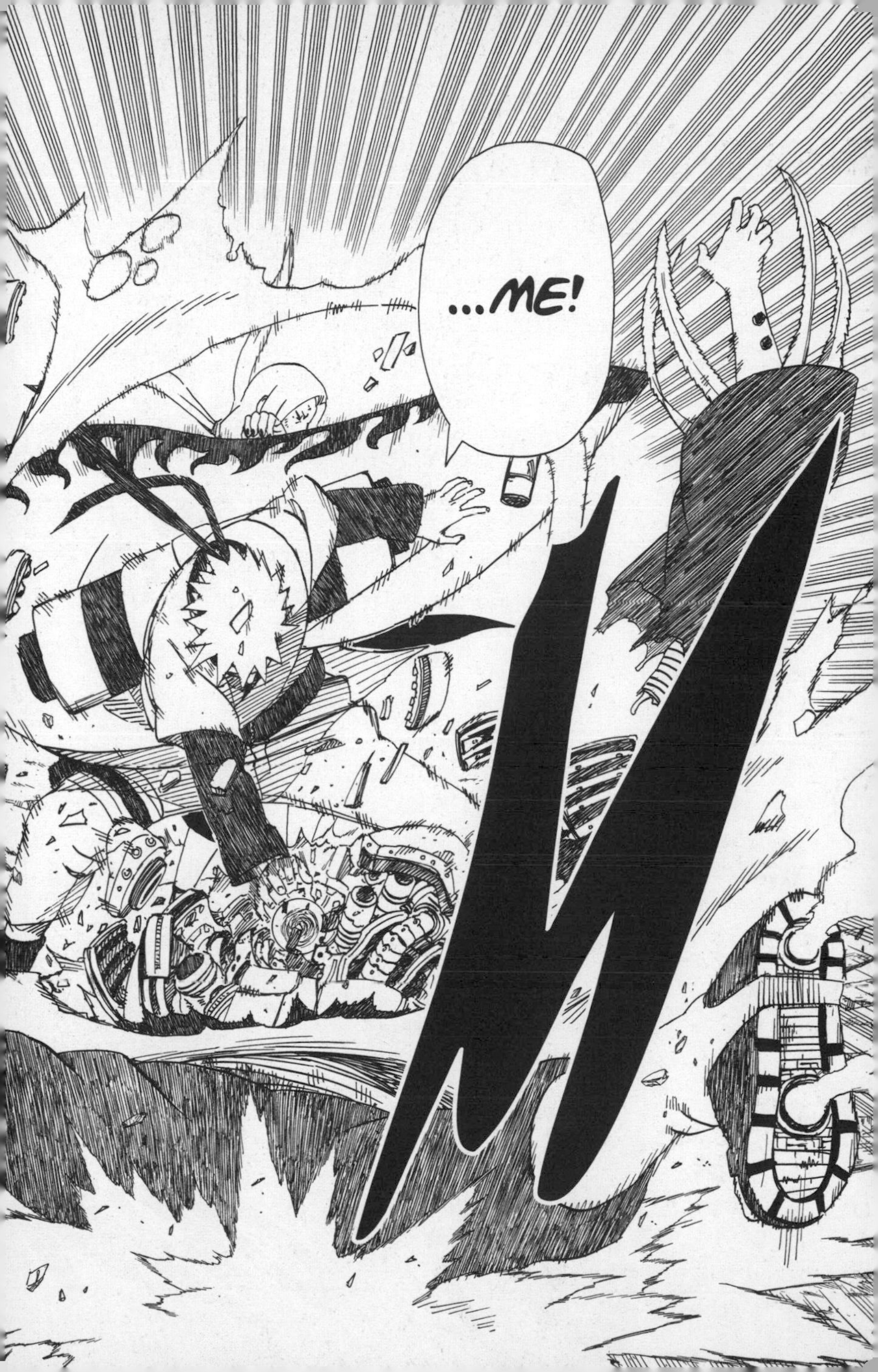
...ME!

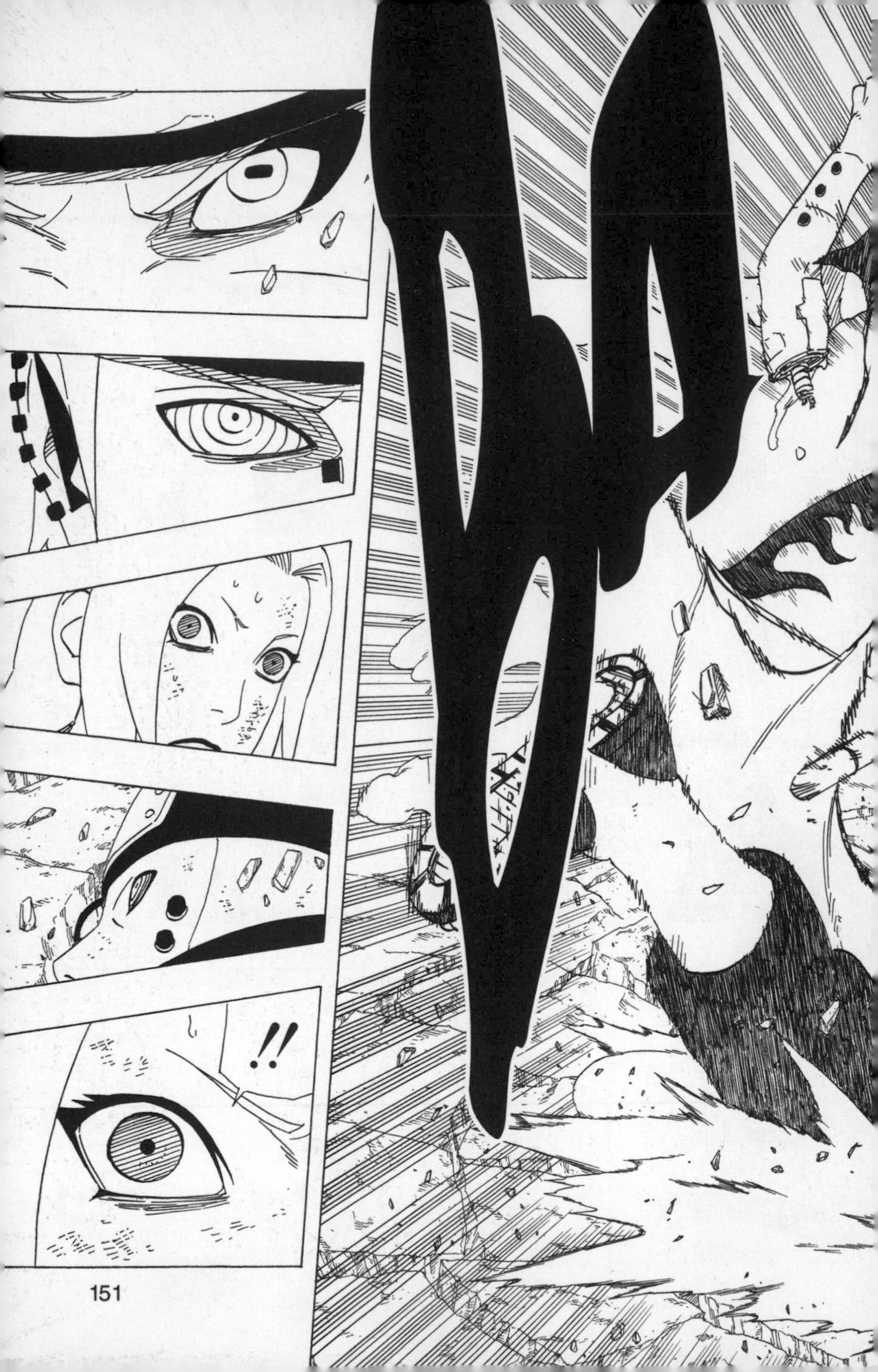
!!

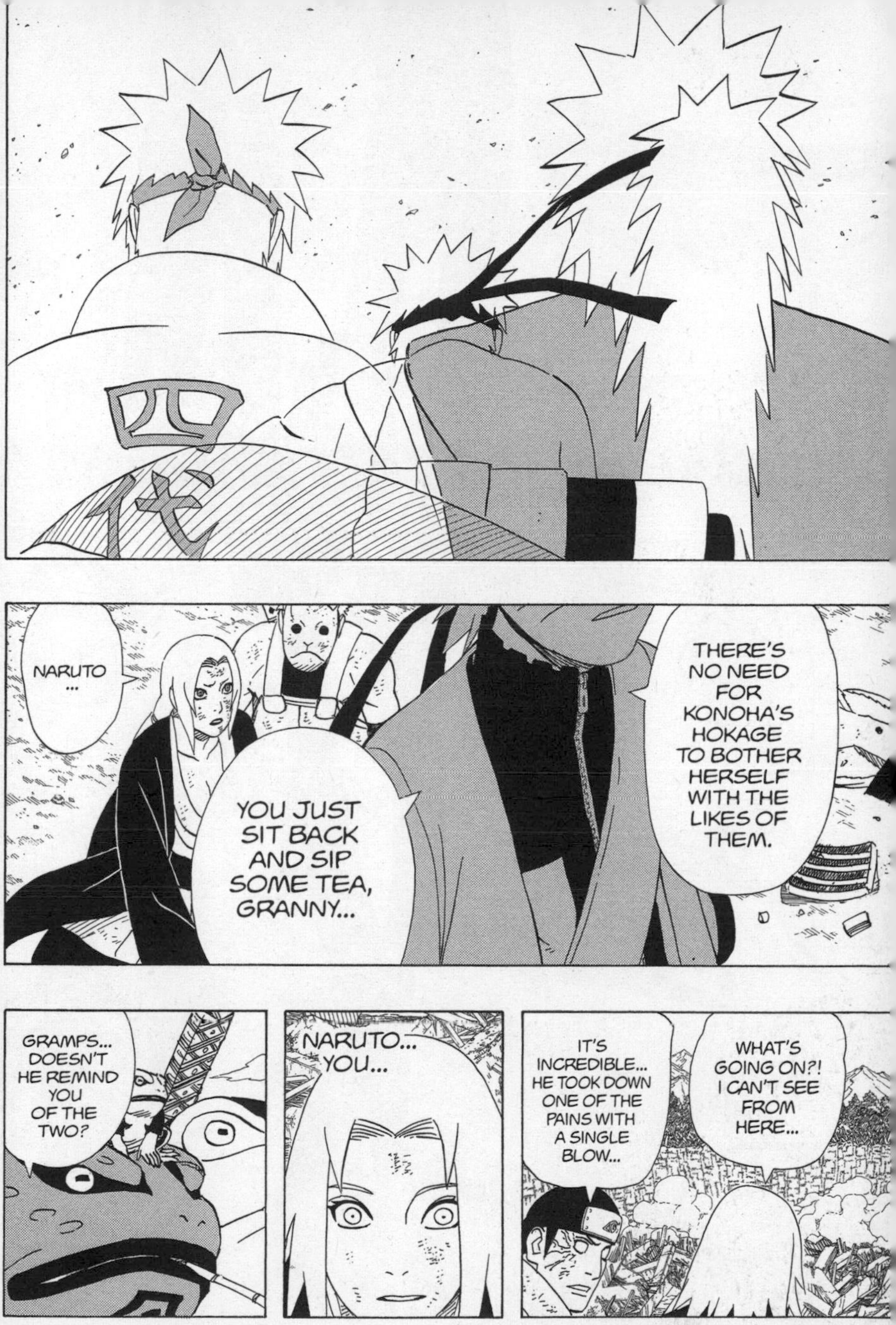
THERE'S NO NEED FOR KONOHA'S HOKAGE TO BOTHER HERSELF WITH THE LIKES OF THEM.
YOU JUST SIT BACK AND SIP SOME TEA, GRANNY...
NARUTO ...
WHAT'S GOING ON?! I CAN'T SEE FROM HERE...
IT'S INCREDIBLE... HE TOOK DOWN ONE OF THE PAINS WITH A SINGLE BLOW...
NARUTO... YOU...
GRAMPS... DOESN'T HE REMIND YOU OF THE TWO?

READ THIS WAY

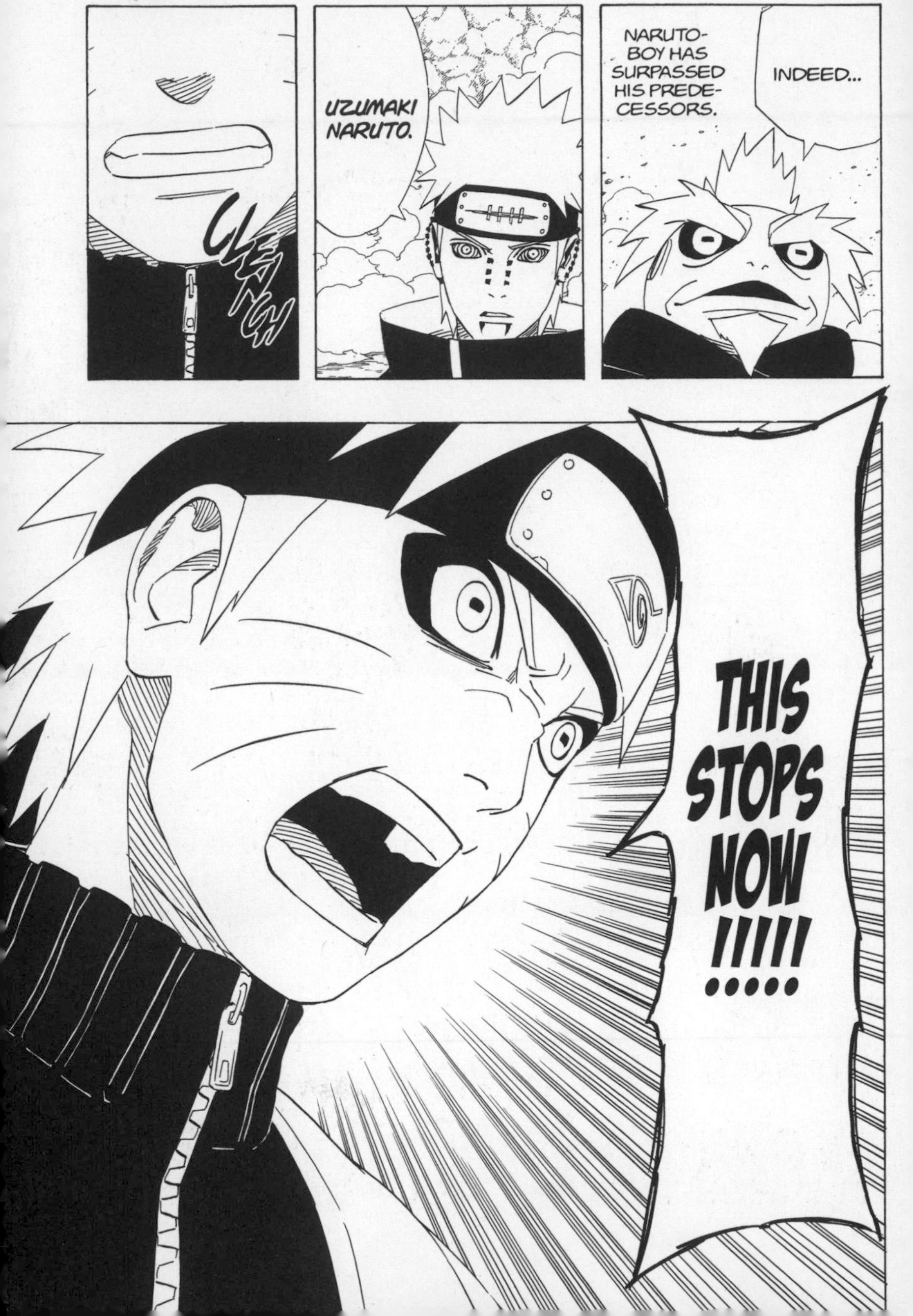
INDEED...
NARUTO-BOY HAS SURPASSED HIS PREDECESSORS.
UZUMAKI NARUTO.
CLENCH
THIS STOPS NOW!!!!!

NARUTO

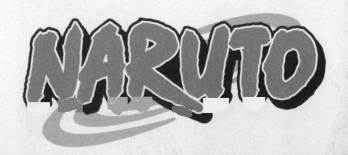

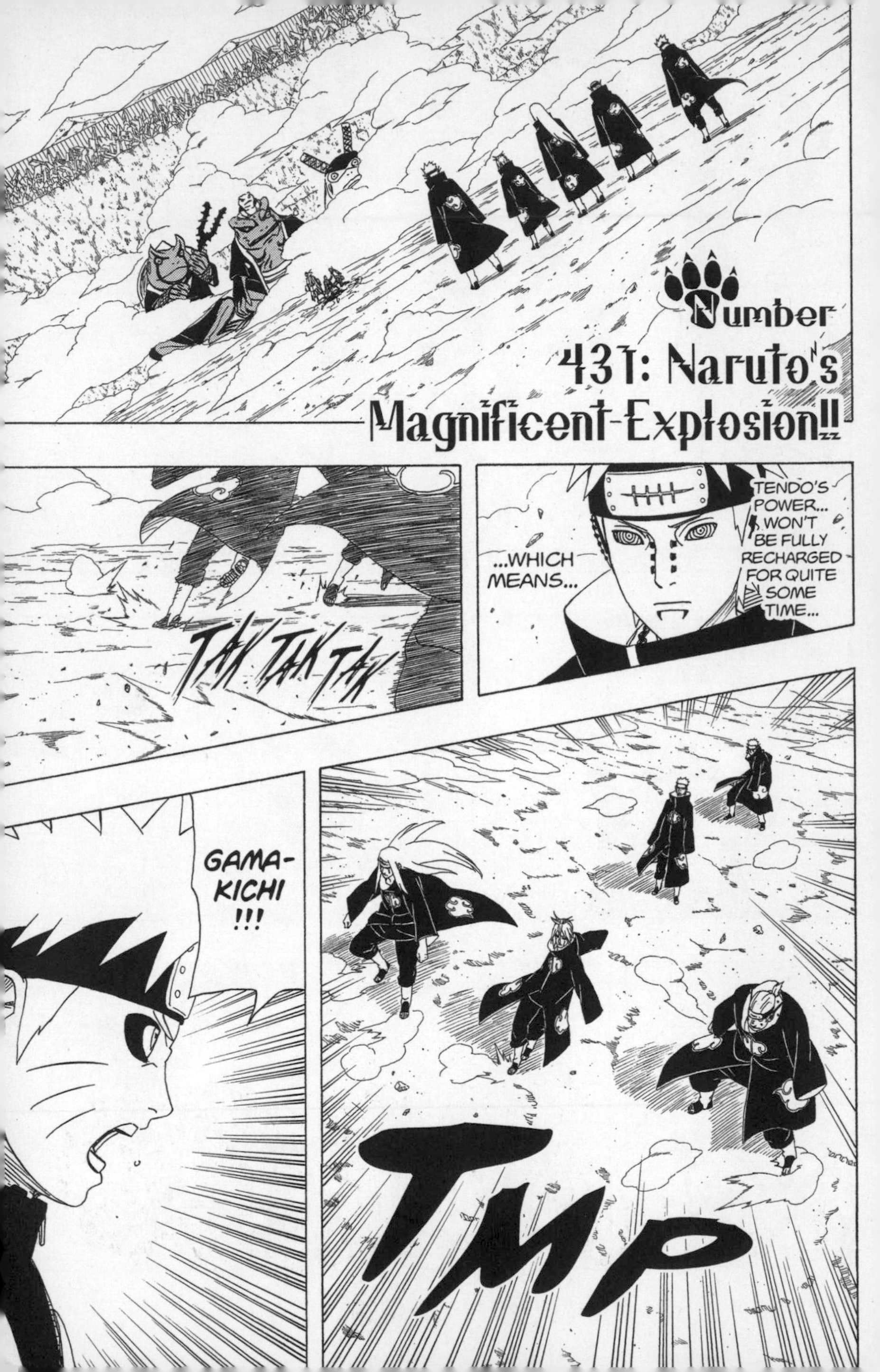
Number 431: Naruto's Magnificent Explosion!!
TENDO'S POWER... WON'T BE FULLY RECHARGED FOR QUITE SOME TIME...
...WHICH MEANS...
TAK TAK TAK
TMP
GAMA-KICHI !!!

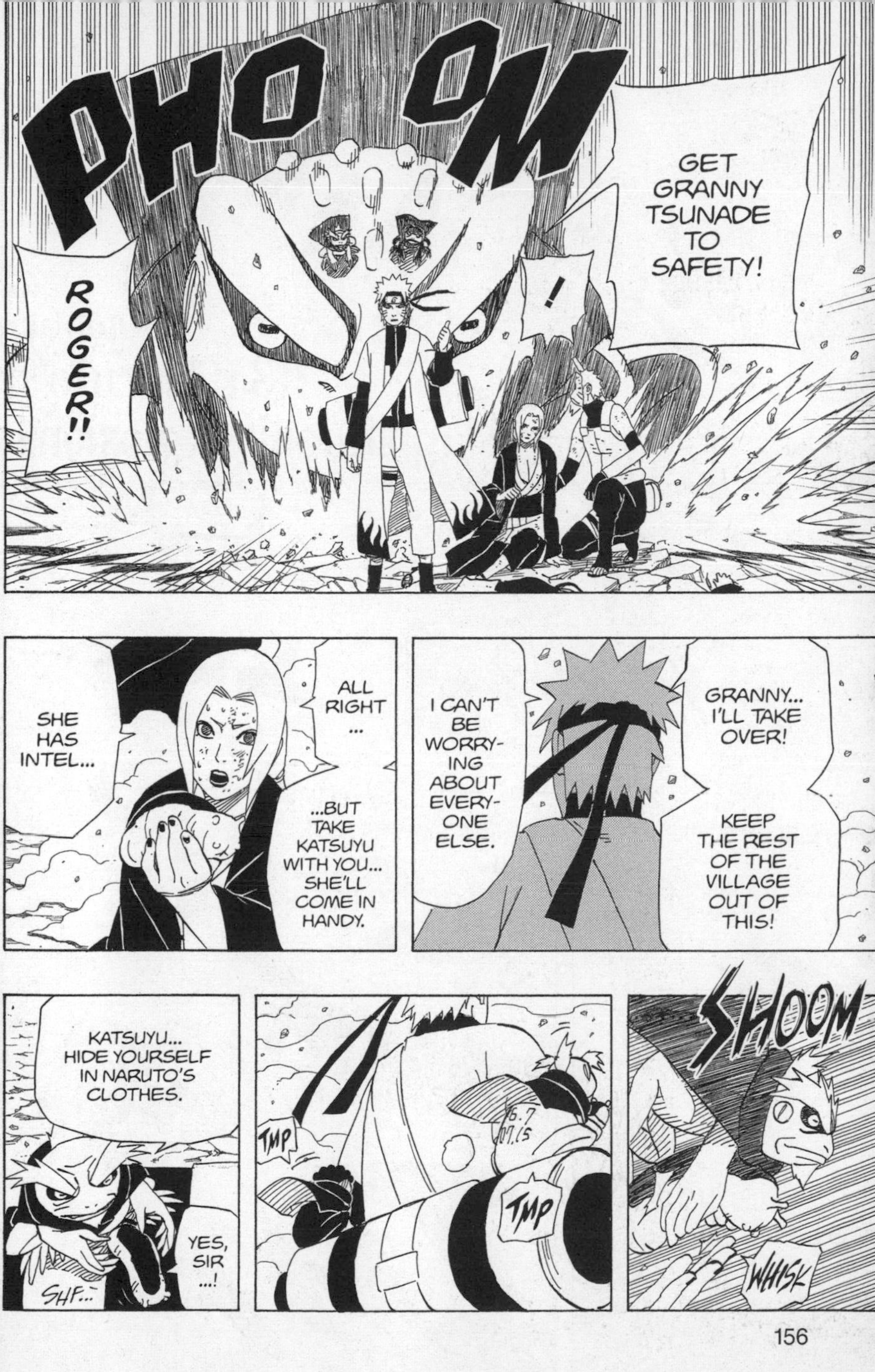
GET GRANNY TSUNADE TO SAFETY!
!
PHOOM
ROGER!!
GRANNY... I'LL TAKE OVER!
KEEP THE REST OF THE VILLAGE OUT OF THIS!
I CAN'T BE WORRYING ABOUT EVERYONE ELSE.
ALL RIGHT ...
...BUT TAKE KATSUYU WITH YOU... SHE'LL COME IN HANDY.
SHE HAS INTEL...
SHOOM
WHISK
TMP
TMP
KATSUYU... HIDE YOURSELF IN NARUTO'S CLOTHES.
YES, SIR ...!
SHF...

READ THIS WAY

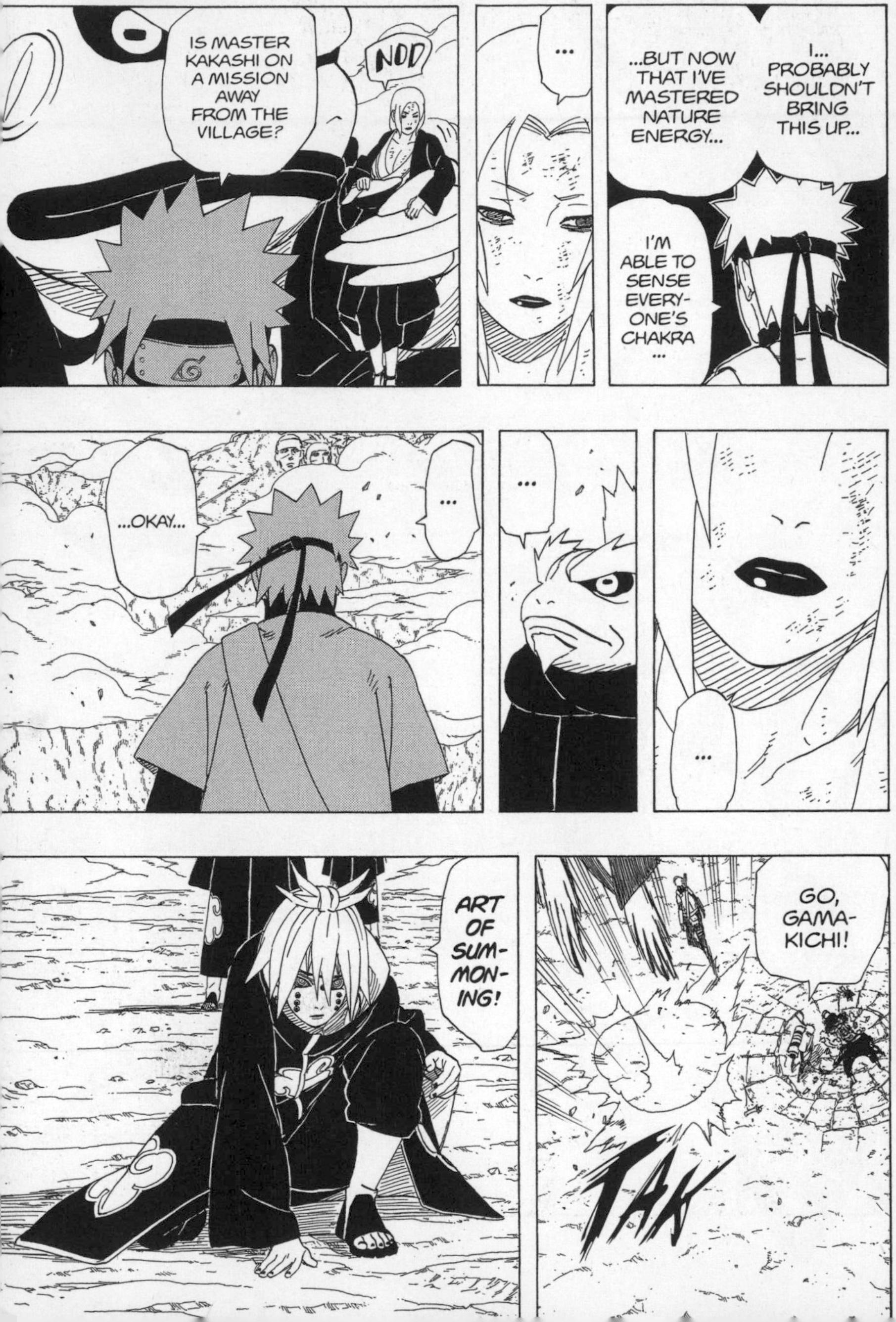
I... PROBABLY SHOULDN'T BRING THIS UP...
...BUT NOW THAT I'VE MASTERED NATURE ENERGY...
I'M ABLE TO SENSE EVERY-ONE'S CHAKRA ...
...
IS MASTER KAKASHI ON A MISSION AWAY FROM THE VILLAGE?
NOD
...
...
...
...OKAY...
GO, GAMA-KICHI!
TAK
ART OF SUM-MON-ING!

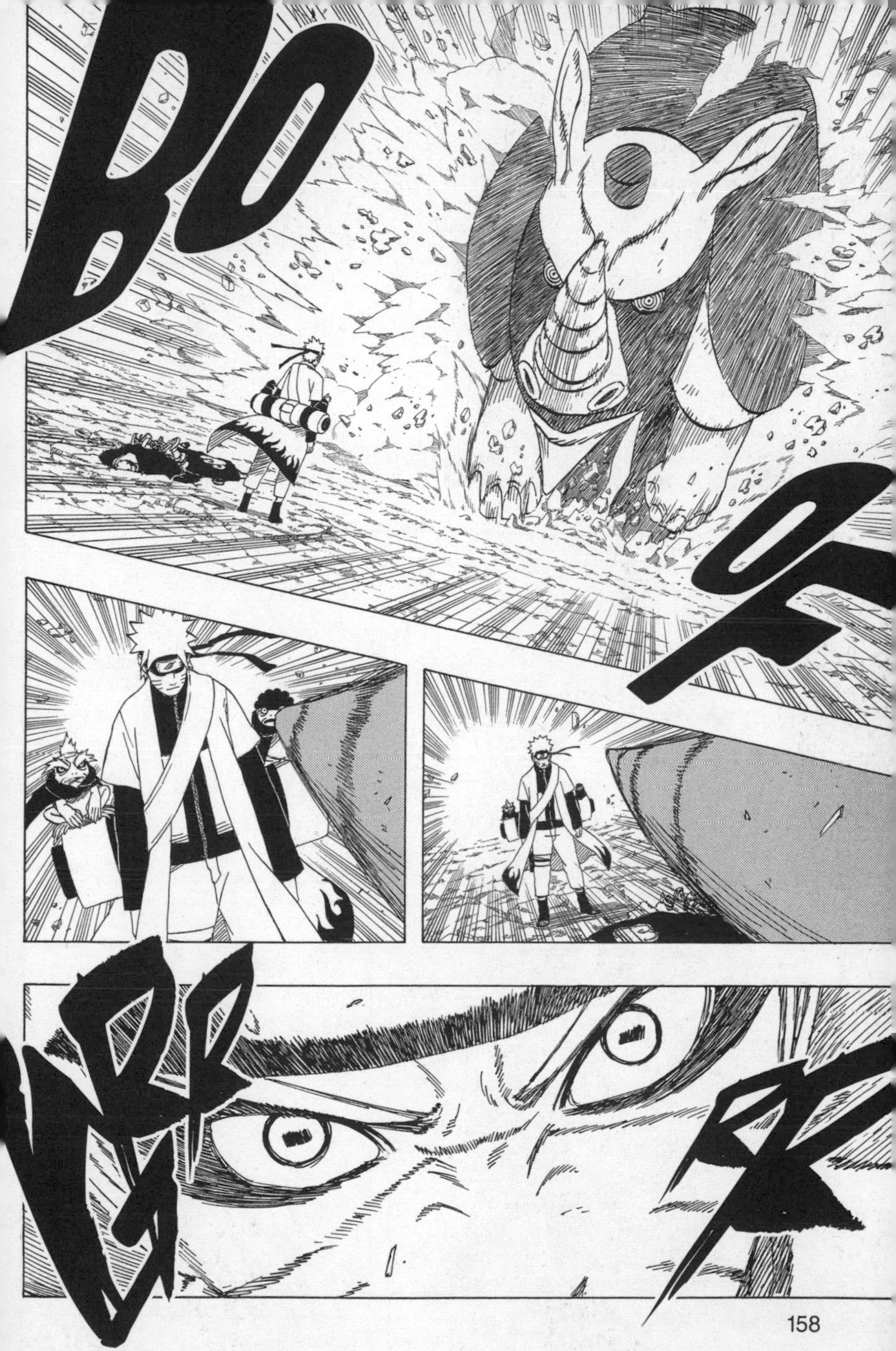
BOOF

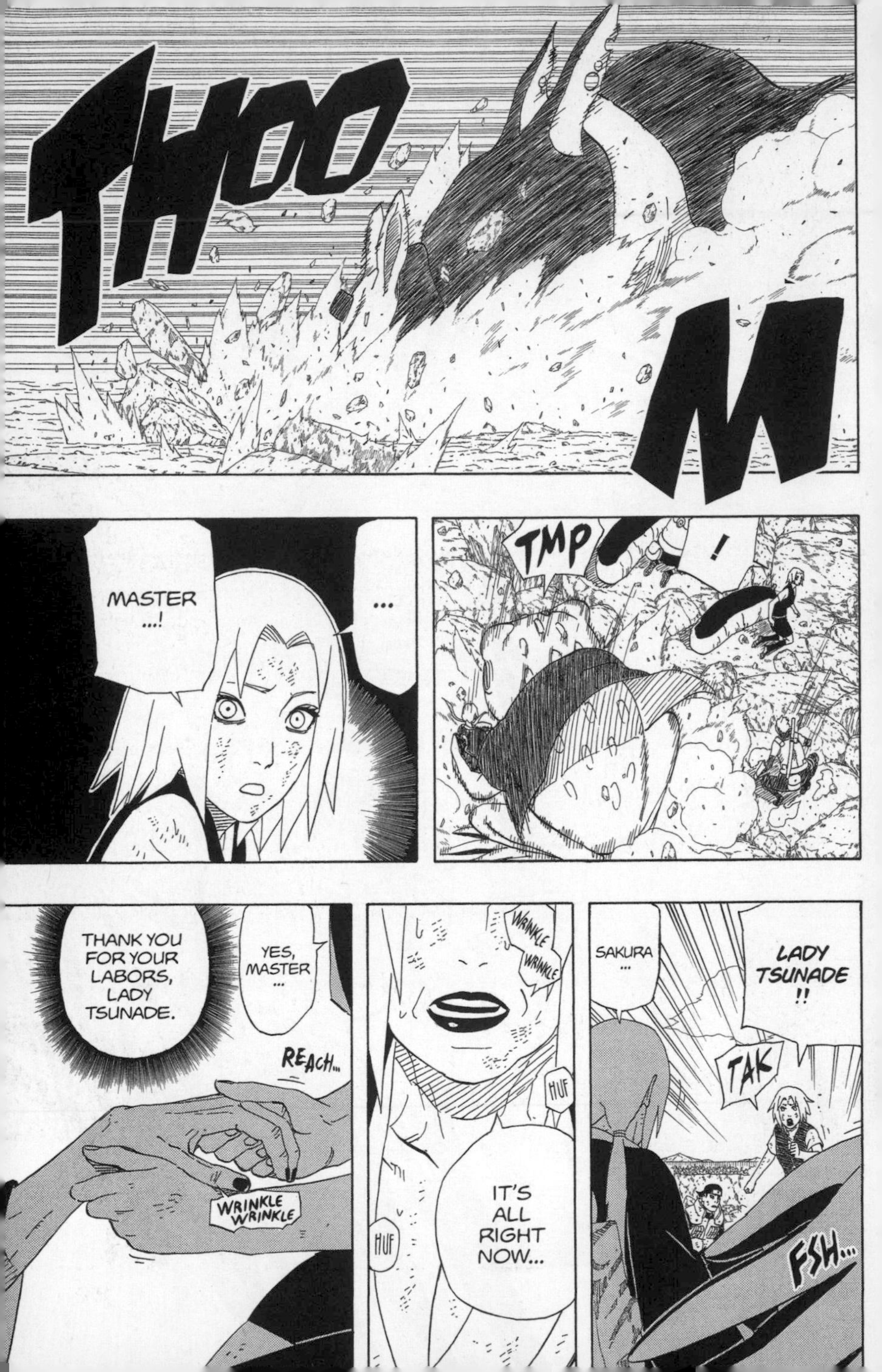
THOOM
TMP
!
MASTER ...!
...
LADY TSUNADE !!
SAKURA ...
TAK
FSH...
WRINKLE WRINKLE
HUF
IT'S ALL RIGHT NOW...
HUF
YES, MASTER ...
THANK YOU FOR YOUR LABORS, LADY TSUNADE.
REACH...
WRINKLE WRINKLE

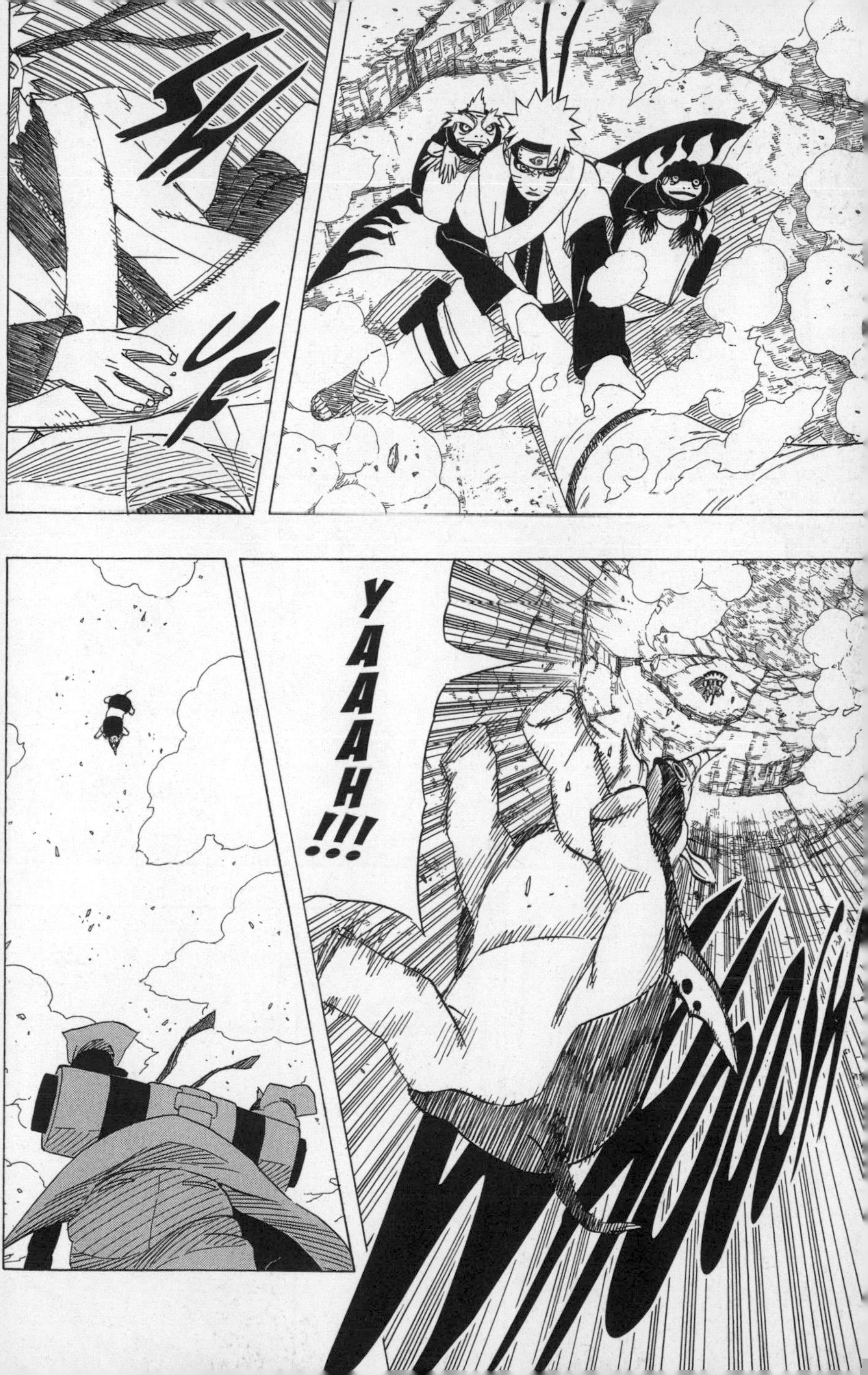
SHUF
YAAAH!!!
WHOOSH

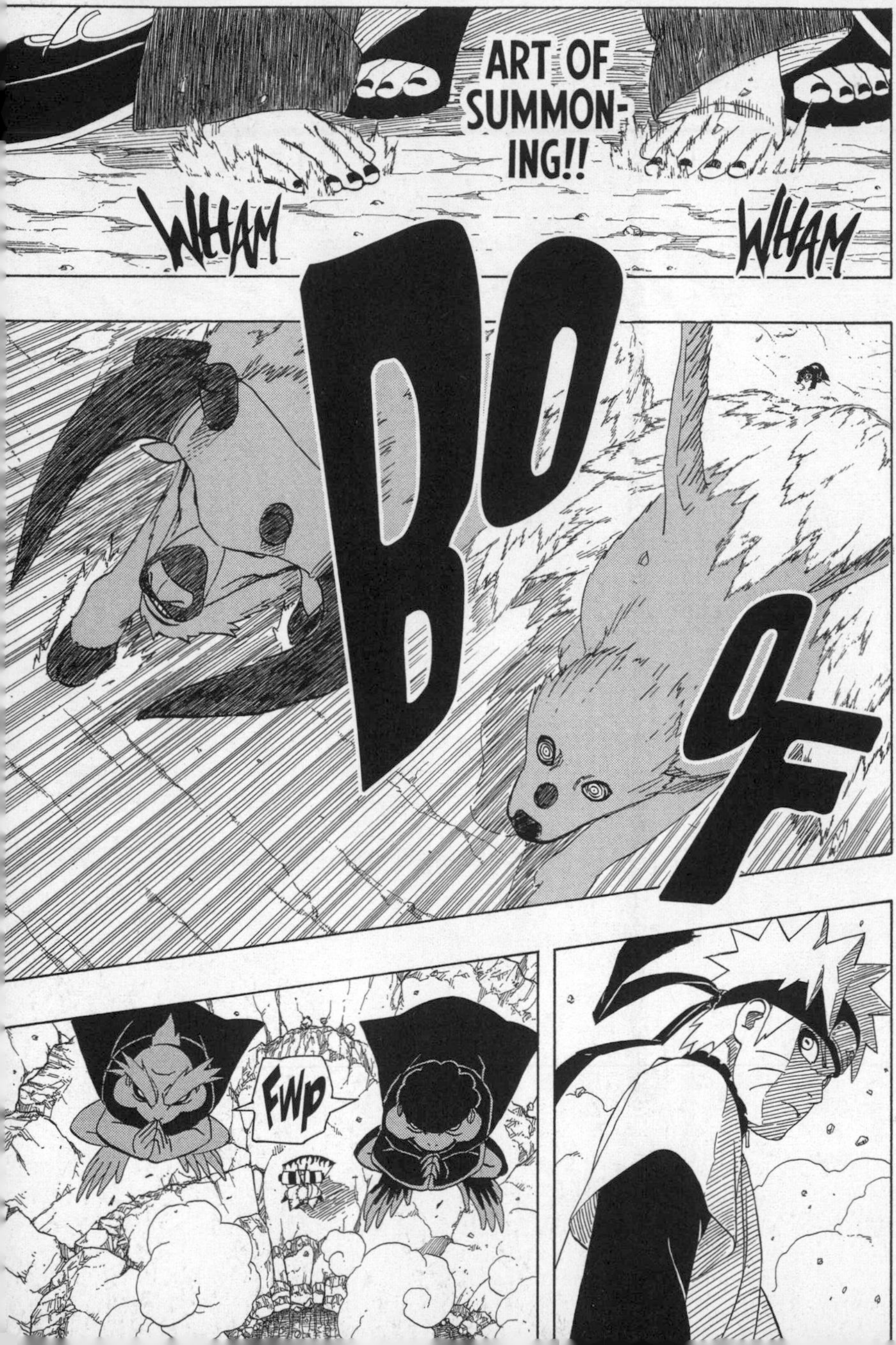
READ THIS WAY
ART OF SUMMONING!!
WHAM
WHAM
BOOF
FWP

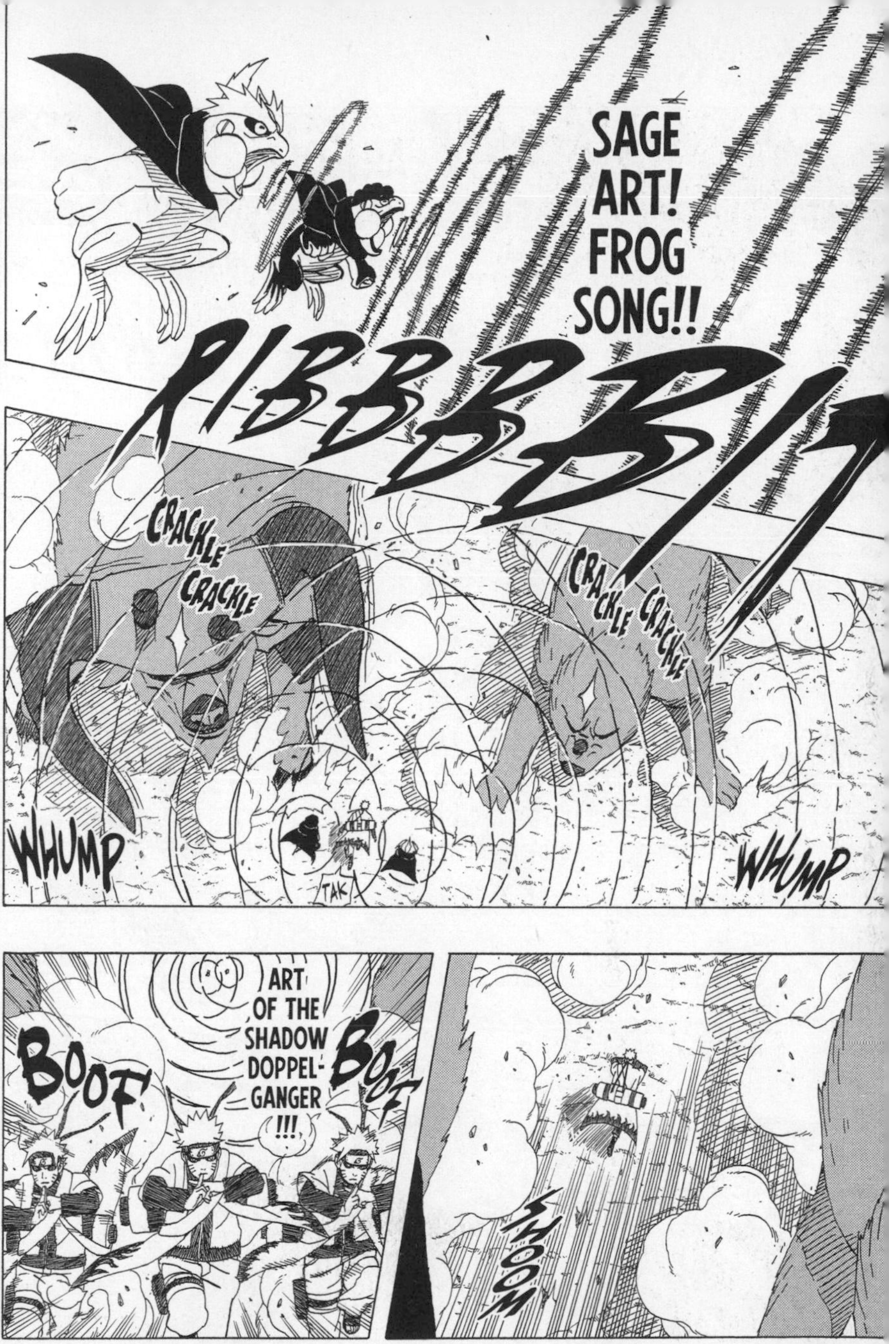
SAGE ART! FROG SONG!!
RIBBBBIT
CRACKLE CRACKLE
CRACKLE CRACKLE
WHUMP
TAK
WHUMP
WHOOM
BOOF
ART OF THE SHADOW DOPPEL-GANGER!!!
BOOF

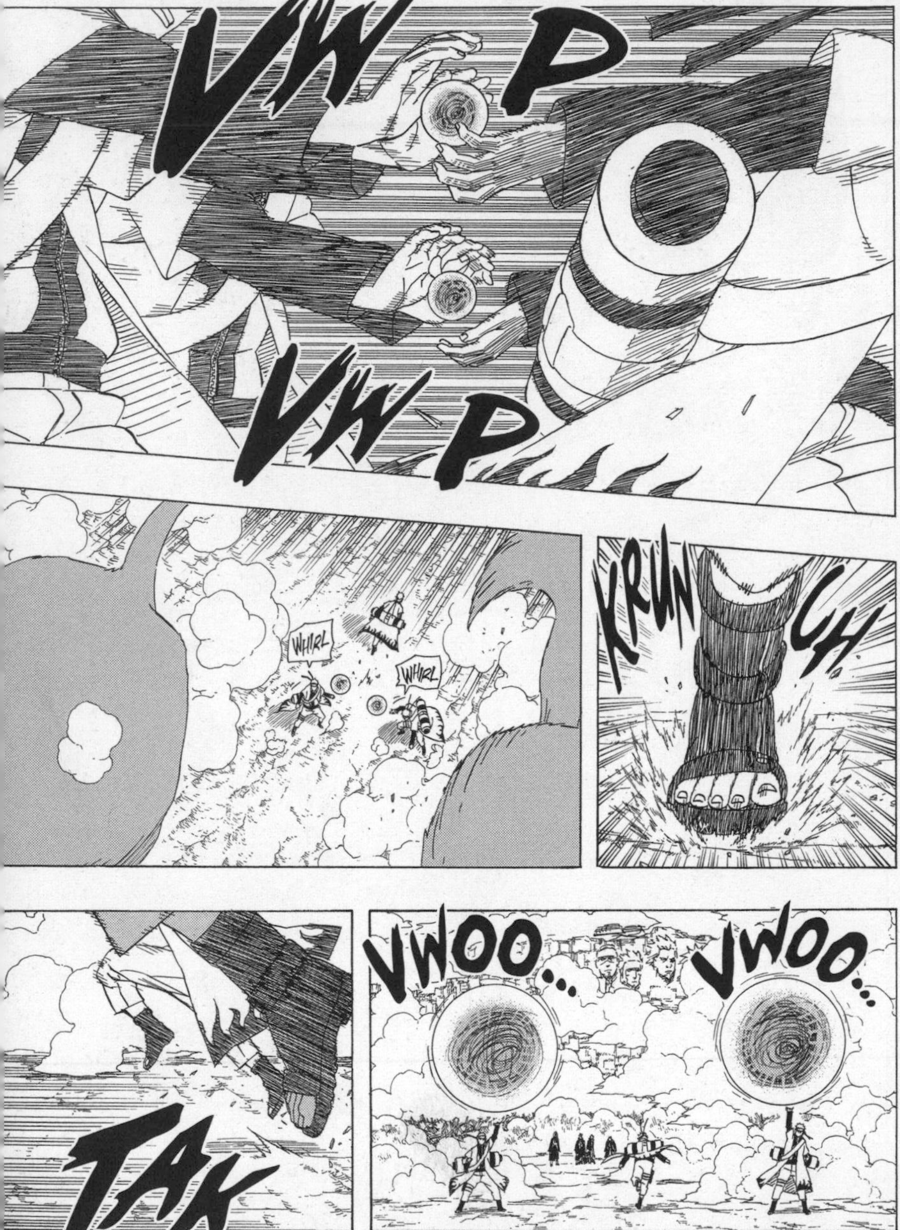
VWP
VWP
KRUNCH
WHIRL
WHIRL
VWOO...
VWOO...
TAK

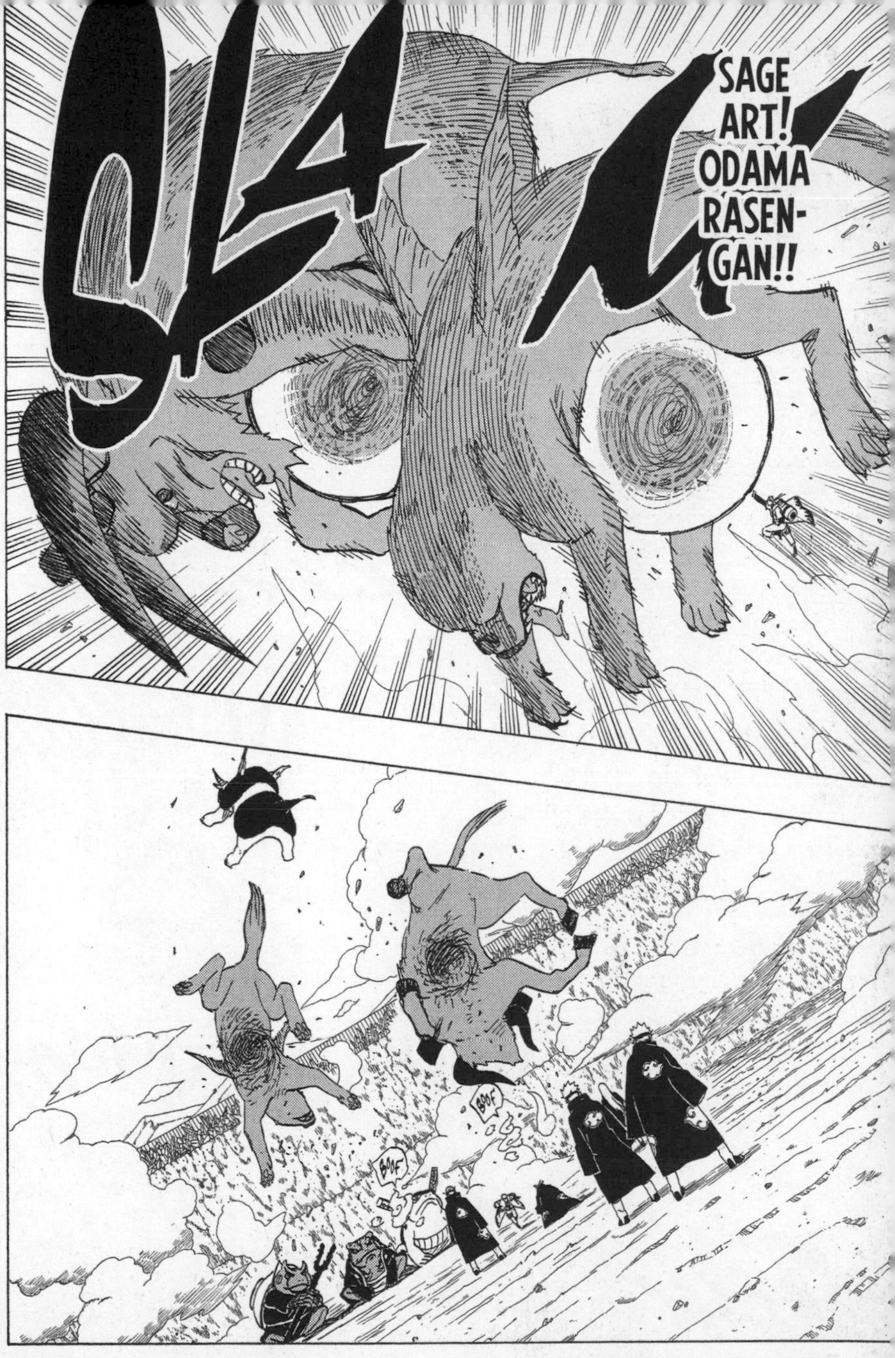
SAGE ART! ODAMA RASEN-GAN!!
BOOF
BOOF

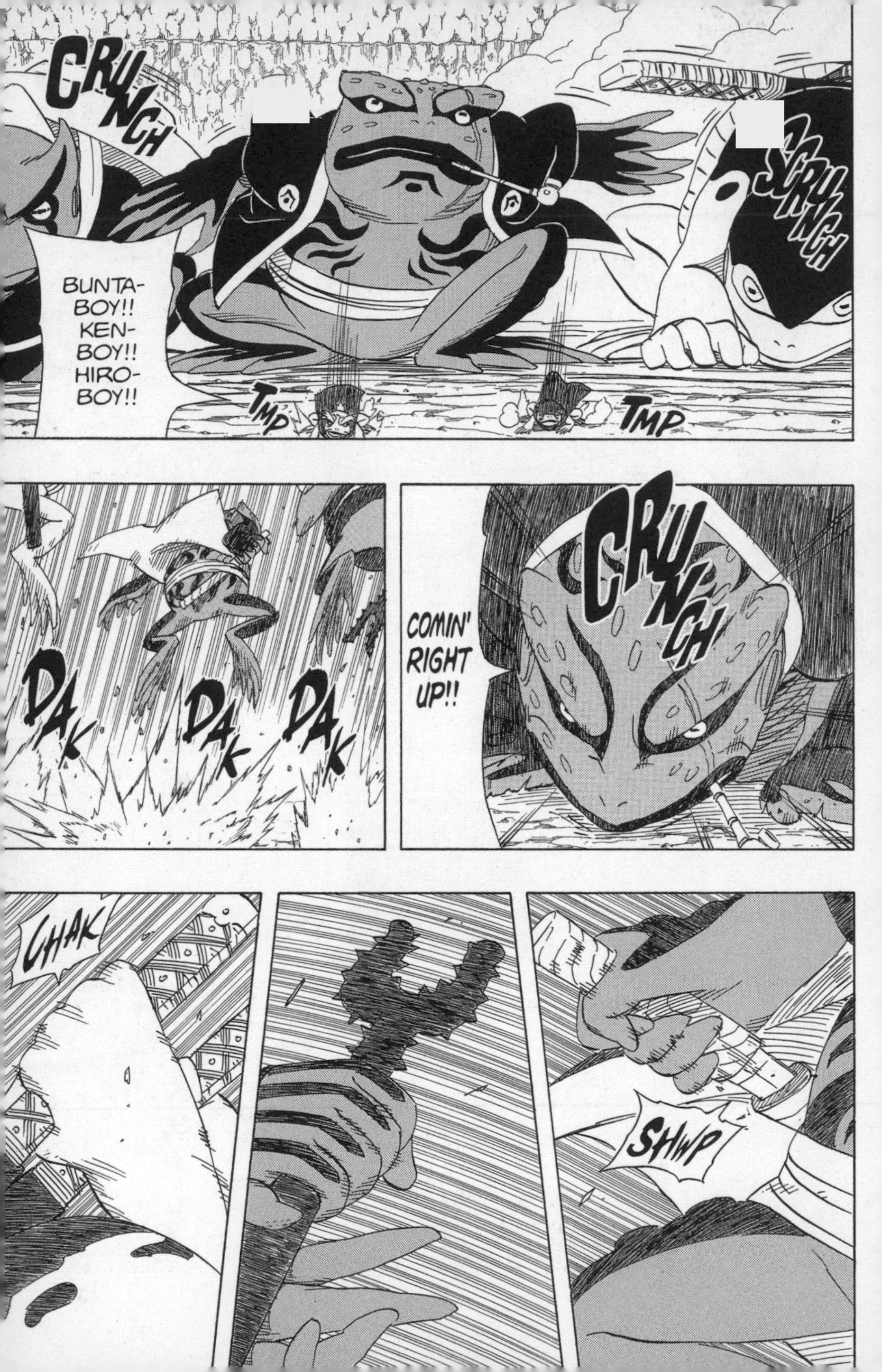

SCRUNCH
CRUNCH
BUNTA-BOY!! KEN-BOY!! HIRO-BOY!!
TMP
TMP
CRUNCH
COMIN' RIGHT UP!!
DAK
DAK
DAK
SHWP
CHAK

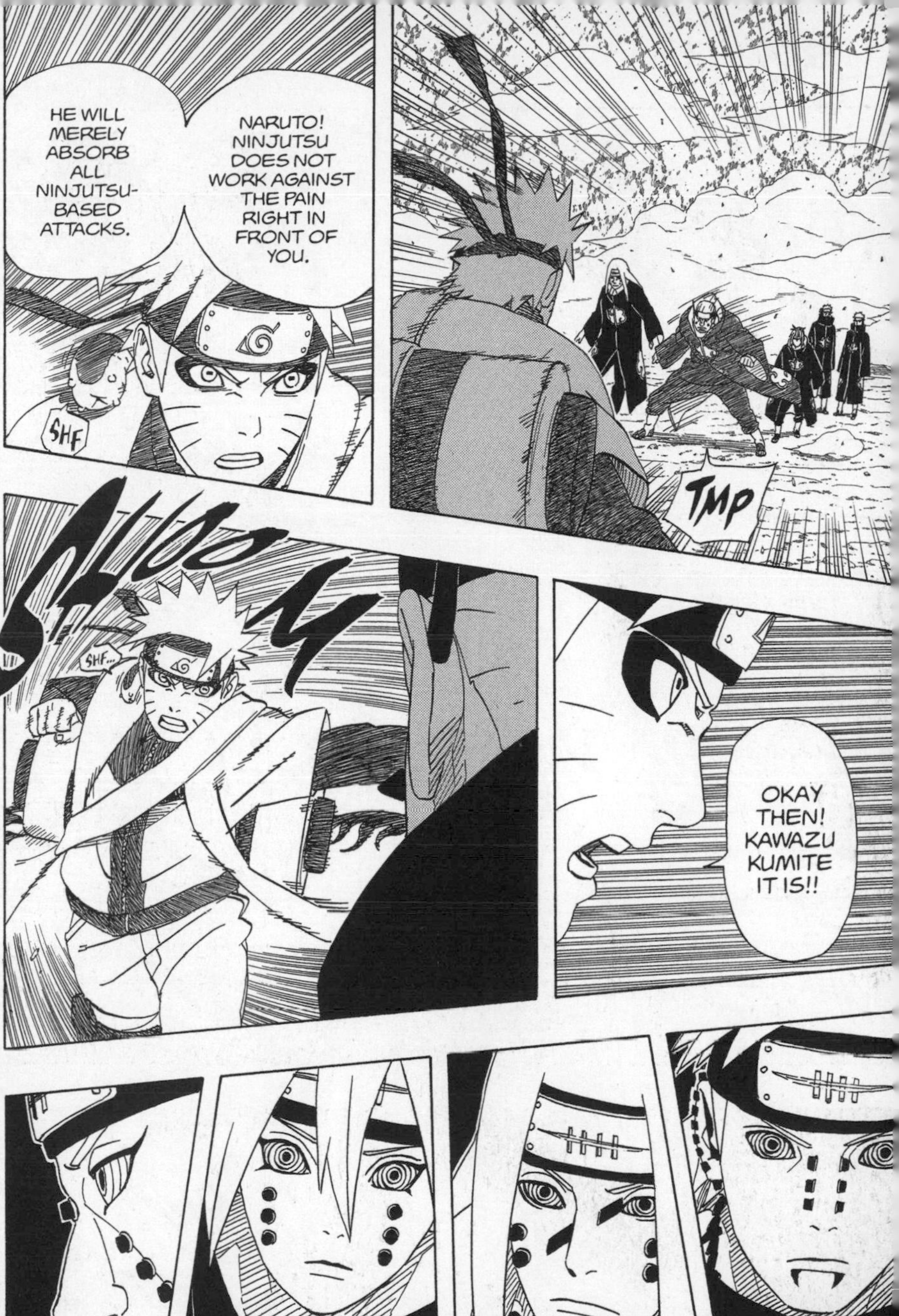
TMP
NARUTO! NINJUTSU DOES NOT WORK AGAINST THE PAIN RIGHT IN FRONT OF YOU.
HE WILL MERELY ABSORB ALL NINJUTSU-BASED ATTACKS.
SHF
OKAY THEN! KAWAZU KUMITE IT IS!!
SHOOM
SHF...

READ THIS WAY

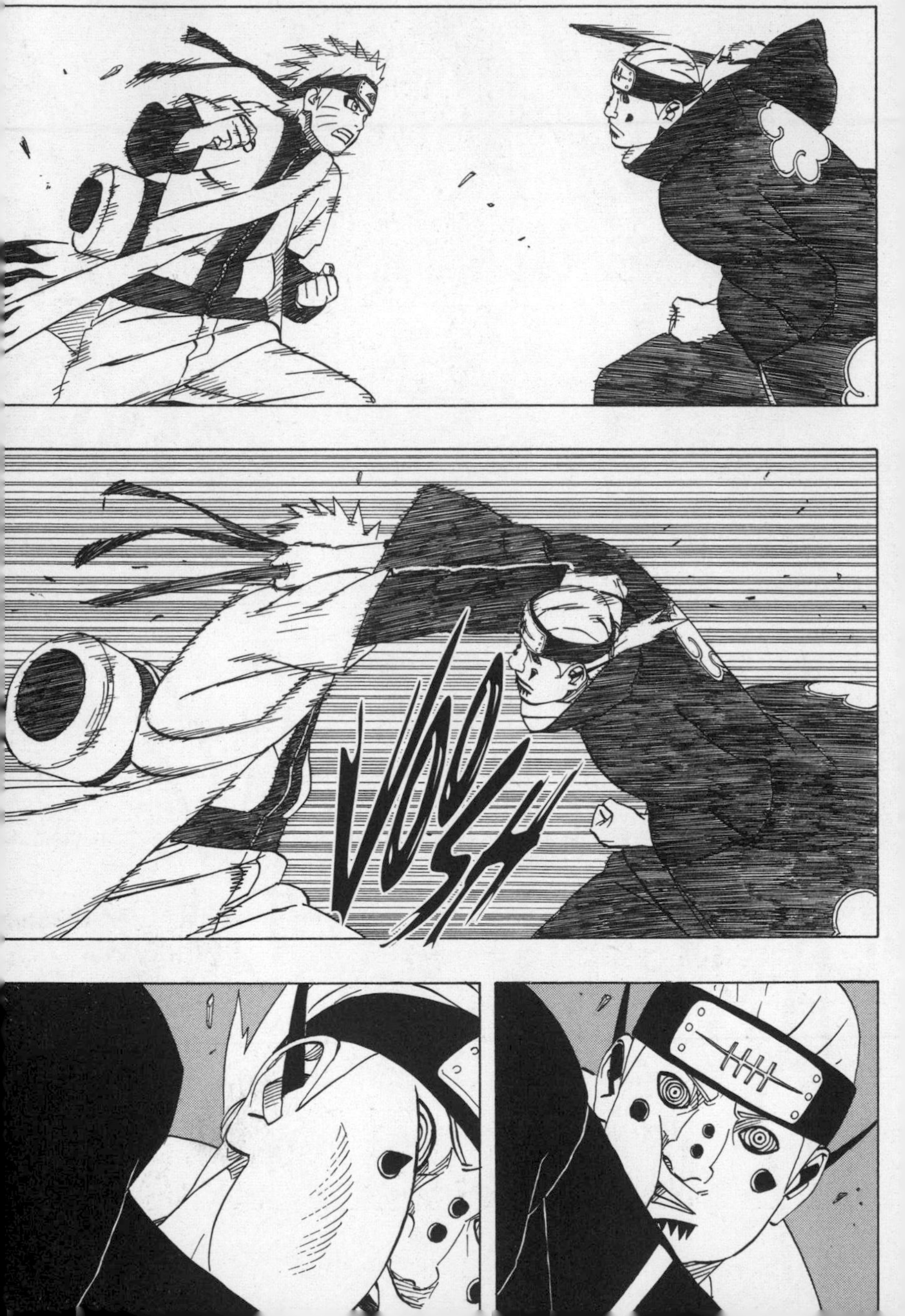
VOOSH

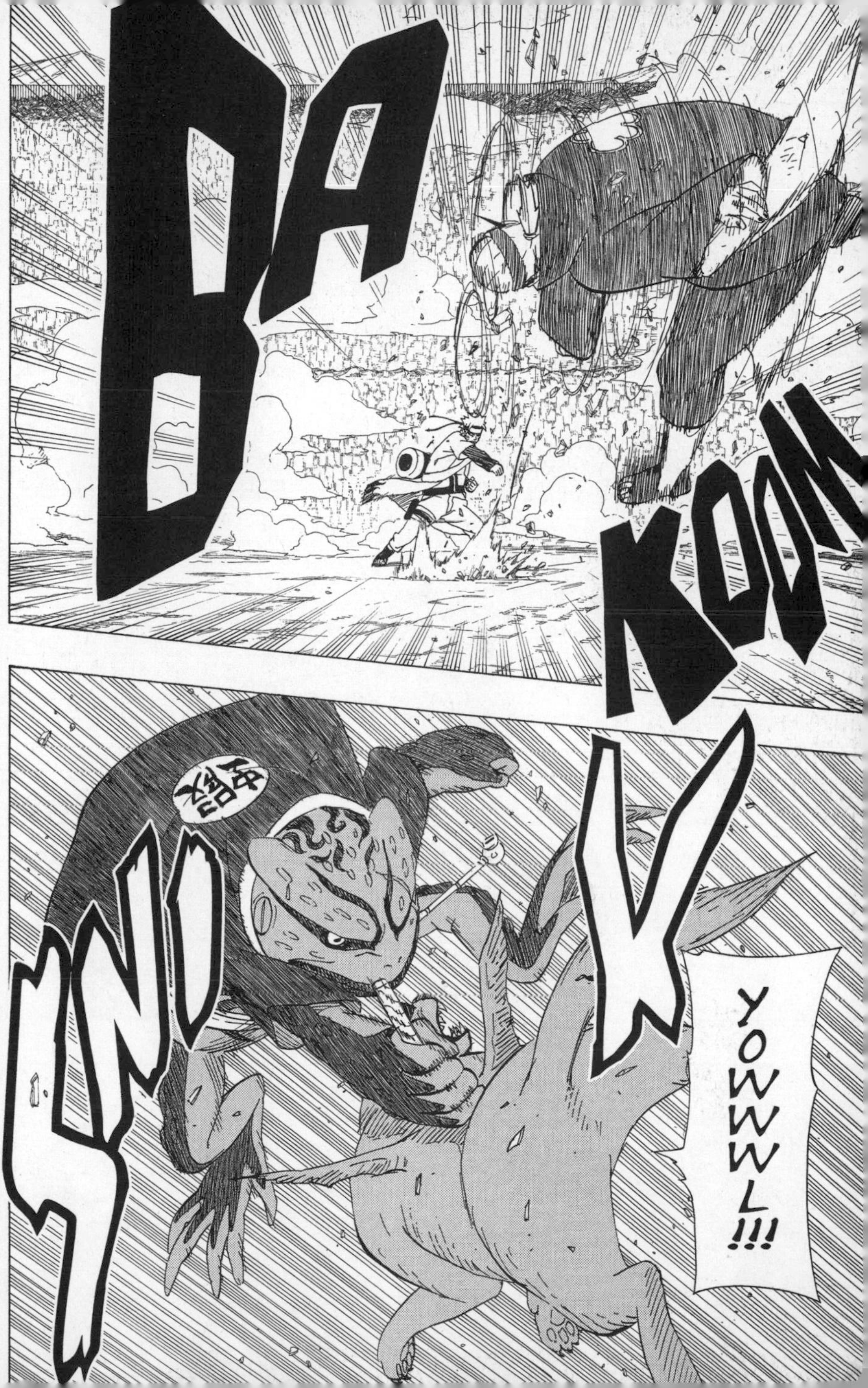
BA
KOOM
YOWWWL!!!
SNIK

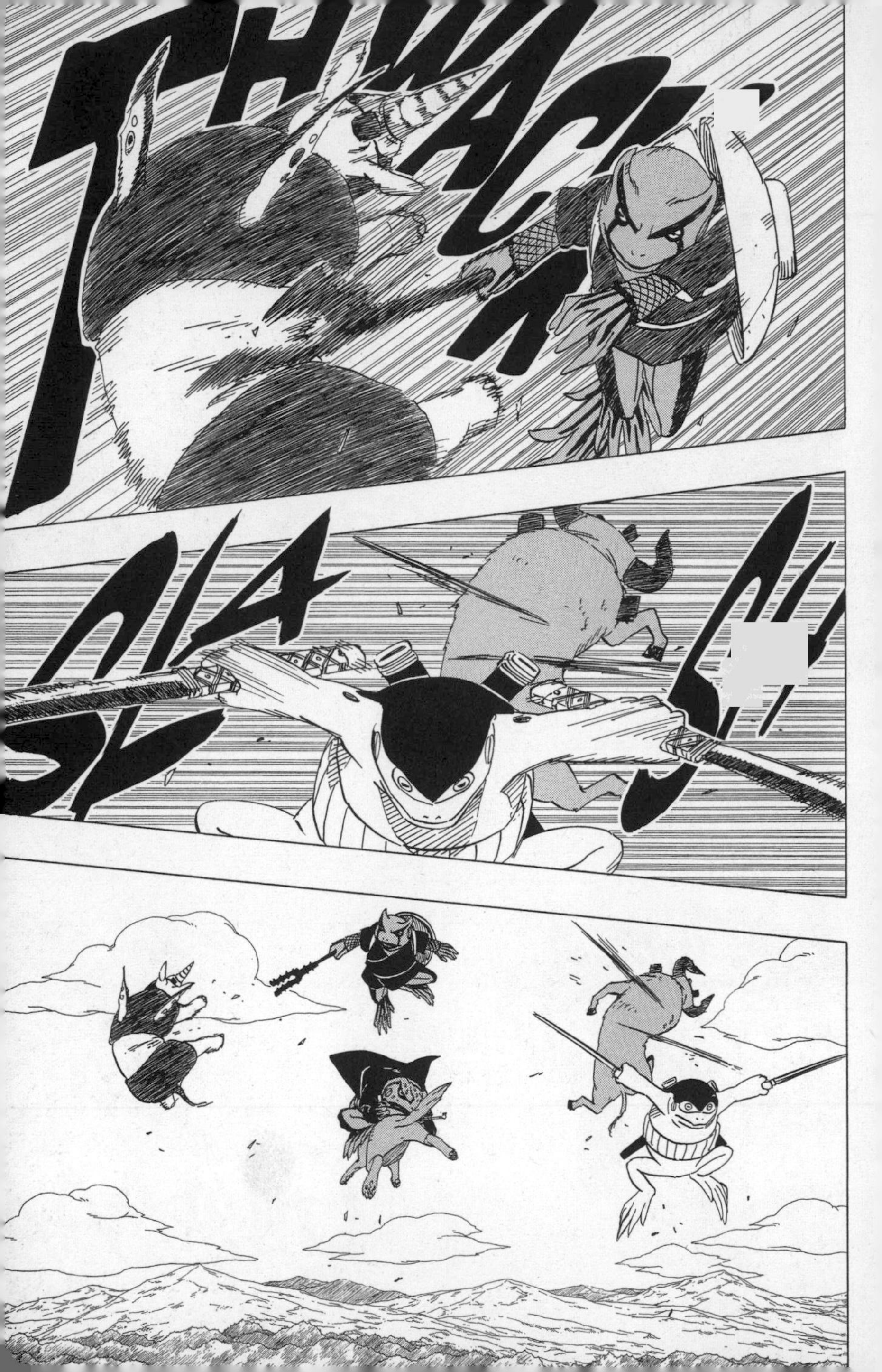
TCHWACK

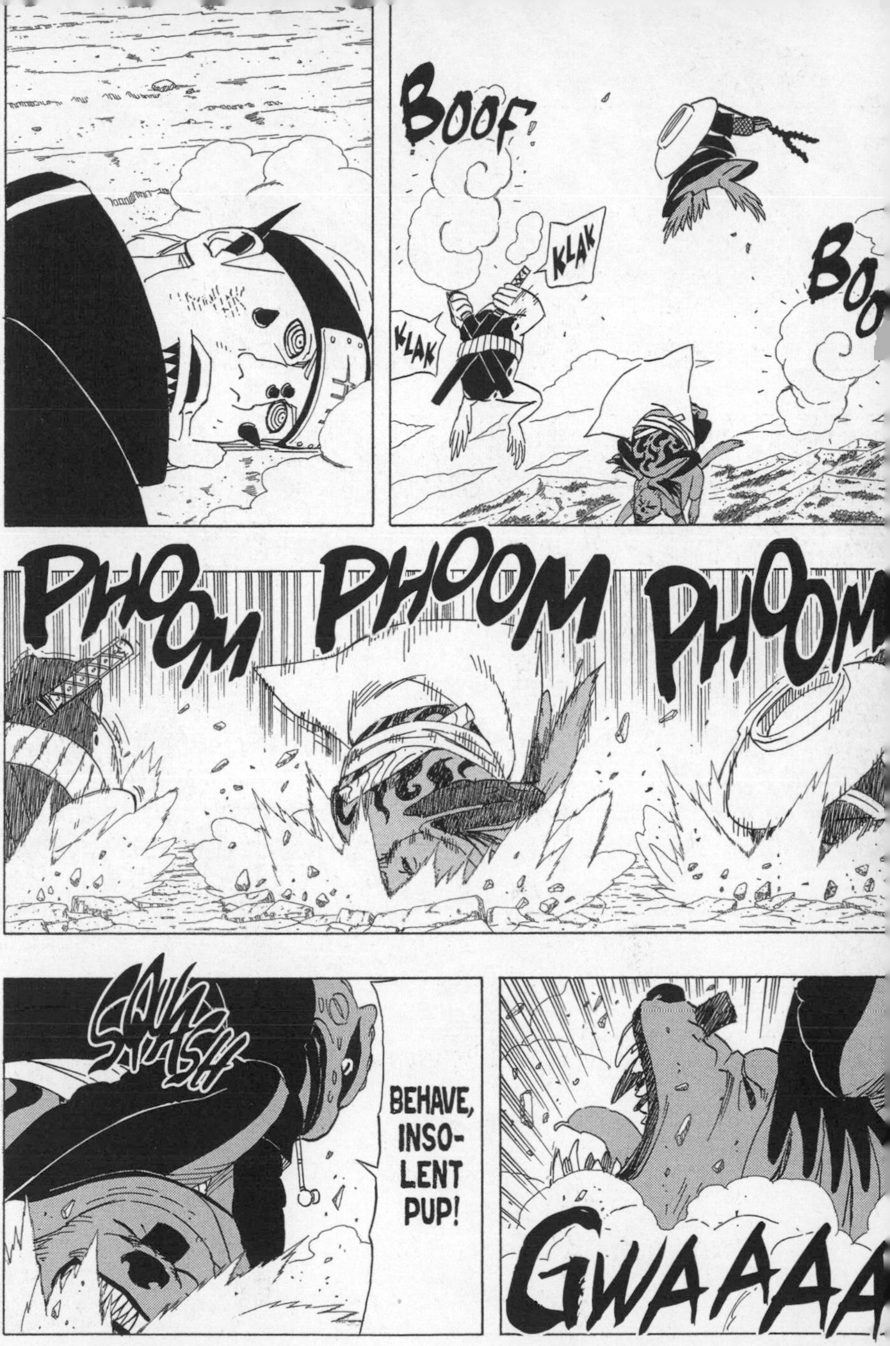
BOO
BOOF
KLAK
KLAK
PHOOM
PHOOM
PHOOM
GWAAAA
SMASH
BEHAVE, INSOLENT PUP!

READ THIS WAY

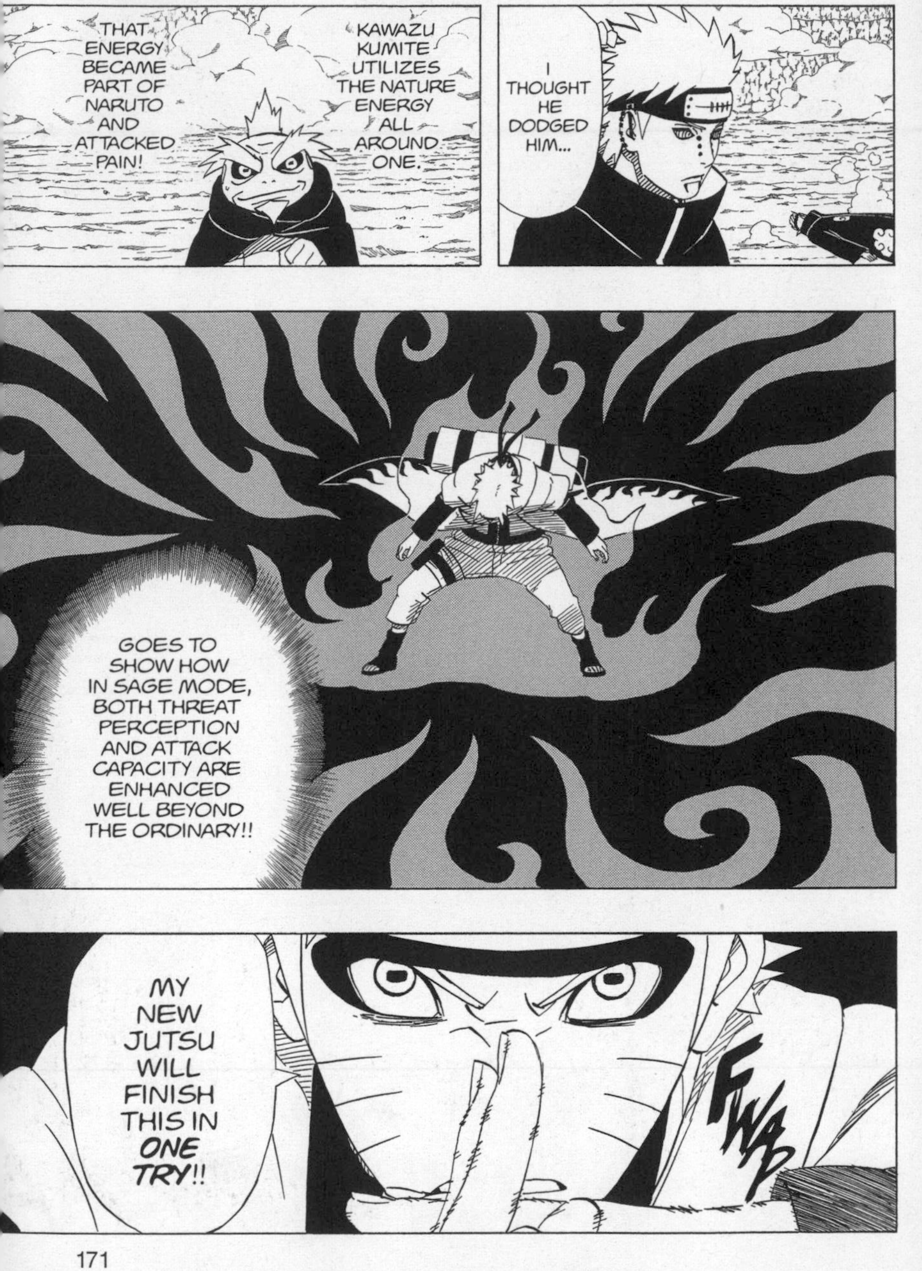

I THOUGHT HE DODGED HIM...
KAWAZU KUMITE UTILIZES THE NATURE ENERGY ALL AROUND ONE.
THAT ENERGY BECAME PART OF NARUTO AND ATTACKED PAIN!
GOES TO SHOW HOW IN SAGE MODE, BOTH THREAT PERCEPTION AND ATTACK CAPACITY ARE ENHANCED WELL BEYOND THE ORDINARY!!
FWAP
MY NEW JUTSU WILL FINISH THIS IN ONE TRY!!

NARUTO

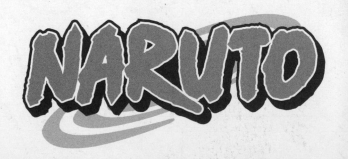

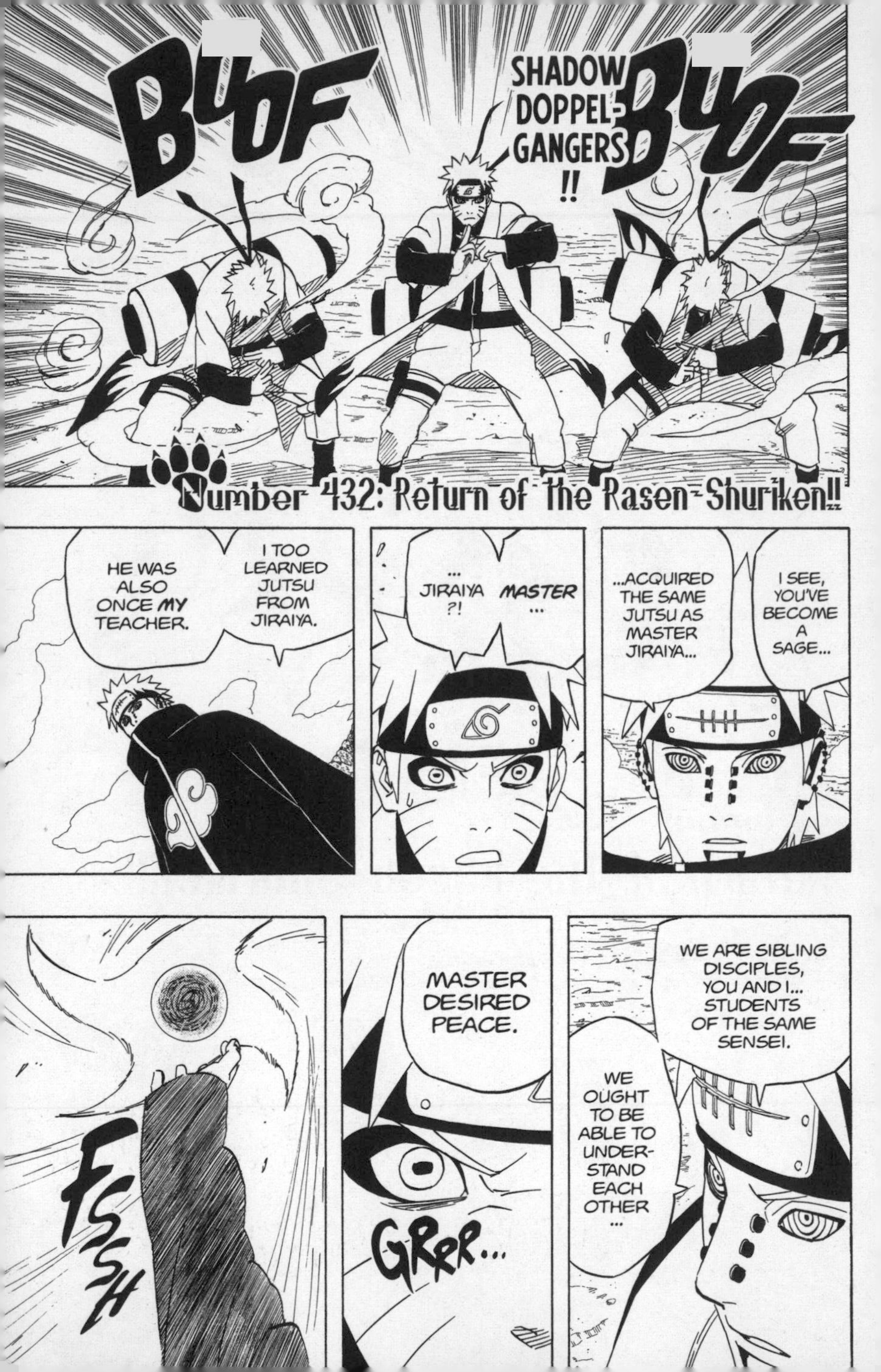
BUOF
SHADOW DOPPEL-GANGERS!!
BUOF
Number 432: Return of the Rasen-Shuriken!!
I SEE, YOU'VE BECOME A SAGE...
...ACQUIRED THE SAME JUTSU AS MASTER JIRAIYA...
MASTER...
...JIRAIYA?!
I TOO LEARNED JUTSU FROM JIRAIYA.
HE WAS ALSO ONCE MY TEACHER.
WE ARE SIBLING DISCIPLES, YOU AND I... STUDENTS OF THE SAME SENSEI.
WE OUGHT TO BE ABLE TO UNDER-STAND EACH OTHER...
MASTER DESIRED PEACE.
GRRR...
FSSH

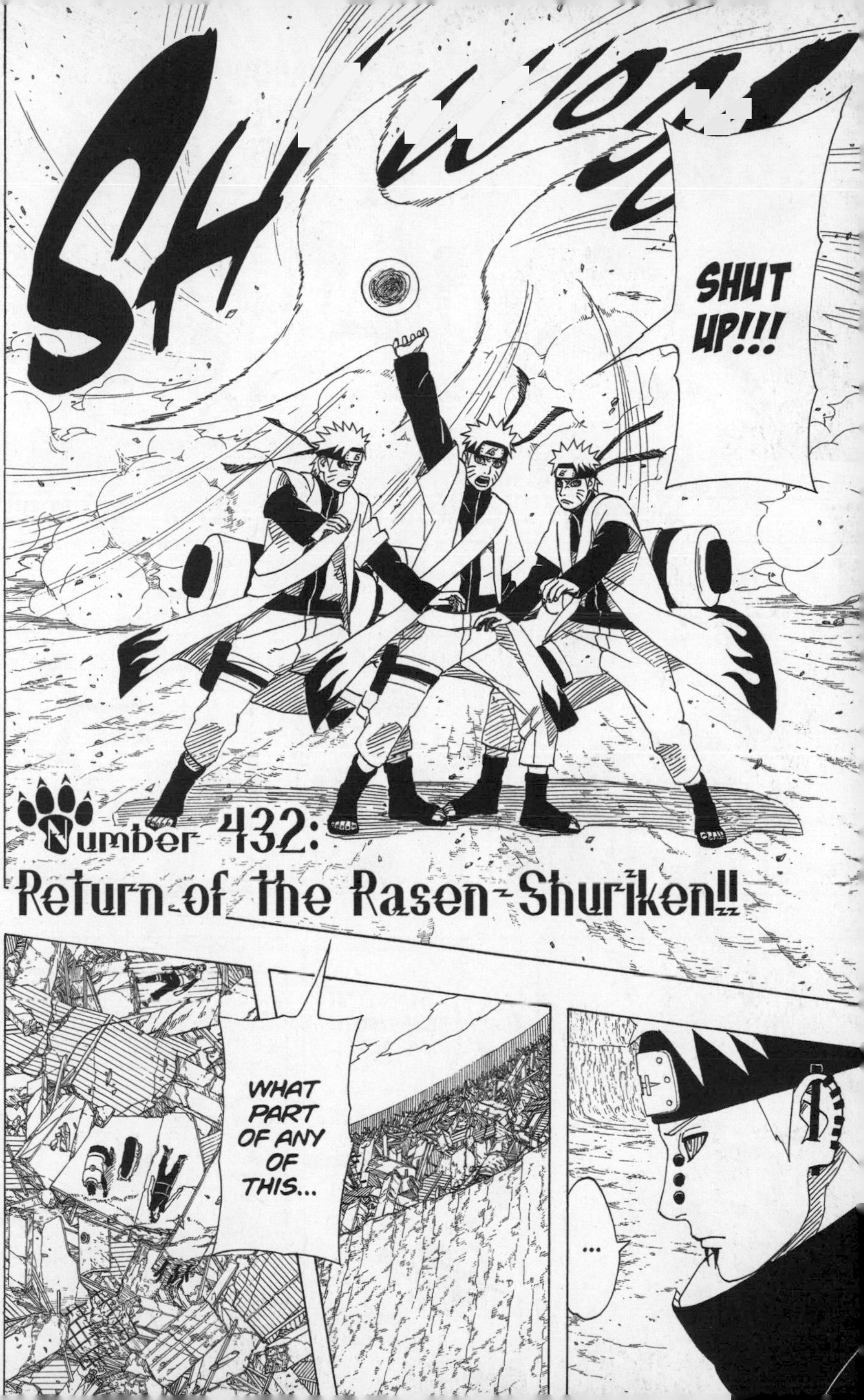
SHUT UP!!!
Number 432:
Return of the Rasen-Shuriken!!
...
WHAT PART OF ANY OF THIS...

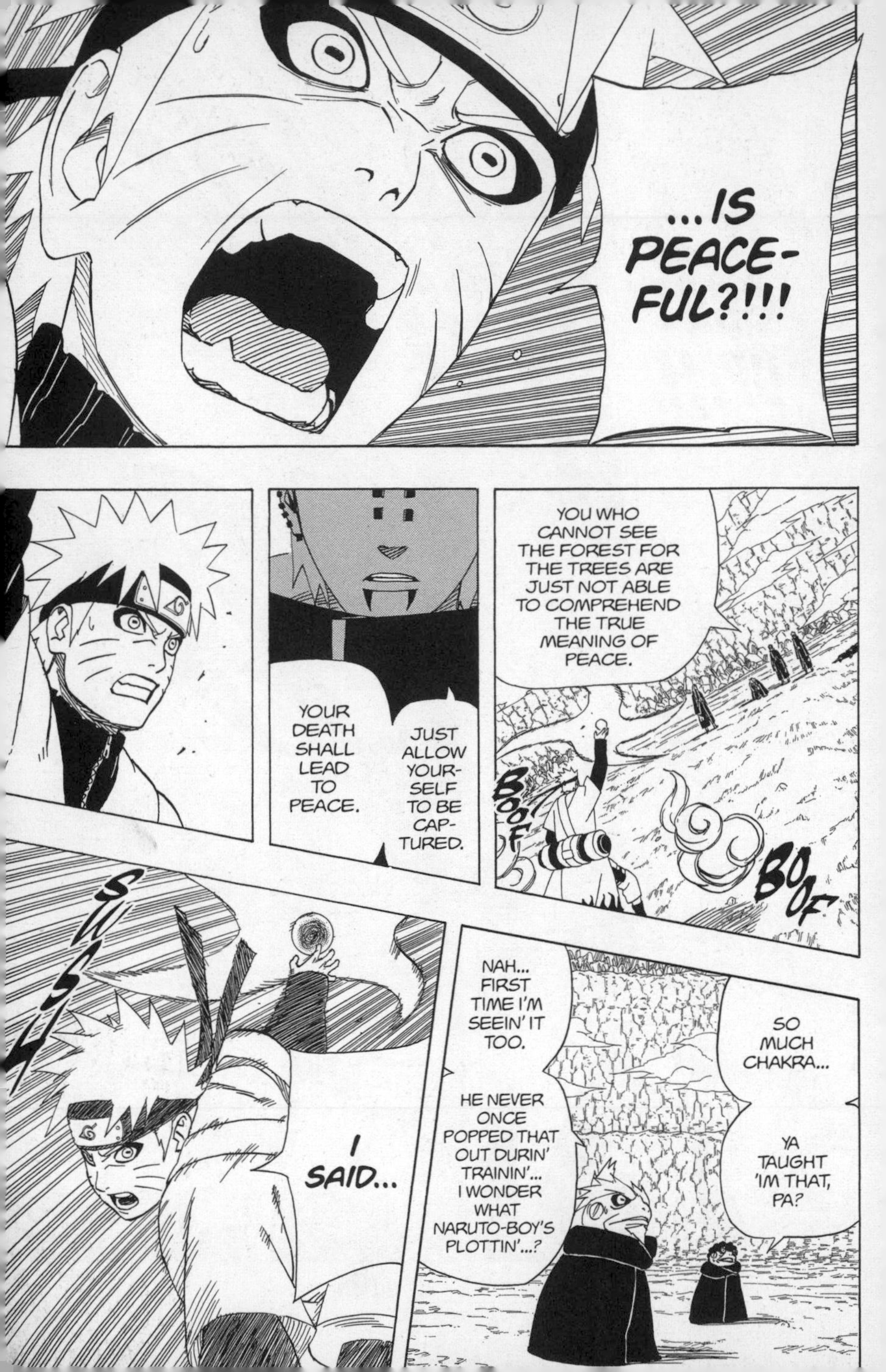
...IS PEACE-FUL?!!!
YOU WHO CANNOT SEE THE FOREST FOR THE TREES ARE JUST NOT ABLE TO COMPREHEND THE TRUE MEANING OF PEACE.
BOOF
BOOF
JUST ALLOW YOUR-SELF TO BE CAP-TURED.
YOUR DEATH SHALL LEAD TO PEACE.
SO MUCH CHAKRA...
YA TAUGHT 'IM THAT, PA?
NAH... FIRST TIME I'M SEEIN' IT TOO.
HE NEVER ONCE POPPED THAT OUT DURIN' TRAININ'... I WONDER WHAT NARUTO-BOY'S PLOTTIN'...?
I SAID...

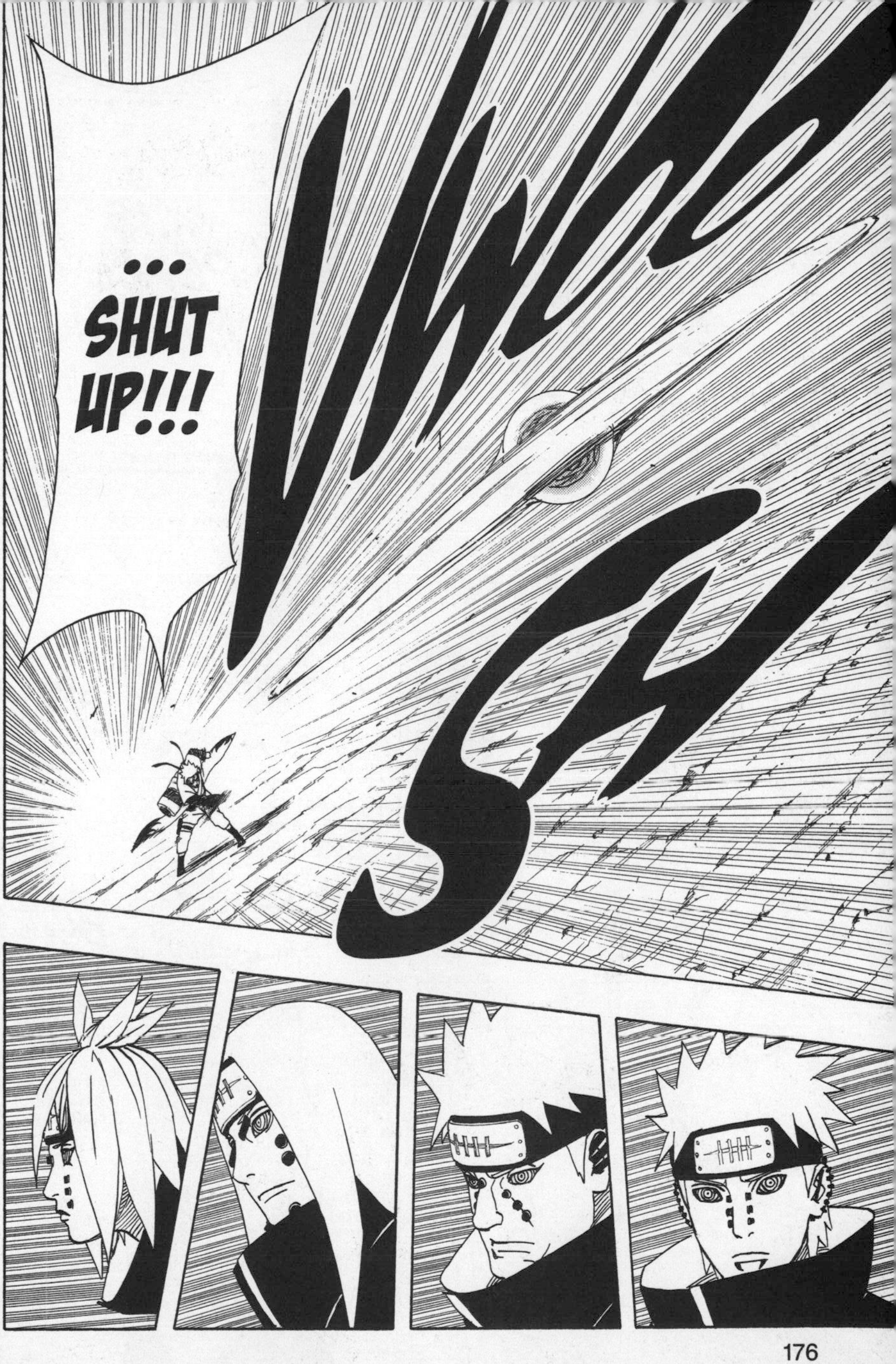
... SHUT UP!!!

READ THIS WAY

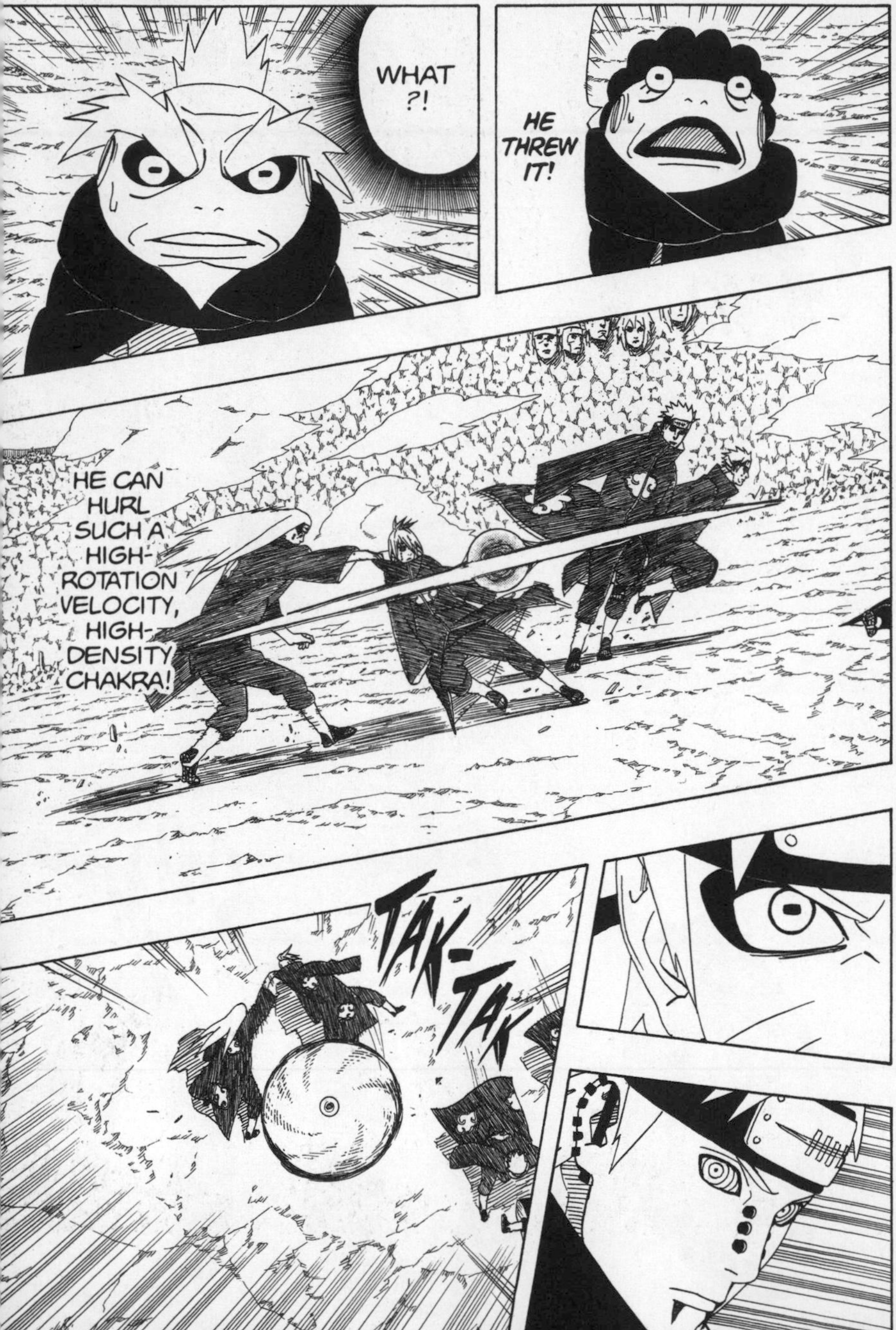
HE THREW IT!
WHAT ?!
HE CAN HURL SUCH A HIGH-ROTATION VELOCITY, HIGH-DENSITY CHAKRA!
TAK-TAK

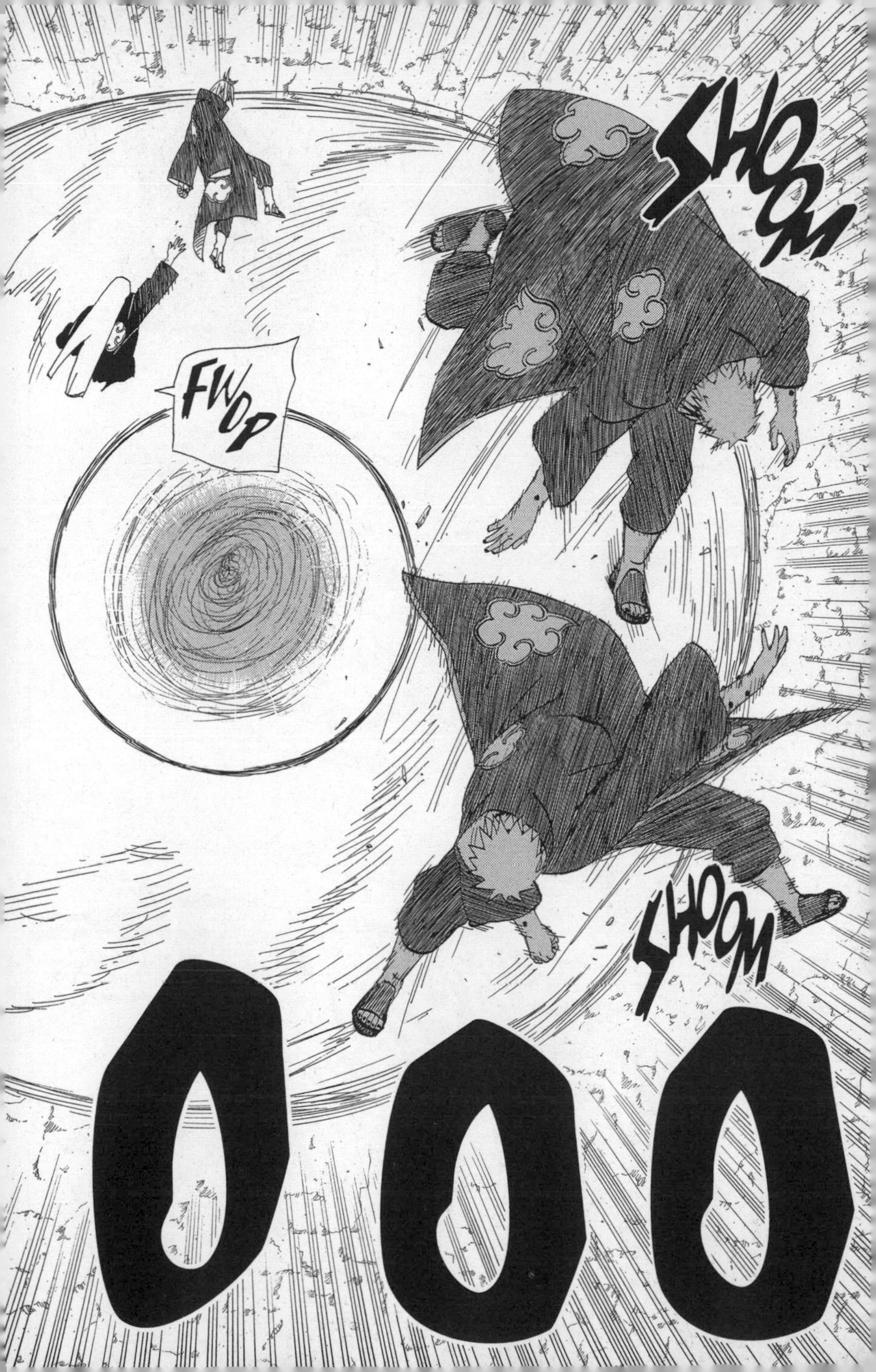
SHOOM
FWOP
SHOOM
OOO

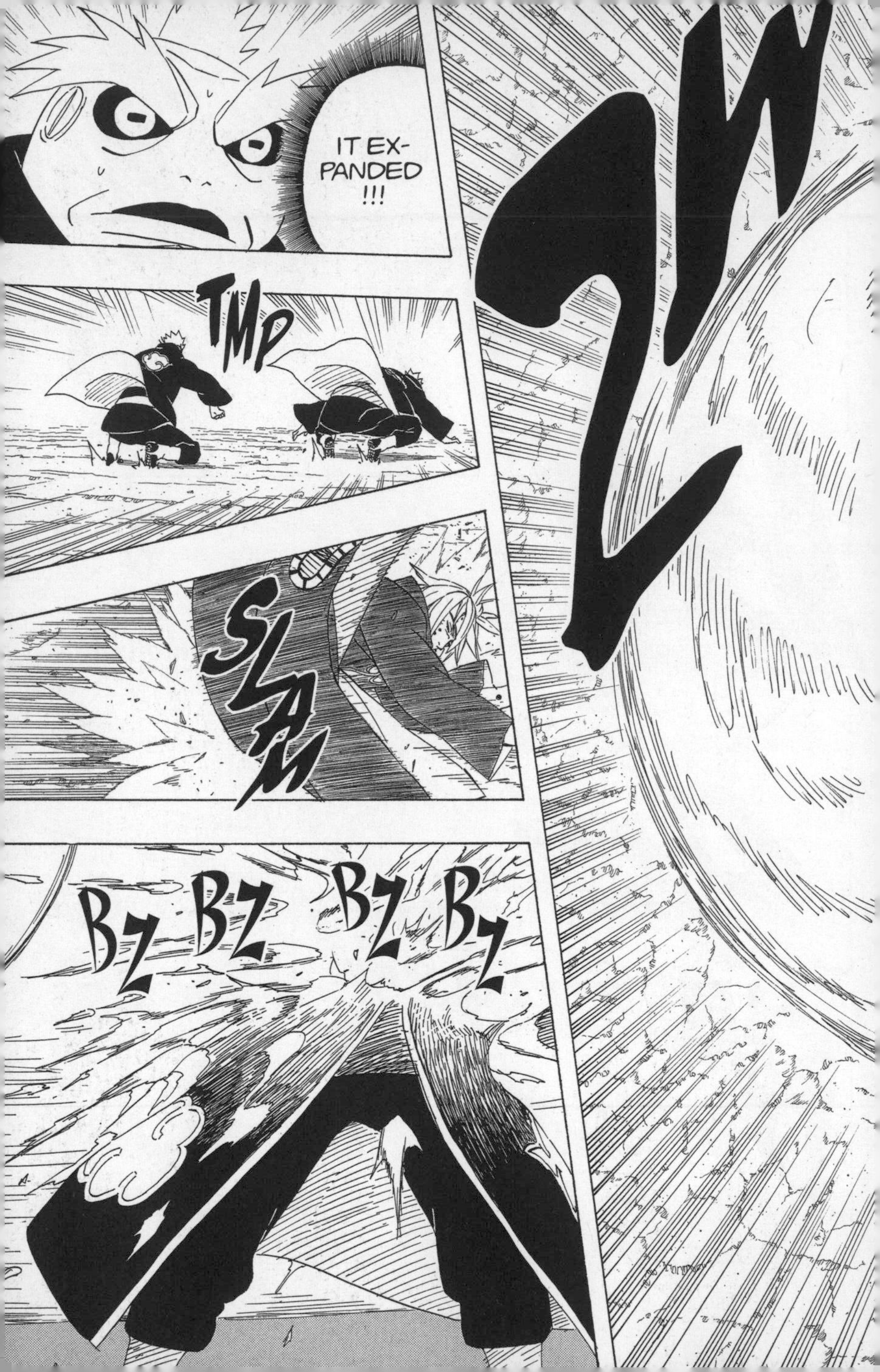
ZW
IT EX-
PANDED
!!!
TMP
SLAM
BZ BZ BZ BZ

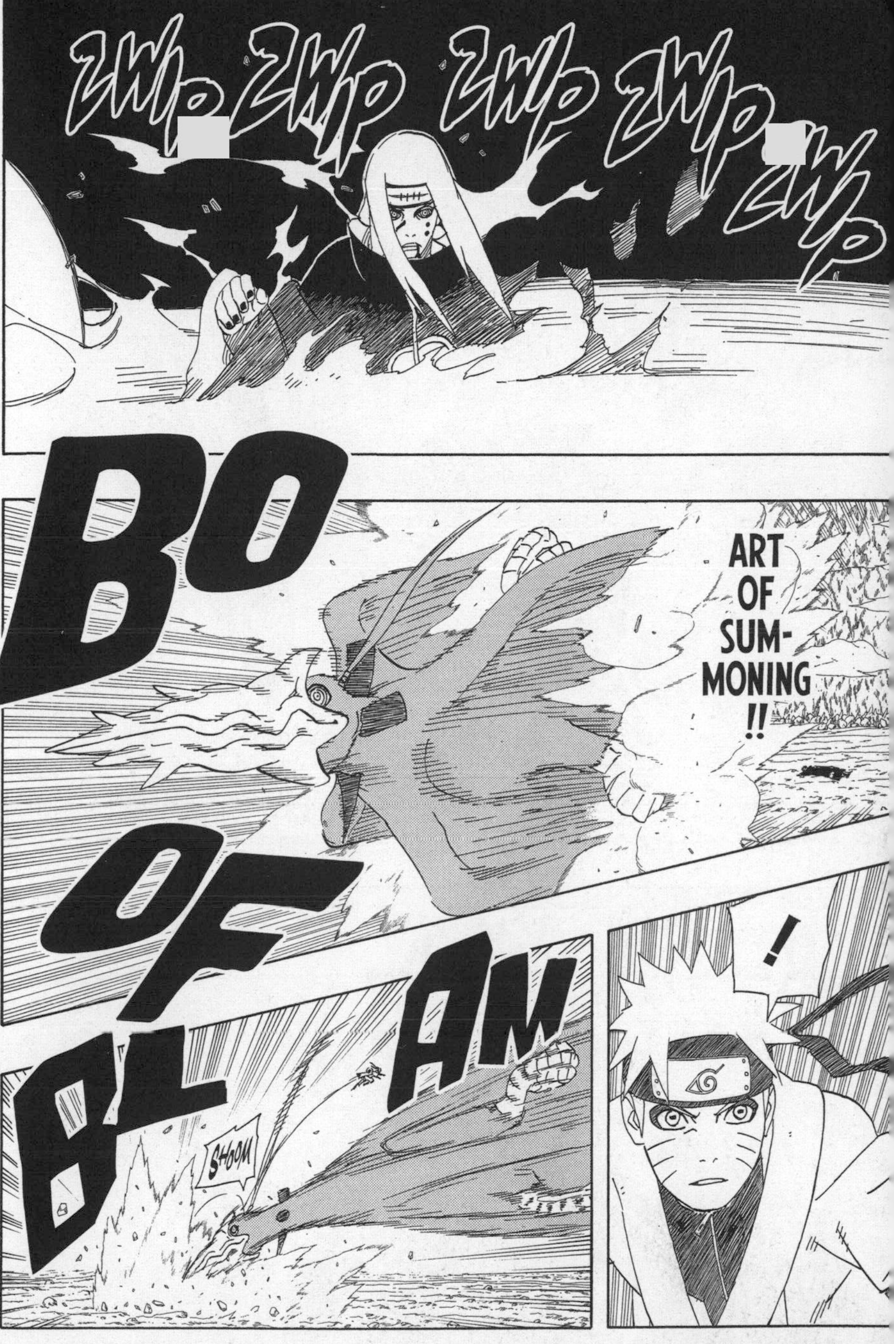
ZWP ZWP ZWP ZWP ZWP
BOOF
ART OF SUM-MONING!!
!
BLAM
SHOOM

READ THIS WAY

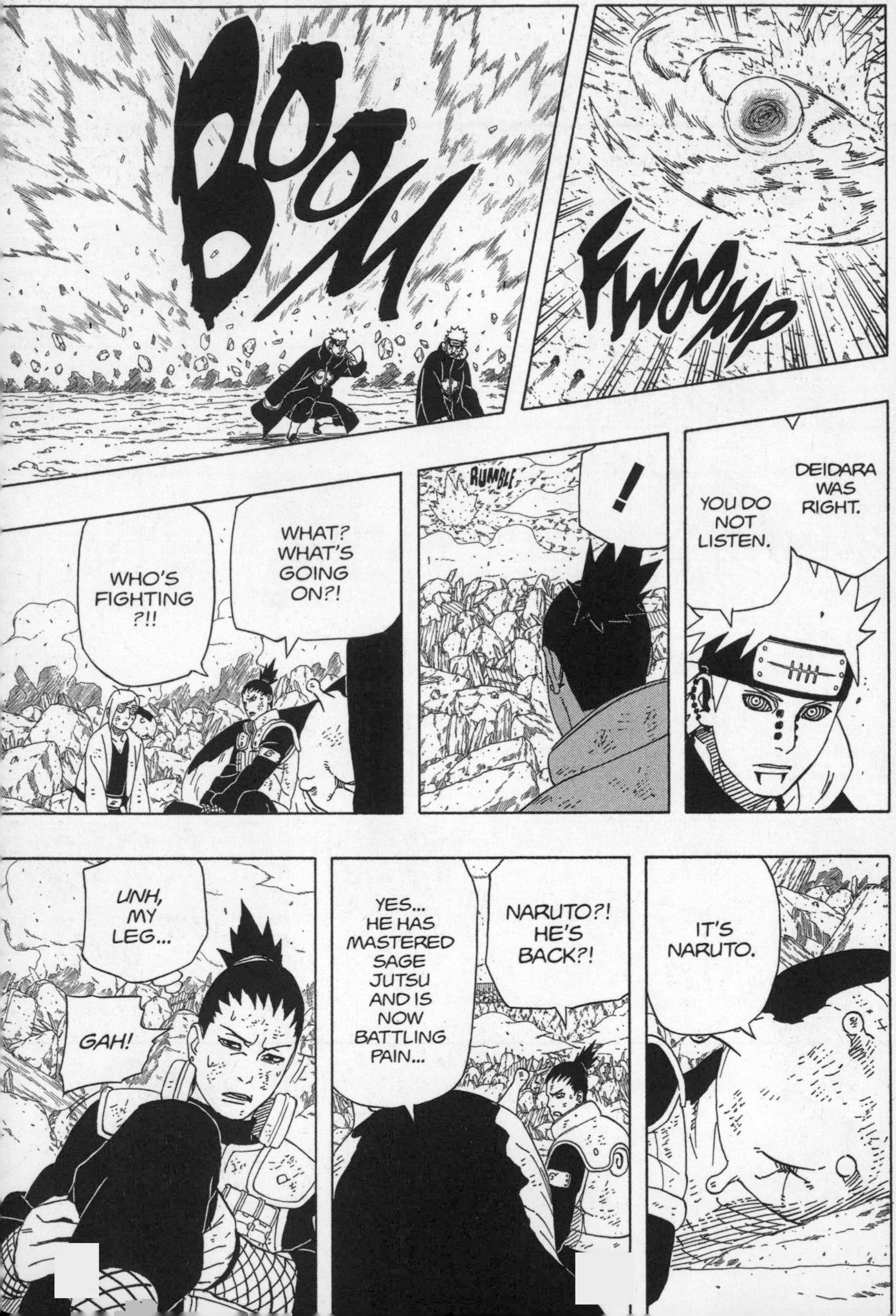
FWOOMP
BOOM
DEIDARA WAS RIGHT.
YOU DO NOT LISTEN.
RUMBLE
!
WHAT? WHAT'S GOING ON?!
WHO'S FIGHTING ?!!
IT'S NARUTO.
NARUTO?! HE'S BACK?!
YES... HE HAS MASTERED SAGE JUTSU AND IS NOW BATTLING PAIN...
UNH, MY LEG...
GAH!

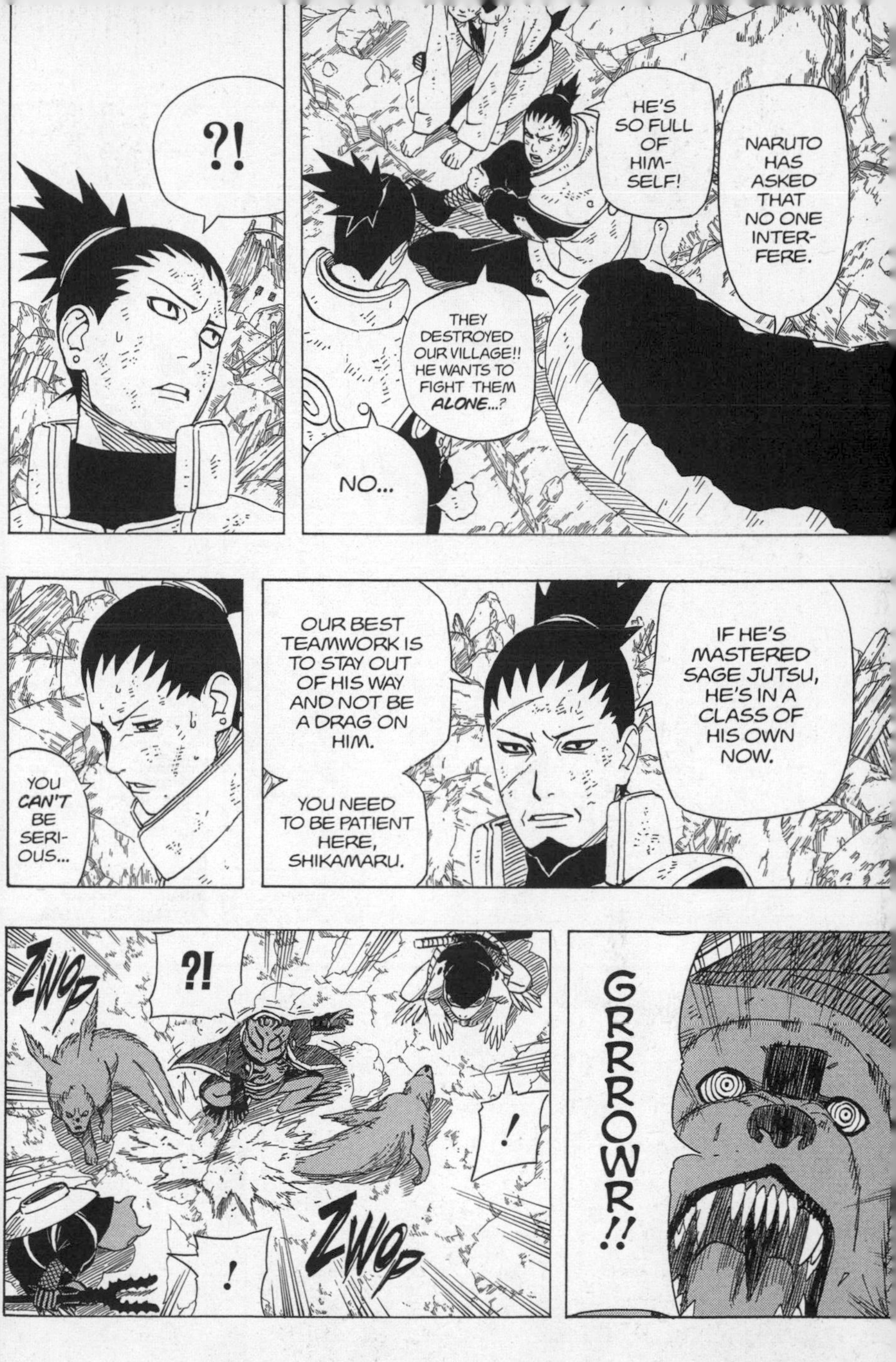
NARUTO HAS ASKED THAT NO ONE INTERFERE.
HE'S SO FULL OF HIMSELF!
THEY DESTROYED OUR VILLAGE!! HE WANTS TO FIGHT THEM ALONE...?
NO...
?!
IF HE'S MASTERED SAGE JUTSU, HE'S IN A CLASS OF HIS OWN NOW.
OUR BEST TEAMWORK IS TO STAY OUT OF HIS WAY AND NOT BE A DRAG ON HIM.
YOU NEED TO BE PATIENT HERE, SHIKAMARU.
YOU CAN'T BE SERIOUS...
GRRROWR!!
?!
ZWOP
!
ZWOP
!

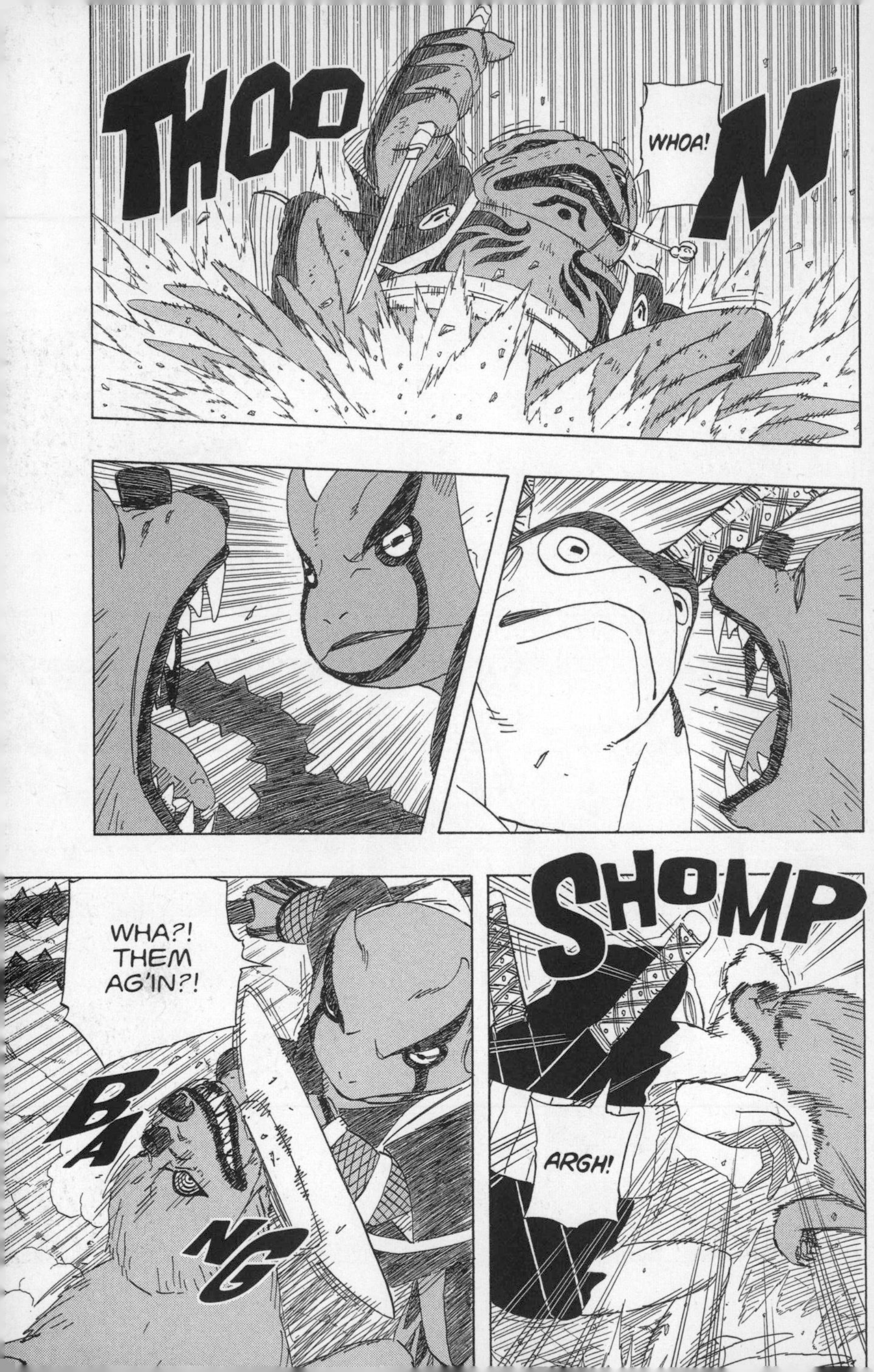
THOOM
WHOA!
SHOMP
ARGH!
WHA?! THEM AG'IN?!
BANG

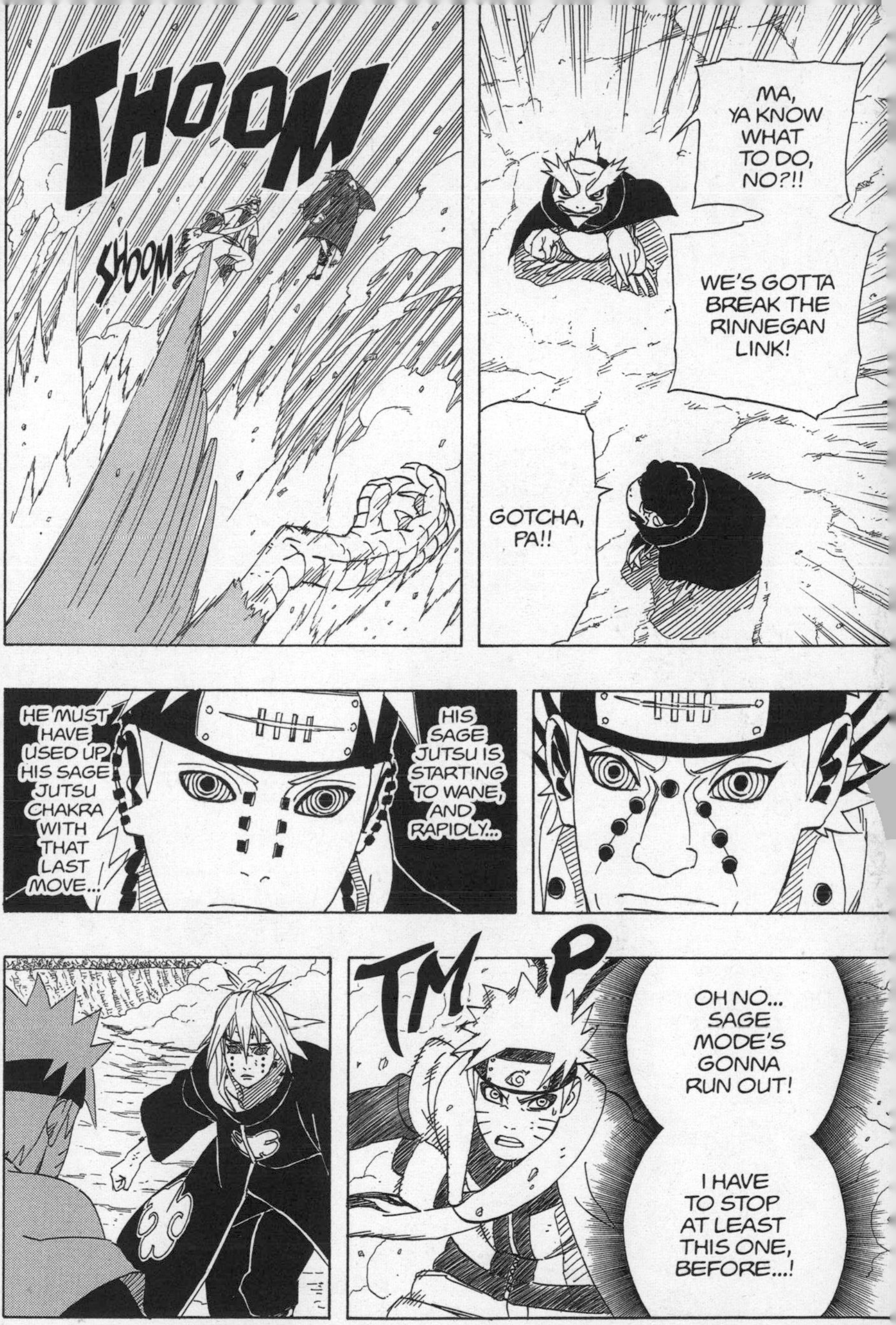
MA, YA KNOW WHAT TO DO, NO?!!
WE'S GOTTA BREAK THE RINNEGAN LINK!
GOTCHA, PA!!
THOOM
SHOOM
HIS SAGE JUTSU IS STARTING TO WANE, AND RAPIDLY...
HE MUST HAVE USED UP HIS SAGE JUTSU CHAKRA WITH THAT LAST MOVE...!
TMP
OH NO... SAGE MODE'S GONNA RUN OUT!
I HAVE TO STOP AT LEAST THIS ONE, BEFORE...!

READ THIS WAY

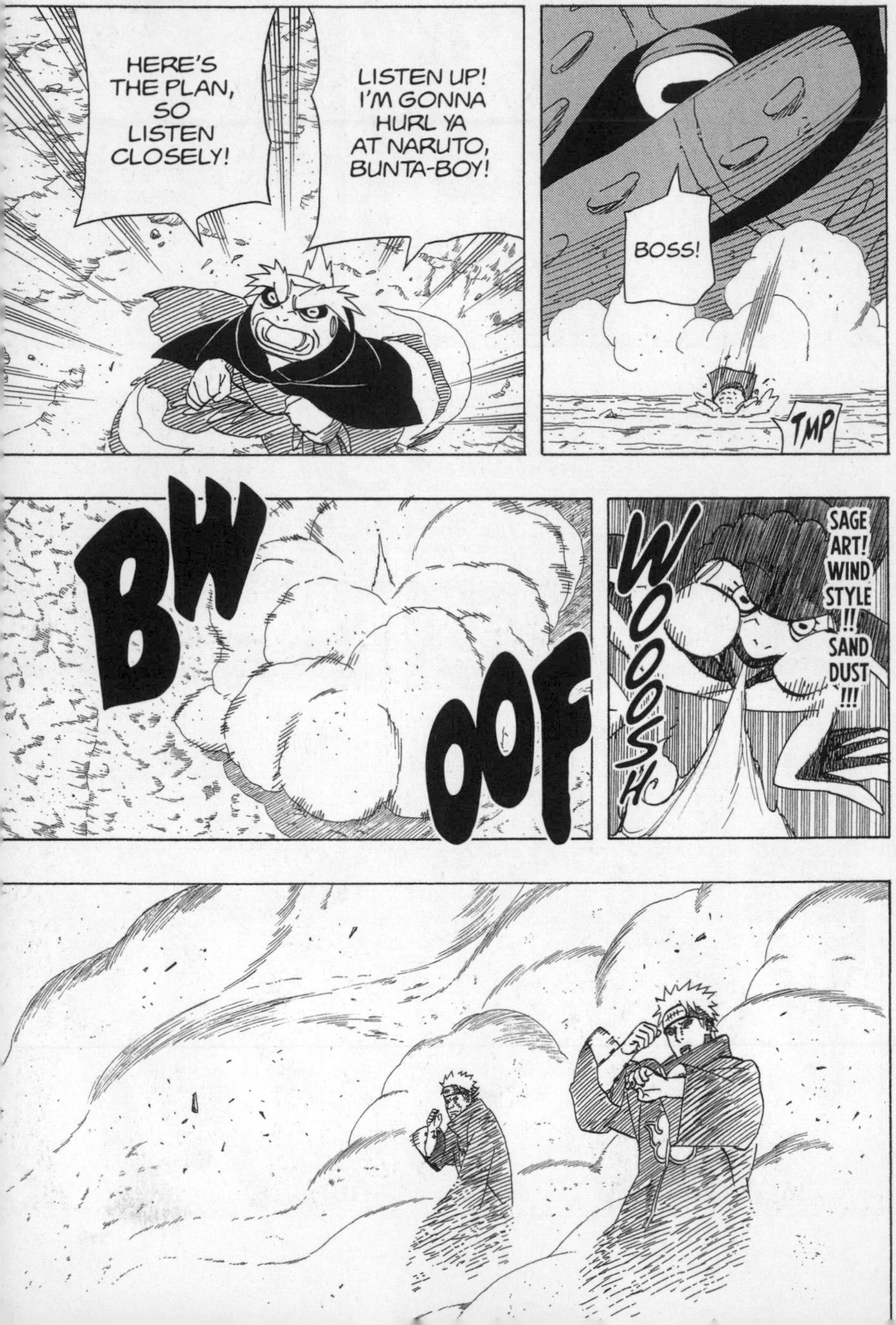

BOSS!
TMP
LISTEN UP! I'M GONNA HURL YA AT NARUTO, BUNTA-BOY!
HERE'S THE PLAN, SO LISTEN CLOSELY!
SAGE ART! WIND STYLE!! SAND DUST!!!
WOOOSH
BWOOF

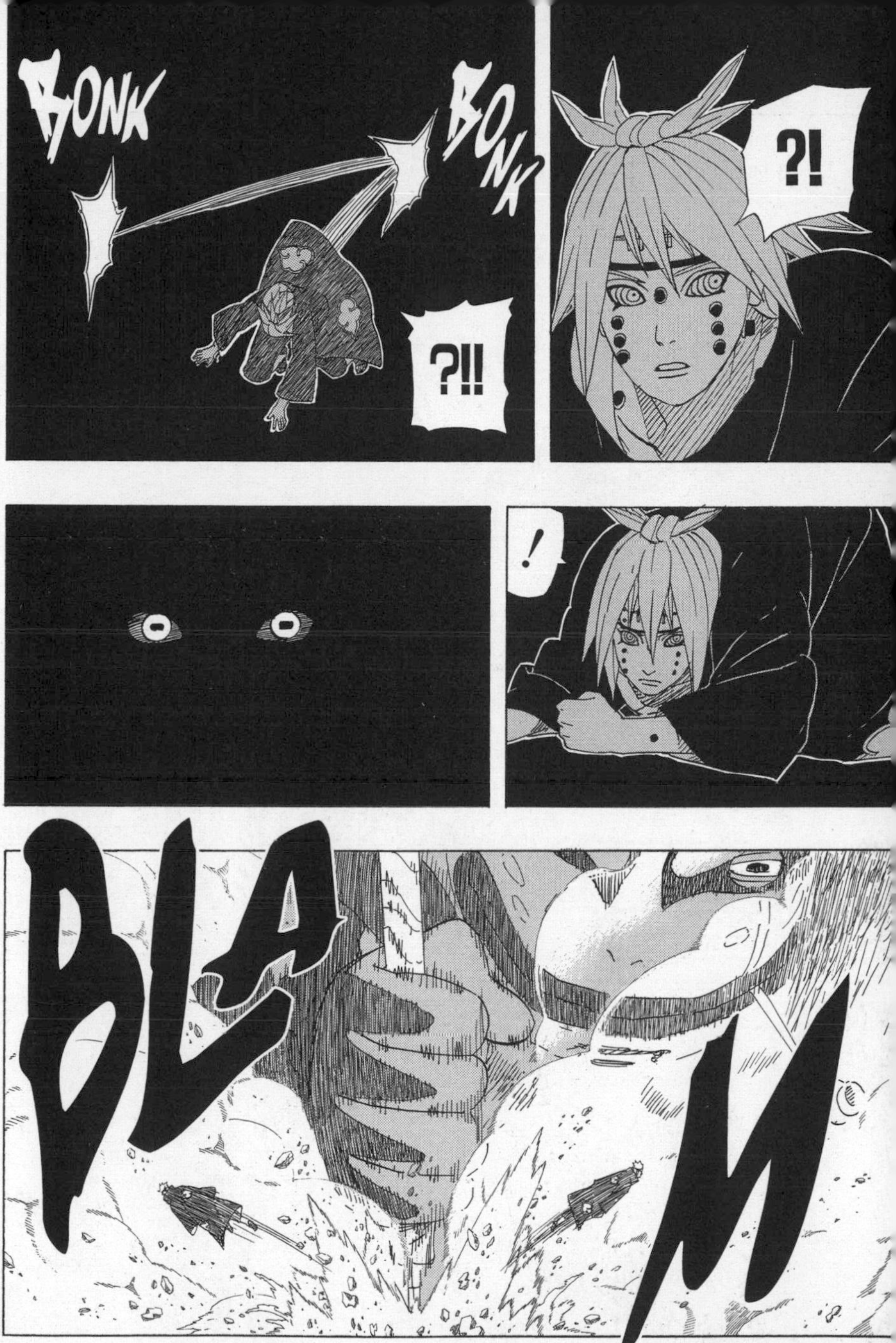
?!
BONK
BONK
?!!
!
BLAM

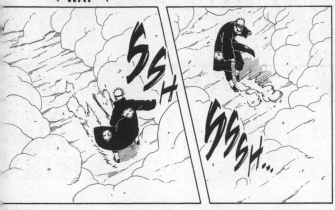

SSSH

SSSSH...

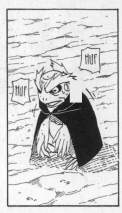

HUF

HUF

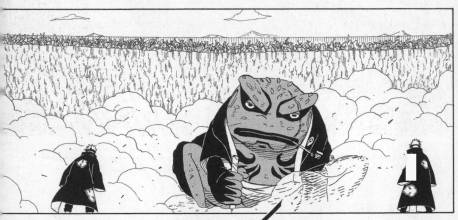

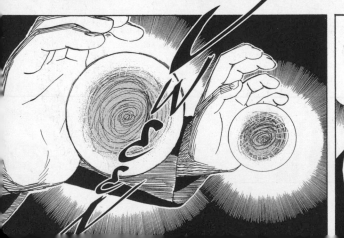

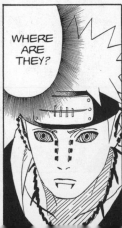

WHERE ARE THEY?

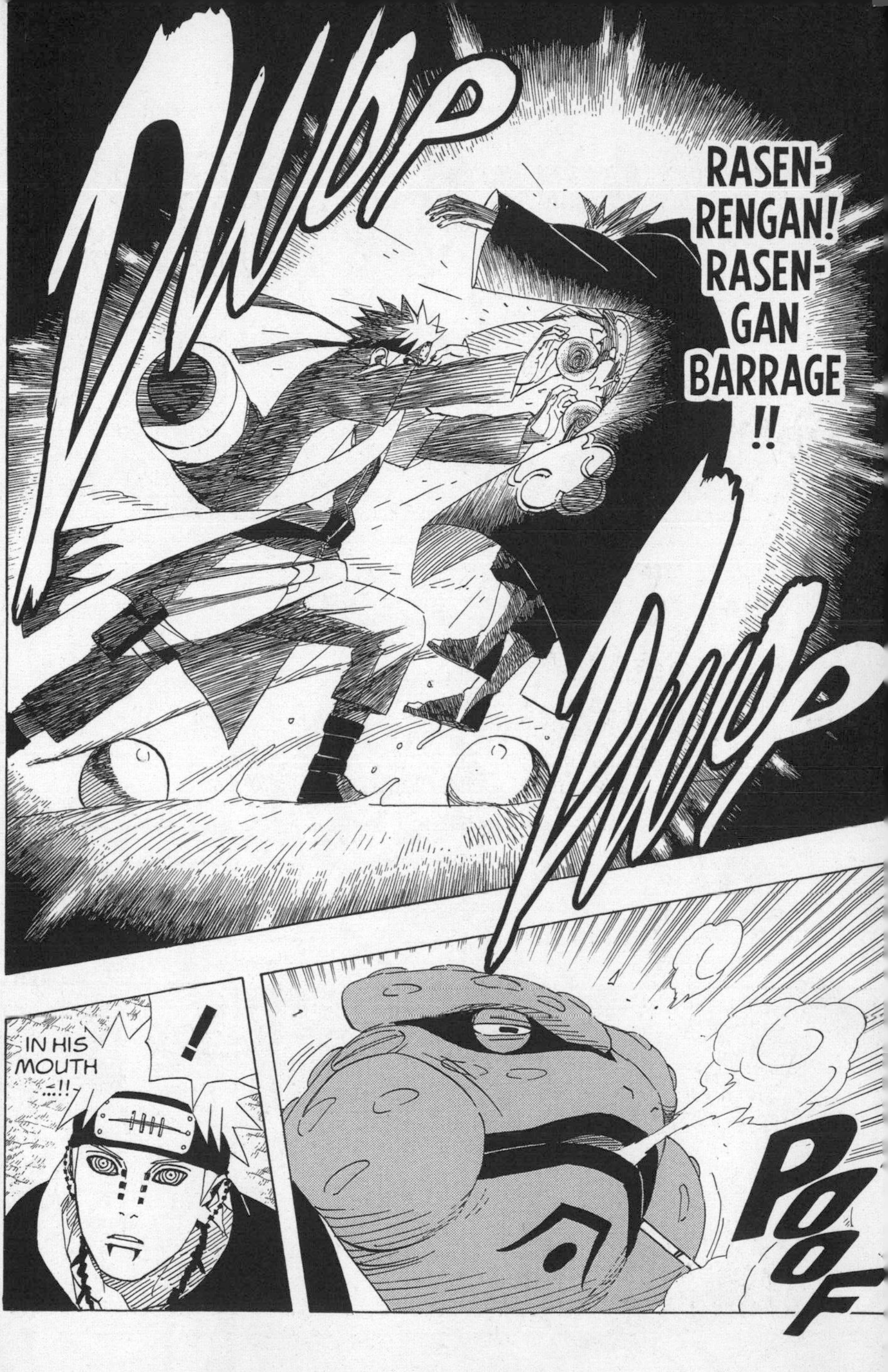
RASEN-RENGAN! RASEN-GAN BARRAGE !!
POOF
!
IN HIS MOUTH ...!!

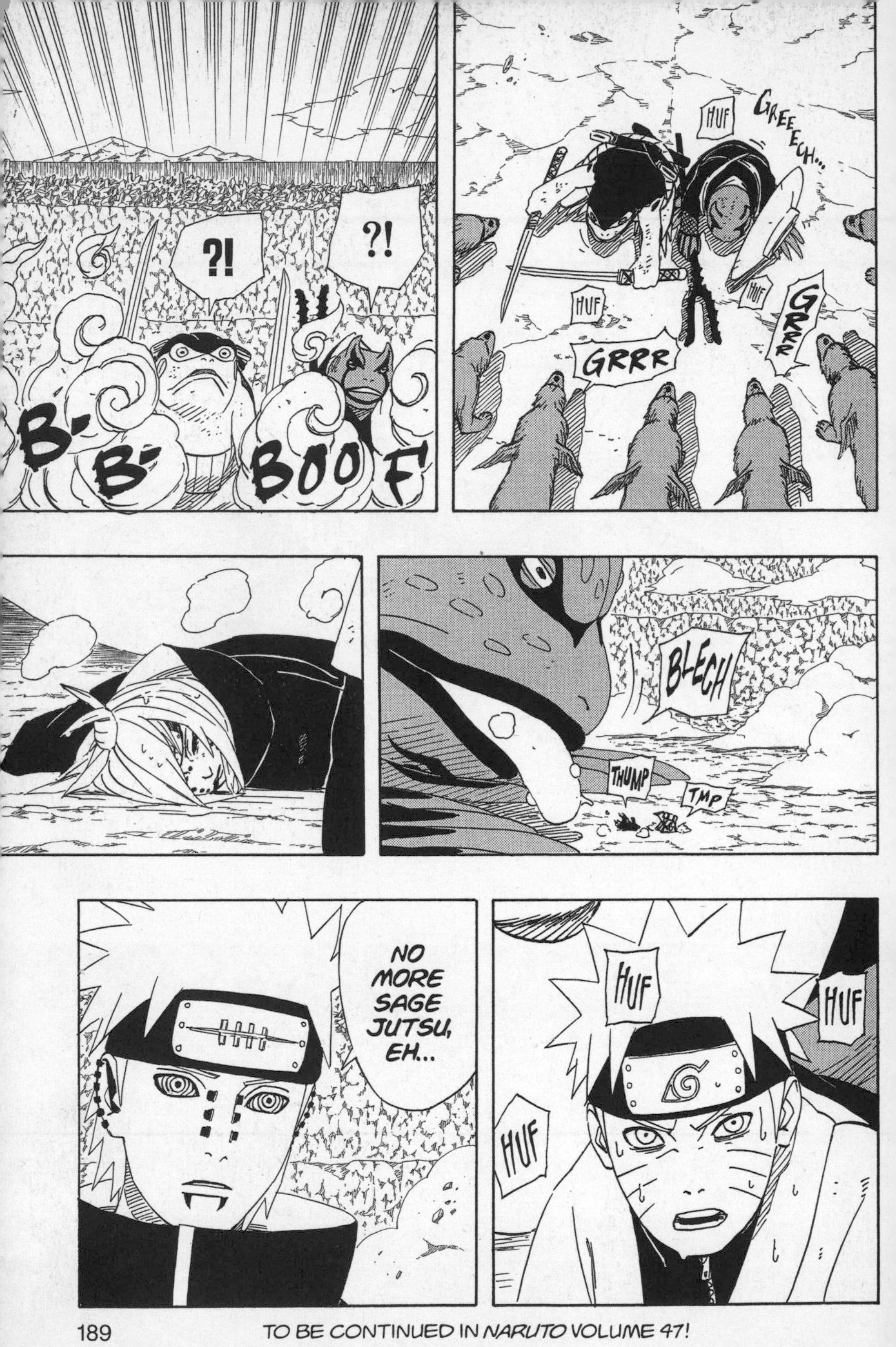
GREEECH...
HUF
HUF
GRRR
HUF
GRRR
?!
?!
B-B-BOOF
BLECH
THUMP
TMP
HUF
HUF
HUF
NO MORE SAGE JUTSU, EH...

TO BE CONTINUED IN *NARUTO* VOLUME 47!

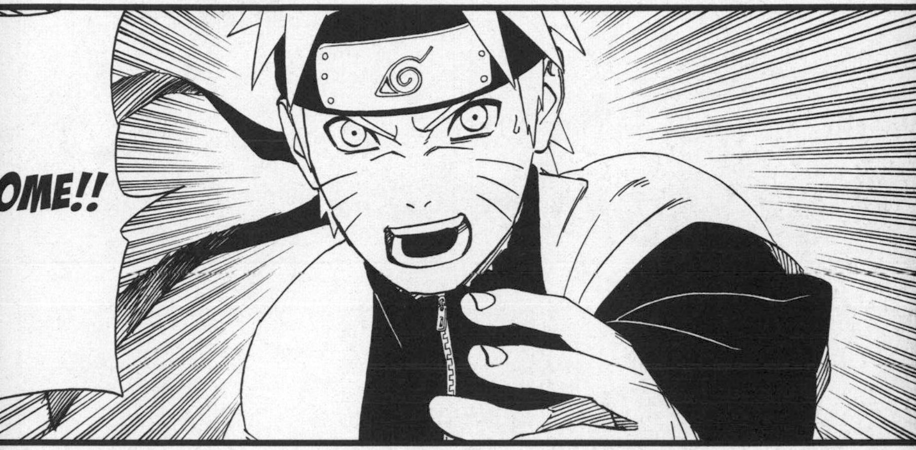
OME!!

IN THE NEXT VOLUME...

CONFESSION

Naruto's transformation kicks into high gear, but it could spell the end of Naruto as we know him! As his friends gather to save him, Naruto learns secrets from all sides. A friend who's rarely spoken up shows unmatched courage. And a famous face from the past could finally hold the key to the secret of Naruto's lineage!

AVAILABLE NOW!

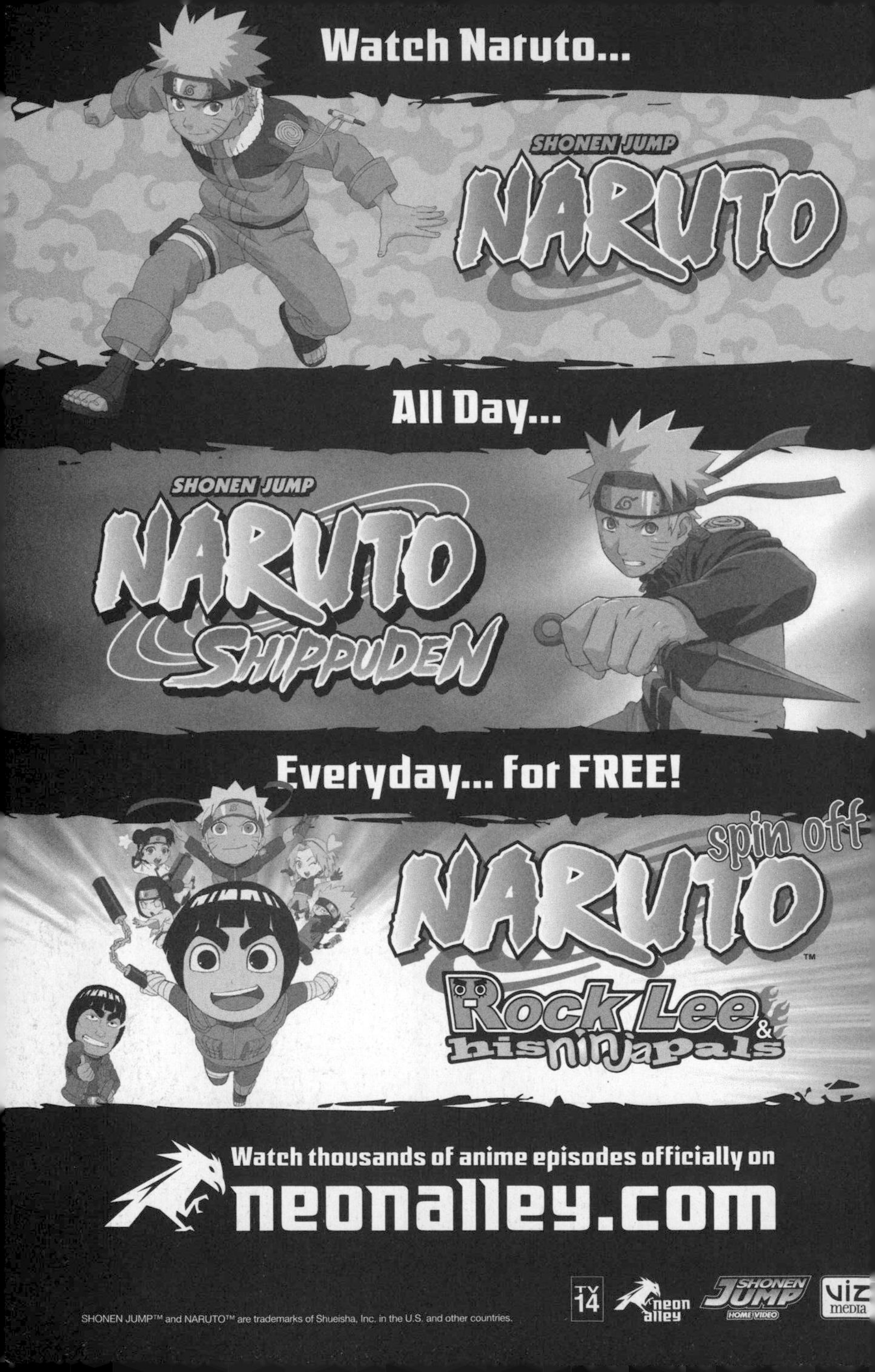
Watch Naruto...
SHONEN JUMP
NARUTO
All Day...
SHONEN JUMP
NARUTO
SHIPPUDEN
Everyday... for FREE!
spin off
NARUTO
TM
Rock Lee & his ninja pals
Watch thousands of anime episodes officially on
neonalley.com
TV 14
neon alley
SHONEN JUMP
HOME VIDEO
viz media
SHONEN JUMP™ and NARUTO™ are trademarks of Shueisha, Inc. in the U.S. and other countries.

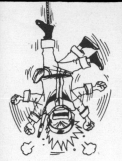

You're Reading in the Wrong Direction!!

Whoops! Guess what? You're starting at the wrong end of the comic!

...It's true! In keeping with the original Japanese format, Naruto is meant to be read from right to left, starting in the upper-right corner.

Unlike English, which is read from left to right, Japanese is read from right to left, meaning that action, sound effects and word-balloon order are completely reversed... something which can make readers unfamiliar with Japanese feel pretty backwards themselves. For this reason, manga or Japanese comics published in the U.S. in English have sometimes been published "flopped"—that is, printed in exact reverse order, as though seen from the other side of a mirror.

By flopping pages, U.S. publishers can avoid confusing readers, but the compromise is not without its downside. For one thing, a character in a flopped manga series who once wore in the original Japanese version a T-shirt emblazoned with "M A Y" (as in "the merry month of") now wears one which reads "Y A M"! Additionally, many manga creators in Japan are themselves unhappy with the process, as some feel the mirror-imaging of their art alters their original intentions.

We are proud to bring you Masashi Kishimoto's Naruto in the original unflopped format. For now, though, turn to the other side of the book and let the ninjutsu begin...!

—Editor

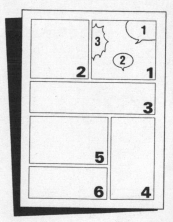